Penguin Education

Phenomenology and Sociology

Edited by Thomas Luckmann

Penguin Modern Sociology Readings

General editor
Tom Burns

Phenomenology and Sociology

Selected Readings

Edited by Thomas Luckmann

Penguin Books

Penguin Books Ltd, Harmondsworth,
Middlesex, England
Penguin Books, 625 Madison Avenue,
New York, New York 10022, U.S.A.
Penguin Books Australia Ltd, Ringwood,
Victoria, Australia
Penguin Books Canada Limited, 2801 John Street,
Markham, Ontario, Canada L3R 1B4
Penguin Books (N.Z.) Ltd, 182–190 Wairau Road,
Auckland 10, New Zealand

First published 1978

Printed in the United States of America by
Kingsport Press, Inc., Kingsport, Tennessee
Set in Monotype Times Roman

Copyright acknowledgements for items in this volume will be
found on page 375.

Contents

Part Two

Contributions to the Theory of Social Action, Communication and Symbolic Realities

Preface

'Phenomenology as a philosophical foundation of modern social science and several recent examples of sociological analysis which builds on that foundation.' This might well have served as an accurate heading for this volume of readings. The actual title, *Phenomenology and Sociology*, indicates less accurately the contents of this volume but it has the advantage of being much shorter. If the 'and' between the terms is not taken as simply connective or additive, it does not misrepresent the nature of this collection of essays. It could perhaps convey that the relation between phenomenology and sociology is the problem to whose clarification the contributions are addressed.

Many signs point to a growing influence of phenomenology on social theory. The attendant misunderstandings and confusions reflect the continued and unresolved tensions between philosophy and science. The real as well as potential enrichment of sociology by phenomenology nevertheless carries the promise of a reconciliation between these two modes of human knowledge that were separated in recent history. Phenomenology, as it was developed by Edmund Husserl from beginnings made by Brentano's psychology in nineteenth-century Germany, but having no direct relation to the phenomenology of Hegel, is a child of the twentieth century. Its impact on modern philosophy is comparable to the consequences of Cartesian and Kantian thought on the philosophy of earlier centuries. In a striking parallel with the success of its great predecessors, Husserl's phenomenology was not merely a new 'system' but a 'new' philosophy, based on a radical shift in perspective and the establishment of a rigorous method of philosophical investigation. Its great significance for the social sciences can be attributed mainly to two facts. The new perspective illuminated the *human* world and the method was applied successfully to the detailed *description* of concrete human experiences.

Despite the scientific rigour of its method and the vast programme of phenomenological research inaugurated by Husserl and continued by the following generations of phenomenologists, phenomenology is not a science in the common understanding of the word. Its perspective is 'egological' (i.e. taking the individual human being as the centre of a system of coordinates on which the experience of the world is mapped) and 'reflexive': it reinstates human experience in its place as the primary datum about the world and it describes this experience by turning and returning to the intentional features of experience. The perspective of egomism science, for excellent historical reasons, is neither based on, nor is it reflexive as, a mode of knowledge. Furthermore, the phenomenological method of attending to experiences precisely as they present themselves, i.e. as a structure of many-layered intentions, is not and cannot be one of the conventional methods of social science. The phenomenological method is more radically descriptive than any method of an empirical science could conceivably be – or could ever want to become.

Phenomenology places between brackets the ontological claims which are an intrinsic trait of our everyday experience and at the same time describes the sources of these claims. It neutralizes, as best as it can without abandoning language as a recording device for its descriptions, the heavy overlay of 'theory' without which scientific as well as common-sense 'facts' are plainly unthinkable. It shows on what conscious activities such theories necessarily rest. Phenomenology describes the constitution of our experiences by recourse to the most direct evidence available. Its criteria of verification differ, however, from those used to good purpose in the social sciences. In contrast to the epistemologically naïve observations and 'measurements' of more or less public events that we practise in the social sciences when we look for 'data', the 'data' of phenomenology are of a more elementary nature. We find them by inspection of our own experiences. By using the methods of phenomenological 'reduction' we proceed step by step from the historically, biographically, socially and culturally concrete features of everyday experience to its elementary structures. This is a procedure that differs from the 'inductive' generalizations of empirical science. Evidently, the results of inspection and 'reduction' can be communicated in a further step to fellow-men. By recourse to evidence of the same kind on their part they can be intersubjectively verified. But this is a different method of verification (or corroboration) from that used in fact or appealed to as an ideal in the social sciences. The goal of phenomenology is to *describe* the *universal* structures of *subjective* orientation in the world, not to explain the *general* features of the *objective* world.

Sociology is not much older than phenomenology. It is a relatively recent discipline in a group of sciences that are, despite a venerable prehistory which goes back at least as far as Aristotle, children of the Modern Age. Rational thought about human affairs is not an invention of our time. But formerly social theory had to contend with religious monopolies on the interpretation of the world, especially, of course, of those sectors of the world that were politically sensitive, i.e. the *polis* and its affairs. From the Athens of Socrates, where the first systematic attempts were made – and suppressed – to employ reason in analysing human conduct, to medieval Islam and Christendom, this monopoly was only rarely relaxed, and it was never abandoned completely. Ever since the Renaissance in Europe, however, it was enforced less rigorously and less and less effectively. The slow but irreversible emancipation of physical science from religious controls carried the promise that the budding social sciences, too, would be allowed to mature without the straightjacket of dogma. But the 'secularization' of traditional social theory did not lead to a new social science in pursuit of an understanding of the social world as a human reality. As soon as social theory was tentatively freed from the constraints of a traditional religious world view it was subjugated by a new cosmology. A Copernican-Galilean-Newtonian view of the world was adopted as the ultimate model for the scientific analysis of social reality.

The conservative opposition to this development retreated in disorder. It took refuge in romantically regressive forms of academically established but intellectually ineffectual political and social philosophy. The 'secularization' of social theory thus resulted in a split between 'philosophical' and 'scientific' approaches to the knowledge of man and society. It failed to prevent the return of *dei ex machinis* into the world of human affairs although the new gods were no longer personal ones. The modern social sciences developed in continuous danger of either forgetting the barely discovered humanity of their subject matter or of defining it as a trivial epiphenomenon of a truer reality.

The controversies between 'religious', 'philosophical' and 'scientific' approaches to the study of man lasted well into the twentieth century and were exacerbated by the infusion of totalitarian ideologies into jurisdictional struggles among intellectuals. A giant step toward a clarification of the issues was taken by Max Weber over half a century ago. He viewed sociology as a science explaining human behaviour in society. But all explanations presupposed interpretations of human actions. These were to be based on historical-typological accounts of the subjective meaning of action. Weber gave *methodological* recognition to the human 'constitution' of the subject matter of the social sciences. Thereby he mediated between the 'positivism' of science and the idealistic 'historicism' of the humanistic disciplines. In the context of American social thought the 'social behaviourism' of George Herbert Mead and his socio-genetic account of the human mind played an analogous part in mediating between the 'behaviouristic' sociology of his time and the philosophy of pragmatism. Neither Max Weber nor Mead was a phenomenologist – *avant-(ou après)-la-lettre*. But their thought played an important part in preventing a lapse of sociology into total reductionism. They prepared the ground for a reorientation of social theory whose philosophical inspiration was Husserl's phenomenology.

Phenomenology appeared as the most suitable candidate for the philosophical foundation of a social science that was willing to define its domain as that of human action and experience, and its goal as the rational and systematic understanding of that domain. By laying bare the universal structures of subjective orientation in the world, phenomenology could provide a general matrix of terms for 'causal', 'functional' or, for that matter, 'dialectical' analyses of typical human actions and their consequences for concrete, i.e. historical, societies. The social sciences face a basic theoretical and methodological problem. The human world, whatever else it may be, is a man-experienced world and in part a man-made world. The objective features of historical social realities rest in some fashion on universal structures of subjective orientation in the world. But precisely how they rest on them, and what precisely these structures are, seem to be questions that an empirical science is not equipped to answer. These questions may be taken as the point of articulation between phenomenology and social theory.

There can be little doubt that the connection between phenomenology and sociology is truly paradigmatic for the present generation of social scientists. Happily or not, in the contemporary state of widespread intellectual disorientation, it is of more than academic interest. In a 'secularized' world, the separation of philosophy and social science contributes heavily to the cosmological uncertainties and confusions created by the definitive emancipation of philosophy and science from religious dogma. Philosophy and science are modes of human knowledge that spring from the same source. They attempt to give answers to the question how a reasonable orientation is possible in a world whose reasonableness is no longer guaranteed by extra-human forces. The differences in perspective, cognitive style and method between these two modes of knowledge should not be confounded. One is based on 'personal' reflection and subjective-intersubjective evidence, the other on 'impersonal' investigation and 'public' evidence. But unless these modes of knowledge overcome their radical alienation from each other they will fail to fulfil their common cosmological function.

*

Be that as it may, the degree to which the contributions collected in this volume illuminated from various points of view the relation between the methods, the goals and the domains of phenomenology and sociology was an important criterion for their selection. It was the main criterion for their inclusion in the first part of the volume. The physical scientist, psychologist and philosopher Aron Gurwitsch, the philosophers Maurice Merleau-Ponty and Alphonse de Waelhens, and other scholars working in the period between the thirties and the sixties continued the work of Husserl in a critique of empiricist psychology and in reconstructing the philosophical foundations of social science. The biologist-philosopher Helmuth Plessner, who with Max Scheler became one of the founding fathers of modern philosophical anthropology, followed an independent but often parallel path. It is, however, undoubtedly the lawyer-economist Alfred Schutz, the student of Max Weber and Edmund Husserl and the friend of Aron Gurwitsch, who is the central figure in the phenomenological reorientation of social theory. The direct influence of his work on sociology in the United States, the European continent and, recently, Great Britain is considerable. Furthermore, the thought of Schutz influenced Harold Garfinkel and Aron Cicourel and is thus one of the sources of what came to be known as ethnomethodology. His teaching at the New School for Social Research in New York City decisively influenced a whole generation of students of philosophy and sociology which included among others Maurice Natanson in the former and Peter Berger in the latter field. Schutz, whose thought synthesizes and continues the key concerns of Edmund Husserl, Max Weber and George Mead in a highly original manner, was little known outside a narrow circle of scholars during his lifetime, but has now become a major influence on modern social theory. His impact is now felt not only in the most varied investigations in the theory of social action, in the sociology of knowledge and other sociological fields, but also, far outside sociology, from political science to literary theory. Some of the recent selections in Part Two will help to give an idea of the range of his influence. Part Two, which is intended as no more than a small sample of work in progress, is therefore much shorter than Part One.

To an extent which I find difficult to assess accurately, the editorial choices were influenced by my theoretical views. Instead of presenting my own position in an introduction, I have chosen to keep the preface short. But I have included in this volume an adapted version of an essay in which I deal directly with the relation between phenomenology and sociology. The reader will be able to judge for himself whether my views were compatible with reasonable principles of selection or whether they unduly distorted them.

Another consideration which influenced the selection was availability. Work in what became known as ethnomethodology, for example, led a subterranean existence for years but recently so many collections of ethnomethodological writing were published – and are easily available to the public – that there seemed no purpose served in reprinting examples of it in this volume. Similarly, some recent work in so-called phenomenological sociology found its way into print. Very much the same can be said about symbolic interactionism, ethnoscience, so-called cognitive anthropology, etc., whose real and acknowledged connections with phenomenology are much less direct than those of 'phenomenological sociology' and 'ethnomethodology' but which are especially interesting as examples of an elective affinity between intellectual traditions of dissimilar origin. They increase the plausibility of the hope that the social sciences could well find a cogent philosophical foundation in phenomenology.

A further factor governing inclusions and omissions was my decision to use only original versions of published papers – unless the author was in a position to edit the paper himself – with the exception of a few essays expressly written or adapted for this volume. Excerpts from books were excluded. I did so for reasons which I consider good, but it must be admitted that this principle eliminated some important work from consideration. The interested reader should therefore give very serious consideration to the list of further reading at the end of the volume.

THOMAS LUCKMANN

Part One

Phenomenology and Convergent Philosophical Foundations of Social Science

1 George Herbert Mead

What Social Objects Must Psychology Presuppose?*

G. H. Mead, 'What Social Objects Must Psychology Presuppose?', *The Journal of Philosophy*, Vol. 7, 1910, pp. 174–80.

There is a persistent tendency among present-day psychologists to use consciousness as the older rationalistic psychology used the soul. It is spoken of as something that appears at a certain point, it is a something into which the object of knowledge in some sense enters from without. It is conceived to have certain functions – in the place of faculties. It is as completely separated from the physical body by the doctrine of parallelism as the metaphysical body was separated from the metaphysical soul by their opposite qualities.

Functional psychology has set itself the programme of assimilating the purposive character of conscious processes – or of consciousness as it is termed – to the evolutionary conception of adaptation, but instead of making consciousness in human individuals a particular expression of a great process, as is demanded of a philosophy of nature, it comes in generally as a new and peculiar factor which even demands a new formula of evolution for its explanation; it involves a new evolution superinduced upon the old.

In spite of much philosophizing, consciousness is identified in current psychological practice with the field which is open to introspection, and the object of knowledge is placed within this field, and related to the physical world – spoken of as an external field of reality – by a parallelistic series. This psychological practice tends to accept the conceptual objects of science, the atoms, molécules, ether vortex rings, ions, and electrons, as the substantial realities of the physical world, and, by implication at

* Given at the meeting of the Psychological Association in Boston, 31 December 1909.

least, to relegate the sensuous content of objects of direct physical experience to this separate field of consciousness. The old-fashioned idealist has then only to point out the thought structure of these hypothetical objects of science to sweep triumphantly, with one stroke of his wand, the whole world of nature within this limited field of the consciousness open to introspection. Whereupon the solipsistic spook arises again to reduce one's world to a nutshell.

The way out of these crude psychological conceptions, in my mind, lies in the recognition that psychical consciousness is a particular phase in development of reality, not an islanded phase of reality connected with the rest of it by a one-to-one relationship of parallel series. This point of view I have elsewhere developed somewhat obscurely and ineffectually, I am afraid.[1]

What I wish to call to your attention in the few moments at my disposal is another phase of this situation which is itself psychological in its character,[2] the presupposition of selves as already in existence before the peculiar phase of consciousness can arise, which psychology studies.

Most of us admit the reality of the objects of direct physical experience until we are too deeply entangled in our psychological analyses of cognition. Unless we subject ourselves to the third degree of criticism, the parallelism of which we speak lies between the processes of brain tissues which can be seen and smelt and handled and the states of consciousness which are conditioned by them. While this admission guarantees the physical bodies of our fellows as equally real, the self is relegated to the restricted field of introspected consciousness and enjoys not the reality of a so-called external object, but only that of a combination of states of consciousness. Into the existence of those states of consciousness in another, we are solemnly told we can only inferentially enter by a process of analogy from the relations of our own introspected states and the movements of our bodies to

1. 'The Definition of the Psychical', University of Chicago Decennial Volumes.
2. I have discussed the implications of this position from a somewhat different point of view in the *Psychological Bulletin*, Vol. VI, No. 12, 15 December 1909.

the movements of other bodies and the hypothetical conscious states that should accompany them. If we approach the self from within, our analysis recognizes, to be sure, its close relationship to, if not its identity with, the organization of consciousness, especially as seen in conation, in apperception, in voluntary attention, in conduct, but what can be isolated as self-consciousness as such reduces to a peculiar feeling of intimacy in certain conscious states, and the self gathers, for some unexplained reason, about a core of certain vague and seemingly unimportant organic sensations – a feeling of contraction in the brow, or in the throat, or goes out to the muscular innervations all over the body which are not involved directly in what we are doing or perceiving. And yet when we proceed introspectively the whole field of consciousness is ascribed to this self, for it is only in so far as we are self-conscious that we can introspect at all.

But what I wish to emphasize is that the other selves disappear as given realities even when we are willing to admit the real objects of physical experience. The self arises within the introspected field. It has no existence outside that introspected field, and other selves are only projects and ejects of that field. Each self is an island, and each self is sure only of its own island, for who knows what mirages may arise above this analogical sea.

It is fair to assume that if we had exact social sciences which could define persons precisely and determine the laws of social change with mathematical exactness, we should accept selves, as there, in the same sense in which we accept physical objects. They would be guaranteed by their sciences. For in the practice of thought, we are as convinced as the Greeks that exact knowledge assures the existence of the object of knowledge.

It is evident that the assumption of the self as given by social science in advance of introspection would materially and fundamentally affect our psychological practice. Consciousness as present in selves would be given as there, outside the field of introspection. Psychological science would have to presuppose selves as the precondition of consciousness in individuals just as it presupposes nervous systems and vascular changes. In actual psychological analysis we should condition the existence and process of states and streams of consciousness upon the normal presence and functioning of these selves, as we condition the appearance and functioning of consciousness upon the normal structure and operation of the physical mechanism, that our psychology presupposes.

In a manner we do this in treatises on mob-psychology, in such a treatise on social psychology as that of Cooley's *Human Nature and the Social Order*. McDougall's *Social Psychology* prepares the way for it in carrying back the processes of consciousness to social impulses and instincts – to those terms in which, somewhat vaguely, selves are stated in an evolutionary theory of society.

The economic man of the dismal science was an attempt to state the self in terms of an objective and exact social science. But fortunately the economic man has proved spurious. He does not exist. The economic man is as little guaranteed by the orthodox political economy, as *realia* were by the metaphysics of scholasticism.

Social science in anthropology, in sociology pure and impure, dynamic and static, has not as yet found its scientific method. It is not able to satisfactorily define its objects, nor to formulate their laws of change and development. Until the social sciences are able to state the social individual in terms of social processes, as the physical sciences define their objects in terms of physical change, they will not have risen to the point at which they can force their object upon an introspective psychology. We can today foresee the possibility of this. Eugenics, education, even political and economic sciences pass beyond the phase of description and look toward the formation of the social object. We recognize that we control the conditions which determine the individual. His errors and shortcomings can be conceivably corrected. His misery may be eliminated. His mental and moral defects corrected. His heredity, social and physical, may be perfected. His very moral self-consciousness through normal and healthful social conduct, through adequate consciousness of his relations to others, may be constituted and established. But without awaiting the development of the social sciences it is possible to indicate in the nature of the consciousness which psychology itself analyses, the presupposition of social objects, whose objective reality is a condition of the consciousness of self.

The contribution that I wish to suggest toward the recognition of the given character of other selves is from psychology itself, and arises out of the psychological theory of the origin of language and its relation to meaning.

This theory, as you know, has been considerably advanced by Wundt's formulation of the relation of language to gesture. From this point of view language in its earliest form comes under that group of movements which, since Darwin, have been called expressions of the emotions. They fall into classes which have been regarded as without essential connection. Either they are elements – mainly preparatory – beginnings of acts – social acts, i.e., actions and reactions which arise under the stimulation of other individuals, such as clenching the fists, grinding the teeth, assuming an attitude of defence – or else they are regarded as outflows of nervous energy which sluice off the nervous excitement or reinforce and prepare indirectly for action. Such gestures, if we may use the term in this generalized sense, act as stimuli to other forms which are already under social stimulation.

The phase of the subject which has not been sufficiently emphasized is the value which these truncated acts, these beginnings of inhibited movements, these gestures, have as appropriate stimulations for the conduct of other individuals. Inevitably, forms that act and react to and upon each other come to prepare for each other's reaction by the early movements in the act. The preliminaries of a dog or cock fight amply illustrate the sensitiveness of such individuals to the earliest perceptible indications of coming acts. To a large degree forms, which live in groups or in the relation of the animals of prey and those they prey upon, act upon these first signs of oncoming acts. All gestures, to whatever class they belong, whether they are the beginnings of the outgoing act itself or are only indications of the attitude and nervous tension which these acts involve, have this value of stimulating forms, socially organized, to reactions appropriate to the attack, or flight, or wooing, or suckling, of another form. Illustrations are to be found in human conduct, in such situations as fencing, where one combatant without reflection makes his parry from the direction of the eye and the infinitesimal change of attitude which are the prelude to the thrust.

Gestures then are already significant in the sense that they are stimuli to performed reactions, before they come to have significance of conscious meaning. Allow me to emphasize further the value of attitudes and the indications of organized preparation for conduct, especially in the change of the muscles of the countenance, the altered breathing, the quivering of tense muscles, the evidence of circulatory changes, in such minutely adapted social groups, because among these socially significant innervations will be found all these queer organic sensations about which the consciousness of the self is supposed to gather as a core.

Human conduct is distinguished primarily from animal conduct by that increase in inhibition which is an essential phase of voluntary attention, and increased inhibition means an increase in gesture in the signs of activities which are not carried out; in the assumptions of attitudes whose values in conduct fail to get complete expression. If we recognize language as a differentiation of gesture, the conduct of no other form can compare with that of man in the abundance of gesture.

The fundamental importance of gesture lies in the development of the consciousness of meaning – in reflective consciousness. As long as one individual responds simply to the gesture of another by the appropriate response, there is no necessary consciousness of meaning. The situation is still on a level of that of two growling dogs walking around each other, with tense limbs, bristly hair, and uncovered teeth. It is not until an image arises of the response, which the gesture of one form will bring out in another, that a consciousness of meaning can attach to his own gesture. The meaning can appear only in imaging the consequence of the gesture. To cry out in fear is an immediate instinctive act, but to scream with an image of another individual turning an attentive ear, taking on a sympathetic expression and an attitude of coming to help, is at least a favourable condition for the development of a consciousness of meaning.

Of course the mere influence of the image, stimulating to reaction, has no more meaning value than the effect of an external stimulus, but in this converse of gestures there is also a consciousness of attitude, of readiness to act in the manner which the gesture implies. In the instance given the cry is part of the attitude of flight. The cry calls out the image of a friendly individual. This image is not merely a stimulus to run toward the friend, but is merged in the consciousness of inhibited flight. If meaning is consciousness of attitude, as Dewey, Royce, and Angell among others maintain, then consciousness of meaning arose only when some gesture that was part of an inhibited act itself called up the image of the gesture of another individual. Then the image of the gesture means the inhibited act to which the first gesture belonged. In a word, the response to the cry has the meaning of inhibited flight.

One's own gestures could not take on meaning directly. The gestures aroused by them in others would be that upon which attention is centred. And these gestures become identified with the content of one's own emotion and attitude. It is only through the response that consciousness of meaning appears, a response which involves the consciousness of another self as the pre-supposition of the meaning in one's own attitude. Other selves in a social environment logically antedate the consciousness of self which introspection analyses. They must be admitted as there, as given, in the same sense in which psychology accepts the given reality of physical organisms as a condition of individual consciousness.

The importance for psychology of this recognition of others, if thus bound up with the psychology of meaning, may need another word of emphasis. Consciousness could no longer be regarded as an island to be studied through parallel relations with neuroses. It would be approached as experience which is socially as well as physically determined. Introspective self-consciousness would be recognized as a subjective phase, and this subjective phase could no longer be regarded as the source out of which the experience arose. Objective consciousness of selves must precede subjective consciousness, and must continually condition it, if consciousness of meaning itself presupposes the selves as there. Subjective self-consciousness must appear *within* experience, must have a function in the development of that experience, and must be studied from the point of view of that function, not as that in which self-consciousness arises and by which through analogical bridges and self-projections we slowly construct a hypothetically objective social world in which to live. Furthermore, meaning in the light of this recognition has its reference not to agglomerations of states of subjective consciousness, but to objects in a socially conditioned experience. When in the process revealed by introspection we reach the concept of self, we have attained an attitude which we assume not toward our inner feelings, but toward other individuals whose reality was implied even in the inhibitions and reorganizations which characterize this inner consciousness.

If we may assume, then, that meaning is consciousness of attitude, I would challenge anyone to show an adequate motive for directing attention toward one's attitudes, in a consciousness of things that were merely physical; neither control over sense-perception nor control over response would be directly forwarded by attention directed toward a consciousness of readiness to act in a given situation. It is only in the social situation of converse that these gestures, and the attitudes they express, could become the object of attention and interest. Whatever our theory may be as to the history of things, social consciousness must antedate physical consciousness. A more correct statement would be that experience in its original form became reflective in the recognition of selves, and only gradually was there differentiated a reflective experience of things which were purely physical.

2 Helmuth Plessner

With Different Eyes

H. Plessner, 'Mit Anderen Augen', *Zwischen Philosophie und Gesellschaft*, Berne: Francke, 1953, pp. 204–17. (Written for an unpublished *Festschrift* for G. Misch, 1948.)

Translated by A. L. Hammond

I

We have long been familiar with the distinction between understanding (*Verstehen*) and explanation (*Erklären*). The conceptual element in each kind of experience has a distinctly and describably different character. Yet this character can be made clear only if the concepts, or the points of view, between which it is sandwiched are identified for each type of experience and it is made clear how and why these elements form its context. If attention had been paid to this in debates for and against understanding, then methodological monism (*Methodenmonismus*) would have had to be defended over a much broader front. Since, however, there was so much partiality for the old scheme of perception, involving sensory foundations, a conceptual middle and an ideally constituted superstructure, the debate was centred almost exclusively around the question of whether it was necessary to distinguish coming to know something through understanding from coming to know it by having it explained, and most discussions were lost in a fog of definitions without the actual point in question being taken any further.

If, however, with Misch,[1] we contrast explanation as knowing *about* something with understanding as actually *knowing* something, then the relationship of viewpoint and concept (if we ignore ideal constructs as a factor for the present) stands midway between them. The materials of sensory appearance, from which we build our personal and historical-social experience of life,

1. 'Die Idee der Lebensphilosophie in der Theorie der Geisteswissenschaften', *Kantstudien*, 1926.

must then be capable of being made transparent to understanding if the mind is capable of penetrating to its essential core.[2] The 'transparency' of material things provides an assurance that there is another way of approaching the problem we are considering, but not that it is infallible.

Our experience of life exposes us to possibilities of error no less than our experience of nature. The struggle against misunderstanding and incomprehension is a lifelong accompaniment to every man's existence and constitutes the problem to which the study of social and mental existence is devoted, albeit this occurs at perpetually shifting levels. Independently of this, however, human material – in documents and monuments, in what is done and left undone, in speech and in work – shows itself to be transparent in nature. This material is not apparent as simply form and colour, sound and force, movement and weight, but it has expressiveness, or reference, or meaning. The natural scientist, because the questions he asks are in terms of what is measurable, starts by comprehending phenomena and their changing forms as signs of a hypothesized relationship which must include indicators for experimental procedures, on the basis of which he can demonstrate whether his hypothesis is true or false. The whole art of 'finding out about things' lies in the particular choice made out of these oblique kinds of approach.

In the human sciences, on the other hand, the student has to start with the possible procedures directly provided by the structure of his material. In deciphering texts or reading a statement, he is attempting to understand the motivations behind human handwork by means of evidence about the objectives which individuals set for themselves out of their own social needs and considerations. In doing so he is guided by the same indications as is anybody who is engaged in human interaction. In his case too, he cannot do without hypotheses when dealing with interrelationships, questions of authorship, the establishment of chronological sequence, the recognition of influences and the

2. Cf. Freyer and Erismann, and, in particular, N. Hartmann, *Das Problem des geistigen Seins*, 1933, pp. 360ff. My own book, which appeared twenty-eight years ago, *Die Einheit der Sinne. Grundlinien einer Ästhesiologie des Geistes*, was a first attempt at a theory of 'transparency'.

construction of causal connections. In special cases when he is concerned with proving authenticity he too has to call upon the help of chemistry and X-ray analysis – perhaps even of astronomy, when it comes to establishing dates. But the material itself calls for interpretation of meaning, not for calculation, because, for all its actuality as a visible, handleable thing, it is really concerned with the human mind. As is the case in personal interaction, mistakes can occur across distances in history because of insensitiveness; there is the possibility of blank misapprehension, narrow-mindedness or dismissiveness, arising out of enthusiasm or affection, or for a thousand personal reasons. These are not dangers which threaten the natural scientist. Both the material with which he is concerned and his methodology ensure that the observer's own being enters only minimally. By contrast, the human scientist's personality, with all its responsive capacities, has to be fully present. Even if he has to keep it under rational control he must nevertheless let it come into play so that his material can make itself apparent to him, and perceive it.

For the human sciences, which are nourished by life-experience and take their direction from it, the problem of the relationship between standpoint and concept is different from what is suggested by the philosophical tradition. It must not be forgotten that the theory of dual composition of the perception of experience, which Kant developed from his inaugural dissertation on the separation of appearance from idea, actually represents a great advance beyond Leibniz, but, like Leibniz, he only takes mathematical and scientific knowledge into account. When the existence of a different kind and a different field of perception is admitted, Kant's dualism inevitably becomes questionable. In any case it has to be restricted to the field of the exact sciences. Moreover, as knowledge of the nature of perception grew within the framework of nineteenth-century physiology and psychology, that knowledge developed not only as a natural science, using experimental laboratory methods, but also in harmony with, and under the influence of, Kantian theory itself; thus the dualistic theory of experience gained a broader basis. The various difficulties with which, in the process, the human sciences were found, the critical reaction of Dilthey, Bergson and Husserl, and, ultimately, of the whole of modern philosophy and psychology which has felt their influence, all helped to bring to light the fictitious character of a doctrine of perception working with isolated sense-impressions. In their different ways they brought into question the feasibility of an approach which disregarded thought and even the mind itself. We are thus brought to consider afresh whether, at least for the human senses, any hard and fast distinction is tenable between two essentially different elements: perception and thought. It may be, of course, that the traditional step-by-step progress from sensation via perception to idea will have to be completely dropped, so far as any theory of experience is concerned, and the antithesis between explanation as 'knowing *about* things' (*cognitio circa rem*) and understanding as 'knowing things' (*cognitio rei*) may therefore come to be regarded in a new light. This question, obviously, touches on the relationship between individual part and whole, the selection of what is significant, the role of value judgements, the subjective conditioning of conceptual structures in the human sciences and other aspects of the basic assumptions of the human sciences.

II

Professional students of the humanities and the human sciences have to deal with objects: texts, works of art, monuments of all kinds, and visual representations which they perceive with their sense organs and, on occasions, have to test, using scientific methods. Since these objects represent the evidence of a human world and the sources of our knowing, a superficial interpretation would identify the point of departure of experience in the human sciences with that of the natural sciences, and our question about the role which 'approach' plays in understanding would be answered by reference to the role which 'approach' plays in scientific explanation. In all this, what is overlooked is the fact that the function of the senses is different in the two cases. They do of course bring us into contact with things, or, if you like, with appearances, but what is the very substratum of observation in one case – that of the natural scientist – represents in another case, say that of the cultural historian, a documentation of human capabilities belonging to a particular historical period. It is only when an analysis of the kind of paper used for an old manuscript treats the document as a physical substratum that the approach of the natural sciences provides any help, although dating its composition is decisive in this case. It has nothing to do with the world of human thought which is invested in this natural object in the form of images and linguistic signs. The clear perception of the natural object in this case, as in many others, does of course bring about contact with the medium by which the human mind has expressed itself, but it does not involve the view of a world of human mentality which is necessary for what our reversal of the classical step-by-step process of perceptual elements has suggested is actually designated for understanding that world. Sense-perception can therefore not be identified with the operative approach we are looking for in studying the structure of experience, nor with the knowledge which this experience sustains.

Where, then, is it to be found? What is it like and what is its function? We will do better to look for some other situations in which our attention is not directed towards people and human relationships. Here, too, normal sense-perception produces the indispensable mode of contact for orientation to milieu, for seeing faces, gestures and movements, for hearing language and for the examination of people's behaviour and actions. In the familiar milieu of our own country we will find everything more or less obvious, so that the unquestioned character of everyday life allows us to appreciate the simplicity and ordinariness of encounters with people and their desires. Everything goes its own way, naturally, as if things could be no different, and we confidently go our own way, along familiar paths, without much regard. Observational alertness is at a very low level, we gradually lose our eye for the curiosities and beauties of city and landscape. Force of habit blunts sensitive appreciation. If, for instance, we walk past the burnt ruins of a house that we have seen standing in its place for the past thirty years, it has to be pushed right under our nose before we are able to surrender our familiar picture to the new reality.

We have to become exiles from the territory of the familiar things we trust before we are able to perceive it anew. Rediscovering new environment, which companionably surrounds us and confronts us as an image, our senses are able to enjoy them afresh, and we can see them again. This alienation is experienced intensely by anyone who has left his home country as a child and returns as a grown man, and perhaps most intensely by the emigrant in the prime of life who becomes aware of the thousand roots sunk in a friendly soil and of his inherited culture strained to breaking point when he discovers anew the whole tradition from which he has sprung – not as his home country would believe, through the spectacles lent him by the friendly country which is sheltering him – but *through other eyes*.

What is true for sense-perception holds true for the approach which is necessary for the consideration of spiritual and intellectual relationships. True awareness is wakened in us only by what is unfamiliar. To be able to look at something, we need distance. However wrong-headed and biased it may be to cling to a scale which begins at the bottom with the vague confusions of conceptual knowledge and at the top offers clarity and specificity of thought, and however true it may be that sense-perception attains a figurative precision of its own as far as intuitive awareness is concerned, this of itself still does not permit us to reach a definition of the concomitant and contradictory functions of perception which lie in understanding. For this we need to introduce the two concepts of familiarity and strangeness. We are then able to say that the functions of intuition and perception and concept in the structuring of human experience are distinguished in terms of strangeness and familiarity. So much so that only what is strange (estranged) comes into 'approach', or intuitive perception, and only what is familiar into 'understanding'.

There are, of course, gradations and connections between these two zones and the functions proper to them. Our search for comprehension applied only to what seems incomprehensible; it is the unfamiliar with which we try to familiarize ourselves, and we can only estrange ourselves from what is commonplace in order to view it, to 'look it over'. Yet the fact that the familiar can be understood and that the unfamiliar can be examined should not be taken as definitive characteristics, nor should we attempt to manipulate them logically without further examination. The comprehensibility of the familiar can become manifest only when the ground is prepared by conceptual understanding. In the same way, the unfamiliar can become strikingly obvious to us only when we have accomplished the first preparative phase of distancing ourselves. Thus the poet, the painter or the scholar successfully interchanges these functions when his deliberately estranged vision catches what has long been familiar and the obvious, or when he grasps what is most alien and remote to his innermost thought.

The world of the familiar and conventional is the self-evident, but this kind of understanding is a meaningful experience to man only when fought for and won. Only when it is won can it be called one's own. But for this new understanding to be won, the first familiarity has to have been lost, and life does not always do us the painful service of removing us from our familiar milieu. That is why the estranged vision of the artist fulfils an indispensable condition for all genuine understanding. It lifts what is invisible in human relations, because it is familiar, into visibility; in this new encounter, understanding is brought into play; so that what is in fact familiar becomes accessible by virtue of being estranged. Without this estrangement there is no understanding; it constitutes a roundabout approach to the familiar, the counterfoil which puts the familiar into perspective as foreground and background and makes it comprehensible.

Any simple optical replication is an example of this. The passport photograph with the head turned slightly to the right under bright lighting turns the familiar face into something simplified, black and white, unfamiliar, and unintentionally distorted. If it is a bad photograph then mechanical distortion misses the point which caricature can make; if it is a good one, then the over-familiarity of the image conceals the individual personality. But the photographer can capture this if he masters the art of portraiture, the art of the indirect approach, of estrangement, which passes from the known to the unknown and back to the familiar. As Webermann rightly remarks, to draw is to leave things out. Thus in any artistic representation which penetrates to the spirit of things through appearances, there must be some distortion about the work, some partiality, selectivity, emphasis – in a word, some distancing mechanism – in order to bring the object to light. With different materials and with different means of expression, the good writer and even the historical scholar will obey the same law. In composing his material he must fashion it with a good dose of selectivity and partiality, but in such a way that his hand can be seen to work selectively if the material is to become alive, as a portrait does, and communicate to us in pictorial terms. The forcefulness of even Hegel, or Marx or Spengler, owes its heightened value to this. It brings things to light; it stimulates the inner eye; it gives us different eyes. Exaggerations and figures of speech, bold constructions, too, fulfil the same function of perceptual counterfoil to understanding.

It is not only learning to look at life with different eyes but at one's own environment, one's own land, one's own tradition and the wider aspects of them in which lies the art of the human sciences, which, activated by genuine, i.e. painful, experience, destroys the familiar, so that it is as if the scales fall from our eyes. It awakens us to new consciousness, liberates the vision and makes it resistant to the refractions and the opacities of prejudice. We have all experienced this: what distancing powers do the historical disciplines not owe to the disturbances which have occurred since 1914? Diligent work along well-trodden paths is appropriate to peaceable times, in which great passions are centred mainly on personal affairs; but the courage for seeing the world afresh is found only in times of desperation, when our very foundations are shaken. Only what is fed in by one's own life-experience can appeal to other people's life-experience; sensitivity comes only from the bitter draught of disillusionment. Pain is the eye of the spirit.

Apart from a few important exceptions, it will be found that fresh enlightenment about human affairs, whether it be in biography or in the demonstration of more significant inter-relationships, has a better chance of occurring in times of turbulence or dangers, or through crises involving gifted individuals, than in the happier times of peace. The force of insight is directly proportional to the misfortunes of an epoch. Between the German-speaking historians and sociologists who were young before 1870 and those who grew up in the German Empire there exists a clear distinction in terms of originality. But neither generation can compare with those who lived through 1848, or were contemporary with Napoleon.

This extremely complex inter-dependency between personal productivity and life-experience in the fields of intellectual and scholarly work is of only partial and occasional relevance to our present problem, which is concerned with the theory of know-ledge. There is a danger, when psychological and sociological influences such as these are incorporated, of the objective status of knowledge (which is already subject to strict limitations) being lost altogether. Does it not put knowledge about human affairs at the arbitrary disposal of personal opinion? The answer to this question is a further question: does the problem thus raised actually take enough account of the difficulties caused by the special nature of human affairs – difficulties with which the systematic historical scholar has to deal in order to make contact at all with his own life and that of others?

Those who, quite rightly, pose this problem, however, may be yet again deceived by an illusory analogy with nature. Natural materials can be before one's eyes, and can be perceived by the senses, *before* theorizing takes over. But the human world cannot be perceived, however concretely it is represented by documents and managements. What can be perceived – seen, heard and felt – is the material embodiments of symbols which may indeed be quite apparent to the initiate, but whose understanding cannot possibly be limited to data they perceive. These data are inter-pretable, but they can be used only as the bare bones of 'evidence' for a rationally verifiable thesis to the extent that they are used in conjunction with whatever corresponds with their own per-sonal experience. So while the historian or the social scientist certainly recognizes the necessity for verification and discussion, and respects the rules of objectivity in every respect, he and his public must not delude themselves into thinking that their theses are inscribed in the book of the world we have lost. In order to be sure of this there would have to be some comprehensive vision of the world of past and present humanity which was comparable to the comprehensive view we have of nature, at least in so far as it is separable from thought (or, in this case, understanding). This is not the case. A view of humankind answering this description does not exist. Phenomenology practises and speaks of Being-in-appearance (*Wesensschau*), of the appearance of the structures of Being. We are not quarrelling with this, but it has only an indirect connection with what we have in mind, of *servicing* understanding and at the same time guiding it. At all events it is not identical with what we have in mind. Misch[3] has made this clear in his critique of Heidegger.

The actual shock of recognition which enters into the attitude we are seeking to examine, the condition of fear and pain necessary for an estranged view of things, is one of the *a priori* conditions for understanding, even when its emotional colouring and personal depth are less in evidence. Conditioning, and conditioned by, experience at one and the same time, this attitude guides and supports historical thought in its search for understanding: *conditioned by* experience, because the veil cast over what is familiar cannot be lifted if there is no shock (which, in untroubled times, passes under the quieter term, experience); *conditioning* experience, because the making of what is estranged visible is the basis and forerunner of reflective understanding. Unquestionably, study of 'the world of the mind' is accomplished under conditions utterly unlike any known in the whole field of the natural sciences. Only this kind of study has to discover the characteristics of what it is examining in such a way that they do not appear directly before it as particulars emanating from the object itself, but in a way that reveals them retrospectively as preconditions of the way in which the object was originally envisaged. The student of 'nature' can afford to omit any explicit representation of the *a priori* which he, no less than the student of human existence, assumes, since what is expressed in this *a priori* contributes nothing to the characteristics of what he wants to study. It can be left aside without involving any loss or damage to the object of study. What he (i.e. the student of the

3. *Lebensphilosophie und Phänomenologie*, Bonn, 1931.

humanities or the social scientist) leaves aside cannot remain ignored without making the object of study defective ... Those basic foundations by means of which it is possible to illuminate the intellectual world have their clearly defined place *within* the world they are designed to illuminate. It is apparent that this is the one situation in which the *a priori*, while expressing the conditions for defining the object, itself initiates the definition of the object. To study something which is not itself of the mind is to know nothing of this kind of limitation.[4]

If, following Litt, we see in Dilthey's triad, 'experience, expression, understanding', the kernel of the selfsame concepts we have been discussing, which 'are accountable for the kind of action in which the subject must be effective if the value of "experience" is to serve as a contribution to his thinking'[5] – i.e. in the value of that experience of living drawn from the human existence of the individual which carries over into the general principles of philosophical understanding and scholarship – then we are back to the traditional sequence for 'all' experience: from intuitive understanding, via concept, to idea. This cannot be replaced simply by Dilthey's triad, which, considering what confronted Dilthey as the *object* of investigation (in this case the processes of the spirit in which the indictive assertions of the human sciences originate,[6] still limits consideration of the problem of intuitive understanding. Once it is understood that this triad is applicable not only to the human sciences (e.g. when interpreting documents and artefacts) but articulates those basic activities indispensable to man's intellectual existence in all its dimensions and aspect and provides the whole foundation of human intellectual being, including even its sensual, physical aspects, only then will we be obliged to agree with Litt[7] that the concepts which were, to begin with, designed to set out exactly what makes the human sciences possible illuminate beyond this the whole fabric of life, which in these sciences is reflecting upon itself and, in the process, the fabric of the reality which those

4. T. Litt, 'Das Allgemeine im Aufbau der geisteswissenschaftlichen Erkenntnis', *Proceedings of the Sächsische Akademie der Wissenschaften,* Phil. Hist. Klasse, 93, 1941, pp. 36 and 35.

5. op. cit., p. 33.   6. Litt, loc. cit.   7. op. cit., p. 36.

sciences take as their object. Clearly, for life-experiences to form so that they can be drawn on not only by the individual but also by a science capable of bridging distances in time, it is necessary for experience to develop alienating forces which can throw familiar circumstances expressively and understandably into an unfamiliar light. This latter once more liberates that reflexive intelligence which reaches its full power in intuitive understanding.

III

Experience, expression and understanding determine human interaction with men and physical objects equally well in familiar and in alienated situations, but what is implicit and taken for granted in a familiar situation becomes articulated in an alien situation and requires artistic or systematic form. 'Understanding' becomes 'understanding discernment', expression is realized in objective terms and the shock of experience releases vision: we see with different eyes. In contemplating with understanding what has become strange, there is at first the question of assuming the right point of view from which to examine human intellectual life, it is the point of view with which historians are continually concerned when they wish to portray a man, an epoch or a whole civilization.

The imagination plays a decisive role in any design modelled by ideas insofar as design is comprehensive, bringing everything into a combined whole around the one energizing centre. Born of disturbance and shock, estrangement releases the possibility of imagination, thought and vision. The historian constructs all that he has understood around his idea into a composition, a portrayal of his vision.

When we compare knowledge of this reflexive kind with the explanatory character of knowledge in the natural sciences, it becomes apparent that the former is deficient so far as any relationship with practical application is concerned, while for the latter it is precisely this area in which it is effective. Understanding also means understanding *about* something (a point which

Heidegger has made use of); it means mastering something, knowing what to do about something, and inherent in this ability is a certain kind of perceptiveness, alertness and insight of the kind recognizable in the craftsman, or the sportsman. With loss of familiarity we lose all easiness in understanding, and a contemplative, theoretical element takes its place, a kind of insight in which the special perceptiveness we have tried to indicate is preponderant. It is possible to identify, in efforts to understand alien and dead civilizations, a positive tendency to exaggerate their qualitative differences and their unintelligibility (meaning that common-sense understanding is impossible) so as to obtain understanding (which in this context means a comprehensive portrayal). In the natural sciences things happen the other way round. Here we begin with uncomprehending observation, which is then accounted for in terms of conceptual description. The mode of thought, to begin with, stays broadly affiliated, qualitatively, to one particular approach, and is therefore impotent, so far as the way things are happening under observation is concerned. There is explanation without, as yet, anything being understood. As soon as there is a successful outline established of a relationship which permits measurement to come into play, explanation loses its descriptive character and throws off the qualitative concepts, which are to a greater or lesser degree connected with the observer's original approach. As it accumulates understanding of the way the things under observation are happening, it is quite simply transposed out of the sphere of the familiar into the language of mathematical symbols.

Cognitio circa rem (knowing about something) is the ability to proceed by mastering the context, the constellation in which the 'thing' in question occurs, expressed in a language which ideally substitutes signs for all natural word-meanings. *Cognitio rei* (knowing something) is perception of the heart of the matter, achieved through distanced and alienating understanding, and expressed in a language, the mastering of which requires close, intimate, and living contact with natural word-meanings and which avoids any symbolic formalization. These are the two directions in which natural science has developed since Galileo and Newton and in which the arts and humanities have developed since the great social theorists, philologists and historians of the eighteenth and nineteenth centuries. The ancient ideal, which had such far-reaching effects, according to which knowledge of nature was to be genuine understanding in the sense of comprehending perception, knowledge of human life, which was grasped so as to serve life, has lost its influence over us. We are masters of a world of nature we no longer understand. We understand a human world of which we are no longer masters.

This divorce of understanding and mastery constitutes the greatest possible danger to the contemporary world, however deeply entrenched modern scientific thought may be and however much the development of the technological marvels of today owes to it. For in his inability to reconcile mastery with understanding, and to reveal to man his place in, and duty towards, a world in which nature and mind meet – an inability which we feel rather than know to exist – man attempts to master mankind in whatever respects he can manage – which means in terms of nature, rather than mind. There is a paradoxical parallel between the subtle penetration of the alienated spiritual and intellectual life of the individual, and the methodical transformation of man which eliminates all his humanity and turns him into a thing, an object, and which casts its shadow in terms of racist ideology. Some 'brave new world' with even greater possibilities for power will be easily managed without much irresponsible falsification. If philosophy does not succeed in achieving a balance between knowledge of the human world and knowledge of nature, between mastery and understanding, no political progress or religious awakening can ward off the dangers threatening mankind for any length of time.

A frequently expressed objection to Dilthey's philosophy of life has been that the total understanding it requires has, so it is said, led to the relativization of the values of the individual and has helped to bring about a crisis of belief, of certainty. In reply, I can offer the following consideration, particularly with respect to the danger I have mentioned. If understanding does reach through to its own actual historical condition and becomes conscious of it, and does not rest until it has become estranged from itself and grasped itself through the distancing eye, it could lead to the growth of a new security and freedom for man. But he must not stop halfway. An uncommitted conception of life or existence which might be regarded as a substructure independent of time or place, and which affects every single thing that men have brought about or can ever bring about, bars the way to an alienating vision of one's own world, if it remains – as happened with existentialism – in some twilight zone between ethics and anthropological analysis. The strength of insight is proven in an experience which is limited. Its fruitful simplicity remains both territory and boundary for understanding. It must start from life-experience and must return to it.

In understanding I have to commit myself, if the object in question is to be reasoned through. The greater the commitment – i.e. the richer and more profound the individual capacity for resonance – the weightier it becomes; so the more difficult the object becomes, the more important it is. Understanding is not the identification of self with others, so that distance is eliminated; it is becoming familiar at a distance which permits one to see the other at one and the same time as other, as something alien. Studying the human mind is bound up with understanding, and understanding diminishes in so far as we rely on familiarity. Nothing is ever finished with.

Something that at one time became perfectly visible because the vision was subject to shock, and, subsequently, to an idea suddenly striking a creative imagination, in traditional terms, fades with the passing of time. It becomes obvious and banal; the vision fades. Different eyes are always necessary to make what has been visible for a long time, but which cannot be sustained, become apparent once more, in a different way. We can always return to sense-perception, regardless of how any particular conceptual scheme treats it. Experiment in the natural sciences is carried out on the selfsame assumption that sense impressions can be identified under certain prescribed conditions. For the observation of the working of the human mind, however, there is no repetition. It cannot be kept still, or unchanged. Once it passes down into tradition, it is framed with the very words used to evoke the object, within the medium of familiarity and is finally buried by it. Somebody else must come, and further shocks and catastrophies happen so as to make the scales fall from their eyes. True vision of men and human affairs is possible, at any time, only when they become something different, and are seen with different eyes.

It is often said, of course, in refutation of this thesis and in defence of the unity of the scientific method, that ultimately every discovery, in whatever field, is dependent on the reconstitution of the observer's point of view, with which it began and to which it returns. It is as though the scales fell from their eyes for the mathematician, the physicist and the biologist, too; nevertheless, the continuity of research is maintained between people and periods despite their different languages and different traditions.

This seems to be an objection, but it is in fact a confirmation of our thesis. Natural scientists and mathematicians are also subject to common human limitations in any particular situation. The solution of a problem is bound up with certain conditions which have to be fulfilled if the general reconstitution of the subject, necessary to produce a solution, is to be successful, quite independently of what 'elements' are involved in the structure of the particular field – numbers, physical or chemical symbols, sense-data, words or some other signifier. It is here, just as in any situation where there are difficulties to be resolved, that imagination enters, something which neither theorists nor practitioners, scholars nor technicians, artists nor statesmen can do without: imagination means an ability to liberate oneself from a given situation *and* to associate oneself with it, an ability which each one must have at his disposal, if only to a modest degree.

But the imaginative factor may be limited, in mathematics and the natural science and in their dependent disciplines, to a creative auxiliary function in the discovery of new relationships, because they have at their disposal identifiable quantities and operative rules based on definition, stipulation or experimental conditions which are independent of explanation. The human sciences are in a quite different situation. Their factual, observable, basis lies in texts and in documents which only an understanding, sympathetic, involvement can make fully accessible. The helping hand of imagination not only contributes to the construction of hypotheses, but to the construction of the original elements to which the hypotheses are applied. If the human scientist is working with material which is incomprehensible without some personal experience of what is expressed in that material, it follows that theory in the human sciences does not develop by following the circular schema: point of view – concept – some overall conception – concept – point of view. The relationship between sense perception and imagination, which is valid for the experience of nature, does not obtain in this case. Perceptual observation becomes auxiliary, and the imagination acquires, in addition to its function in the theoretical structuring of understanding, the simultaneous task of representing afresh a reality which is irrevocably dead, along with the people who lived then. It is for the imagination to produce the objects wherein understanding is to be fulfilled.

Bringing what is irrevocably past into the present can only be accomplished in a language which it is impossible to formalize, since it has to appeal to the power of the imagination. Thus the following two assertions can be made: it is for the imagination to produce whatever objects are inherent in texts and artefacts, so that they are present, and understanding may be achieved; secondly, producing such objects is something which cannot be done apart from the living commonalty of language, or be preserved from decay. It has to be done over and over again, and always as if it were looked at for the first time.

3 Edmund Husserl

The Origin of Geometry*

E. Husserl, *The Crisis of European Sciences and Transcendental Phenomenology*, trans. D. Carr, Evanston: Northwestern University Press, 1970, pp. 353–78.

The interest that propels us in this work makes it necessary to engage first of all in reflections which surely never occurred to Galileo. We must focus our gaze not merely upon the ready-made, handed-down geometry and upon the manner of being which its meaning had in his thinking; it was no different in his thinking from what it was in that of all the late inheritors of the older geometric wisdom, whenever they were at work, either as pure geometers or as making practical applications of geometry. Rather, indeed, above all, we must also inquire back into the original meaning of the handed-down geometry, which continued to be valid with this very same meaning – continued and at the same time was developed further, remaining simply 'geometry' in all its new forms. Our considerations will necessarily lead to the deepest problems of meaning, problems of science and of the history of science in general, and indeed in the end to problems of a universal history in general; so that our problems and expositions concerning Galilean geometry take on an exemplary significance.

Let it be noted in advance that, in the midst of our historical meditations on modern philosophy, there appears here for the first time with Galileo, through the disclosure of the depth-problems of the meaning-origin of geometry and, founded on

---

* This manuscript was written in 1936 and was edited and published (beginning with the third paragraph) by Eugen Fink in the *Revue internationale de philosophie*, Vol. I, No. 2 (1939), under the title 'Der Ursprung der Geometrie als intentional-historisches Problem'. It appears in Biemel's edition of the *Crisis* as 'Beilage III', pp. 365–86. The first paragraphs suggest it was meant for inclusion in the *Crisis*.

this, of the meaning-origin of his new physics, a clarifying light for our whole undertaking: namely, the idea of seeking to carry out, in the form of historical meditations, self-reflections about our own present philosophical situation in the hope that in this way we can finally take possession of the meaning, method, and beginning of philosophy, the *one* philosophy to which our life seeks to be and ought to be devoted. For, as will become evident here, at first in connection with one example, our investigations are historical in an unusual sense, namely, in virtue of a thematic direction which opens up depth-problems quite unknown to ordinary history, problems which, however, in their own way, are undoubtedly historical problems. Where a consistent pursuit of these depth-problems leads can naturally not yet be seen at the beginning.

The question of the origin of geometry (under which title here, for the sake of brevity, we include all disciplines that deal with shapes existing mathematically in pure space-time) shall not be considered here as the philological-historical question, i.e. as the search for the first geometers who actually uttered pure geometrical propositions, proofs, theories, or for the particular propositions they discovered, or the like. Rather than this, our interest shall be the inquiry back into the most original sense in which geometry once arose, was present as the tradition of millennia, is still present for us, and is still being worked on in a lively forward development;[1] we inquire into that sense in which it appeared in history for the first time – in which it had to appear, even though we know nothing of the first creators and are not even asking after them. Starting from what we know, from our geometry, or rather from the older handed-down forms (such as Euclidean geometry), there is an inquiry back into the submerged original beginnings of geometry as they necessarily must have been in their 'primally establishing' function. This regressive inquiry unavoidably remains within the sphere of generalities, but, as we shall soon see, these are generalities which can be richly explicated, with prescribed possibilities of arriving at

1. So also for Galileo and all the periods following the Renaissance, continually being worked on in a lively forward development, and yet at the same time a tradition.

particular questions and self-evident claims as answers. The geometry which is ready-made, so to speak, from which the regressive inquiry begins, is a tradition. Our human existence moves within innumerable traditions. The whole cultural world, in all its forms, exists through tradition. These forms have arisen as such not merely causally; we also know already that tradition is precisely tradition, having arisen within our human space through human activity, i.e. spiritually, even though we generally know nothing, or as good as nothing, of the particular provenance and of the spiritual source that brought it about. And yet there lies in this lack of knowledge, everywhere and essentially, an implicit knowledge, which can thus also be made explicit, a knowledge of unassailable self-evidence. It begins with superficial commonplaces, such as: that everything traditional has arisen out of human activity, that accordingly past men and human civilizations existed, and among them their first inventors, who shaped the new out of materials at hand, whether raw or already spiritually shaped. From the superficial, however, one is led into the depths. Tradition is open in this general way to continued inquiry; and, if one consistently maintains the direction of inquiry, an infinity of questions opens up, questions which lead to definite answers in accord with their sense. Their form of generality – indeed, as one can see, of unconditioned general validity – naturally allows for application to individually determined particular cases, though it determines only that in the individual that can be grasped through subsumption.

Let us begin, then, in connection with geometry, with the most obvious commonplaces that we have already expressed above in order to indicate the sense of our regressive inquiry. We understand our geometry, available to us through tradition (we have learned it, and so have our teachers), to be a total acquisition of spiritual accomplishments which grows through the continued work of new spiritual acts into new acquisitions. We know of its handed-down, earlier forms, as those from which it has arisen; but with every form the reference to an earlier one is repeated. Clearly, then, geometry must have arisen out of a *first* acquisition, out of first creative activities. We understand its persisting manner of being: it is not only a mobile forward process from one set of acquisitions to another but a continuous synthesis in which all acquisitions maintain their validity, all make up a totality such that, at every present stage, the total acquisition is, so to speak, the total premise for the acquisitions of the new level. Geometry necessarily has this mobility and has a horizon of geometrical future in precisely this style; this is its meaning for every geometer who has the consciousness (the constant implicit knowledge) of existing within a forward development understood as the progress of knowledge being built into the horizon. The same thing is true of every science. Also, every science is related to an open chain of the generations of those who work for and with one another, researchers either known or unknown to one another who are the accomplishing subjectivity of the whole living science. Science, and in particular geometry, with this ontic meaning, must have had a historical beginning; this meaning itself must have an origin in an accomplishment: first as a project and then in successful execution.

Obviously it is the same here as with every other invention. Every spiritual accomplishment proceeding from its first project to its execution is present for the first time in the self-evidence of actual success. But when we note that mathematics has the manner of being of a lively forward movement from acquisitions as premises to new acquisitions, in whose ontic meaning that of the premises is included (the process continuing in this manner), then it is clear that the *total* meaning of geometry (as a developed science, as in the case of every science) could not have been present as a project and then as mobile fulfilment at the beginning. A more primitive formation of meaning necessarily went before it as a preliminary stage, undoubtedly in such a way that it appeared for the first time in the self-evidence of successful realization. But this way of expressing it is actually overblown. Self-evidence means nothing more than grasping an entity with the consciousness of its original being-itself-there (*Selbst-da*). Successful realization of a project is, for the acting subject, self-evidence; in this self-evidence, what has been realized is there, *originaliter*, as itself.

But now questions arise. This process of projecting and successfully realizing occurs, after all, purely within the *subject* of the inventor, and thus the meaning, as present *originaliter* with its whole content, lies exclusively, so to speak, within his mental space. But geometrical existence is not psychic existence; it does not exist as something personal within the personal sphere of consciousness; it is the existence of what is objectively there for 'everyone' (for actual and possible geometers, or those who understand geometry). Indeed, it has, from its primal establishment, an existence which is peculiarly supertemporal and which – of this we are certain – is accessible to all men, first of all to the actual and possible mathematicians of all peoples, all ages; and this is true of all its particular forms. And all forms newly produced by someone on the basis of pregiven forms immediately take on the same objectivity. This is, we note, an 'ideal' objectivity. It is proper to a whole class of spiritual products of the cultural world, to which not only all scientific constructions and the sciences themselves belong but also, for example, the constructions of fine literature.[2] Works of this class do not, like tools (hammers, pliers) or like architectural and other such products, have a repeatability in many like exemplars. The Pythagorean theorem, indeed all of geometry, exists only once, no matter how often or even in what language it may be expressed. It is identically the same in the 'original language' of Euclid and in all 'translations'; and within each language it is again the same, no matter how many times it has been sensibly uttered, from the original expression and writing-down to the innumerable oral utterances or written and other documentations. The sensible utterances have spatio-temporal individuation in the world like all corporeal occurrences, like everything embodied in bodies as such; but this is not true of the spiritual form itself, which is called an 'ideal object' (*ideale Gegenständlichkeit*). In a certain way ideal objects do exist objectively in the world, but it is only in

2. But the broadest concept of literature encompasses them all; that is, it belongs to their objective being that they be linguistically expressed and can be expressed again and again; or, more precisely, they have their objectivity, their existence-for-everyone, only as signification, as the meaning of speech. This is true in a peculiar fashion in the case of the objective sciences: for them the difference between the original language of the work and its translation into other languages does not remove its identical accessibility or change it into an inauthentic, indirect accessibility.

virtue of these two-levelled repetitions and ultimately in virtue of sensibly embodying repetitions. For language itself, in all its particularizations (words, sentences, speeches), is, as can easily be seen from the grammatical point of view, thoroughly made up of ideal objects; for example, the word *Löwe* (lion) occurs only once in the German language; it is identical throughout its innumerable utterances by any given persons. But the idealities of geometrical words, sentences, theories – considered purely as linguistic structures – are not the idealities that make up what is expressed and brought to validity as truth in geometry; the latter are ideal geometrical objects, states of affairs, etc. Wherever something is asserted, one can distinguish what is thematic, that about which it is said (its meaning), from the assertion, which itself, during the asserting, is never and can never be thematic. And what is thematic here is precisely ideal objects, and quite different ones from those coming under the concept of language. Our problem now concerns precisely the ideal objects which are thematic in geometry: how does geometrical ideality (just like that of all sciences) proceed from its primary intrapersonal origin, where it is a structure within the conscious space of the first inventor's soul, to its ideal objectivity? In advance we see that it occurs by means of language, through which it receives, so to speak, its linguistic living body (*Sprachleib*). But how does linguistic embodiment make out of the merely intrasubjective structure the *objective* structure which, e.g. as geometrical concept or state of affairs, is in fact present as understandable by all and is valid, already in its linguistic expression as geometrical speech, as geometrical proposition, for all the future in its geometrical sense?

Naturally, we shall not go into the general problem which also arises here of the origin of language in its ideal existence and its existence in the real world grounded in utterance and documentation; but we must say a few words here about the relation between language, as a function of man within human civilization, and the world as the horizon of human existence.

Living wakefully in the world we are constantly conscious of the world, whether we pay attention to it or not, conscious of it as the horizon of our life, as a horizon of 'things' (real objects), of our actual and possible interests and activities. Always standing out against the world-horizon is the horizon of our fellow men, whether there are any of them present or not. Before even taking notice of it at all, we are conscious of the open horizon of our fellow men with its limited nucleus of our neighbours, those known to us. We are thereby co-conscious of the men on our external horizon in each case as 'others'; in each case 'I' am conscious of them as 'my' others, as those with whom I can enter into actual and potential, immediate and mediate relations of empathy; this involves a reciprocal 'getting along' with others; and on the basis of these relations I can deal with them, enter into particular modes of community with them, and then know, in a habitual way, of my being so related. Like me, every human being – and this is how he is understood by me and everyone else – has his fellow men and, always counting himself, civilization in general, in which he knows himself to be living.

It is precisely to this horizon of civilization that common language belongs. One is conscious of civilization from the start as an immediate and mediate linguistic community. Clearly it is only through language and its far-reaching documentations, as possible communications, that the horizon of civilization can be an open and endless one, as it always is for men. What is privileged in consciousness as the horizon of civilization and as the linguistic community is mature normal civilization (taking away the abnormal and the world of children). In this sense civilization is, for every man whose we-horizon it is, a community of those who can reciprocally express themselves, normally, in a fully understandable fashion; and within this community everyone can talk about what is within the surrounding world of his civilization as objectively existing. Everything has its name, or is namable in the broadest sense, i.e. linguistically expressible. The objective world is from the start the world for all, the world which 'everyone' has as world-horizon. Its objective being presupposes men, understood as men with a common language. Language, for its part, as function and exercised capacity, is related correlatively to the world, the universe of objects which is linguistically expressible in its being and its being-such. Thus men as men, fellow men, world – the world of which men, of which we, always talk and can talk – and, on the other hand, language, are inseparably intertwined; and one is always certain of their inseparable relational unity, though usually only implicitly, in the manner of a horizon.

This being presupposed, the primally establishing geometer can obviously also express his internal structure. But the question arises again: How does the latter, in its 'ideality', thereby become objective? To be sure, something psychic which can be understood by others (*nachverstehbar*) and is communicable, as something psychic belonging to this man, is *eo ipso* objective, just as he himself, as concrete man, is experienceable and namable by everyone as a real thing in the world of things in general. People can agree about such things, can make common verifiable assertions on the basis of common experience, etc. But how does the intrapsychically constituted structure arrive at an inter-subjective being of its own as an ideal object which, as 'geometrical', is anything but a real psychic object, even though it has arisen psychically? Let us reflect. The original being-itself-there, in the immediacy (*Aktualität*) of its first production, i.e. in original 'self-evidence', results in no persisting acquisition at all that could have objective existence. Vivid self-evidence passes – though in such a way that the activity immediately turns into the passivity of the flowingly fading consciousness of what-has-just-now-been. Finally this 'retention' disappears, but the 'disappeared' passing and being past has not become nothing for the subject in question: it can be reawakened. To the passivity of what is at first obscurely awakened and what perhaps emerges with greater and greater clarity there belongs the possible activity of a recollection in which the past experiencing (*Erleben*) is lived through in a quasi-new and quasi-active way. Now if the originally self-evident production, as the pure fulfilment of its intention, is what is renewed (recollected), there necessarily occurs, accompanying the active recollection of what is past, an activity of concurrent actual production, and there arises thereby, in original 'coincidence', the self-evidence of identity: what has now been realized in original fashion is the same as what was previously self-evident. Also coestablished is the capacity for repetition at will with the self-evidence of the identity (coincidence of identity) of the structure throughout the chain of repetitions. Yet even with this, we have still not gone beyond the subject and his subjective, evident capacities; that is, we still have no 'objectivity' given. It does arise, however – in a preliminary stage – in understandable fashion as soon as we take into consideration the function of empathy and fellow mankind as a community of empathy and of language. In the contact of reciprocal linguistic understanding, the original production and the product of one subject can be *actively* understood by the others. In this full understanding of what is produced by the other, as in the case of recollection, a present coaccomplishment on one's own part of the presentified activity necessarily takes place; but at the same time there is also the self-evident consciousness of the identity of the mental structure in the productions of both the receiver of the communication and the communicator; and this occurs reciprocally. The productions can reproduce their likenesses from person to person, and in the chain of the understanding of these repetitions what is self-evident turns up as the same in the consciousness of the other. In the unity of the community of communication among several persons the repeatedly produced structure becomes an object of consciousness, not as a likeness, but as the one structure common to all.

Now we must note that the objectivity of the ideal structure has not yet been fully constituted through such actual transferring of what has been originally produced in one to others who originally reproduce it. What is lacking is the *persisting existence* of the 'ideal objects' even during periods in which the inventor and his fellows are no longer wakefully so related or even are no longer alive. What is lacking is their continuing-to-be even when no one has consciously realized them in self-evidence.

The important function of written, documenting linguistic expression is that it makes communications possible without immediate or mediate personal address; it is, so to speak, communication become virtual. Through this, the communalization of man is lifted to a new level. Written signs are, when considered from a purely corporeal point of view, straightforwardly, sensibly experienceable; and it is always possible that they be inter-subjectively experienceable in common. But as linguistic signs they awaken, as do linguistic sounds, their familiar significations. The awakening is something passive; the awakened signification is thus given passively, similarly to the way in which any other activity which has sunk into obscurity, once associatively awakened, emerges at first *passively* as a more or less clear memory. In the passivity in question here, as in the case of memory, what is passively awakened can be transformed back,[3] so to speak, into the corresponding activity: this is the capacity for reactivation that belongs originally to every human being as a speaking being. Accordingly, then, the writing-down effects a transformation of the original mode of being of the meaning-structure, e.g. within the geometrical sphere of self-evidence, of the geometrical structure which is put into words. It becomes sedimented, so to speak. But the reader can make it self-evident again, can reactivate the self-evidence.[4]

There is a distinction, then, between passively understanding the expression and making it self-evident by reactivating its meaning. But there also exist possibilities of a kind of activity, a thinking in terms of things that have been taken up merely receptively, passively, which deals with significations only passively understood and taken over, without any of the self-evidence of original activity. Passivity in general is the realm of things that are bound together and melt into one another associatively, where all meaning that arises is put together passively. What often happens here is that a meaning arises which is apparently possible as a unity – i.e. can apparently be made self-evidence through a possible reactivation – whereas the attempt at actual reactivation can reactivate only the individual members of the combination, while the intention to unify them into a whole, instead of being fulfilled, comes to nothing; that is,

3. This is a transformation of which one is conscious as being in itself patterned after what is passively awakened.

4. But this is by no means necessary or even factually normal. Even without this he can understand; he can concur 'as a matter of course' in the validity of what is understood without any activity of his own. In this case he comports himself purely passively and receptively.

the ontic validity is destroyed through the original consciousness of nullity.

It is easy to see that even in ordinary human life, and first of all in every individual life from childhood up to maturity, the originally intuitive life which creates its originally self-evident structures through activities on the basis of sense-experience very quickly and in increasing measure falls victim to the *seduction of language*. Greater and greater segments of this life lapse into a kind of talking and reading that is dominated purely by association; and often enough, in respect to the validities arrived at in this way, it is disappointed by subsequent experience.

Now one will say that in the sphere that interests us here – that of science, of thinking directed toward the attainment of truths and the avoidance of falsehood – one is obviously greatly concerned from the start to put a stop to the free play of associative constructions. In view of the unavoidable sedimentation of mental products in the form of persisting linguistic acquisitions, which can be taken up again at first merely passively and be taken over by anyone else, such constructions remain a constant danger. This danger is avoided if one not merely convinces oneself *ex post facto* that the particular construction can be reactivated but assures oneself from the start, after the self-evident primal establishment, of its capacity to be reactivated and enduringly maintained. This occurs when one has a view to the univocity of linguistic expression and to securing, by means of the most painstaking formation of the relevant words, propositions, and complexes of propositions, the results which are to be univocally expressed. This must be done by the individual scientist, and not only by the inventor but by every scientist as a member of the scientific community after he has taken over from the others what is to be taken over. This belongs, then, to the particulars of the scientific tradition within the corresponding community of scientists as a community of knowledge living in the unity of a common responsibility. In accord with the essence of science, then, its functionaries maintain the constant claim, the personal certainty, that everything they put into scientific assertions has been said 'once and for all', that it 'stands fast', forever identically repeatable with self-evidence and usable for further theoretical or practical ends – as indubitably reactivatable with the identity of its actual meaning.[5]

However, two more things are important here. First: we have not yet taken into account the fact that scientific thinking attains new results on the basis of those already attained, that the new ones serve as the foundation for still others, etc. – in the unity of a propagative process of transferred meaning.

In the finally immense proliferation of a science like geometry, what has become of the claim and the capacity for reactivation? When every researcher works on his part of the building, what of the vocational interruptions and time out for rest, which cannot be overlooked here? When he returns to the actual continuation of work, must he first run through the whole immense chain of groundings back to the original premises and actually reactivate the whole thing? If so, a science like our modern geometry would obviously not be possible at all. And yet it is of the essence of the results of each stage not only that their ideal ontic meaning in fact comes later than that of earlier results but that, since meaning is grounded upon meaning, the earlier meaning gives something of its validity to the later one, indeed becomes part of it to a certain extent. Thus no building block within the mental structure is self-sufficient; and none, then, can be immediately reactivated by itself.

This is especially true of sciences which, like geometry, have their thematic sphere in ideal products, in idealities from which more and more idealities at higher levels are produced. It is quite different in the so-called descriptive sciences, where the theoretical interest, classifying and describing, remains within the sphere of sense-intuition, which for it represents self-evidence. Here, at least in general, every new proposition can by itself be 'cashed in' for self-evidence.

5. At first, of course, it is a matter of a firm direction of the will, which the scientist establishes in himself, aimed at the certain capacity for reactivation. If the goal of reactivatability can be only relatively fulfilled, then the claim which stems from the consciousness of being able to acquire something also has its relativity; and this relativity also makes itself noticeable and is driven out. Ultimately, objective, absolutely firm knowledge of truth is an infinite idea.

How, by contrast, is a science like geometry possible? How, as a systematic, endlessly growing stratified structure of idealities, can it maintain its original meaningfulness through living reactivatability if its cognitive thinking is supposed to produce something new without being able to reactivate the previous levels of knowledge back to the first? Even if this could have succeeded at a more primitive stage of geometry, its energy would ultimately have been too much spent in the effort of procuring self-evidence and would not have been available for a higher productivity.

Here we must take into consideration the peculiar 'logical' activity which is tied specifically to language, as well as to the ideal cognitive structures that arise specifically within it. To any sentence structures that emerge within a merely passive understanding there belongs essentially a peculiar sort of activity best described by the word 'explication'.* A passively emerging sentence (e.g. in memory), or one heard and passively understood, is at first merely received with a passive ego-participation, taken up as valid; and in this form it is already our meaning. From this we distinguish the peculiar and important activity of explicating our meaning. Whereas in its first form it was a straightforwardly valid meaning, taken up as unitary and undifferentiated – concretely speaking, a straightforwardly valid declarative sentence – now what in itself is vague and undifferentiated is actively explicated. Consider, for example, the way in which we understand, when superficially reading the newspaper, and simply receive the 'news'; here there is a passive taking-over of ontic validity such that what is read straightway becomes our opinion.

But it is something special, as we have said, to have the intention to explicate, to engage in the activity which articulates what has been read (or an interesting sentence from it), extracting one by one, in separation from what has been vaguely, passively received as a unity, the elements of meaning, thus bringing the total validity to active performance in a new way on the basis of the individual validities. What was a passive meaning-pattern has now become one constructed through active production. This activity, then, is a peculiar sort of self-evidence; the structure

* *Verdeutlichung*, i.e. making explicit.

arising out of it is in the mode of having been originally produced. And in connection with this self-evidence, too, there is communalization. The explicated judgement becomes an ideal object capable of being passed on. It is this object exclusively that is meant by logic when it speaks of sentences or judgements. And thus the *domain of logic* is universally designated; this is universally the sphere of being to which logic pertains insofar as it is the theory of the sentences or propositions in general.

Through this activity, now, further activities become possible – self-evident constructions of new judgements on the basis of those already valid for us. This is the peculiar feature of logical thinking and of its purely logical self-evidences. All this remains intact even when judgements are transformed into assumptions, where, instead of ourselves asserting or judging, we think ourselves into the position of asserting or judging.

Here we shall concentrate on the sentences of language as they come to us passively and are merely received. In this connection it must also be noted that sentences give themselves in consciousness as reproductive transformations of an original meaning produced out of an actual, original activity; that is, in themselves they refer to such a genesis. In the sphere of logical self-evidence, deduction, or inference in forms of consequence, plays a constant and essential role. On the other hand, one must also take note of the constructive activities that operate with geometrical idealities which have been explicated but not brought to original self-evidence. (Original self-evidence must not be confused with the self-evidence of 'axioms'; for axioms are in principle already the results of original meaning-construction and always have this behind them.)

Now what about the possibility of complete and genuine reactivation in full originality, through going back to the primal self-evidences, in the case of geometry and the so-called 'deductive' sciences (so called, although they by no means merely deduce)? Here the fundamental law, with unconditionally general self-evidence, is: if the premises can actually be reactivated back to the most original self-evidence, then their self-evident consequences can be also. Accordingly it appears that, beginning with the primal self-evidences, the original genuineness must propagate itself through the chain of logical inference, no matter how long it is. However, if we consider the obvious finitude of the individual and even the social capacity to transform the logical chains of centuries, truly, in the unity of one accomplishment, into originally genuine chains of self-evidence, we notice that the above law contains within itself an idealization: namely, the removal of limits from our capacity, in a certain sense its infinitization. The peculiar sort of self-evidence belonging to such idealizations will concern us later.

These are, then, the general essential insights which elucidate the whole methodical development of the 'deductive' sciences and with it the manner of being which is essential to them.

These sciences are not handed down ready-made in the form of documented sentences; they involve a lively, productively advancing formation of meaning, which always has the documented, as a sediment of earlier production, at its disposal in that it deals with it logically. But out of sentences with sedimented signification, logical 'dealing' can produce only other sentences of the same character. That all new acquisitions express an actual geometrical truth is certain *a priori* under the presupposition that the foundations of the deductive structure have truly been produced and objectified in original self-evidence, i.e. have become universally accessible acquisitions. A continuity from one person to another, from one time to another, must have been capable of being carried out. It is clear that the method of producing original idealities out of what is prescientifically given in the cultural world must have been written down, and fixed in firm sentences prior to the existence of geometry; furthermore, the capacity for translating these sentences from vague linguistic understanding into the clarity of the reactivation of their self-evident meaning must have been, in its own way, handed down and ever capable of being handed down.

Only as long as this condition was satisfied, or only when the possibility of its fulfilment was perfectly secured for all time, could geometry preserve its genuine, original meaning as a deductive science throughout the progression of logical constructions. In other words, only in this case could every geometer be capable of bringing to mediate self-evidence the meaning borne by every sentence, not merely as its sedimented (logical) sentence-meaning but as its actual meaning, its truth-meaning. And so for all of geometry.

The progress of deduction follows formal-logical self-evidence; but without the actually developed capacity for reactivating the original activities contained within its fundamental concepts, i.e. without the 'what' and the 'how' of its prescientific materials, geometry would be a tradition empty of meaning; and if we ourselves did not have this capacity, we could never even know whether geometry had or ever did have a genuine meaning, one that could really be 'cashed in'.

Unfortunately, however, this is our situation, and that of the whole modern age.

The 'presupposition' mentioned above has in fact never been fulfilled. How the living tradition of the meaning-formation of elementary concepts is actually carried on can be seen in elementary geometrical instruction and its textbooks; what we actually learn there is how to deal with *ready-made* concepts and sentences in a rigorously methodical way. Rendering the concepts sensibly intuitable by means of drawn figures is substituted for the actual production of the primal idealities. And the rest is done by success – not the success of actual insight extending beyond the logical method's own self-evidence, but the practical successes of applied geometry, its immense, though not understood, practical usefulness. To this we must add something that will become visible further on in the treatment of historical mathematics, namely, the dangers of a scientific life that is completely given over to logical activities. These dangers lie in certain progressive transformations of meaning[6] to which this sort of scientific treatment drives one.

By exhibiting the essential presuppositions upon which rests the historical possibility of a genuine tradition, true to its origins, of sciences like geometry, we can understand how such sciences can vitally develop throughout the centuries and still not be genuine.

6. These work to the benefit of logical method, but they remove one further and further from the origins and make one insensitive to the problem of origin and thus to the actual ontic and truth-meaning of all these sciences.

The inheritance of propositions and of the method of logically constructing new propositions and idealities can continue without interruption from one period to the next, while the capacity for reactivating the primal beginnings, i.e. the sources of meaning for everything that comes later, has not been handed down with it. What is lacking is thus precisely what had given and had to give meaning to all propositions and theories, a meaning arising from the primal sources which can be made self-evident again and again.

Of course, grammatically coherent propositions and concatenations of propositions, no matter how they have arisen and have achieved validity – even if it is through mere association – have in all circumstances their own logical meaning, i.e. their meaning that can be made self-evident through explication; this can then be identified again and again as the same proposition, which is either logically coherent or incoherent, where in the latter case it cannot be executed in the unity of an actual judgement. In propositions which belong together in one domain and in the deductive systems that can be made out of them we have a realm of ideal identities; and for these there exist easily understandable possibilities of lasting traditionalization. But propositions, like other cultural structures, appear on the scene in the form of tradition; they claim, so to speak, to be sedimentations of a truth-meaning that can be made originally self-evident; whereas it is by no means necessary that they actually have such a meaning, as in the case of associatively derived falsifications. Thus the whole pre-given deductive science, the total system of propositions in the unity of their validities, is first only a claim which can be justified as an expression of the alleged truth-meaning only through the actual capacity for reactivation.

Through this state of affairs we can understand the deeper reason for the demand, which has spread throughout the modern period and has finally been generally accepted, for a so-called 'epistemological grounding' of the sciences, though clarity has never been achieved about what the much-admired sciences are actually lacking.[7]

7. What does Hume do but endeavour to inquire back into the primal impressions of developed ideas and, in general, scientific ideas?

As for further details on the uprooting of an originally genuine tradition, i.e. one which involved original self-evidence at its actual first beginning, one can point to possible and easily understandable reasons. In the first oral cooperation of the beginning geometers, the need was understandably lacking for an exact fixing of descriptions of the prescientific primal material and of the ways in which, in relation to this material, geometrical idealities arose together with the first 'axiomatic' propositions. Further, the logical superstructures did not yet rise so high that one could not return again and again to the original meaning. On the other hand, the possibility of the practical application of the derived laws, which was actually obvious in connection with the original developments, understandably led quickly, in the realm of praxis, to a habitually practised method of using mathematics, if need be, to bring about useful things. This method could naturally be handed down even without the ability for original self-evidence. Thus mathematics, emptied of meaning, could generally propagate itself, constantly being added to logically, as could the methodics of technical application on the other side. The extraordinarily far-reaching practical usefulness became of itself a major motive for the advancement and appreciation of these sciences. Thus also it is understandable that the lost original truth-meaning made itself felt so little, indeed, that the need for the corresponding regressive inquiry had to be reawakened. More than this: the true sense of such an inquiry had to be discovered.

Our results based on principle are of a generality that extends over all the so-called deductive sciences and even indicates similar problems and investigations for all sciences. For all of them have the mobility of sedimented traditions that are worked upon, again and again, by an activity of producing new structures of meaning and handing them down. Existing in this way, they extend enduringly through time, since all new acquisitions are in turn sedimented and become working materials. Everywhere the problems, the clarifying investigations, the insights of principle are *historical*. We stand within the horizon of human civilization, the one in which we ourselves now live. We are constantly, vitally conscious of this horizon, and specifically as a temporal horizon implied in our given present horizon. To the one human civilization there corresponds essentially the one cultural world as the surrounding life-world with its peculiar manner of being; this world, for every historical period and civilization, has its particular features and is precisely the tradition. We stand, then, within the historical horizon in which everything is historical, even though we may know very little about it in a definite way. But it has its essential structure that can be revealed through methodical inquiry. This inquiry prescribes all the possible specialized questions, thus including, for the sciences, the inquiries back into origin which are peculiar to them in virtue of their historical manner of being. Here we are led back to the primal materials of the first formation of meaning, the primal premises, so to speak, which lie in the prescientific cultural world. Of course, this cultural world has in turn its own questions of origin, which at first remain unasked.

Naturally, problems of this particular sort immediately awaken the total problem of the universal historicity of the correlative manners of being of humanity and the cultural world and the *a priori* structure contained in this historicity. Still, questions like that of the clarification of the origin of geometry have a closed character, such that one need not inquire beyond those prescientific materials.

*

Further clarifications will be made in connection with two objections which are familiar to our own philosophical-historical situation.

In the first place, what sort of strange obstinacy is this, seeking to take the question of the origin of geometry back to some undiscoverable Thales of geometry, someone not even known to legend? Geometry is available to us in its propositions, its theories. Of course we must and we can answer for this logical edifice to the last detail in terms of self-evidence. Here, to be sure, we arrive at first axioms, and from them we proceed to the original self-evidence which the fundamental concepts make possible. What is this, if not the 'theory of knowledge', in this case specifically the theory of geometrical knowledge? No one would think of tracing the epistemological problem back to such a supposed Thales. This is quite superfluous. The presently available concepts and propositions themselves contain their own meaning, first as non-self-evident opinion, but nevertheless as true propositions with a meant but still hidden truth which we can obviously bring to light by rendering the propositions themselves self-evident.

Our answer is as follows. Certainly the historical backward reference has not occurred to anyone; certainly theory of knowledge has never been seen as a peculiarly historical task. But this is precisely what we object to in the past. The ruling dogma of the separation in principle between epistemological elucidation and historical, even humanistic-psychological explanation, between epistemological and genetic origin, is fundamentally mistaken, unless one inadmissibly limits, in the usual way, the concepts of 'history', 'historical explanation', and 'genesis'. Or rather, what is fundamentally mistaken is the limitation through which precisely the deepest and most genuine problems of history are concealed. If one thinks over our expositions (which are of course still rough and will later of necessity lead us into new depth-dimensions), what they make obvious is precisely that what we know – namely, that the presently vital cultural configuration 'geometry' is a tradition and is still being handed down – is not knowledge concerning an external causality which effects the succession of historical configurations, as if it were knowledge based on induction, the presupposition of which would amount to an absurdity here; rather, to understand geometry or any given cultural fact is to be conscious of its historicity, albeit 'implicitly'. This, however, is not an empty claim; for quite generally it is true for every fact given under the heading of 'culture', whether it is a matter of the lowliest culture of necessities or the highest culture (science, state, church, economic organization, etc.), that every straightforward understanding of it as an experiential fact involves the 'co-consciousness' that it is something constructed through human activity. No matter how hidden, no matter how merely 'implicitly' co-implied this meaning is, there belongs to it the self-evident possibility of explication, of 'making it explicit' and clarifying it. Every explication and every transition from making explicit to making self-evident (even perhaps in cases where one stops much too soon) is nothing other than historical disclosure; in itself, essentially, it is something historical, and as such it bears, with essential necessity, the horizon of its history within itself. This is of course also to say that the whole of the cultural present, understood as a totality, 'implies' the whole of the cultural past in an undetermined but structurally determined generality. To put it more precisely, it implies a continuity of pasts which imply one another, each in itself being a past cultural present. And this whole continuity is a *unity* of traditionalization up to the present, which is our present *as* a process of traditionalizing itself in flowing-static vitality. This is, as has been said, an undetermined generality, but it has in principle a structure which can be much more widely explicated by proceeding from these indications, a structure which also grounds, 'implies', the possibilities for every search for and determination of concrete, factual states of affairs.

Making geometry self-evident, then, whether one is clear about this or not, is the disclosure of its historical tradition. But this knowledge, if it is not to remain empty talk or undifferentiated generality, requires the methodical production, proceeding from the present and carried out as research in the present, of differentiated self-evidences of the type discovered above (in several fragmentary investigations of what belongs to such knowledge superficially, as it were). Carried out systematically, such self-evidences result in nothing other and nothing less than the universal *a priori* of history with all its highly abundant component elements.

We can also say now that history is from the start nothing other than the vital movement of the coexistence and the inter-weaving of original formations and sedimentations of meaning.

Anything that is shown to be a historical fact, either in the present through experience or by a historian as a fact in the past, necessarily has its *inner structure of meaning*; but especially the motivational interconnections established about it in terms of everyday understanding have deep, further and further reaching implications which must be interrogated, disclosed. All merely factual history remains incomprehensible because, always merely drawing its conclusions naïvely and straightforwardly from facts, it never makes thematic the general ground of meaning upon which all such conclusions rest, has never investigated the immense structural *a priori* which is proper to it. Only the disclosure of the essentially general structure[8] lying in our present and then in every past or future historical present as such, and, in totality, only the disclosure of the concrete, historical time in which we live, in which our total humanity lives in respect to its total, essentially general structure – only this disclosure can make possible historical inquiry (*Historie*) which is truly understanding, insightful, and in the genuine sense scientific. This is the concrete, historical *a priori* which encompasses everything that exists as historical becoming and having-become or exists in its essential being as tradition and handing-down. What has been said was related to the total form 'historical present in general', historical time generally. But the particular configurations of culture, which find their place within its coherent historical being as tradition and as vitally handing themselves down, have within this totality only relatively self-sufficient being in traditionality, only the being of non-self-sufficient components. Correlatively, now, account would have to be taken of the subjects of historicity, the persons who create cultural formations, functioning in totality: creative personal civilization.[9]

In respect to geometry one recognizes, now that we have pointed out the hiddenness of its fundamental concepts, which have become inaccessible, and have made them understandable as such in first basic outlines, that only the consciously set task of discovering the historical origin of geometry (within the total problem of the *a priori* of historicity in general) can provide the method for a geometry which is true to its origins and at the same

8. The superficial structure of the externally 'ready-made' men within the social-historical, essential structure of humanity, but also the deeper structures which disclose the inner historicities of the persons taking part.

9. The historical world is, to be sure, first pregiven as a social-historical world. But it is historical only through the inner historicity of the individuals, who are individuals in their inner historicity, together with that of other communalized persons. Recall what was said in a few meagre beginning expositions about memories and the constant historicity to be found in them (pp. 49 f., above).

time is to be understood in a universal-historical way; and the same is true for all sciences, for philosophy. In principle, then, a history of philosophy, a history of the particular sciences in the style of the usual factual history, can actually render nothing of their subject matter comprehensible. For a genuine history of philosophy, a genuine history of the particular sciences, is nothing other than the tracing of the historical meaning-structures given in the present, or their self-evidences, along the documented chain of historical back-references into the hidden dimension of the primal self-evidences which underlie them.[10] Even the very problem here can be made understandable only through recourse to the historical *a priori* as the universal source of all conceivable problems of understanding. The problem of genuine historical explanation comes together, in the case of the sciences, with 'epistemological' grounding or clarification.

We must expect yet a second and very weighty objection. From the historicism which prevails extensively in different forms today I expect little receptivity for a depth-inquiry which goes beyond the usual factual history, as does the one outlined in this work, especially since, as the expression '*a priori*' indicates, it lays claim to a strictly unconditioned and truly apodictic self-evidence extending beyond all historical facticities. One will object: what naïveté, to seek to display, and to claim to have displayed, a historical *a priori*, an absolute, supertemporal validity, after we have obtained such abundant testimony for the relativity of everything historical, of all historically developed world-apperceptions, right back to those of the 'primitive' tribes. Every people, large or small, has its world in which, for that people, everything fits well together, whether in mythical-magical or in European-rational terms, and in which everything can be explained perfectly. Every people has its 'logic' and, accordingly, if this logic is explicated in propositions, 'its' *a priori*.

However, let us consider the methodology of establishing

10. But what counts as primal self-evidence for the sciences is determined by an educated person or a sphere of such persons who pose new questions, new historical questions, questions concerning the inner depth-dimension as well as those concerning an external historicity in the social-historical world.

historical facts in general, thus including that of the facts supporting the objection; and let us do this in regard to what such methodology presupposes. Does not the undertaking of a humanistic science of 'how it really was' contain a presupposition taken for granted, a validity-ground never observed, never made thematic, of a strictly unassailable type of self-evidence, without which historical inquiry would be a meaningless enterprise? All questioning and demonstrating which is in the usual sense historical presupposes history (*Geschichte*) as the universal horizon of questioning, not explicitly, but still as a horizon of implicit certainty, which, in spite of all vague background-indeterminacy, is the presupposition of all determinability, or of all intention to seek and to establish determined facts.

What is historically primary in itself is our present. We always already know of our present world and that we live in it, always surrounded by an openly endless horizon of unknown actualities. This knowing, as horizon-certainty, is not something learned, not knowledge which was once actual and has merely sunk back to become part of the background; the horizon-certainty had to be already there in order to be capable of being laid out thematically; it is already presupposed in order that we can seek to know what we do not know. All not-knowing concerns the unknown world, which yet exists in advance for us *as* world, as the horizon of all questions of the present and thus also all questions which are specifically historical. These are the questions which concern men, as those who act and create in their communalized coexistence in the world and transform the constant cultural face of the world. Do we not know further – we have already had occasion to speak of this – that this historical present has its historical pasts behind it, that it has developed out of them, that historical past is a continuity of pasts which proceed from one another, each, as a past present, being a tradition producing tradition out of itself? Do we not know that the present and the whole of historical time implied in it is that of a historically coherent and unified civilization, coherent through its generative bond and constant communalization in cultivating what has already been cultivated before, whether in cooperative work or in reciprocal interaction, etc.? Does all this not announce a universal 'knowing' of the horizon, an implicit knowing that can be made explicit systematically in its essential structure? Is not the resulting great problem here the horizon toward which all questions tend, and thus the horizon which is presupposed in all of them? Accordingly, we need not first enter into some kind of critical discussion of the facts set out by historicism; it is enough that even the claim of their factualness presupposes the historical *a priori* if this claim is to have a meaning.

But a doubt arises all the same. The horizon-exposition to which we recurred must not bog down in vague, superficial talk; it must itself arrive at its own sort of scientific discipline. The sentences in which it is expressed must be fixed and capable of being made self-evident again and again. Through what method do we obtain a universal and also fixed *a priori* of the historical world which is always originally genuine? Whenever we consider it, we find ourselves with the self-evident capacity to reflect – to turn to the horizon and to penetrate it in an expository way. But we also have, and know that we have, the capacity of complete freedom to transform, in thought and fantasy, our human historical existence and what is there exposed as its life-world. And precisely in this activity of free variation, and in running through the conceivable possibilities for the life-world, there arises, with apodictic self-evidence, an essentially general set of elements going through all the variants; and of this we can convince ourselves with truly apodictic certainty. Thereby we have removed every bond to the factually valid historical world and have regarded this world itself merely as one of the conceptual possibilities. This freedom, and the direction of our gaze upon the apodictically invariant, results in the latter again and again – with the self-evidence of being able to repeat the invariant structure at will – as what is identical, what can be made self-evident *originaliter* at any time, can be fixed in univocal language as the essence constantly implied in the flowing, vital horizon.

Through this method, going beyond the formal generalities we exhibited earlier, we can also make thematic that apodictic aspect of the prescientific world that the original founder of geometry had at his disposal, that which must have served as the material for his idealizations.

Geometry and the sciences most closely related to it have to do with space-time and the shapes, figures, also shapes of motion, alterations of deformation, etc., that are possible within space-time, particularly as measurable magnitudes. It is now clear that even if we know almost nothing about the historical surrounding world of the first geometers, this much is certain as an invariant, essential structure: that it was a world of 'things' (including the human beings themselves as subjects of this world); that all things necessarily had to have a bodily character – although not all things could be mere bodies, since the necessarily coexisting human beings are not thinkable as mere bodies and, like even the cultural objects which belong with them structurally, are not exhausted in corporeal being. What is also clear, and can be secured at least in its essential nucleus through careful *a priori* explication, is that these pure bodies had spatio-temporal shapes and 'material' (*stoffliche*) qualities (colour, warmth, weight, hardness, etc.) related to them. Further, it is clear that in the life of practical needs certain particularizations of shape stood out and that a technical praxis always aimed at the production of particular preferred shapes and the improvement of them according to certain directions of gradualness.

First to be singled out from the thing-shapes are surfaces – more or less 'smooth', more or less perfect surfaces; edges, more or less rough or fairly 'even'; in other words, more or less pure lines, angles, more or less perfect points; then, again, among the lines, for example, straight lines are especially preferred, and among the surfaces the even surfaces; for example, for practical purposes boards limited by even surfaces, straight lines, and points are preferred, whereas totally or partially curved surfaces are undesirable for many kinds of practical interests. Thus the production of even surfaces and their perfection (polishing) always plays its role in praxis. So also in cases where just distribution is intended. Here the rough estimate of magnitudes is transformed into the measurement of magnitudes by counting the equal parts. (Here, too, proceeding from the factual, an essential form becomes recognizable through a method of variation.) Measuring belongs to every culture, varying only according to stages from primitive to higher perfections. We can always presuppose some measuring technique, whether of a lower or higher type, in the essential forward development of culture, as well as the growth of such a technique, thus also including the art of design for buildings, of surveying fields, pathways, etc.; such a technique is always already there, already abundantly developed and pregiven to the philosopher who did not yet know geometry but who should be conceivable as its inventor. As a philosopher proceeding from the practical, finite surrounding world (of the room, the city, the landscape, etc., and temporally the world of periodical occurrences: day, month, etc.) to the theoretical world-view and world-knowledge, he has the finitely known and unknown spaces and times as finite elements within the horizon of an open infinity. But with this he does not yet have geometrical space, mathematical time, and whatever else is to become a novel spiritual product out of these finite elements which serve as material; and with his manifold finite shapes in their space-time he does not yet have geometrical shapes, the phoronomic shapes; his shapes, as formations developed out of praxis and thought of in terms of gradual perfection, clearly serve only as bases for a new sort of praxis out of which similarly named new constructions grow.

It is evident in advance that this new sort of construction will be a product arising out of an idealizing, spiritual act, one of 'pure' thinking, which has its materials in the designated general pregivens of this factual humanity and human surrounding world and creates 'ideal objects' out of them.

Now the problem would be to discover, through recourse to what is essential to history (*Historie*), the historical original meaning which necessarily was able to give and did give to the whole becoming of geometry its persisting truth-meaning.

It is of particular importance now to bring into focus and establish the following insight: only if the apodictically general content, invariant throughout all conceivable variation, of the spatio-temporal sphere of shapes is taken into account in the idealization can an ideal construction arise which can be understood for all future time and by all coming generations of men and thus be capable of being handed down and reproduced with the identical intersubjective meaning. This condition is valid far beyond geometry for all spiritual structures which are to be unconditionally and generally capable of being handed down. Were the thinking activity of a scientist to introduce something 'time-bound' in his thinking, i.e. something bound to what is merely factual about his present or something valid for him as a merely factual tradition, his construction would likewise have a merely time-bound ontic meaning; this meaning would be understandable only by those men who shared the same merely factual presuppositions of understanding.

It is a general conviction that geometry, with all its truths, is valid with unconditioned generality for all men, all times, all peoples, and not merely for all historically factual ones but for all conceivable ones. The presuppositions of principle for this conviction have never been explored because they have never been seriously made a problem. But it has also become clear to us that every establishment of a historical fact which lays claim to unconditioned objectivity likewise presupposes this invariant or absolute *a priori*.

Only through the disclosure of this *a priori* can there be an *a priori* science extending beyond all historical facticities, all historical surrounding worlds, peoples, times, civilizations; only in this way can a science as *aeterna veritas* appear. Only on this fundament is based the secured capacity of inquiring back from the temporarily depleted self-evidence of a science to the primal self-evidences.

Do we not stand here before the great and profound problem-horizon of reason, the same reason that functions in every man, the *animal rationale*, no matter how primitive he is?

This is not the place to penetrate into those depths themselves.

In any case, we can now recognize from all this that historicism, which wishes to clarify the historical or epistemological essence of mathematics from the standpoint of the magical circumstances or other manners of apperception of a time-bound civilization, is mistaken in principle. For romantic spirits the mythical-magical elements of the historical and prehistorical aspects of mathematics may be particularly attractive; but to cling to this merely historically factual aspect of mathematics is precisely to lose oneself to a sort of romanticism and to overlook the genuine problem, the internal-historical problem, the epistemological problem. Also, one's gaze obviously cannot then become free to recognize that facticities of every type, including those involved in the historicist objection, have a root in the essential structure of what is generally human, through which a teleological reason running throughout all historicity announces itself. With this is revealed a set of problems in its own right related to the totality of history and to the full meaning which ultimately gives it its unity.

If the usual factual study of history in general, and in particular the history which in most recent times has achieved true universal extension over all humanity, is to have any meaning at all, such a meaning can only be grounded upon what we can here call internal history, and as such upon the foundations of the universal historical *a priori*. Such a meaning necessarily leads further to the indicated highest question of a universal teleology of reason.

If, after these expositions, which have illuminated very general and many-sided problem-horizons, we lay down the following as something completely secured, namely, that the human surrounding world is the same today and always, and thus also in respect to what is relevant to primal establishment and lasting tradition, then we can show in several steps, only in an exploratory way, in connection with our own surrounding world, what should be considered in more detail for the problem of the idealizing primal establishment of the meaning-structure 'geometry'.

4 Aron Gurwitsch

Galilean Physics in the Light of Husserl's Phenomenology

A. Gurwitsch, 'Galilean Physics in the Light of Husserl's Phenomenology', in *Galileo, Man of Science*, ed. Ernan McMullin, New York: Basic Books, 1967, pp. 388–401.

Husserl's analysis of Galilean physics, on which I am to comment, is contained in his book *Die Krisis der Europäischen Wissenschaften und die Transzendentale Phänomenologie*. A translation true to the spirit rather than the letter might render the title as *The Crisis of Western Sciences and Transcendental Phenomenology*. 'European' was not meant by Husserl to be taken geographically; rather, he took it to have an historical sense as referring to the Occidental world, understood as the scene of an unfolding and a unified intellectual development. To this, his last work, Husserl devoted the closing years of his life, but he was unable to bring it to completion.[1] In Husserl's lifetime, the first third of what was later to become the book appeared in the form of an article under the same title.[2] The discussion of Galileo occupies the centre of this article.

Both the article and the book have the subtitle: 'An introduction to phenomenological philosophy'. The subtitle indicates the general perspective in which Husserl places his analysis of modern science or, as Husserl calls it, the 'science of Galilean style'. His intention was to open up a new avenue of approach to phenomenological philosophy. The novelty of this approach consisted in the fact that, in contradistinction to his earlier writings, he takes his departure from certain basic problems that beset modern science or, more accurately, from the very existence of this science of 'modern style' itself. It appears legitimate to

1. It was edited in 1954 by Walter Biemel at the Husserl Archives, and appears as Volume 6 of the *Husserliana* series.
2. In the little-known and long extinct periodical, *Philosophia*, Belgrade, 1, 1936.

isolate, or at least to concentrate upon, his analysis of Galileo, and this is what I shall try to do. When read in this light, Husserl's book acquires a significance of the first order for the philosophy of science. It marks a turning-point in the development of this discipline and inaugurates a new phase in its history.

Three phases in the philosophy of science

Roughly speaking, one can distinguish two phases in the philosophy of science prior to the appearance of Husserl's work. The first phase extends approximately from the middle of the seventeenth century to the middle of the eighteenth century. Descartes' *Meditations on first philosophy* may be considered as a representative document of this first period. Descartes sets out to provide a foundation for, and a validation of, the new science. It is to rest upon and be guided by the following thesis: The universe is not as it appears in common experience; its nature and structure do not lay themselves open to perception; on the contrary, they have to be uncovered by means of mathematical notions. In reality, then, the universe is not as it seems to be, but as it is conceived and constructed by the mathematical physicist.

We children of the twentieth century may find it difficult to realize the boldness of this thesis because we are heirs to a tradition of science which we have come to take for granted as something definitely possessed, rather than as something to be acquired and justified. We hardly see any necessity, therefore, for a justification of the thesis upon which modern science rests. In the seventeenth century, the situation was quite different. The men of that day were not heirs but inaugurators, to whom the legitimacy of their endeavour presented a real problem. Descartes' solution to this problem was to have recourse to the Divine veracity in order to guarantee the validity of the principle that whatever is clearly and distinctly perceived is true. It was on the basis of this principle that mathematical knowledge and the geometrical conception of the external world seemed to him to be justified. Along similar lines, though in some respects differently from Descartes, Malebranche conceived of the intellectual life of man, insofar as he engages himself in genuinely cognitive endeavours, as some kind of participation in the intellectual life of the Deity. Galileo in a famous passage speaks in the same vein.

The second period in the development of the philosophy of science began in the year 1748, when Leonhard Euler, the great Swiss mathematician, submitted to the Royal Prussian Academy of Berlin a memoir entitled *Réflexions sur l'espace et le temps*. This memoir, which concerns itself with the problems of absolute motion, absolute space, and absolute time, is Euler's contribution to the discussion regarding the nature of space, which had been going on for over a century, and in which Descartes, Malebranche, the Cambridge neo-Platonists, Newton and his followers, Leibniz, Berkeley, and others had taken part. Euler grants that philosophy must concern itself with the fundamental concepts of the sciences, especially of physics. However, the decision as to whether or not a given concept should be admitted among these falls under the competence of physics rather than of philosophy. If it appears that the laws of dynamics, especially the law of inertia, require for their formulation the notions of absolute space and absolute time, then these notions (as well as that of absolute motion which they immediately imply) must be admitted as valid. They derive their right of citizenship from the part they play within the theoretical context of physics. Against such a decision, which is based upon the theoretical exigencies of physics, no appeal is possible. Consequently, philosophy must accept this decision, and accommodate its constructions and theories accordingly.

Euler's memoir contains a 'declaration of independence' on the part of physics with regard to philosophy. Such a claim to autonomy was made possible by the accomplishments of the science of physics during the preceding century and a half, and it expresses a self-confidence rooted in those accomplishments. Euler's memoir opened up the second phase of the philosophy of science, a phase in which science is no longer considered as in need of justification and validation, but on the contrary, as a given fact simply to be accepted. The phrase 'science as a fact' is, as a rule, associated with the name of Kant. But what Kant did was to provide an elaborate realization of the programme which Euler had not only anticipated but conceived in a rather concrete fashion. Husserl's *Crisis of Western Sciences* thus marks the beginning of a third phase in the philosophy of science. Whereas in the second phase science was accepted as a fact, in the third phase it appears as a *problem*. It is under this historical perspective, I suggest, that Husserl's discussion of Galileo can best be understood.

Two preliminary remarks are worth making. In the first place, this attribution of a problematic status to science must not be mistaken for the expression of an 'anti-scientific spirit'. Awareness of problems which beset the very existence of modern science is something quite different from hostility toward science itself. I feel impelled to apologize for this truism. Yet judging by what one reads, it seems necessary to insist upon it. Hostility to science was totally alien to Husserl, whose own scholarly career had begun in mathematics. It was, in fact, because of his training in, and first-hand acquaintance with, modern mathematical science that Husserl was not prepared to listen in an attitude of superstitious awe to slogans about 'Science' or 'Scientific Method'.

In the second place, Husserl was not an historian of science and never made any claim to be one, even though he presented his views on 'science as a problem' in the form of an analysis of Galileo's work. One may doubt whether he ever gave to the study of Galileo's writings that time and attention which a professional historian would devote to them as a matter of course. Cassirer's discussion of Galileo in *Das Erkenntnisproblem in der Philosophie und Wissenschaft der neueren Zeit* may well have been one of Husserl's main sources of information. He remarks himself that he does not distinguish between Galileo's own contributions and those made by his predecessors (nor those made by his successors, one might add). As a matter of fact, he ascribes some ideas to Galileo with which Descartes or Huygens should have been credited instead. In the face of such historical inaccuracies of fact, it may not be out of place to recall the judgement of an authority in the history of science, the late Alexandre Koyré, who once remarked to me that even though Husserl was not a historian either by training or by temperament, or by direction of interest, his analysis provides the key for a profound and radical understanding of Galileo's work. At any rate, we can assume that when Husserl speaks of 'Galileo', he does not really mean the historical figure bearing that name. Rather, as he says himself, he uses the name as a symbol. It symbolizes for him the 'spirit of modern physics', a spirit of which the real Galileo was, of course, a pioneer. This is what he means by a 'physics of Galilean style'. He submits this physics to a critique, not (once again be it said) a criticism.

Galilean physics as a problem

Let us approach this topic from different angles, since it has many facets. Husserl compares scientific activity, as it has developed during the last three centuries, to the functioning of a machine. He has in mind not so much the machines of industry as the 'machines' of the logician or mathematician, i.e. the symbolic procedures which have proved of such paramount importance for the development and formalization of mathematics. Such algorithmic procedures can be applied in a purely mechanical fashion, their use demanding no more than the observance of formal rules of operation. Methods of science, once invented, tend to become formalized and to undergo a process of 'technization' of this sort, in the course of which their application becomes a matter of routine. We possess scientific methods; we operate and manipulate, and we invent new and better – that is, more effective – methods. In this way, results of the highest importance from both the theoretical and the practical points of view are obtained. If by an 'understanding' of science no more is meant than the successful application of methodical procedures, there seems to be no difficulty. In fact, the 'technician of science' – a term not meant in any pejorative sense, but simply to denote someone whose exclusive interest lies in practical achievement – might simply rest his case on the successful operation of the scientific 'machine', since it yields results of the kind he wishes to obtain.

Not so the philosopher, whose very *raison d'être* is to raise radical questions, radical in the etymological sense of going to the roots. The philosopher cannot be satisfied with the actual working of the machine, he must wonder why and how it functions. From the machine as a fact here and now, he will go back to the mechanism which makes it work, to the principles involved in its construction, to the conditions upon which this construction depends. To express this less metaphorically, we have to inquire into the presuppositions which underlie the elaboration of science of the Galilean style, presuppositions from which that science derives its sense and which defines, in consequence, its limitations. They are well concealed, and remain so as long as one adopts what I have called the attitude of the scientific technician. Since they determine the sense of scientific activity, to make them explicit is to elucidate the meaning of science itself. What is in question is not the meaning of particular scientific conceptions and theories, like quantum physics or the theory of relativity, but rather the meaning of modern science in its entirety, the meaning in particular, of that progressive mathematization of nature which Galileo first conceived.

A question that must occur to anyone who has to deal with science in its historic aspect is: why did the mathematization of nature start around 1600 and in Italy? Why did it not start before then, or in another civilization? Why not in Greece, or in Rome, where the engineers were of a remarkably high level of competence? Why did it not start during the Middle Ages? It would obviously be silly to try to explain this in terms of some sort of intellectual inferiority during those periods. To answer the question, one would have to turn to a historically oriented sociology of knowledge. But I am raising the question merely for the purpose of emphasizing that the existence of science of the modern style must not be taken for granted. For many centuries, a highly civilized mankind got along without the mathematical conception of nature. To be sure, there were the Pythagoreans and there was Archimedes. But these thinkers left no enduring imprint upon the intellectual development that immediately followed them.

Physics and the *Lebenswelt*

The mathematical conception of nature is, therefore, not essential to the human mind. In direct experience, nature does not present itself as a mathematical system. There has been a discrepancy from the beginning between the universe constructed by physical science and the world given to us in immediate (mainly perceptual) experience. This latter is the world into which we are born, within which we find ourselves at every moment of our lives, no matter what activities we are engaged in, and no matter what goals and aims we are pursuing. Within that world, we encounter our fellow men, to whom we stand in relations of the most diverse kinds. With the ways of this world – the 'life-world' (*Lebenswelt*) as Husserl calls it – we have acquired, both through education and through personal experience, a familiarity of a very special sort. The objects which we encounter in this world have human significance; they present themselves as tools, as utensils to be handled in specific ways in order that desired results may be obtained. Moreover, they exhibit certain intrinsic properties of their own. For instance, over there is a blue chair. In the *Lebenswelt* we take our bearings from perceptual experience and thus unhesitatingly consider the blue colour to be a property intrinsic to the chair. Unless we have studied physics or are indirectly influenced by it, it would not occur to us to regard the colour as a subjective phenomenon, a content of our consciousness, on the same footing as, say, a feeling of joy, a desire, or the like. What is at issue here is not merely the substitution for the colour of processes that are completely describable in mathematical terms, like wave-length, frequency, velocity of propagation, and the consequent replacement of qualitative differences by quantitative ones. Of equal importance is the ever-growing alienation of the universe of physics from the world of perceptual experience. The physics of the nineteenth century, even the field theories of Faraday and Maxwell, still made use of models that had intuitive content and lent themselves to visualization. Lines of force were conceived by analogy with rubber bands which stretch and contract. Contemporary physics, however, relies on constructs of a totally abstract nature which have to be treated according to algorithmic rules of operation alone. They no longer have a visualizable content, and no intuitive significance is claimed for them. What in the beginning appeared as a discrepancy has grown into an ever-widening gulf.

In an earlier phase of the modern period, the constructions of mathematical physics were not simply regarded as models, meant for convenience of systematization, prediction or even explanation. On the contrary, they were thought to express the true state of affairs, the real nature of the external world. By means of his mathematically expressed theories, the physicist was believed to pierce through the veil of perceptual appearance and thus to describe nature as it really is. This realistic interpretation of physics finds few defenders today, yet so recent and so great a physicist as Max Planck still adhered to it.

We seem somehow to be confronted with two realms. One is the realm of reality, of nature as mathematically conceived and constructed; the other is the world of appearances. Malebranche speaks of '*illusions naturelles*'. They are natural, because they are grounded in the real condition of things, on the basis of which they occur in regular fashion. (The explanation of this regularity is, incidentally, one of the principal tasks of the science of psychology in the specific modern sense.) But they *are* illusions, since they do not correspond to the true state of affairs. Nevertheless, the persistence of these illusions is most remarkable. Despite the rapid development of science, the perceptual world continues to be its familiar self. To the physicist and layman alike, things continue to exhibit chromatic qualities as though they were intrinsic to the things themselves. On a summer evening by the seashore, we still see the sun dipping into the ocean, all our knowledge of astronomy notwithstanding. Such facts point to some sort of priority on the part of the *Lebenswelt*. After all, scientific theories must be verified by means of observations, which, even if reduced to mere pointer readings, are still perceptual experiences. One might object that this priority holds good only *quo ad nos*: to arrive at the universe as it really is, we naturally have to take our departure from the world as it appears to us. Even if this objection were to be granted, the original point is still strong enough to make it worthwhile to inquire into those general features of the world of common experience which provide the initial motivation for constructing a mathematical conception of nature. Then we shall have to ask further what else, in addition to that motivation, is required for the actual elaboration of a mathematical physics.

Three features of the *Lebenswelt*

Fortunately for us, it is not necessary to present a full analytic description of the general structure of the *Lebenswelt*. This would be a very arduous task indeed, the more so as no complete and exhaustive analysis of it has yet been made, though many authors in recent decades have made valuable additions to Husserl's pioneer work. For our purposes, a few major points from Husserl's analysis will suffice. In the first place, the world of everyday experience is extended in space and time; these constitute a comprehensive frame in which all the existents of our experience can be related in spatial and in temporal terms with one another. Furthermore, things exhibit spatial forms. Trees, for instance, present a cylindrical shape. The phrase 'cylindrical shape' is, of course, not meant to be understood in a strictly geometrical sense, but rather as indicating a physiognomic aspect of spatial form. It does not denote a determinate figure, but rather a generic type of spatial configuration, one that within limits not precisely defined allows variation and deviation. Going beyond Husserl's analysis, it may be noted that psychologists, especially of the Gestalt school, have long used terms like 'circularity' or 'rectangularity' in this physiognomic sense, when they speak, for instance, of a circle as 'bad' or of one right angle as 'better than another'. From a strictly geometrical point of view, such phrases would be nonsense; they make good sense, however, when applied to the phenomenal aspects of perceptual experience. This experience is always affected by some vagueness and indefiniteness; its determinations only hold by and large. (For reasons to be made clear in a moment, I avoid speaking of 'approximation'.) One might, perhaps, characterize perceptual experience by saying that it is determinate as to type, but that there will ordinarily be some latitude about the manner in which the type is particularized.

In the second place, the 'life-world' exhibits various regularities. As far back as we can remember, we have been familiar with the alternation of day and night and with the change of the seasons. Living in the northern hemisphere, we have always known that in July it is hotter than in February and we act accordingly in choosing our clothing. Things, as Husserl expressed it, have their habits of behaviour. It is not from science, either Aristotelian or Galilean, that we learn that stones, when lifted and released, fall down. It is a matter of everyday experience in the life-world that water can be boiled and that, when further heated, it evaporates. Generally speaking, the life-world exhibits universal causality of a certain style. Events hang together with each other; occurrences of one type are regularly followed by occurrences of another type. Familiarity with such regularities, that is, with the 'style' of the universal causality, is of paramount importance for our existence and the practical conduct of our lives. It, and it alone, permits anticipations. Because of this familiarity, we know fairly well what to be prepared for in the near future; we can often influence the course of affairs to bring something about. As the late Alfred Schutz has shown in his penetrating analyses, all activities within the life-world are dominated throughout by the pragmatic motive. Since causal connections come to our attention originally on account of their pragmatic significance, it is natural that this same significance should determine the degree of accuracy with which these connections will be established and described. That is to say, our familiarity with particular causal connections as well as with the universal style of causality in the life-world is affected by the kind of indefiniteness and vagueness already commented upon, which thus appears to be a general feature of perceptual experience.

Finally, things in the life-world present themselves, as Husserl expresses it, in a certain relativity with respect to the experiencing subjects. All of us perceive the same objects in this room, but each one of us sees them from his own point of observation. The same things appear under a variety of changing aspects. The exigencies of social life make adjustment of these differences absolutely necessary. Some are considered to be irrelevant and are therefore ignored; others are handled by what Schutz calls the 'interchangeability of the standpoints', or the 'reciprocity of perspectives'. Intersubjective agreement is brought about in a number of different ways, into the details of which we have not time to enter. All of us find ourselves living, therefore, in one and the same life-world. The pragmatic motive still retains its predominance here, since it is essentially related to the concrete conditions under which a certain social group exists. Hence the intersubjective life-world remains subject to a degree of relativity, no longer, to be sure, with regard to this or that individual, but with respect to the social group in question, however small or large.

Geometry and dualism in Greek thought

Greek philosophy claimed to discover an opposition between the multifarious appearances involved in perpetual change and an immutable realm of existence, forever persisting in strictest self-identity. This latter was called 'Being-as-it-is-in-itself', *ontos on*. To this distinction there corresponded one between *epistémé* and *doxa*. *Doxa* covers our beliefs about appearances, and is thus changeable. *Doxa* is necessary (and also sufficient) for the practical conduct of affairs in the realm of appearances. It depends upon the situation in which the subject finds himself, on his interests and plans. The Greek term, '*doxa*', thus conveys something of the relativity and indeterminateness that we have seen to characterize our relation with the life-world. *Epistémé*, on the other hand, is knowledge in the genuine and emphatic sense. Since it is concerned with Being-as-it-is-in-itself, it is free from all relativity with regard to subjects, their standpoints, and the vicissitudes of their lives. Because of the persistent self-identity of this Being, genuine knowledge is perpetually true, under all circumstances and for everyone. Whereas the domain of opinion is that of persuasion and plausibility (i.e. of rhetoric in the classical sense of that term), these qualifications have no place in the domain of *epistémé*, where only cogent argument and conclusive demonstration count. Either a thesis can be fully demonstrated, e.g. by proving that its negation leads to contradictions and absurdities, or it has no right to be advanced at all. If any disagreement appears, it can, at least in principle, be definitely resolved. Otherwise the argument would not have the permanent and universal binding force claimed for it.

These correlated notions of Being-as-it-is-in-itself and *epistémé* are important to us on account of their bearing upon Greek geometry and its consequent philosophical significance. In view of the importance of geometry for Galileo's work we must try to trace its far-off origins in the practices of the life-world. Every society, however primitive, possesses an art of measurement. The degree of accuracy obtainable in measurement will depend, of course, upon the techniques available. Furthermore, like every other activity in the life-world, measuring is dominated by the pragmatic motive. The degree of accuracy desired depends upon the purpose at hand, which is always of a practical nature. This leads to more skilful uses of a particular technique, as well as to the invention of new techniques. All these improvements are made in view of practical purposes; they are carried out within a horizon of practicality or, as Husserl calls it, a horizon of finiteness.

While this is going on, a jump may occur by means of which the power of the pragmatic motive is broken and the horizon of finiteness transcended. Husserl gives the example of a craftsman working on wooden planks, so as to make them planer and smoother. In the course of this, the idea may arise of perfect planeness, of planeness as an ideal of perfection. The notions of straightness, circularity, and the rest can be reached in the same way. But then the corresponding terms gradually come to denote geometrical figures in the strict sense, now understood as ideal entities located at infinity, ideal 'limit-poles'. Spatial shapes and configurations encountered or deliberately produced in perceptual experience may then be compared with the ideal limit-poles. Naturally, they fall short of the ideal. No perceived spatial shape can ever coincide with the strict geometrical figure with which we may correlate it. Here it is appropriate to speak of *approximation*. We have a series of perceptual spatial configurations and a term totally outside the series, to which they can be said to approximate to a greater or lesser degree. (This is in marked contrast with what we saw of the merely typical determinations of the spatial shapes given in perceptual experience, where no ideal limit-pole is involved.) Not surprisingly, the perceptual configurations are now given the ontological status of imitations. The ideal geometrical figures are conceived as originals, which the perceived entities (in Plato's metaphor) strive unsuccessfully to attain. In a beautiful passage in the *Republic*, Plato compares the relation between outlines drawn in the sand and the geometrical figures of the mathematician, with the relation between shadows thrown on water and the objects throwing the shadows.

Geometrical figures conceived as ideal entities may well pass for beings-in-themselves. Free from every ambiguity, exempt from all change and variation, they persist in self-identity, irrespective of knowing subjects. Whereas measurements in the life-world admit of varying degrees of accuracy, geometrical determinations are made with exactness. Exactness implies the absence both of fluctuation and of any restriction in terms of practical purpose. In Euclid's axiomatization of geometry a small number of fundamental propositions, as well as some elementary methods of construction, were explicitly specified. From them, various properties of plane figures can be cogently demonstrated. Thus an infinity of exact spatial forms are situated relatively to one another by means of a single coherent theory, coherent because deductively developed. Geometry thus perfectly exemplifies the ideal of *epistémé*. Mastery of the methods of geometrical reasoning allows one to reach results that are permanently and universally valid. All relativity with regard to subjects and their situations is overcome.

The Platonism of Galilean physics

Galileo inherited not only geometry as a body of technical knowledge, but also the Platonic interpretation of geometry as embodying the ideal of true knowledge. Here I must touch upon a topic frequently treated elsewhere in these essays, namely the Platonism of Galileo. I was greatly interested in the views of my colleagues on this issue, even though I tended to disagree with them. Following Cassirer, Koyré and Crombie, I still persist in considering Galileo as a 'Platonist' and, going even further, I maintain that the whole of modern physics – the 'physics of Galilean style' – is of Platonic inspiration. This involves a wider sense of the term 'Platonism' to be sure, but one I think to be preferable. Galileo, it is true, did not espouse the mathematical speculations of the *Timaeus*. Platonism, however, need not necessarily be construed in the narrow sense of endorsing all the doctrines found in the writings of Plato. I will take it to signify the defence of a two-world theory, of a distinction between two realms of unequal ontological status. One domain is assumed to be subordinated to the other and to lead a merely borrowed existence; it has to be explained in terms of the domain of higher order. Galileo's work may be said to mark a turning-point in the historical development of 'Platonism' in this sense of the term; it was thoroughly transformed and renewed by him.

Galileo's acceptance of geometry as the model of knowledge is in Husserl's view his fundamental presupposition. One might even speak of a 'prejudice', since Galileo makes use of a Platonic conception of genuine knowledge and a corresponding conception of true Being, without attempting in any way to justify them, without apparently even noticing that they required justification. The sort of reflection we made in the last section on the origins of geometrical concepts was very far indeed from Galileo's mind. Once geometry be accepted as the standard of knowledge, it follows that, if a science of nature is to be possible at all, it will somehow *have* to be conceived after the model of geometry. Galileo's Platonism appears in the distinction between the perceptual appearance of nature and its true, that is its mathematical, structure. The disclosure of this structure is the task of the new science of physics which proceeds to a thoroughgoing mathematization of nature. Spatio-temporal occurrences must, in consequence, be idealized, that is, referred to exact mathematical relationships. If motion be simply considered as change of spatial position in time, an exhaustive mathematical treatment of mechanics becomes possible, though this will require the redefinition of the concepts of velocity and acceleration. This is necessary because these concepts already had roles in describing the life-world, where, however, they denote quantities only roughly estimated, just as in the case already noted, of spatial configurations. The mathematization of motion leads to the study of the different possible forms of motion, among which uniformly accelerated motion proves to be of special interest. Mathematically expressed hypotheses are developed and tested against observation in order to ascertain which hypothesis applies to a given case, e.g. that of freely falling bodies.

Testing the consequences of such hypotheses against experiential data requires measurement, eventually under laboratory conditions. The accuracy of the measurement once again depends upon the available techniques, with improved techniques yielding results of increasing accuracy. It seems very like the situation we have already seen regarding measurement in the life-world, independently of geometrical idealization. This idealization bestows, however, a radically new sense upon the results of measurement. No longer do the increasingly accurate results obtained by means of improving techniques stand side by side with one another, each fully justified by the practical purpose for which it is intended. By being referred to an ideal limit-pole, the results of measurement come to be interpreted as *approximations*, in the strict sense of forming a sequence which converges toward a true and exact value. Technically speaking, measurement is still carried on under the conditions prevailing in the life-world; its interpretation, however, is placed – as Husserl puts it – under a 'horizon of infinity'.

For this reason, the perfectibility of measuring techniques now begins to acquire the overtone of an *unlimited* perfectibility. We have already seen that the art of measurement in the life-world prepared the way for geometrical idealization. Now the relationship is in a sense reversed. Geometrical (and more generally, mathematical) idealization comes to inspire the application of measuring techniques, in that the idea of mathematical exactness yields incentives not only for the obtaining of increasingly closer approximations, but also for the contrivance of 'better' techniques. Mathematical idealization thus provides a built-in method for improving upon itself, as it were, without direct reference to any practical purposes, hence with the sense of a possibly unlimited, i.e. an infinite, progress.

Thus far the idealization and mathematization of only the spatial and temporal aspects of the life-world have been considered. Things encountered in perceptual experience exhibit, in addition to these aspects, qualitative properties – colour, temperature, and so forth – which fill the spatial forms. These properties do not lend themselves to quantification. A certain red may be said to be 'brighter' than another, but it is not possible to go beyond rough estimates of this sort and to ask 'how much brighter?', expecting an answer in numerical terms. There is only one geometry, and it is related to space, not to qualities. This becomes clear if one notes that any spatial shape can be conceived as a limited portion of the one, unique, all-encompassing space, whereas there is no universal qualitative form into which all qualitative configurations might be inserted in an analogous manner. Hence if a mathematization of qualities is possible at all, it can, at best, only be contrived in an indirect way. It is to this indirect mathematization that we must now turn. Husserl associates it too with Galileo, though it would be historically more correct to mention Descartes and, especially, Huygens. As we have already seen, Galileo's name is for Husserl a symbol.

Indirect mathematization of the qualities requires that they be correlated with occurrences which, because they are describable in spatio-temporal terms, are capable of direct mathematization. Take, for instance, the Pythagorean discovery of the dependence of the pitch of a musical note upon the length of the vibrating cord. This dependence by itself does not warrant the conclusion that the note heard is a mere subjective datum and that all that exists in reality are the vibrations of the cord. Rather we have here the regular correlation of one occurrence with a different one, an instance of the 'universal causality' found in the life-world. As far as our experience of that causality goes, events of one kind are known to depend upon events of a different kind; changes in one respect are accompanied by changes in other respects. This, however, gives us no reason to assume that qualitative phenomena are causally dependent upon spatio-temporal occurrences in some simple unilateral way.

But this is just what *has* been assumed as physics has continued to progress. It has become more or less taken for granted that qualitative phenomena are produced by processes that interact with our sense-organs and are definable in spatio-temporal terms exclusively. Qualitative phenomena and their changes are thought both to reveal and to conceal the true state of affairs. They reveal it, because as effects of quantitative processes, they point to these processes, and can be read as their symptoms, at least by the physicist who has learned to decipher the language. They conceal the true state of affairs (so it is said) because of the utter hetero-geneity between the symptom itself and that of which it is a symptom. Nature as it *really* is (by contrast with its perceptual appearance) is mathematical structure, perhaps a plurality of such structures, and it matters but little whether the structures are comparatively simple, as in the early phases of modern science, or extremely complex and abstract, as in contemporary physics.

Mathematics and Nature

What logical status should be assigned to the thesis that nature is mathematical throughout? Obviously, it is not a formulation of empirical findings, nor is it arrived at by generalization from experience. On account of its generality, it cannot pass for a law of nature; in fact, every determinate law of nature is one of its particular specifications. Because of its generality, it cannot be considered as an hypothesis in the usual sense. If, as Husserl does, one calls it a 'hypothesis', one must, following him, underline its peculiar nature. One might speak of it as the 'hypothesis underlying hypotheses', as a 'regulative idea' in the sense of Kant, as a methodological norm which directs the formulation of scientific hypotheses and guides all scientific activities, theoretical and experimental alike. A 'hypothesis' of this kind cannot be defended by direct argument, but can only be sub-stantiated by the continuing success of the methodological norm itself. And this means on-going, never-ending work. The thesis that nature is mathematical throughout can be confirmed only by the entire historical process of the development of science, a steady process in which nature comes to be mathematized pro-gressively. No matter how far the process has advanced, that is, no matter what confirmation the thesis has already received, it still remains an hypothesis in the sense of being in need of further substantiation. The distinction between nature as it is conceived by science at a moment of its history, and nature as it actually is in scientific truth must never be overlooked. This last phrase does not denote a concealed reality lying behind the appearances in the life-world and waiting to be discovered, but rather a goal to be reached, or more correctly, to be approximated to asymptotically.

Instead of stating that nature is mathematical, it is more appropriate to say that nature lends itself to mathematization. This is not just a matter of words. The latter formulation brings out the point that mathematization does not necessarily mean the disclosure of a pre-given, though yet hidden, reality. On the contrary, it suggests an accomplishment yet to be achieved, a universe yet to be constructed. Science takes on this task and, under the guidance of its own methodological norms, constructs its universe by means of a complex continuing process of idealization and mathematization. The resulting universe is the product of a methodological procedure, a 'tissue of ideas' (*Ideenkleid*), which must never be mistaken for reality itself. Reality is, and always remains, the life-world, no matter how vast the possibilities of systematization and prediction that have been opened up by the development of science of the Galilean style.

This science is certainly one of the greatest accomplishments of the human mind. Coming from Husserl's pen, this phrase is no pious declamation, but rather suggests a problem for future research. It is at this point that the analysis of Galilean physics flows into the mainstream of phenomenology. As a product of the mind, science of the Galilean style requires phenomenological clarification. Because of the role of the life-world as the presupposition of scientific construction, the problems which (if one is to be systematic) have to be attacked first, are those related to the life-world itself and the experience through which it presents itself, i.e. perceptual experience. Subsequently, a phenomenological account must be given of the higher intellectual processes which, like idealization, formalization, and so on, are basic to the construction of pure mathematics and the mathematization of nature.

I hope you will forgive me for not going beyond these sketchy hints for a phenomenological philosophy of science. And you must forgive me also for saying, in conclusion, that notwithstanding the voluminous recent literature on the philosophy of science (whose value I do not in the least belittle), we do not yet possess a philosophy of science in a truly radical sense. Husserl's analysis of Galileo's physics indicates the direction in which a 'radical' (i.e. a properly rooted) philosophy of science must develop. Ten years after the appearance of Husserl's work, I can just begin to see something of its outlines. As always in the case of Husserl's writings, at the end of work accomplished, more work is looming on the horizon. The work will be long and hard but – I am convinced – most rewarding.

5 Hermann Lübbe

Positivism and Phenomenology: Mach and Husserl*

H. Lübbe, 'Positivism and Phenomenology: Mach and Husserl', in *Beiträge zur Philosophie und Wissenschaft*, Berne: Francke, 1960, pp. 161–84.

Translated by A. L. Hammond

Ernst Mach had the misfortune to provide philosophical backing for two or three Russians whose political line met with Lenin's displeasure politically.[1] Orthodox Marxists since then have known him as the man who inaugurated a 'reactionary philosophy'. Positive recognition has of course been accorded him in the tradition of the Viennese circle.[2] On the other hand the rest of German philosophy has almost forgotten him, as it has forgotten critical empiricism as a whole. This is astonishing, since the work of Mach, and of Richard Avenarius too, was far from being ephemeral. The journal of the school of critical empiricism – the *Vierteljahrsschrift für wissenschaftliche Philosophie* – continued to be published for almost forty years, from 1877 to 1916, and the number of contributors, which included well-known people such as Alois Riehl, Joseph Petzold and Max Heinze, was far from small. Yet the methodology of empirical criticism and its philosophy of perception remained isolated, particularly in comparison with the transcendental philosophical theory of knowledge of the neo-Kantians, and Avenarius and Mach could not compete with the dominant position in German philosophy

---

* Abbreviated by author from *Beiträge zur Philosophie und Wissenschaft. Wilhelm Szilasi on his 70th Birthday*, Munich, 1960, pp. 161–84. Reprinted in Hermann Lübbe, *Bewusstsein in Geschichten. Studien zur Phänomenologie der Subjektivität; Mach-Husserl-Schapp-Wittgenstein*, Freiburg: Rombach, 1972, pp. 33–62.

1. V. I. Lenin: *Materialism and Empiriocriticism. Critical remarks concerning a reactionary philosopher*, 1909.

2. Cf. V. Kraft: *Der Wiener Kreis. Der Urspung des Neopositivismus. Ein Kapitel der jüngsten Philosophiegeschichte*, Vienna, 1950, particularly pp. 7–9.

held by Hermann Cohen, Paul Natorp, Wilhelm Windelband or Heinrich Rickert up to the First World War. The fact that Avenarius did not have much influence outside his own school can certainly be explained by the abstruse language of his works: a monstrous collection of neologisms ('principal coordination', 'vital difference') and superfluous symbols with pretensions to exactitude ('T' = fellow-man), diagrammatic mannerisms which degenerated into a mere stylistic device, designed to demonstrate the scientific qualities of his method; this kind of thing tended to make him unpalatable. Mach, however, wrote brilliantly. Alongside Helmholtz, perhaps, or Harnack, he belongs among the founders of a clear style of unpretentious, scholarly presentation and communication, so that we could say of him that he initiated a new era in the history of German style. Hence, too, his mastery of the art of popularization, so rare in Germany. But simple clarity in the way he presented his works alone could not win him an influence over German philosophy commensurate with their significance (though Robert Musil made the works of Mach, which 'were full of the most brilliant expositions', the subject of his dissertation).[3] They bore that damaging label, 'positivist'. As against this, what the essay attempts to do is to demonstrate that Ernst Mach and other critical empiricists, regardless of their 'positivism', belong in the tradition of phenomenology. This is not always clear.

However, it must be said that Husserl himself, in his search for new phenomenological 'foundations for pure logic and of a theory of knowledge', expressly dissociates himself from empiricism, including it in the 'dominant trend in logic' from which he wished to depart.[4] Husserl devoted a whole chapter of a polemical kind to Mach and Avenarius in his *Prolegomena*.[5] And it is indeed against the positivistic principle of 'economy of thought' (*Denkökonomie*) that he addresses himself. The

3. R. Musil, *Beitrag zur Beurteilung der Lehren Machs*, Berlin: Diss, 1908.
4. E. Husserl, *Logische Untersuchungen*, Vol. I, 'Prolegomena zur reinen Logik', Halle, 1913, p. vii. (*Logical Investigations*, trans. with an Introduction by J. N. Findlay, New York: Humanities Press, 1970. *Editor's note*)
5. ibid., Chapter nine: 'Das Prinzip der Denkökonomie und die Logik', pp. 192–210.

positivism of the economy of thought does of course play an important role in empiricism, and Husserl did recognize that it was here that a decisive difference from his phenomenological idea of a pure logic was to be found. What does 'economy of thought' mean in positivism? Very generally it is an interpretation of the theoretical and specifically scientific achievements of man by analogy with technology (*technische Praxis*). Technology is 'economic' in nature in so far as the smaller the expenditure of effort necessary to achieve a fixed practical goal, the nearer perfection it is thought to be. The same applies to theoretical – and in particular, scientific – relationships between man and reality. Firstly, human praxis and theory are united in that they both serve the same purpose – survival. Mach is Darwinist in regarding theoretical ability as the supreme means for achievement in life. And theoretical knowledge serves survival in that it preserves experience; theory is precisely what preserved experience is – i.e. experience translated into the preservable and communicable form of a judgement which is, as it were, made once and for all, and which thus saves us the trouble of repeating the experience. According to Mach, this is what the meaning of theory, in terms of economic praxis, consists of. Its significance is increased, however, when theory as knowledge is detached from the totality of praxis, through the process of division of labour, and the acquisition of knowledge of reality based on experience comes to be the goal of a specific and highly differentiated praxis, even of a knowledge in the technical exploration of which people who have not had the relevant experience directly can take part themselves. Knowledge, thus defined, is perfected anew in the sense of economical practice, not only by continually encompassing increasingly wide areas of reality through experience, but especially by generalizing individual experiences, by discovering functional dependencies between constituent parts of experience, and so forth, so that ultimately an ever-increasing stock of experience, reduced to more and more simplified theoretical forms, can be their means, so more subject to rational control.

Even before Mach, Avenarius had propounded this economy of thought interpretation of scientific theory in his 'Habilitation' thesis. It bore the title 'Philosophy as thinking about the world in accordance with the principle of least effort'.[6] This 'principle' runs as follows: the intelligence 'applies to an apperception no more effort than is necessary, and gives preference, from among a number of possible apperceptions, to that which produces the same result with a smaller expenditure of effort, or else produces greater effect with the same expenditure of effort'.[7] According to Avenarius, the procedure of both individual sciences and philosophy, and indeed all sciences, which is immanent in this principle, is articulated in philosophy more clearly than anywhere else, since philosophy is 'the endeavour to think in a scientific way, with the least expenditure of effort, about the totality of everything which has been revealed by experience'.[8] Thinking must be *economically* viable. It is from desire to increase this economic viability that it draws the energy to go on with the enterprise, or, conversely, to withdraw from it, when it discovers that it has merely complicated the relationship between man and reality, as happened, for example, in the case of metaphysics (metaphysics being, as it were, in the red on the accounts of scientific progress). The analogy of scientific theory, understood in these terms, with technico-economic praxis, is expressed fittingly in the term 'the economics of thinking' (*Denkökonomie*). Mach introduced it. It is thought to have come to him as a result of his acquaintance with the economist E. Hermann at Munich.[9] He apparently chose the term in order to point out, by means of the expression itself, that the gulf between the praxis of everyday life and the highly specialized praxis of science did not exist. To what extent is the praxis of everyday life conducted economically? To the extent that it seeks to avoid unnecessary expenditure. Economy is praxis 'excluding purposeless activity'.[10] According to Mach,

6. R. Avenarius, *Philosophie als Denken der Welt gemäss dem Princip des kleinsten Kraftmasses. Prolegomena zu einer Kritik der reinen Erfahrung*, Leipzig, 1876.

7. ibid., pp. iii f.   8. ibid., p. 21.

9. E. Mach, *Die Leitgedanken meiner naturwissenschaftlichen Erkenntnislehre und ihre Aufnahme durch die Zeitgenossen*, Leipzig, 1919, p. 8; cf. also 'Die ökonomische Natur der physikalischen Forschung', in *Populätwissenschaftliche Vorlesungen*, Leipzig, 1896, pp. 203–30.

10. E. Mach, *Die Leitgedanken . . .*, p. 4.

knowledge must be thought of in the same way. What does the physicist do, for example? He systematizes his experiences, he experiments, he measures, for example, the dependent relationship of a frictionless fall on the duration of time. He then has a scale of measurement. He notices a functional relationship between the values on the scale, reduces it to a formula and thus arrives at a 'law of gravity'. This 'law', according to Mach, has no possible ontological or transcendental reality *sui generis*, something which would need prior philosophical explanation in terms of the conditions of its possibility. It is (and again we take the example of a law of gravity) more 'a very simple and summary indication of the way that all falling bodies may be portrayed in thought'. It is a 'complete substitute for a tabulation which may be as extensive as you wish, and which, thanks to the formula, can at any moment be most easily reproduced, without the memory being in the least overburdened'.[11] The 'law' is simply an instrument of economics of thought, 'experience economically organized so as to be ready for use'.[12]

Husserl opposed the economics of thought of the critical empiricists by showing what it is not capable of. But the critical instruments he used in no way blinded him to the positive aspects of the theory. He expressly praises the fact that philosophical economy can 'throw a clear light on the anthropological bases of different research methods'.[13] In particular he agrees with Mach's economistic interpretation of the operation of mathematics: 'The problem [is], how are mathematical disciplines possible, disciplines in which not just relatively simple thoughts but veritable edifices of thought and combinations of thoughts interconnected in a thousand ways are activated with supreme freedom and, as a result of further research, become increasingly complex.' Mathematics has reached this point as a result of the development of techniques of operating which in fact are 'in the nature of philosophical-economical measures'.[14] Mach had shown that even the most elementary mathematical operations presuppose and include the mastery of such techniques. When it comes to

11. E. Mach, 'Die ökonomische Natur . . .', p. 210.
12. ibid., p. 220.   13. E. Husserl, op. cit., p. 19.   14. ibid., p. 198.

the multiplication, we make use of the results of previous arithmetic operations instead of repeating them each time, or if we make use of logarithm tables, we economize, and instead of carrying out further arithmetical operations, substitute operations executed long before, etc.: we are, on such occasions, increasing the productivity of the calculator by employing techniques which are, in the economic sense, purpose-built. The analogy with technology holds true in a further sense in that the accuracy of a calculation does not depend on whether the subject who is carrying it out knows of or has himself had the experiences which are condensed in the formula of the operation – just as operating a machine does not depend on the operative's knowledge of mechanics. Mach goes on: 'There is no disputing the fact that the most elementary, like the most advanced, mathematics is economically designed to exploit previous mathematical experience available to us.'[15] Husserl certainly did not dispute it. He recognized the role played by economy of thought in the 'constitution of the idea of technical methods in human knowledge'.[16] He took over Mach's idea that a certain proportion of human scientific praxis could be interpreted by analogy with mechanical praxis.[17] This cognitive activity is 'mechanistic' or 'mechanical' – Husserl's words – in that subject, possessing fixed cognitive methods, as it were reaches one result after another without this activity being fed back in the sense of improving his methodically determined cognitive *capacity*. A reasoning subject who solves problem after problem according to a prescribed procedure is efficacious, in this particular sense. Since, as subject, he remains unchanged in the process he could, for the self-same reason, theoretically be replaced by a machine. Mach glimpsed in the construction of cognitive machines – such as calculating machines – the most recent consequences of economy of thought.[18,19]

15. E. Mach, 'Die ökonomische Natur . . .', p. 212.
16. E. Husserl, op. cit., p. 202.
17. ibid., p. 198: 'The "practico-logical reflexivity of the scientist" proceeds economically in that it produces incomparably more effective mechanisms of thought than would naturally occur . . .'
18. E. Mach: 'Die ökonomische Natur . . .', p. 213.
19. In contrast to this kind of knowledge, which is described in structural terms by Mach and Husserl, non-mechanistic knowledge would be defined

The exposition of the way in which Husserl agrees with Mach's analysis of the economic nature of scientific cognitive praxis serves merely to provide the background against which he delivered his attack, made all the more decisive, on the conclusions Mach drew from this analysis for his theory of knowledge. For Mach, the process by which the laws of nature comprehend, in a uniform and comprehensive fashion, a multiplicity of empirical data is perhaps nothing more than a technical instrument for mastering this multiplicity in economically expedient, theoretical terms. Husserl says the opposite: the 'economy of thought' position is one which asserts that, within the framework of the study of human thought and action, the multiplicity of empirical data can be subsumed under one single unifying schema. The multiplicity of empirical fact and the singleness of scientific knowledge are not unified through economic praxis; on the contrary, economic praxis is located within the ultimate set of conditions which determine empirical fact and scientific knowledge. We can of course call a logarithm table an instrument of economy of thought. But the logarithm itself, as a mathematical construct, is not rooted in the economic pragmatics of human survival. The latter simply makes use of it. The (*a priori*) validity of the mathematical and the logical is itself 'the

by the fact that its subject experiences a change and, in particular, an increase in his cognitive capacities while exploiting his knowledge, and therefore, as subject, undergoes change. Hermeneutic knowledge is of this kind. Anyone who wishes to understand, for example, a man's career is at the very beginning obliged in doing so to identify with his object imaginatively in order to be able to understand him. He finds himself trapped in a contradiction: in his first approach to his object he needs the very capacity for understanding that can only be achieved through the process of investigation. This 'hermeneutic circle' is resolved by repetition; i.e. the attempt to comprehend the object is repeated in that the attempt is conditioned by the understanding that has been gained during a previous attempt. This repetition is not mechanical, i.e. it is not a repetitive cognitive process following methodically fixed operations – it is in the modern sense of the word dialectic. It is a way of developing cognition or possibilities of understanding a learning process. It is self-evident that the structures of hermeneutic knowledge are not to be found in Mach's economy of thought theory of a natural science, but it is complementary, so to speak, to Dilthey's theory of the human sciences.

precondition of any meaningful account of economy of thought and so cannot possibly be evidence of explanation which follows the doctrines of economy of thought'.[20] Husserl's structural argument against economy of thought is on the same lines as that which he uses against psychologism: just as psychologism in its analysis of, say, closure as a psychological act mistakes the ideal character of the *form* of closure itself, economy of thought in its analysis of the economic nature, say, of experimentation mistakes the logical-ideal conditions which make it a meaningful activity in the first place. (It is precisely on this point that Husserl knew that he was at one with the neo-Kantians and against psychologism and economy of thought.)[21]

Husserl's fundamental critique of economistic positivism definitely locates empiriocriticism on the same side against which he set out to formulate phenomenology as a new philosophical method and science. Hence, so far as we have gone, it is not yet clear in what sense Mach and Avenarius can be said to have prepared the way for phenomenology. But the critique of economy of thought is not the only one which Husserl thought about, and uttered, concerning the relationship between phenomenology and empiriocriticism. In the Amsterdam lectures on phenomenological psychology[22] he places Mach (alongside the physiologist, Hering) expressly among those who had earlier made use of phenomenological method: 'At the turn of the century in philosophy's struggle to find a rigorously scientific method, a new science made its appearance with a new method of philosophical together with psychological enquiry. The new science was called *phenomenology*, since it arose from one particular radical treatment of the phenomenological methods which had already been worked out and made use of by a few natural scientists and psychologists. The attraction of this method for men like Mach and Hering lay in a reaction against the loss of theoretical foundations which threatened the "exact" sciences;

20. E. Husserl, op. cit., p. 208.
21. Cf. *Logische Untersuchungen*, p. 156 footnote 1, and p. 169 footnote 1.
22. Manuscript folio II 1 of the Husserl archives, now published in *Husserliana* 9 (1968), pp. 302–49.

Hermann Lübbe 97

it was a reaction against theorizing in conceptual forms and in speculative mathematics which were remote from observations, and which did not in any legitimate sense make for clarity of insight and theoretical effectiveness.'[23] Even in his later work, on the crisis of European science, Husserl does not name Avenarius (alongside Schuppe) as representative of a position fundamentally opposed to phenomenology, as he had in the 'Prolegomena', but rather as the representative of a philosophical concern which prepared the way for phenomenological transcendentalism, without, of course, following it up in a sufficiently radical way.[24] We may presume from this that Husserl, when he made Mach's 'Analysis of Perception', which anticipated phenomenology to an extraordinary extent, the basis of his seminar,[25] did this in the intention of joining with a related field.

Husserl himself notes one particular feature of Mach's critical empiricism which relates him to phenomenology when he says, in the Amsterdam lectures, that the 'attraction' of the phenomenological methods applied by Mach lies in the 'reaction' against the 'loss of theoretical foundations which threatened' the natural sciences. In the event, phenomenology and empiriocriticism made common cause in their criticism of the persistent philosophical dogmatism of the natural sciences. Both attacked a procedure by which any data specifically related to consciousness were treated as non-existent so that it could be asserted that physical-physiological data were the only proper reality. Anyone, for example, who describes sight as an optical physiological process is no longer talking about 'seeing' as it is everybody who actually 'sees'. This misinterpretation of the 'intentional immanent data of consciousness' in the domain of physics and physio-

23. ibid., p. 302.

24. E. Husserl, 'Die Krisis der europäischen Wissenschaften und die transzendentale Phänomenologie', ed. W. Biemel, The Hague, 1954 (*Husserliana* 6), p. 198. (*The Crisis of European Sciences and Transcendental Phenomenology*, Evanston: Northwestern University Press, 1970. *Editor's note*)

25. Rudolf Böhm enumerates those themes in Husserl's writings which are based on earlier or even contemporary authors in his editorial introduction to Edmund Husserl, *Erste Philosophie* (1923/24), Part One, 'Kritische Ideengeschichte', The Hague, 1956, pp. xxvii ff.

logy is attacked by Husserl as the arch-failure of 'Naturalism'.[26] There is an analogous significance in Mach's fight against 'metaphysics'. The 'fight against metaphysics' is in the first place no more, or less, than a reaffirmation of the slogan which almost completely ruled German philosophy of the second half of the nineteenth century. But the special meaning it held for Mach is understood only when we know what 'metaphysics' he was opposing. Just as we cannot understand Kant's critique of metaphysics without knowing that its target was the metaphysical school of the eighteenth century, we cannot understand Mach's critique of metaphysics without knowing the materialistic pseudo-metaphysics of the natural sciences that it was aimed at. One of the most important facts in the history of philosophy around the middle of the nineteenth century, without which the 'criticism' of such tendencies which dominated German universities after about 1870 would be incomprehensible, is that the 'victor' which triumphed in the 'collapse of the metaphysical systems' of German idealism was not pure natural science nor even a philosophical theory of science related to it, but the antimetaphysics of Büchner, Vogt and Moleschott. These people were natural scientists, physiologists and zoologists, and they used their knowledge as an arsenal of arguments in favour of a cryptometaphysical materialism. The words attributed to Vogt 'that thoughts bear the same relationship to the brain as gall, for example, bears to the liver or urine to the kidneys' is a significant and frequently quoted example of the disappearance of all reality in the material process which takes place in this pseudometaphysics. Moreover this dogmatic materialism born of the natural sciences is far from being confined, historically speaking, to the period of the so-called materialism controversy (1854). It was dominant in most areas of science and general education into the first part of the twentieth century, and, ultimately, inflated into a universal world-view; it attained its greatest influence in Haeckel's monism. This is demonstrated by the existence of the 'Monist Association' with

26. Cf. E. Husserl, 'Philosophie als strenge Wissenschaft' in *Logos 11*, 1910, p. 289–341: 'Naturalistische Philosophie'. ('Philosophy as a Rigorous Science', in *Phenomenology and the Crisis of Philosophy*, ed. and trans. Quentin Lauer, New York: Harper & Row, 1965. *Editor's note*)

its pseudo-religious ritual, and by Wilhelm Ostwald's 'Sunday Scientific Sermons'. Mach, himself a physicist and physiologist of repute, developed his philosophical and methodological work out of a critique of this dogmatic materialism which functioned as an artificial metaphysics-substitute. 'Most natural scientists today cultivate, as philosophers, a 150-year-old materialism, the inadequacy of which has been seen through long ago not only by professional philosophers but by anyone not too far removed from philosophical thought'.[27] It is in this context, therefore, that we should read the 'preliminary anti-metaphysical remarks', with which Mach opened his 'Analysis of the Sensations'. These pages are not what today, in our historical situation in philosophy, we might suppose to have been suggested by Mach's positivism – instead, they are from the very outset directed against a 'physicalism' which saw itself as materialistic; thus, 'physics, despite its important developments, is yet only a part of a greater sum of knowledge and cannot exhaust this material (viz. the analysis of the sensations) with the intellectual means at its disposal, which were created for limited purposes'.[28] Even Avenarius's major work, *Kritik der reinen Erfahrung*,[29] is no less directed in the same sense against the lack of self-criticism in science and in support of a purification of its methodological assumptions from implicit cryptometaphysics. We must therefore accept the fact that empiriocriticism and phenomenology share the self-same interest in the face of the false appeal of materialism and naturalism to physics and physiology and in their assertion of the independence of a reality of the mind and of consciousness which cannot be contained within materialistic or naturalistic categories; and that it was necessary to found a methodically independent science ordered in terms of this reality.[30]

Avenarius, who otherwise can hardly be credited with one worthwhile phrase, coined the slogan for these anti-materialistic

27. E. Mach, *Erkenntnis und Irrtum*, Leipzig, 1917.
28. E. Mach, *Die Analyse der Empfindungen und das Verhältnis des Psychischen zum Physischen*, Jena, 1918, p. 1.
29. R. Avenarius, *Kritik der reinen Erfahrung*, 2 vols., Leipzig, 1888,1890.
30. This line of thought is not confined either to Mach or to Husserl. It can be said to encompass Wilhelm Schuppe's 'philosophy of immanence', as well as Dilthey's psychology.

tendencies; it was, he said, a question of founding a 'human concept of the world' (*menschlicher Weltbegriff*).[31] This term in fact is appropriate for many decades of phenomenological thought up to and including Heidegger's fundamental ontological definition of world-concept. How Husserl is implicated in this context is less easy to see, if we regard his phenomenology as extending from his critique of psychologism and from his intention to found a 'pure logic'; it becomes easier, however, if we start from Husserl's analysis of intentional experiences in the fifth of the *Logical Investigations*, and if we consider that Husserl, particularly in the *Cartesian Meditations*, extends phenomenology[32] into an analysis of the 'historical nature of consciousness' and finally, in his later work, on the *Crisis of European Science*, outlines the programme of an 'ontology of the living world'. In this regard, the critical empiricist notion of a world-concept takes its place at the beginning of the development of phenomenological tradition in the history of philosophy. The content of this world-concept is best understood through the difference between it and that other world-concept, from which it is distinguished by the attribute 'human' (or, rather, 'natural'). This other concept is the one which was evolved philosophically from the consequences of the theory of the natural sciences, in particular the physical and physiological theory. And this concept is, in very general terms, negatively defined, in that it reduces subjectivity as such to vanishing point. It is where subjectivity still persists that the problem arises. In this general form the problem is of course older than phenomenology or critical empiricism. Even Kant's critique of practical (i.e. moral) philosophy is at heart an answer to the problem of the possibility and reality of the subjective, called moral freedom, on the assumption that natural science asserts that 'objective reality' is an unbroken, causally determined, material process carrying on infinitely through time and space.

31. R. Avenarius, *Der menschliche Weltbegriff*, Leipzig, 1927.
32. cf. L. Landgrebe, 'Das Problem der Geschichtlichkeit des Lebens und die Phänomenologie Husserls' (1932), in L. Landgrebe, *Phänomenologie und Metaphysik*, Hamburg, 1949, pp. 50 ff.; H. Lübbe, 'Das Ende des phänomenologischen Platonismus', in *Tijdschrift voor Philosophie*, 16, 1954, pp. 639–66.

Thus for Kant the problem which arose from the concurrence of a natural science which made everything objective, alongside experience of the subjective, was focused crucially on the antithesis: causal necessity – moral freedom. In the second half of the nineteenth century the problem was enlarged in one particular respect, and this enlargement involved one of the decisive preconditions for the development of the kind of questions posed by phenomenology. At that time research in the natural sciences began to develop in previously unsuspected ways, not least in zoology, anatomy and physiology. And it was precisely these sciences which gathered more and more precise knowledge about the way in which human life was conditioned by natural causes. What the materialism of the Enlightenment had dogmatically asserted was now demonstrated in concrete terms and in many different ways. What happened was that the human being, as subject, was regarded as reducible in his entirety to object. This inevitably had an especially profound influence on questions concerning the theory of knowledge. For a theory of knowledge requires a subject, knowledge of which is, at times, knowledge itself. How can this subject be defined over against physical and physiological objectivity? It becomes an insubstantial 'inwardness', the relationship of which to objective reality is then problematical.[33] If we pose this problem in terms of a question about the physiological conditioning of psychic 'inwardness', it is suceptible to many kinds of empirical research. One can, for example, in the framework of experimental psychology, such as Fechner founded, investigate how the subjective strength of sensations is related to the objective strength of a stimulus and attempt to reduce this relationship to the form of a law, etc. One can ask where subjective powers like memory, hearing or movement are located, etc. Such questions need not, in principle, give rise to difficulties. Difficulties do arise, however, if one goes on from this point to try to arrive at a theory of perception. The question then is how awareness of external objects is possible at all for the 'inward' subject. To begin

33. R. Avenarius, 'Bemerkungen zum Begriff des Gegenstandes der Psychologie', in *Vierteljahrsschrift für wissenschaftliche Philosophie* 18, 1894, pp. 137–61 (1st Article), pp. 150 ff.: 'Das "Innere" als Gegenstand der Psychologie'.

with, the subject, with its definition as something 'inner', has no reference at all to the outside world; there are a few sensations which are directly given to it, as subject, and to which objectively material processes in the body correspond. How from this does the conscious subject arrive at those objects which are, so to speak, outside the four walls of his own body? Of course these external objects have an effect on the body and set off processes, the subjective aspect of which is again in the form of sensations. But these effects are themselves quite objective, of course, and therefore do not explain how external objects as such can be the content of subjective awareness. It was precisely over this point that Helmholtz through his self-awareness became a Kantian: the categories of causality, which are *a priori* certainties so far as the experiencing subject is concerned, provide the way for allowing consciousness of external objects, in that he grasps his sensations in themselves as produced by these categories. They are just the same as the causal categories. Of course it would be nonsensical to try to assert some kind of similarity between the objects as they really are and the sensation that they cause. How can we imagine external, material reality being reconstituted in the subjective medium of the sensations? There is no existential analogy to bridge this gulf. Thus Helmholtz remains a Kantian revisionist in that for him the object becomes an unknowable thing in itself, to which its subjective appearance is related simply as a sign. Sensations of light and colour are only symbols for relationships with reality; they bear just as little or as much similarity or reference to the latter as the name of a person or his signature bears to the person himself. They tell us, by means of similarity or dissimilarity in their appearance, whether we are dealing with the same objects or different objects, just as in stories of strangers and strange towns, we can tell from their names being similar or dissimilar whether the same people and places are being mentioned, or different ones.[34]

The epistemological conclusions which Helmholtz drew from his physical and physiological research, thereby clearing the way

34. H. Helmholtz, 'Über die Natur der menschlichen Sinnesempfindungen' (1852) in *Wissenschaftliche Abhandlungen*, Vol. 2, Leipzig, 1883, pp. 591–609.

for his conversion to Kant, may or may not be correct. It is, however, certain that in perception, so far as the perceiving is concerned, the entire apparatus with the help of which, according to Helmholtz, the inward subject relates to external objects remains undiscoverable. It is excluded from the domain of physics and physiology; but it is not a phenomenal reality. The conscious subject knows absolutely nothing about the fact that he comes to know a real object through some inference about it made by subjective perception. Consciousness has not the slightest clue that the things it is conscious of are not the things themselves but something quite different which is related to them simply as a sign. Helmholtz of course does not deny the distinction between how consciousness appears to itself and how it is described, in epistemological terms, in physiological research. He regards it very definitely as the task of his own branch of science to explain what perception 'specifically' is, and how it functions. But Helmholtz did not see that it was precisely at a time when theory about what reality actually is had become so irrevocably distant from what this reality knew of itself, that the need arose for showing what constituted this latter kind of knowing. A scientific explanation of consciousness which shows it as something quite different from what it seems to be to the man who has it, demands some attempt to describe what it really is, in analytical terms, and not just to 'explain' it. The phenomenological position is fundamentally dedicated to this problem. This makes clear the significance of the critical empiricist demand for the foundation of a 'human' or 'natural' concept of the world as preceding, and in anticipating, decades of phenomenological research. At bottom it is a demand for the elementary reality of human experience to be taken as the object of theory; it is precisely this experience which is left out of discussion when explanation is couched in terms of physics and of physiology. Of course critical empiricism is a long way from satisfying this demand in any detail. But the ground is laid, and the critical empiricists themselves (particularly Mach) made good progress along phenomenological lines. The present paper will be limited to the discussion of this particular aspect.

There is only one chapter in Mach's 'Analysis of the Sensations' which deals with 'preconceptions'.[35] By this Mach means the explanation in terms of physics and physiology of the psychological phenomena we have mentioned. He talks about the constraints on research which have frequently arisen from the fact that categories and conceptions have been treated as interchangeable. Particularly great, however, is the 'confusion arising from transposing preconceived notions from the field of physics into the field of psychology'. The physicist may of course investigate the optics of the human eye and throw light on the problem of the inversion of the retinal image by investigating the internal structure of the eye. On the other hand, when this formulation of the problem is carried over into psychology, it creates confusion. 'The question why we *see* the inverted retinal image as *upright* has no meaning as a psychological problem ... For the experiencing subject, such a question just cannot arise.' At this point the phenomenological character of the critical empiricist thesis becomes particularly clear. Mach observed that, beyond whatever may be asserted by the optical and physiological theory of sight, there still remains the act of seeing itself, as the subject's own act; that in seeing, retinas and even inverted images on them are simply not involved, and that, precisely because of this, seeing must itself be made the object of theorizing of a different kind from what obtains in physics and physiology. Mach demonstrates the same point again with respect to the 'well-known theory of the after-image', current at that time, particularly after Helmholtz. The optician may certainly look for a visible object along the straight lines stretching out from the retinal point and the eyes' focal point. Nevertheless, once more 'no such problem exists' for the seeing subject himself. In sum, 'the extrapolation of the experience of after-images into a whole theory of the psychological origin of the external world' is founded, generally speaking, 'on a mistaken application of the point of view which obtains in physics'.[36] 'The world, therefore, does not consist of puzzling beings which, by means of some reciprocal exchange with another equally puzzling being, the I, produce the only accessible "sensations"', Mach resumes.[37] The world of colour,

35. E. Mach, *Die Analyse der Empfindungen*, pp. 31–7.
36. ibid., pp. 31 ff.   37. ibid., p. 24.

sound, space and time is, according to Mach, an immediate datum, which cannot be grasped perceptually or cognitively 'by a process of psychological projection or of logical conclusions and constructions'[38] or present essential problems of what 'reality' or 'actuality' may be hidden behind the colour we see or the sound we hear. Husserl in his exhaustive study of the major works of critical empiricist philosophy,[39] underlined the remarks I have quoted, and in the margin, agreeing with Mach, observes that the investigation of consciousness and perception is directly concerned with the analysis of the immediate datum of the relationship between the elements of reality, as they occur in consciousness and perception; to explain human perception phenomenologically it is completely unnecessary and not 'advisable' even as Avenarius says in the sense of the neo-Kantian theory of scientific methodology 'to reflect immediately or exclusively complex and specialized forms of highly developed "scientific" knowledge'. It is rather a question of first 'keeping an eye on ordinary life, and on perception, just on its own, without self-consciousness, *out of which* what is scientific has evolved and thereby seeing the relationship of scientific to pre-scientific forms and means of perception'.[40] Husserl picked out this passage also to underline, and in effect it does seem to point directly towards the kind of phenomenological work that was carried out in Husserl's circle particularly during the Göttingen period, and of which Wilhelm Schapp's phenomenology of

38. ibid., p. 26.

39. As is revealed by his marginal notes and underlinings, Husserl worked particularly intensively on Mach's *Beiträge zur Analyse der Empfindungen*, Jena, 1886, and moreover, on the extended version of his book *Die Analyse der Empfindungen*, 3rd ed., Jena, 1902; then on Avenarius's 'Habilitation' thesis: *Philosophie als Denken der Welt gemäss dem Princip des kleinsten Kraftmasses*, Leipzig, 1876; on his major work, *Kritik der reinen Erfahrung*, Vol. I, Leipzig, 1888; and on his work on the human concept of the world, Leipzig, 1891; also, finally, on Schuppe's *Grundriss der Erkenntnistheorie und Logik*, Berlin, 1894, on the same work in the second edition of 1910, on Schuppe's treatise on the relationship of body and soul, Wiesbaden, 1902, as well as on his work on human thought, Berlin, 1870. Dr Walter Biemel, of Cologne, was kind enough to inform me of these volumes and to help me obtain them from the Husserl Archives at Löwen.

40. R. Avenarius, *Kritik der reinen Erfahrung*, Vol. I, Leipzig, 1888, p. ix.

consciousness can be cited as one of the most significant ex-amples.[41]

It now becomes easier to describe the structure of that world, the concept of which Avenarius called 'natural' or 'human'. It is at first negatively defined, in that the subjective is not reduced to a physically and physiologically defined objectivity in it. It is rather the world of the subject himself, the subjective world, where the subject is now no longer shrunk to a mere 'inwardness' in the face of a physical and physiological objectivity. It is there-fore a subjective world in the sense of being not in the first instance so divided from the other subject, derived from per-ceived reality, that there is any problem as to how (in the act of consciousness) the two can come into contact with each other. It is from this reciprocal reference that the analysis of the human world-concept proceeds, which is at the same time also an analysis of the concept of the subject, within which the subject itself is so conceived that it is always in and of its world. This Heideggerian structural formula of being-in-the-world exactly fits the critical empiricist concept of the subject if we disregard the fact that in Heidegger the practical relations between man and reality are included, whereas critical empiricism hardly went beyond the analysis of sensation and conscious perception.

What had previously, under the rather invidious label of a 'division' or 'gulf between subject and object', been problematic is already approaching comprehensibility with critical empiri-cism. This philosophical school represents the start of an ana-lytical theory of consciousness which is retained within conscious-ness itself, instead of approaching its object in such a way that it reduces the phenomena it is faced with to something else which does not of itself come within the field of consciousness. The formulation is one which arises from an insight into the insoluble difficulties over which a theory of perception comes to grief when it seeks to explain perception in terms of a process of a physical and physiological nature which supposedly connects an external object and an internal subject. In this latter view, what the characteristics are – a subject, moreover, which is the perceiving

41. W. Schapp, *Beiträge zur Phänomenologie der Wahrnehmung*, Göttin-gen, 1910.

subject as such, related to something which it knows to be different from itself – disappeared completely. The real world, which the subject is 'inside', and which, in turn, has its existence 'within' the subject, is completely lost. Husserl first remarked on the singularity of the manner in which subject and object have this mutual reference, and are, in the act of perceiving, encompassed phenomenally within each other, in a reference to Brentano in his analysis of 'intentional experiences'. The structure of these experiences is such that in them the reference of the subject is to something else. This other, whatever it is, is, in so far as it is intentional, a moment of experience. It would nevertheless be nonsensical to ascribe a 'mental', 'immanent' existence to it; for, within experience, e.g. when experience relates to an object perceived in space, it is treated straightforwardly as that object. In intentional acts, such as perception, the subject refers to an objective, real world which is independent of himself. This is exactly what we would mean if we put it the other way round, making the world, as it were, the intended moment of these acts, the thing to which they refer.[42] If we have made this peculiar structure clear, it will be possible to recognize the contradiction inherent in any attempt to try and construct the perception of objectivity out of those 'physiological effects (sensations)' brought about by physical processes in the body: 'I do not see colour sensations, but coloured things, I do not hear sensations of sound, but the song a woman is singing, etc.'[43]

The distinction between the colour itself and the sensation of colour is, according to Husserl, a distinction only 'superficially self-evident'; it rests on the old traditional notion which at the epistemological level is inherent in the false antithesis 'internally conscious image – extra conscious being-in-itself'.[44] The objection Husserl raises to this discussion, which is actually transposed from the formulation of problems in physiological terms into physiology, is that 'all reference to its objectivity is contained within the phenomenological being of consciousness in itself',[45]

42. Cf. also E. Husserl, *Logische Untersuchungen*, Vol. 2: 'Untersuchungen zur Phänomenologie und Theorie der Erkenntnis', Part I, 2, revised ed., Halle, 1913, pp. 364 ff.: 'Bewusstsein als intentionales Erlebnis'.
43. ibid., p. 374.   44. ibid., p. 374.   45. ibid., p. 423.

and 'that the intentional object of a notion is *the same* as its real object and in any given case, as its external object, and that it is nonsensical to distinguish between the two'.[46] This phenomeno-logical argument against dualism in the theory of perception is completely analogous to the critical attacks Mach made again and again on the 'duplication' of the world into two: being-in-itself and a world which is within the subject, either in the sense of an image or of a symbolic substitution. (Incidentally it is in the context of these critical attacks that Mach repeatedly and expressly mentions Avenarius as associated with him.)[47] Admit-tedly, in Mach, it is all rather embryonic, and stated only in rudimentary form, whereas with Husserl and his disciples a far-reaching analysis is fully developed. Mach stands at the beginning of a philosophical road, which he guesses will lead to a point at which people will be able to be simply astonished at 'how we could believe that colours and sounds which are around us suddenly find their way inside our physical world, composed of atoms, and how we once upon a time could be surprised that what clatters and bangs so emptily out there can sing and sparkle here inside our head . . .'[48]

Mach is of course not the only one who, even before the turn of the century, anticipated Husserl by raising objections to the duplication of the world into an 'external' world and a sub-ordinate 'internal' one, to would-be 'explanations' of what exists in the consciousness in terms of physical and physiological processes, as well as to the theoretical constructions of perception which became necessary given these assumptions, and went on to postulate a new theory which analyses and describes what exists phenomenally in perception as such. Mach is one of several contemporaries who saw, and set down in explicit terms, the new problems with which the historical situation of scientific know-ledge confronted the theory of perception. Besides his Zürich colleague Avenarius, to whom he referred most frequently, there

46. ibid., p. 425.
47. E. Mach, *Die Analyse* . . . op. cit., pp. 38 ff., 'Mein Verhältnis zu R. Avenarius und anderen Forschern'.
48. E. Mach, *Populärwissenschaftliche Vorlesungen*, Leipzig, 1896, pp. 229 f.

was, in particular, Wilhelm Schuppe, whose work he felt pointed in the same direction. They each dedicated work to the other,[49] and each expressed agreement with the other in correspondence.[50] Schuppe too participated in the criticism of a theory of sensation which did away with its phenomenal object and stationed it inside the brain, and of the doctrine of the external projection of sensation, which then became necessary in order to join together again what was actually found in sensation as such.[51] 'I *reject* subjective sensation which has been differentiated ... from the content of sensation ... as a fiction, which confuses the meaning of the concepts.'[52] Schuppe continues, and moves, like Mach, towards a Husserlian concept of intention by saying: 'This universe, so utterly real, with its sun, moon and stars, and this earth with all its rocks and animal life, its fiery mountains, and so on – this is all contained within consciousness, except that we must not say "just" contained within consciousness,'[53] 'for in this "only" stands just that isolating division of subjective consciousness and objective external world which provokes "unending duplication" and which still clings to the present generation of philosophers like original sin'.[54] Thus Schuppe also is one of those who initiated the specifically phenomenological viewpoint and in a desert of sham problems showed the way to the 'promised land' of pure phenomena, towards which Husserl knew he was heading.[55,56]

49. Mach dedicated *Erkenntnis und Irrtum*, 1905, to Schuppe; Schuppe responded in the second edition of his *Grundriss der Erkenntnistheorie und Logik*, 1910.

50. Letters from Richard Avenarius and Ernst Mach to Wilhelm Schuppe in *Erkenntnis* 6, 1936, pp. 73–80.

51. W. Schuppe, *Erkenntnistheoretische Logik*, Bonn, 1878, p. 59.

52. ibid., p. 65.   53. ibid., p. 70.

54. W. Schuppe, 'Die Bestätigung des naiven Realismus. Open letter to Prof. Dr Richard Avenarius' (1893), in R. Avenarius, *Der menschliche Weltbegriff*, Leipzig, 1927, pp. 135–74.

55. Cf. E. Husserl, 'Persönliche Aufzeichnungen', in *Philosophy and Phenomenological Research* 16, ed. W. Biemel, 1956, pp. 293–302.

56. R. Zocher gives detailed information about the relationship between Schuppe's and Husserl's thought in *Husserls Phänomenologie und Schuppes Logik. Ein Beitrag zur Kritik des intuitionistischen Ontologismus in der Immanenzidee*, Munich, 1932.

Next, of course, comes Dilthey, who independently of contemporary philosophies such as critical empiricism and the philosophy of immanence, and in the completely different context of an attempt to found the methodological and objective independence of the human sciences as opposed to the natural sciences,[57] criticized the illusory theoretical problems of perception which arise when the subject is opposed to the 'external world' in such a way that 'philosophy ... is presented with the task of finding a proof, which will reach through *inference* by means of *causality* into what lies *beyond consciousness*'.[58] This critique of Dilthey's became an important step in the development of phenomenological thought, particularly for Heidegger's analysis of existence[59] because the basis from which it proceeds is a theory of the subject which sees the latter not merely in the restricted sense of a subject of conscious awareness and perception, but rather more than this, as a subject of the total life-process to which 'will, conflict, work, need, satisfaction' belong as 'recurrent invigorating elements' and which at the same time also 'provides the arena for mental events'.[60] Inasmuch as it constitutes the life-process, the subject is from the very beginning never isolated from the 'external world'; it lives in it and experiences it in the sense that it is a reality on its own, independent of the subject, and this independence affirms its reality in relation to the subject as soon as the latter sets out to incorporate it into its life-process. 'Externality is constructed in the mind not by playing a subordinate role under the heading of causation: on the contrary, the presence of this force is a datum of existence to us in our experience of limitation and opposition; we then have to interpret this force as something external, separate from

57. L. Landgrebe, 'Wilhelm Diltheys Theorie der Geisteswissenschaften (Analyse ihrer Grundbegriffe)', in *Jahrbuch für Philosophie und phänomenologische Forschung* 9, 1928, pp. 237–366.

58. W. Dilthey, 'Beiträge zur Lösung der Frage vom Ursprung unseres Glaubens an die Realität der Aussenwelt und seinem Recht' (1890), in *Gesammelte Schriften*, Vol. V, Leipzig and Berlin, 1924, pp. 91–138.

59. For Heidegger's critical proximity to Dilthey, compare M. Heidegger, *Sein und Zeit*, Tübingen, 1957 ed., pp. 209 ff.: 'Realität als ontologisches Problem'.

60. Dilthey, op. cit., p. 131.

ourselves.'[61] The old problem of how to explain that the two separate realms of the subjective and the objective meet in the process of perception is precisely reversed in Dilthey, and the problem is rather the process by which the subject achieves experience of something that possesses a reality independent of itself and is thus, in this sense, objective. The problem lies in the process through which the subject learns to distinguish itself, as it were, from what it is not and proceeds to form itself into a subject which is then practically and theoretically related as such to objectivity. Dilthey proposes the analysis of this process as the content of a new theory which, in antithesis to the old constructions of theories of perception, concerns itself with how the subject is related to the object only in so far as the relationship 'is given in the experience of life'.[62] There is no doubt that with this Dilthey is moving towards phenomenology.

Admittedly, experiencing reality as objective through experiencing its resistance does not, of course, happen in practical matters only, in which some change of circumstance is sought, but just as much in perception, which simply lets what is perceived remain unchanged. Perception, too, perceives the objective as such only so long as the independence of the object from the subject is revealed by the changes which take place in perception when the perceiving subject moves in relation to the object perceived. 'If I move my eye to the right and the object does not follow me, I acquire awareness of its being independent of my will.'[63] Dilthey thus saw the unique role played by kinaesthetics in the phenomenological constitution of human perception and went on to discuss it: 'The displacement in perspective of images when one shifts position, the way in which other people perceive these images ... from where they stand and the corresponding qualitative changes in objects are things which take us by surprise every day, and only when we can make them subject to known and uniform conditions are they substantiated as legitimate. It is the force of this legitimacy which controls each individual impression, and which consequently strikes us as something alien and autonomous.'[64] In Husserl's great *Phänomenologische*

61. loc. cit.   62. ibid., p. 133.   63. ibid., p. 109.
64. ibid., p. 116.

Untersuchungen zur Konstitution, which fill the second book of *Ideas*, the same phenomenology of kinaesthetics plays a central role;[65] it shows how consciousness reaches 'objective reality' through kinaesthetic experience. It is where Dilthey's and Husserl's analysis is brought to bear on kinaesthetic experience, in the sense that the basis of a specifically phenomenological research is unmistakably attained, and when the theory moves into the sphere of a concept of the subject, in the light of which questions about the possibility of perceiving the external world, about the relationship between perception and the object perceived, and so forth are shown to be unreal problems. And it must be said that Mach, even before Dilthey and Husserl, had reached this level of phenomenological enquiry; because his analysis of sensation is, in fact, none other than an analysis of how the dual dependency of sense experience on the self and on what is experienced creates for us awareness of the self and of its existence in the phenomenal totality of reality.

Interest then shifts to the realms of the individual senses: the realms of sight, of hearing and of touch, as distinct from geometric space, the conditions under which the notion of geometric space is developed, inner experience of time – all of them problems which belong among the classic objects of phenomenological research. Thus Mach, to give but a few examples, exhaustively investigated how geometric congruence is related to perceptual congruence, and went from this to show how geometric space and perceptual space prove to be two different structures, that, for example, the latter does not display anything like the same characteristics in different connections as those of the former;[66] how, to take one instance, evenly distributed colour on a motionless body, despite the phenomena of shading, can only be seen as evenly distributed if the specific tactile space is so to speak seen along with it; how, in darkened tactile space, orientation is achieved by movement; how it is this experience of movement

65. E. Husserl, *Ideen zu einer reinen Phänomenologie und phänomenologischen Philosophie*, Second Book: *Phänomenologische Untersuchungen zur Konstitution*, ed. M. Biemel, The Hague, 1952 (*Husserliana*, 4), pp. 55 ff.: 'Die Aistheta in Bezug auf den aisthetischen Leib'.

66. Cf. E. Mach, *Die Analyse . . .*, op. cit., pp. 87 ff.

above all which opens up to us the spacial world of rigid bodies, and that it is only on the basis of this that we can gain the notion of geometric space.[67] Finally, Mach carried out detailed investigations into how time is experienced. In his efforts to free himself from the 'thought patterns of physics' in which he had been 'caught', he also managed, in the process, to separate time as experienced, according to its own specific structure, from time as defined by the homogeneity of its intervals, as in physics.[68] Husserl studied these investigations closely, as his personal copy of Mach's *Beiträge zur Analyse der Empfindungen* testifies, and it is certain that he learnt here a lot of what appears in his own works, as analogous, particularly in his *Phänomenologische Untersuchungen zur Konstitution*, as well as in the 'Vorlesungen zur Phänomenologie des inneren Zeitbewusstseins'. On the other hand, we must not of course overlook the fact that, when it came to details, Mach remained completely imbued with the concepts of biology and natural science, much more so than was Husserl in psychologism in the *Logische Untersuchungen*. But this should not prevent us from recognizing Mach as among those who developed a specifically phenomenological position, in that they concentrated on the subject itself, and along with it the world of its perception and life, in contrast to those scientists who reduced all subjectivity to something other than what that subjectivity knew itself to be.

To my knowledge Mach is the only man to whom something like a picture of the phenomenological approach occurred. On page 15 of his *Analyse der Empfindungen* there is a figure showing a man lying on a couch with his legs crossed; he is apparently a scholar, since on the wall of his room to his left are rows of folio volumes. All that we can see of him is from about the chest level but we can also see, somehow, that the eye with which the observer looks into the picture, through the window which is open in front of him, on to the countryside, is also the left eye of the scholar himself. Hence his neck and head cannot be seen but only the tip of his nose and, indistinctly, the bridge of the nose

67. Cf. E. Mach, *Beiträge zur Analyse der Empfindungen*, Jena, 1886, p. 100.
68. ibid., pp. 103ff.

which frames the right-hand side of the picture and which continues upwards, enclosing the picture there as his brow, under which his bushy eyebrows are just visible. The scene is cut off at the bottom by a lengthy moustache-end. The left-hand side of the picture is open and unframed, the row of books disappearing behind one's back into the invisible. This drawing is an illustrated criticism of the divorce of subject from object which renders theory of perception quite incapable of relating one to the other. The drawing demonstrates how, even in the simple process of seeing, there is no phenomenal world in which the subject itself is not already present, and that there is no subject which is not already present in the world.

It does not follow from the fact that it was Mach who showed the way for phenomenology that the positivists of the Vienna Circle were wrong in claiming him as a forerunner. The truth is that there are different approaches coexistent in Mach's works which diverged later into antithetical extremes: into neopositivism on the one hand and, on the other, into the later phenomenological tradition represented by Heidegger.[69] One of the approaches has been discussed in the present paper, and concerns the analysis of the phenomenally given 'natural' or 'human' world, to use Avenarius's somewhat programmatic statement. It is this which stretches through classical phenomenology to the fundamental ontology of Heidegger and to Husserl's later plan for an analysis of the 'living world'. The other is the specifically positivistic approach of clearing the traditional methodological and categorical scientific apparatus of its confusing superfluities, originating in metaphysics, and to re-define science as a system of statements which describe efficiently, i.e. economically, how reality is built up out of irreducible 'elements' of sense experience. Mach was not aware of the fact that he was freeing himself from the doctrine of perception with one hand and clinging to the conceptual apparatus of the physical sciences on the other, while thinking he could construct any process of perception out of elementary sense data. In practice he did nothing of the kind;

69. Cf. Carnap's polemic against Heidegger: R. Carnap, 'Überwindung der Metaphysik durch logische Analyse der Sprache', in *Erkenntnis* 2, 1931, pp. 219–41.

in practice he analysed, for example, hearing a melody by referring to temporal phenomena, which became evident and comprehensible through hearing over time, instead of trying, for instance, to deduce the melody heard from more elementary aural sequences and thereafter explaining how the melody might exist as such. However, Mach's design for a scientific methodology undoubtedly amounts to an insistence that every theory must be based on the unshakeable facts provided by 'atoms' of sense data ('elements'). In this Mach denies what he always in practice assumes in his analyses, namely that phenomenal data as a totality do have their parts, but that these parts are defined by the totality, and not vice versa, with the totality constructed from the parts. In this he demonstrates how difficult it is to maintain the phenomenological approach as opposed to the physicists' mode of thinking. His problem was that of Husserl himself at a much more developed stage of phenomenological studies, when the latter tried, in his analysis of the constitution of reality, to found the animal world on material nature and the intellectual world in its turn on the animal, in terms of a natural science approach, only of course to realize later that phenomenologically things were, so to speak, the other way round – that phenomenologically the intellectually determined 'living world' is primary to the extent that the abstraction, in the natural sciences, of subjectivity, and its reduction to the material, is conditioned by this world, reading 'conditioned', this time, in the sense of 'historically preceding'.[70] So it was with Mach's scientific positivism that the representatives of the neopositivistic 'scientific interpretation of the world', organized as the 'Ernst Mach society', associated themselves.[71] They maintain that here they stand 'resolutely' on the 'basis of simple human experience'.[72] There can be no doubt about their resoluteness. It is doubtful, however, whether the 'basis of simple human experience' is not merely the distant reflection of the kind of terminology which was valid for Mach

70. Cf. L. Landgrebe, 'Seinsregionen und regionale Ontologien in Husserls Phänomenologie', in *Studium Generale* 9, 1956, pp. 313–24.

71. Cf. *Wissenschaftliche Weltauffassung. Der Wiener Kreis,* ed. Verein Ernst Mach, Vienna, 1929.

72. ibid., p. 29.

and Avenarius in connection with that part of their work which prepared the way for phenomenology in the way we have described. It is doubtful, moreover, whether we reach any basis of simple human experience if, following Mach, we break reality up into supposedly elementary atomic sense data, or whether we are talking about the same 'experience' in the kind of science which, for Carnap, is formulated out of recorded propositions in which the elementary atomic data are set down.[73] Here again the subject and its 'human experience' is expelled from the realm of theory, and its specific experiential reality, such as it knows it to be, is attributed to something which is not to be found in this reality as such. Once again, it was against the expulsion of the subject, and its 'human experience' from the framework of theory, and the attribution of specific experiential reality which it knows to something outside that reality, that Mach took his stand in those writings that prefigured phenomenology. And if anyone should ask where the subjective is then to be found, once it no longer has any place in theory, Carnap refers him to lyric poetry and music.[74]

Phenomenological philosophy of course stands at the opposite pole to this neopositivist approach in that it seeks to perceive as theory precisely what natural science theory excludes. We must not omit to note, however, that philosophical thinking, phenomenological in origin, in a new phase of its development, in the ideas of the later Heidegger, confirms positivism in so far as it expressly disclaims any scientific quality in the classical sense and willingly confers this quality on the exact, positive sciences, as their distinguishing feature, while changing itself into a 'mythical discourse' and continuing to contemplate the 'second coming' of Being. This, the final arbitrary limitation imposed by positivism on theory, is welcomed, it seems, because this self-limitation

73. For the theory of recorded proposition sentences, cf. R. Carnap, 'Die physikalische Sprache als Universalsprache der Wissenschaft', in *Erkenntnis* 2, 1931, pp. 432–65. M. Schlick has already criticized, from within the Vienna circle itself, the recorded propositions: M. Schlick: 'Über das Fundament der Erkenntnis', ibid., 1934 (4), pp. 79–99.

74. R. Carnap, 'Überwindung der Metaphysik durch logische Analyse der Sprache', ibid., 1931 (2), pp. 219–441.

leaves room for a 'return of a vanished mythical world' in the face of which thought becomes poetry.[75] On the other hand, what should also be kept in mind is what associates Mach with Husserl: the pathos of a rationality which yet does not see itself as so hardened that it has to hold aloof from the 'true world' in which men live.

75. W. Brocker, *Dialektik, Positivismus, Mythologie*, Frankfurt-am-Main, 1958.

6 Alfred Schutz

Phenomenology and the Social Sciences*

A. Schutz, 'Phenomenology and the Social Sciences', in *Collected Papers*, Vol. 1, The Hague: Nijhoff, 1962; originally in *Philosophical Essays in Memory of Edmund Husserl*, ed. M. Farber, Cambridge, Mass.: Harvard University Press, 1940.

The significance of Husserl's phenomenology for the foundation of the social sciences will presumably become fully known only when the Husserl manuscripts which are relevant to this problem have been published. To be sure, the published works already contain the most important themes of thought pertaining to this subject. Husserl was constantly concerned with them from the time of writing the sixth *Logical Investigation*. But these important implicit themes remain scarcely noticed, not only because the extensive discoveries of phenomenology in the realm of pure logic and the general theory of knowledge have taken first place in the public discussions, but also because only in the later writings of the master has the problem of the social sciences been attacked systematically.

Even in these later writings Husserl proceeded with great hesitation. As is known, he had completed a second volume of the *Ideas* in 1913, as far as proof-reading. In this volume the problems of personality, intersubjectivity, and culture were to have been treated. Just before publication, misgivings concerning the result of his work befell this scholar, who was always a model of conscientiousness. He recognized that the attack on these prob-

* *Author's note.* I wish to express my gratitude to Professor Richard H. Williams of the University of Buffalo for the great interest and the untiring efforts which he has devoted to the translation of my essay. The task of reproducing faithfully Husserl's language, which in the original German offers serious difficulties even to German readers, is, I believe, really creative work. To Professor Marvin Farber I am deeply indebted for his kind interest and his careful supervision of the text. To Professor Fritz Machlup I owe valuable suggestions concerning the English rendition.

lems presupposed carrying out still further analyses, especially the clarification of the constitutive activities of consciousness.

It was first in the *Formal and Transcendental Logic* (1929) that an avenue of approach was opened to this new thematic field, but again it proceeded from the point of view of purely logical problems. In this work can also be found[1] the starting-points toward considerations which were carried further in the postscript to the English translation of the *Ideen* and in the fifth *Cartesian Meditation* (both in 1931), and which would have found their complete presentation in an extensive series of essays planned under the title 'The Crisis of European Sciences and Transcendental Phenomenology'.[2] In the last conversations which the writer had the good fortune of having with Husserl, he repeatedly designated this series of essays as the summary and the crowning achievement of his life work. He was working continuously on them during the last three years of his life, but only the first essay appeared, in the journal *Philosophia* (Belgrade, 1936). Then death took the pen from Husserl's hand and only the penetrating fragment which appeared in the *Revue internationale de philosophie*[3] on 'The Question about the Origin of Geometry' gives an indication of the extent of the work which had been begun in this period.

In the following paragraphs of this essay an attempt will be made to trace in concise form the initial phases of a phenomenological foundation of the social sciences which are contained in the writings referred to above. Following this, in the second part of the essay, the question concerning the independence of the social sciences will be raised and, going beyond Husserl, an inquiry will be made concerning the contribution which phenomenology can make to their concrete methodological problems.

1. See especially *Formale und transzendentale Logik*, Secs. 94 ff.; *Formal and Transcendental Logic*, trans. Dorion Cairns, The Hague: Nijhoff, 1969.

2. *Die Krisis der europäischen Wissenschaften und die transzendentale Phänomenologie*, ed. Walter Biemel, The Hague: Nijhoff, 1957; *The Crisis of European Sciences and Transcendental Phenomenology*, trans. with an Introduction by David Carr, Evanston: Northwestern University Press, 1970. (*Editor's note*)

3. Brussels, 1939, 1, 2. (Reprinted here, pages 42–70. *Editor's note*)

It goes without saying that all this must be limited to inadequate intimations.

I

All sciences, be they related to objects of nature or to so-called cultural phenomena, are, for Husserl, a totality of human activities, namely, those of scientists working together. The fact of science itself belongs to that realm of objects which must be clarified by the methods of the cultural sciences, which in German are referred to as *Geisteswissenschaften*. Furthermore, the basis of meaning (*Sinnfundament*) in every science is the pre-scientific life-world (*Lebenswelt*) which is the one and unitary life-world of myself, of you, and of us all. The insight into this foundational nexus can become lost in the course of the development of a science through the centuries. It must, however, be capable in principle of being brought back into clarity, through making evident the transformation of meaning which this life-world itself has undergone during the constant process of idealization and formalization which comprises the essence of scientific achievement. If this clarification fails to occur, or if it occurs to an insufficient degree, and if the idealities created by science are directly and naïvely substituted for the life-world, then in a later stage in the development of science those problems of foundation and those paradoxes appear from which all positive sciences are suffering today; they ought to be remedied by an *ex post facto* critique of knowledge which comes too late.

Phenomenological philosophy claims to be a philosophy of man in his life-world and to be able to explain the meaning of this life-world in a rigorously scientific manner. Its theme is concerned with the demonstration and explanation of the activities of consciousness (*Bewusstseinsleistungen*) of the transcendental subjectivity within which this life-world is constituted. Since transcendental phenomenology accepts nothing as self-evident, but undertakes to bring everything to self-evidence, it escapes all naïve positivism and may expect to be the true science of mind (*Geist*) in true rationality, in the proper meaning of this term.

However, a whole series of difficult problems is already revealed by this point of departure. We shall select a few of the groups of problems treated by Husserl which are especially relevant to our topic.

1) First of all, how can a transcendental philosophy, such as constitutive phenomenology, risk the assertion that the life-world as viewed within the natural attitude remains its basis of meaning while at the same time the troublesome effort of phenomenological reduction is needed in order to bracket this natural world? This reduction thus creates the prerequisite of the investigation of the contributive intentionalities in which the world is constituted for transcendental subjectivity.

2) If the life-world as viewed within the natural attitude remains the basis of meaning of transcendental phenomenology, then not only I but also you and everyone belong to this life-world. My transcendental subjectivity, in the activities of which this world is constituted, must thus from the beginning be related to other subjectivities, in relation to the activities of which it authorizes and rectifies its own. And to this life-world, which is characterized as the single and unitary life-world of us all, belong indeed all the phenomena of social life from the simple Thou-relation to the most diverse types of social communities (including all the sciences as a sum total of the accomplishments of those who are engaged in science). In short, all that constitutes our own social world in its historical actuality, and all other social worlds concerning which history gives us knowledge, belongs to it. But must not the attempt to constitute the world from the activities of transcendental subjectivity necessarily lead to solipsism? Can it explain the problem of the *alter ego* and thereby of all social phenomena which are founded on the interaction of man with his fellows in the real life-world?

3) Can the assertion be justified that positive sciences have naïvely substituted idealities for the life-world, and thus have lost the connection with their basis of meaning, in view of the unquestionable success of the natural sciences and especially of

mathematical physics in the control of this life-world? And is a special cultural science (*Geisteswissenschaft*) at all thinkable which would not necessarily refer to natural science, since the entire world of mind (*Geist*) seems to be based on things of the natural world and the psychical appears only in psychophysical connections? Must not, rather, a single style be demanded for all sciences which claim to be exact, and is not this style of the unified science precisely that of the mathematical sciences, whose remarkable successes, even in their practical application, we must always gratefully admire?

4) If in fact the phenomenological method is able to prove its legitimate claim to the establishment of the cultural sciences, and if in this way it succeeds in bringing to light a style of thought peculiar to these sciences by an analysis of the constitutive activities of the transcendental subjectivity, would such a proof yield any contribution at all to the solution of the methodological problems of the concrete sciences of cultural phenomena (law, the economic and social world, art, history, etc.), since all these sciences are related to that mundane sphere which transcendental phenomenology has bracketed? Can any help at all be expected from phenomenology for the solution of all these questions? Is it not rather an affair of a psychology oriented to everyday life to solve this problem?

In the following paragraphs we shall attempt to draw together the answers to these questions which Husserl has given in diverse places in the writings cited above.

Ad 1. It should be pointed out at once that there is widespread misunderstanding to the effect that transcendental phenomenology denies the actual existence of the real life-world, or that it explains it as mere illusion by which natural or positive scientific thought lets itself be deceived. Rather, for transcendental phenomenology also there is no doubt that the world exists and that it manifests itself in the continuity of harmonious experience as a universe. But this indubitability must be made intelligible and the manner of being of the real world must be explained. Such a radical explanation, however, is only possible by proving the relativity of this real life-world, and of any imaginable life-world, to the transcendental subjectivity which alone has the ontic sense of absolute being.[4]

In order to uncover this sphere of the transcendental subjectivity at all, the philosopher, beginning his meditation within the natural attitude, must undertake that change in attitude which Husserl calls phenomenological epoché or transcendental phenomenological reduction. That is to say, he must deprive the world which formerly, within the natural attitude, was simply posited as being, of just this posited being, and he must return to the living stream of his experiences of the world. In this stream, however, the experienced world is kept exactly with the contents which actually belong to it. With the execution of the epoché, the world in no way vanishes from the field of experience of the philosophically reflecting ego. On the contrary, what is grasped in the epoché is the pure life of consciousness in which and through which the whole objective world exists for me, by virtue of the fact that I experience it, perceive it, remember it, etc. In the epoché, however, I abstain from belief in the being of this world, and I direct my view exclusively to my consciousness of the world.

In this universe of the experiencing life of the transcendental subjectivity I find my entire cogitations of the life-world which surrounds me, a life-world to which also belong my life with others and its pertinent community-forming processes, which actively and passively shape this life-world into a social world. In principle all of these experiences found in my conscious life, if they are not themselves originarily giving and primally founding experiences of this life-world, can be examined concerning the history of their sedimentation. In this way, I can return fundamentally to the originary experience of the life-world in which the facts themselves can be grasped directly.

To interpret all this by showing the intentional accomplishments of the transcendental subjectivity makes up the enormous area of work of constitutive phenomenology. It is thus a true science of mind (*Geist*), and claims to be a method, in fact the only method, which seriously means to be a radical explanation of the world through mind.

4. Husserl, 'Nachwort zu meinen *Ideen*', *Jahrbuch für Philosophie und phänomenologische Forschung*, Vol. XI, 1930, pp. 562ff.

Ad 2. But this life-world, which has constantly been referred to above, and which may only be constituted by the activities of my transcendental subjectivity, is certainly not my private world. To be sure, Others, fellow-men, also belong to it, indeed not only as other bodies or as objects of my experience of this world but as *alter egos*, that is to say, as subjectivities which are endowed with the same activities of consciousness as am I. The world which is experienced after the completion of the reduction to my pure life of consciousness is an intersubjective world, and that means that it is accessible to everyone. All cultural objects (books, tools, works of all sorts, etc.) point back, by their origin and meaning, to other subjects and to their active constitutive intentionalities, and thus it is true that they are experienced in the sense of 'existing there for everybody'. (Of course, this is only true 'for everybody' who belongs to the corresponding community of culture – but that is a problem of a quite different character, which will be discussed later.)

Thus, for phenomenology the problem of the experience of Others need not be a dark corner which, to use a beautiful expression of Husserl,[5] is feared only by children in philosophy because the spectre of solipsism or psychologism and relativism haunts it. The true philosopher, however, must light up this dark corner rather than run away from it.

In the fifth *Cartesian Meditation* Husserl offered the following solution of the problem, which we shall attempt to render in its main outline, as far as possible in his own words.[6]

After the execution of the epoché I can first eliminate from the

5. *Formale und transzendentale Logik*, p. 210.

6. For this purpose we have not used the French translation but the original unpublished German manuscript.* A critique of the Husserlian establishment of the transcendental subjectivity, against which, in my opinion, certain important objections can be raised, must wait for another publication.†

* *Cartesianische Meditationen und Pariser Vorträge*, ed. S. Strasser, The Hague: Nijhoff, 1950. (*Cartesian Meditations*, The Hague: Nijhoff, 1969. *Editor's note*)

† See Alfred Schutz, 'Das Problem der transzendentalen Intersubjektivität bei Husserl', *Philosophische Rundschau*, 5, 2, 1957, pp. 81–107. ('The Problem of Transcendental Intersubjectivity in Husserl', *Collected Papers*, Vol. III, The Hague: Nijhoff, 1966, pp. 51–91. *Editor's note*)

thematic field within the transcendental universal sphere all the constitutive activities which are immediately or mediately related to the subjectivity of Others. In this way I reduce the universe of my conscious life to my own transcendental sphere (*transzendentale Eigensphäre*), to my concrete being as a monad. What is left by the abstractive elimination of the sense of other subjectivity is a uniformly connected stratum of the phenomenon 'world' – Husserl calls it the primordial sphere – which is no longer a world objectively existing for everybody, but is my world belonging peculiarly to me alone. And thus, in the truest sense, it is my private world.

Within this reduced world-phenomenon, one object is distinguished from all others. I call it my body, and it is distinguished by the fact that I can control it in action and that I attribute sensorial fields to it in conformity with my experience. If I reduce other human beings in a similar way, I get peculiar corporealities; if I reduce myself as a human being, I get 'my body' and 'my mind' or me as a psychophysical unity, and in it my personal I which functions in my body, or which acts on and endures the exterior world by means of it. Now, in this reduced exterior world the 'Other' also appears as a corporeality, but as a corporeality which I apprehend as a body, and indeed as a body of *another* by a process of appresentative pairing.[7]

The other corporeality, once experienced, continues indeed to manifest itself as a body through its changing but always concordant gestures, which appresentatively indicate a psychical side. This psychical side, at first only indicated by appresentation, has

7. By *appresentation* Husserl understands a process of analogy, but this process is in no sense a conclusion by analogy. By it an actual experience refers back to another experience which is not given in actuality and will not be actualized. In other words the appresented does not attain an actual presence. For instance, by looking at the obverse of an object the reverse is appresented. *Pairing* ('*accouplement*' in the French translation) is a principal form of passive synthesis, which means of association. Its characteristic is that two data, distinguishable each from the other, are presented in the unity of consciousness; they constitute as a pair a phenomenological unity of similarity established by pure passivity, although they appear distinct and regardless of whether or not they are noticed. Cf. *Méditations Cartésiennes*, Sec. 50 and 51.

to be fulfilled by original experience. In this way an Other is appresentatively constituted in my monad as an ego that is not 'I myself' but a second ego which mirrors itself in my monad. This second ego, however, is not simply there and given in and of itself, but is an *alter ego*; it is an Other which, in accordance with his constitutive sense, refers back to me, the ego of this *alter ego*. This 'Other' is nevertheless not simply a duplicate of myself. The alien corporeality that is apperceived as an 'Other' appears in my monadic sphere above all in the mode of the 'there' (*illic*), while my own body is in the mode of the absolute 'here' (*hic*). That which becomes appresented in this way does not derive from my own sphere of peculiarity; it is a coexistent ego in the mode of the *illic* and therefore an *alter ego*.

The first communality which exists between me, the primordial psychophysical I, and the appresentatively experienced Other, and which forms the foundation of all other intersubjective communities of a higher order, is the community of Nature, which belongs not only to my primordial sphere but also to that of the Other. There is, however, the difference that the Other's world of Nature is seen as *illic* from my point of view, which is to say that the Other gets that aspect from it, which I should get if I myself were not *hic* but *illic*. In this way, every natural thing which is experienced or which can be experienced in my primordial sphere obtains a new appresentative stratum, namely, as the same natural thing in the possible manners of its givenness for the Other.

Starting from myself as the original constitutive monad, I thus get other monads, that is, Others as psychophysical subjects. These Others are not merely related by means of associative pairing to my psychophysical being in their capacity as being bodily opposite me; rather it is a question of an objective equalization, a mutual interrelatedness of my existence and that of all Others. For, as the body of the Other is appresented by me as an Other, so my body is experienced by the Other as his Other, and so forth. The same thing obtains for all subjects, that is, for this open community of monads which Husserl has designated as transcendental intersubjectivity.

It should be stressed that this transcendental intersubjectivity exists purely in me, the meditating ego. It is constituted purely from the sources of my intentionality, but in such a manner that it is the *same* transcendental intersubjectivity in every single human being (only in other subjective manners of appearance) in his intentional experiences. In this constitution of the transcendental intersubjectivity that of the single and uniformly objective world is also executed, and along with it the constitution of those peculiarly mental objectivities, especially those types of social communities, which have the character of personalities of a higher order.

Of special importance for our topic is the constitution of the specifically human, and that means cultural, worlds in their peculiar manner of objectivity.[8] According to Husserl, accessibility for everyone belongs in essence to the constitutive sense of Nature, of corporeality and of the psychophysical human being. *But the world of culture is of a limited kind of objectivity*, and with this it should be borne in mind that the life-world is given to me, and to everyone who retains the natural attitude primarily as his cultural world, namely, as a world of signification which the human being in question historically takes a part in forming. The constitution of the world of culture, similar to the constitution of any 'world', including the world of one's own stream of experience, has the lawful structure of a constitution, oriented with respect to a 'null point' (*Nullglied*), i.e. to a personality. Here am I and my culture; it is accessible to me and to my cultural companions as a kind of experience of Others. Other cultural humanity and other culture can become accessible only by a complicated process of understanding, namely, on the basic level of the common Nature, which, in its specific spatio-temporal structure, constitutes the horizon of being for the accessibility to all the manifold cultural phenomena. As Nature is thus concretely and uniformly constituted, so human existence itself is referred to an existent life-world as a realm of practical activity, which, from the first, is endowed with human significations. All this is in principle accessible to the explication of a phenomenological constitutive analysis which, proceeding from the apodictic ego, must finally reveal the transcendental meaning of the world

8. In this connection see especially *Méditations Cartésiennes*, Sec. 58.

in its full concretion, which is the continuous life-world of us all.

Ad 3. It was stated above that the natural sciences generally, and especially the natural sciences which use mathematics, have lost their relation to their basis of meaning, namely the life-world. How can this reproach be justified, when it has just been shown that it is precisely this universal Nature which constitutes itself concretely and uniformly in intersubjectivity, and which must almost be considered as the form of access to the worlds of other culture, in their manner of oriented constitution? We may reply first of all that Nature as the object of the natural sciences does not mean precisely the same thing as Nature as a constitutive element of the life-world. That which the naïvely living human being takes for natural reality is not the objective world of our modern natural sciences; his conception of the world, as valid for him in its subjectivity, obtains with all its gods, demons, etc. *Nature in this sense, as an element of the life-world, is thus a concept which has its place exclusively in the mental* (geistig) *sphere.* It constitutes itself in our everyday meaningful experience as this experience develops in our historically determined being.

Let us take geometry as an example. When we, in our perceptual life-world, direct our view by abstraction to merely spatial and temporal figures we experience, it is true, 'solids'. However, they are not the ideal solids of geometry, but they are solids as we actually realize them, with the same content which is the true content of our experience.[9] To the world which is pre-given to our everyday experience belongs the spatio-temporal form, in which are included the corporeal figures ordered within it, and in which we ourselves live in conformity with our personal, bodily manner of being. But here we find nothing of geometrical idealities, of geometrical space or of mathematical time with all their forms.[10] Concretely empirical figures are given to us, in our life-world, merely as forms of a material, of a 'sensory fullness'; thus they are given with that which is represented by the so-called specific sense-qualities (colour, odour, etc.). But pure geometry deals with solids in the corporeal world only in pure abstraction; that is to say, only with abstract figures in the spatio-temporal framework, which are, as Husserl recognizes, purely ideal

9. Husserl, 'Krisis', pp. 98ff.   10. ibid., pp. 125ff.

'meaning figures', meaning-creations of the human mind. This is not to say that geometrical existence is psychological or personal existence in the personal sphere of consciousness. On the contrary, geometrical existence is of the same kind as the existence of meaning-structures, and it is objective for everyone who is a geometer or understands geometry.

Geometrical figures, axioms, and propositions, just as most structures of the world of culture, have an *ideal objectivity*; they can always be *reactivated* as identically the same. That is to say, the meaning-producing activity which has led to their sedimentation can be re-executed. But reactivation in this sense is also explication of the meaning which lies implicated in the abbreviations of this sedimentation, by referring it back to the primal evidence. The possibility always remains open for examining the primal evidence of a tradition, for example, of geometrical or of any other deductive science, which works on through the centuries. If this does not occur, then the original activities which are found within the fundamental concepts of this deductive science and their foundation in pre-scientific materials remain undisclosed. The tradition in which these sciences are handed down to us is then emptied of meaning, and the basis of meaning to which these sciences refer, namely the life-world, is forgotten.[11] But according to Husserl, this is the situation in modern times not only with respect to geometry and mathematics, including all natural sciences using mathematics, but also with respect to traditional logic.[12]

The fundamental idea of modern physics is that nature is a *mathematical* universe. Its ideal is exactitude, which means an ability to recognize and determine the things of nature in absolute identity, as the substratum of an absolutely identical, methodically unequivocable and discernible character. In order to achieve this ideal, physics makes use of measurement and of the mathematical methods of calculation and formulae. In this way it seeks to create an entirely new kind of prediction for the cor-

11. Husserl, 'Die Frage nach dem Ursprung der Geometrie', pp. 203–25, and especially pp. 209–17. (Reprinted here, pp. 42–70. *Editor's note*)

12. In relation to this last point, about logic, cf. *Formale und transzendentale Logik*, Sec. 73–81, Sec. 94ff.

poreal world, and to be able to calculate the occurrences in this world in terms of a compelling necessity. But on the one hand, the sensory fullness of solids in the life-world and the changes of this fullness are not capable of being mathematized, and on the other hand, pre-scientific intuitable nature does not lack this predictability. In the world perceptible by our senses, changes in the spatio-temporal positions of solids, changes in their form and fullness, are not accidental and indifferent, but they are dependent on each other in sensuously *typical* ways. The basic style of our visible immediate world is empirical. This universal, and indeed causal, style makes possible hypotheses, inductions, and predictions, but in pre-scientific life they all have the character of the approximate and typical.[13] Only when the ideal objectivities become substituted for the empirical things of the corporeal world, only when one abstracts or co-idealizes the intuitable fullness, which is not capable of mathematization, does the *fundamental hypothesis* of the entire realm of mathematical natural science result, namely, that a universal inductivity might prevail in the intuitable world, an inductivity which suggests itself in everyday experience but which remains concealed in its infinity. Consequently, this universal causality of the mathematical sciences is also an idealization. Now it is doubtless true, says Husserl, that in the remarkable structure of the natural sciences this hypothesis holds good in infinity, and precisely in its prediction of events in the life-world. But in spite of all verification it still remains a hypothesis and thus an unclarified supposition of mathematical natural science.

The natural scientist, in unquestioned tradition, accepts the inherited idealizations and unclarified suppositions as technics (τεχνή) without becoming conscious of the shift which the originally living meaning of the aim to get knowledge of the world itself has experienced.[14] In the process of mathematization of the natural sciences, says Husserl, we measure the life-world for a well-fitting garment of ideas. In just this way we get possibilities for a prediction which goes far beyond the accomplishments of everyday anticipation, concerning the occurrences in the intuitable life-world. But everything which represents the life-world to

13. Cf. 'Krisis', pp. 101–5.   14. 'Krisis', pp. 113–16 and pp. 132 ff.

the natural scientists as 'objectively actual and true nature' is clothed by this garment of symbols and disguised. The cloak of ideas has the effect that we take a method to be true being, in order infinitely to improve upon the *raw* predictions which are the only ones possible within the actual experiences of the life-world. But the proper meaning of methods, formulae, and theories remains unintelligible as long as one does not reflect about the historical meaning belonging to their primordial establishment.

With the enormous success of the mathematical natural sciences has come the fact that modern philosophy and critique of knowledge generally perceive the prototype of scientific thought in their methods. The consequence is a dualistic cleavage into a real and self-contained corporeal world, and a mental world, which latter, however, remains dependent upon the natural world and is not brought to any independent status in its own right. The further consequence is that even this mental world ought to be explained *more geometrico* according to the unclarified rationalism of the mathematical natural sciences, or, as Husserl terms it, by means of physicalistic rationalism. Above all, psychology ought to be treated objectivistically, where objectivistic should mean that in the realm of the world which is self-evidently given through experience one will search for the 'objective truths' without inquiring about the subjective activities of the mind, out of which alone the ontic sense of the pre-given life-world is constituted. For the life-world is a subjective formation resulting from the activities of the experiencing pre-scientific life. Inasmuch as the intuitable life-world, which is purely subjective, has been forgotten in the thematic interest of natural science, and also of objectivistic psychology, the working subject, namely the human being himself who is pursuing his science, has in no way become thematic. It is only in purely cultural scientific knowledge that the scientist does not become confounded by the objection of the self-disguise of his activity. It is consequently erroneous if the social sciences contend with the natural sciences for an equal warrant. As soon as they grant to the natural sciences their objectivity as their own independent attribute, the social sciences themselves fall into objectivism, for only mind (*Geist*) has being in itself and is independent. To regard nature as something in itself alien to mind and then to found the cultural sciences on the natural sciences, and thus supposedly to make them exact, is an absurdity. The cultural scientists, blinded by naturalism, have completely neglected even to raise the problem of a universal and true cultural science.

Ad 4. But is it an affair of the cultural sciences at all, in the sense of that term as used today, to make inquiries concerning the problem of a universal science of the mind in Husserl's sense? Is this task not specifically a philosophical, or more properly a phenomenological problem that becomes visible only in the transcendental sphere, and thus only after that mundane world, which alone is the topic and ought to be the topic of all efforts of the concrete sciences of culture, has been bracketed? The ideal of history, to recount the past 'as it then actually was' (von Ranke), is also, with certain modifications, the ideal of all other sciences of culture, i.e. to determine what society, the state, language, art, economy, law, etc. actually are in our mundane life-world and its historicity, and to determine how the meaning of each can be made intelligible in the sphere of our mundane experience. And should not an appeal be made to psychology in this sphere for a solution of the problem of a universal cultural science?

For Husserl there is also no doubt that all the hitherto existing cultural and social sciences are related in principle to phenomena of mundane intersubjectivity. Hence, the transcendental constitutive phenomena, which only become visible in the phenomenologically reduced sphere, scarcely come within the view of the cultural sciences. However, a psychology from which a solution of the problems of the cultural sciences might be expected must become aware of the fact that it is not a science which deals with empirical facts. It has to be a science of essences, investigating the correlates of those transcendental constitutional phenomena which are related to the natural attitude. Consequently, it has to examine the invariant, peculiar, and essential structures of the mind; but that is to say it examines their *a priori* structure.[15] The concrete description of the spheres of

15. 'Nachwort zu meinen *Ideen*', p. 553; cf. p. 14 of Boyce Gibson's translation of *Ideas*.

Alfred Schutz 133

consciousness as it has to be undertaken by a true descriptive psychology within the natural attitude remains, however, the description of a closed sphere of the intentionalities. That is to say, it requires not only a concrete description of the experiences of consciousness, as in the Lockean tradition, but also necessarily the description of the conscious (intentional) 'objects in their objective sense'[16] found in active inner experiences. But such a true *psychology of intentionality* is, according to Husserl's words, nothing other than a *constitutive phenomenology of the natural attitude*.[17]

In this eidetic mundane science (thus in the psychological apperception of the natural attitude), which stands at the beginning of all methodological and theoretical scientific problems of all the cultural and social sciences, all analyses carried through in phenomenological reduction essentially retain their validation. It is precisely here that the tremendous significance of the results achieved by Husserl for all the cultural sciences lies.

II

In the above résumé of some of the most important lines of thought of the later philosophy of Husserl, the concept of the life-world is revealed in its entire and central significance as the basis of meaning of all sciences, including natural sciences and including also philosophy in so far as it wishes to appear as an exact science. Thus, every reflection finds its evidence only in the process of recurring to its originally founding experience within this life-world, and it remains the endless task of thought to make intelligible the intentional constitution of the contributive subjectivity in reference to this its basis of meaning. We, however, who live naïvely in this life-world, encounter it as already constituted. We are, so to speak, born into it. We live in and endure it, and the living intentionality of our stream of consciousness supports our thinking, by which we orient ourselves practically in this life-world, and our action, by which we intervene in it.

Our everyday world is, from the outset, an intersubjective

16. ibid., p. 565.   17. ibid., p. 567.

world of culture. It is intersubjective because we live in it as men among other men, bound to them through common influence and work, understanding others and being an object of understanding for others. It is a world of culture because, from the outset, the life-world is a universe of significations to us, i.e. a framework of meaning (*Sinnzusammenhang*) which we have to interpret, and of interrelations of meaning which we institute only through our action in this life-world. It is a world of culture also because we are always conscious of its *historicity*, which we encounter in tradition and habituality, and which is capable of being examined because the 'already-given' refers back to one's own activity or to the activity of Others, of which it is the sediment. I, the human being born into this world and naïvely living in it, am the centre of this world in the historical situation of my actual 'Now and Here'; I am the 'null point toward which its constitution is oriented'.[18] That is to say, this world has significance and meaning first of all by me and for me.

In what follows we intend to try to clarify this topic by drawing from Husserl's course of ideas some fundamental consequences not found in his own writings, for the knowledge of the structure of the social sciences.

This world, built around my own I, presents itself for interpretation to me, a being living naïvely within it. From this standpoint everything has reference to my actual historical situation, or as we can also say, to my pragmatic interests which belong to the situation in which I find myself here and now. The place in which I am living has not significance for me as a geographical concept, but as my home. The objects of my daily use have significance as my implements, and the men to whom I stand in relationships are my kin, my friends, or strangers. Language is not a substratum of philosophical or grammatical considerations for me, but a means for expressing my intentions or understanding the intentions of Others. Only in reference to me does that relation to Others obtain its specific meaning which I designate with the word 'We'. In reference to Us whose centre I am, Others stand out as 'You', and in reference to You, who refer back to me, third parties stand out as 'They'. My social world with the *alter egos*

18. Cf. above, pp. 128–9.

in it is arranged, around me as the centre, into associates (*Um-welt*), contemporaries (*Mitwelt*), predecessors (*Vorwelt*), and successors (*Folgewelt*),[19] whereby I and my different attitudes to Others institute these manifold relationships. All this is done in various degrees of *intimacy* and *anonymity*.

Furthermore, the life-world is arranged into fields (*Zentren*) of different relevance according to my current state of interest, each one of which has its own peculiar centre of density and fullness, and its open but interpretable horizons. In this connection, the categories of *familiarity* and *strangeness* and the very important category of *accessibility* enter into consideration. This last category refers to the grouping of my environments according to (1) that which actually lies within the extent of my reach, seeing and hearing, or has once lain there and might at will be brought back into actual accessibility; (2) that which is or was accessible to others and might thus potentially be accessible to me if I were not here (*hic*) but there (*illic*);[20] (3) the open horizons of that which in free variation can be thought of as attainable.

To this it should be added that I assume everything which has meaning for me also has meaning for the Other or Others with whom I share this, my life-world, as an associate, contemporary, predecessor, or successor. This life-world presents itself also to them for interpretation. I know about their perspectives of relevance and their horizons of familiarity or strangeness; indeed I also know that with segments of my meaningful life I belong to the life-world of Others as Others belong to my life-world. All this is a manifold orientation for me, the naïve human being. I

19. The translation of these terms follows the usage in an article by Alfred Stonier and Karl Bode concerning Dr Schutz's work, 'A New Approach to the Methodology of the Social Sciences', *Economica*, Vol. IV, 1937, pp. 406–24. These terms are developed at length in Dr Schutz's *Der sinnhafte Aufbau der sozialen Welt*, Vienna, 1932, 2nd ed. 1960. The *Umwelt* is the immediate world within which direct and relatively intimate experience of Others is possible. The *Mitwelt* is a world of mediate, but contemporary, experience within which indirect and relatively anonymous experience of Others can be obtained. The *Vorwelt* refers to experiences of the historical past. The *Folgewelt* refers to the future, of which no experience is possible, but toward which an orientation may exist. (*Translator's note*)

20. Cf. above, pp. 126–7.

posit meaningful acts in the expectation that Others will interpret them meaningfully, and my schema of positing is oriented with respect to the Others' schema of interpretation. On the other hand, I can examine everything which, as a product of Others, presents itself to me for meaningful interpretation as to the meaning which the Other who has produced it may have connected with it. Thus, on these reciprocal acts of positing meaning and of interpretation of meaning, my social world of mundane intersubjectivity is built; it is also the social world of Others, and all other social and cultural phenomena are founded upon it.

All this is self-evident to me in my naïve life just as it is self-evident to me that the world actually exists and that it is actually *thus*, as I experience it (apart from deceptions which subsequently in the course of experience prove to be mere appearances). No motive exists for the naïve person to raise the transcendental question concerning the actuality of the world or concerning the reality of the *alter ego*, or to make the jump into the reduced sphere. Rather, he posits this world in a *general thesis* as meaningfully valid for him, with all that he finds in it, with all natural things, with all living beings (especially with human beings), and with meaningful products of all sorts (tools, symbols, language systems, works of art, etc.). Hence, the naïvely living person (we are speaking of healthy, grown-up, and wide-awake human beings) automatically has in hand, so to speak, the meaningful complexes which are valid for him. From things inherited and learned, from the manifold sedimentations of tradition, habituality, and his own previous constitutions of meaning, which can be retained and reactivated, his *store of experience* of his life-world is built up as a closed meaningful complex. This complex is normally unproblematical for him, and it remains controllable by him in such a way that his momentary interest selects from this store of experience those things which are relevant to the demand of the situation. The experience of the life-world has its special style of verification. This style results from the process of the harmonization of all single experiences. It is co-constituted last but not least, by the perspectives of relevance and by the horizons of interest which are to be explicated.

All that has been said so far, however, is no more than chapter-headings for an extensive exploration. For the present, it will suffice to keep firmly in mind that a special motivation is needed in order to induce the naïve person even to pose the question concerning the meaningful structure of his life-world, even *within the general thesis*. This motivation can be very heterogeneous; for example, a newly appearing phenomenon of meaning resists being organized within the store of experience, or a special condition of interest demands a transition from a naïve attitude to a reflection of a higher order. So-called rational action can be given as an example of the latter. Rational action is given when all the ends of action and all the means which will lead to it are clearly and distinctly presented, as, for example, in the case of economic action. If such a motivation for leaving the natural attitude is given, then by a process of reflection the question concerning the structure of meaning can always be raised. One can always reactivate the process which has built up the sediments of meaning, and one can explain the intentionalities of the perspectives of relevance and the horizons of interest. Then all these phenomena of meaning, which obtain quite simply for the naïve person, might be in principle exactly described and analysed even *within the general thesis*. To accomplish this on the level of mundane intersubjectivity is the task of the mundane cultural sciences, and to clarify their specific methods is precisely a part of that constitutive phenomenology of the natural attitude of which we have been speaking. Whether one will call this science Intentional Psychology or, better, General Sociology, since it must always be referred back to mundane intersubjectivity, is a quite secondary question.

All science presumes a special attitude of the person carrying on science; it is the attitude of the disinterested observer. In this manner it is distinguished above all from the attitude of the person who lives naïvely in his life-world and who has an eminently practical interest in it. With the transition to this attitude, however, all categories of experience of the life-world undergo a fundamental modification. As a disinterested observer, not as a private person, which certainly he also is, the scientist does not participate in the life-world as an actor, and he is no longer carried along by the living stream of intentionalities. The person living naïvely in the life-world can become, as we have said, motivated so as to raise the question concerning the structure of its meaning. But, although he reflects in this manner, he in no way loses his practical interest in it, and he still remains the centre, the 'null point', of this his world, which is oriented with regard to him. *But to make up his mind to observe scientifically this life-world means to determine no longer to place himself and his own condition of interest as the centre of this world, but to substitute another null point for the orientation of the phenomena of the life-world.* What this null point is and how it comes to be constituted as a type (economic man, subject of law, etc.) depends upon the particular problem-situation which the scientist has chosen. The life-world, as an object of scientific investigation, will be for the investigator *qua* scientist predominantly the life-world of Others, the observed. This does not alter the fact that the scientist, who is *also* a human being among human beings in this single and uniform life-world and whose scientific work is in itself a working-together with Others in it, constantly refers and is obliged to refer in his scientific work to his own experience of the life-world. But it must always be clearly borne in mind that the disinterested observer has to a certain extent departed from the living stream of intentionalities. *Together with the substitution of another null point for the framework of orientation, every meaning-reference which was self-evident to the naïve person, in reference to his own I, has now undergone a fundamental specific modification.*[21] It remains for each social and cultural science to develop the type of such modification proper to it, that is, *to work out its particular methods.* In other words, each of these sciences must give the equation of transformation according to which the

21. For example, the social scientist does not study the concrete action (*Handeln*) of human beings, like you and me and everyone in our daily lives, with our hopes and fears, mistakes and hates, happiness and misery. He analyses only certain definite sequences of activity (*Handlungsabläufe*) as types, with their means-end relations and their chains of motivation; and he constructs (obviously, according to quite definite structural laws) the pertinent ideal personality types with which he peoples the segment of the social world he has selected as an object of his scientific research.

phenomena of the life-world become transformed by a process of idealization.

For idealization and formalization have just the same role for the social sciences as the one which Husserl has stated for the natural sciences, except that it is not a question of *mathematizing the forms* but of developing a *typology of 'fullnesses'* (*Füllen*). Also, in the social sciences the eminent danger exists that their idealizations, in this case typologies, will not be considered as methods but as true being. Indeed this danger is even greater in the sciences which deal with the human being and his life-world, because they are always obliged to work with a highly complex material involving types of a higher order. This material does not refer back immediately to the subjective activity of individuals, which is always the chief problem if it is in the sphere of mundane apperception.

In relation to these problems it is the great contribution of Max Weber[22] in his 'verstehende Soziologie' to have given the principles of a method which attempts to explain all social phenomena in the broadest sense (thus all objects of the cultural sciences) in relation to the 'intended meaning' which the actor connects with his action. At the same time, he has given the main characteristics of the style of method of these sciences in his theory of the ideal type and its laws of formation. But, it seems to me, these methods can only become fully intelligible by means of the far-reaching investigations of a constitutive phenomenology of the natural attitude.

Such a science will find more than a guide in Husserl's investigations in the area of transcendental phenomenology, for, as we have already said, in essence all analyses carried out in phenomenological reduction must retain their validation in the correlates of the phenomena investigated within the natural sphere. Therefore, it is to be the task of this science to apply the whole treasure of knowledge opened up by Husserl to its own area. We mention only Husserl's analysis of time, his theory of signs and symbols, of ideal objects, of occasional judgements, and finally his teleological interpretation of history. To develop the

22. An excellent presentation of his theory is to be found in English in Talcott Parsons, *The Structure of Social Action*, New York, 1937.

programme of such a science, even in its main characteristics, beyond the mere suggestion given above, would go far beyond our present limits.[23]

23. I have presented several of the main principles in *Der sinnhafte Aufbau der sozialen Welt*, Vienna 1932, 2nd ed. 1960. (*The Phenomenology of the Social World*, Evanston, Northwestern University Press, 1967. *Editor's note*)

7 Maurice Merleau-Ponty

The Philosopher and Sociology*

M. Merleau-Ponty, 'Le Philosophe et la sociologie', in *Signes*, Paris: Gallimard, 1960, pp. 123–42.

Translated by David Fernbach

Philosophy and sociology have lived for a long time in a state of mutual separation. If this has made it possible to conceal their rivalry, it is only by denying them any common ground, restricting their growth, making each incomprehensible to the other, and thus putting culture in general in a situation of permanent crisis. But as always happens in the end, the spirit of research has brushed aside these taboos, and it now seems that the progress of each side enables us today to re-examine their interrelation.

We should like to draw attention here to those meditations of Husserl which he devoted to this set of problems. The reason we see Husserl as exemplary is that it is he more than anyone else who has felt how all forms of thought are in a certain sense solidary with one another; that there is therefore no need to destroy the human sciences in order to establish philosophy, nor to destroy philosophy in order to establish the human sciences; that every science contains an implicit ontology and that every ontology anticipates a specific kind of knowledge; finally, that it is up to us to come to terms with this state of affairs in such a way that both philosophy and science[1] become possible . . .

It may be that this separation of philosophy and sociology has never been upheld in quite the way that we have just put it.

---

* This article was first translated into English by Richard C. McCleary, in *Signs*, Evanston: Northwestern University Press, 1964; reprinted in *Phenomenology, Language and Sociology*, Selected Essays, ed. John O'Neill, London: Heinemann, 1974.

1. In French, '*science*' refers to any disciplined and organized body of knowledge or mode of inquiry; thus history, as well as physics, sociology, as well as biology, are 'sciences'; in German, too, the term '*Wissenschaft*' has the same inclusive reference. (*Translator's note*)

Fortunately enough, the actual work of philosophers, and of sociologists, respectively, has often been less exclusive than their principles. But this separation is still part of a certain understanding common to both philosophers and sociologists, which, by referring philosophy and the human sciences to what it believes to be their pure type, ends up by compromising both scientific knowledge and philosophical reflection.

While it is an acknowledged fact that all major philosophies seek to consider the human mind both in itself *and in its various aspects* (ideas and their development, understanding and sense-perception), there is a certain myth which presents philosophy as the authoritarian assertion of the mind's absolute autonomy. In this interpretation philosophy is no longer a process of questioning. It is rather a fixed body of doctrines, set up in order to ensure an absolutely *unbound* mind the enjoyment of itself and its ideas. On the other hand, there is a myth which presents scientific knowledge, the science of things in the world, as arising from the mere collection of facts, not to mention the science of this science, so that my sociology of knowledge (itself conceived in empiricist fashion) would have to close the universe of facts in on itself by inserting into it the very ideas that we invent in order to interpret these facts, thus, as it were, ridding us of our own selves. These two myths are both antagonists and accomplices. Opposed in this way, philosophers and sociologists are at least agreed on a boundary line that ensures they will never meet; if this *cordon sanitaire* were removed, philosophy and sociology would destroy one another. Thus up to now they have done battle for the human mind in a cold-war state of separation.

In such an atmosphere, any research that seeks to take account of both of ideas and of facts is bound to be somewhat disjointed, since on one side facts, instead of being understood as stimulants and guarantors of constructive effort that would link up their internal dynamic, are elevated into a state of peremptory grace from which everything else is expected to follow, while on the other side ideas are dispensed on principle from any confrontation with our experience of the world, of other people, and of ourselves. The interaction of facts and ideas is rejected as a bastard procedure – neither science nor philosophy – which would deprive scientists of the final interpretation of the very facts that they themselves discovered, while confronting philosophy with the threat of the ever-provisional results of scientific research...

We must realize the *obscurantist* effects of this rigour. If investigations of a 'mixed' character really have the drawbacks just mentioned, this would mean that the philosophical perspective and the scientific perspective were mutually exclusive, and that philosophy and sociology could be certain of their results only on condition that they ignored one another. The scientist would thus have to be prohibited the 'idealization' of brute fact which is in fact the very essence of his work. He would have to dispense with the deciphering of signs that is his very *raison d'être*, and with the construction of intellectual models without which there would be no more sociology today than there was physics before Galileo. He would have to put on the blinkers of Baconian or Millian induction, even if his own research evidently avoided these canonical recipes. He would have to pretend to approach social facts as if they were something foreign to him, as if his study of them owed nothing to the experience of inter-subjectivity that he has as a social subject. Under the pretext that sociology is in fact no longer conducted simply on the basis of this lived experience, but that it analyses, explains and objectifies it, that it undermines our initial awareness of social relations and finally makes those relations in which we live appear as a specific variant of a dynamic process, whose existence we did not originally even suspect and which can only be grasped by contact with other cultural formations – under this pretext, objectivism forgets the other evidence that it is impossible for us to expand our experience of social relations and form an idea of actual social relations save by analogy or by contrast with those that we have experienced ourselves, in other words by an *imaginary variation* of these; this variation undoubtedly gives these relations a new significance, just as the fall of a body on an inclined plane is cast in a new light by the pure idea of free fall, but it is our own experience of social relations that provides this imaginary variation with the only sociological meaning that it can have. Anthropology shows us that there are certain cultures in which children treat certain other close relatives as their 'parents', and facts of this kind eventually enable us to draw a diagram of the kinship system of the culture in question. However, these kinds of correlations give us only an outline or contour of kinship in this culture, a division of behaviour that is given the nominal definition of 'kinship' into certain significant points X, Y, Z that are still anonymous, in the sense that they do not yet have any sociological meaning. The formulae in which they are described could just as well represent a physical or chemical process of the same form, so long as we have not managed to place ourselves in the institution thus defined, understood the style of kinship which these facts all allude to, understood *in what sense* it is that certain subjects in this culture perceive other subjects of their own generation as their 'parents', thus so long as we have not grasped the basic personal and interpersonal structure, the institutional relations with nature and with other people, that make possible the established correlations. Once again, though the underlying dynamic of the social group is certainly not *given* to us by our limited experience of social life, it is still only by a process of de-centring and re-centring the latter that we manage to represent this dynamic to ourselves, just as the generalized concept of number remains 'number' for us only via the link that ties it to the whole number of simple arithmetic. Similarly, on the basis of the Freudian conception of pregenital sexuality, we can build up a table of the various possible modes in which the child's bodily orifices can be emphasized, and in this table, those which are actually emphasized in our own cultural system and have been described by Freudian analysts will figure as particular variants out of a large number of possible alternatives which may well be selected by cultures still unknown to us. But a table of this kind tells us *nothing* about the relations with others and with nature that define these cultural types, unless we refer back to the psychological significance of the mouth, the anus or the genital apparatus on the basis of our own lived experience, so as to see, in the different uses that different cultures make of these, different crystallizations of an original polymorphism of the body as vehicle of being-in-the-world. This table provides us only with an invitation to imagine, on the basis of our experience of our own bodies, other bodily techniques. That which is actually realized in ourselves is never reducible to the status of simply one possibility among all others, since it is on the basis of this privileged experience, in which we come to know the body as 'structuring' principle, that we can glimpse other 'possibilities', different as these might be. It is important never to cut socio- logical investigation off from our own experience as social subjects (which of course includes not only what we have our- selves experienced, but also behaviour that we perceive via the actions, accounts and writings of other people), since the for- mulae of sociology can only begin to represent the social from the point that the correlations that they express are linked together and put inside a certain unique *vision* of society and nature that is specific to the society in question, and that has become, even when it is quite different from current official conceptions, the clandestine institution or principle of its entire outward func- tioning. If objectivism or scientism were ever to succeed in depriving sociology of all recourse to meanings, it would only protect it from 'philosophy' by closing to it any understanding of its object. We might then perhaps have mathematical treat- ments of social phenomena, but we would never have the mathematics *of* the society in question. The sociologist begins to do philosophy to the extent that he takes it on himself not simply to note down facts, but rather to understand them. At the stage of interpretation, he is himself already a philosopher. This means that the professional philosopher is not disqualified from reinter- preting facts which he has not himself observed, if these facts say something different from or something more than the scientist saw in them. As Husserl put it, the eidetic of the physical object did not begin with phenomenology, but with Galileo. Reciprocally, the philosopher has the right to read and interpret Galileo.

This separation that we are arguing against is just as damaging to philosophy as it is to the development of science. How can a philosopher with some degree of awareness seriously propose that philosophy be prohibited the company of science? For in the last analysis, philosophy always has to think *about something*: the square drawn in the sand, the donkey, the horse and the mule, the cubic foot of volume, cinnabar, the Roman state, the hand plunged into iron filings ... The philosopher thinks his experience and his world. How, save by an arbitrary edict, could he be given the right to forget what science says about the same experience and the same world? What the collective noun 'science' refers to is nothing more than a systemative arrangement, a methodological exercise – broader or narrower, more or less far-seeing – of the same experience that begins with our very first perception. Science is a set of means for perceiving, imagining and ultimately living, oriented towards the same truth whose necessity is established in us by our first experiences. It may be that science purchases its precision at the cost of a certain schematization. But the remedy for this is to confront science with the integrity of experience, rather than to oppose to it a philosophical knowledge that comes from God knows where.

The great merit of Husserl, as his philosophy came to maturity, and to an ever greater extent as he continued his effort, is to have defined, with his 'vision of essences', 'morphological essences' and 'phenomenological experience', a field and an attitude of investigation in which philosophy and science could actually meet together. It is well known that Husserl began by maintaining a rigorous difference between the two, and he always held to this. As we see it, however, his idea of a psycho-phenomenological parallelism (we might say, more generally, his thesis of a parallelism between positive science and philosophy, which leads to each assertion made by the one corresponding to an assertion made by the other) actually leads us to the idea of a *reciprocal envelopment*. As far as the social is concerned, the final question is to know how this can be both a 'thing' of which one can have unprejudiced knowledge, and at the same time a 'meaning' such that those societies that we have knowledge of only provide an opportunity for its appearance; how the social can both exist in itself and in us. Now that we have entered this labyrinth, we shall follow the steps that Husserl takes towards his final conceptions, in which these steps are both preserved and superseded.

At the start of his work, Husserl staked a claim for philosophy in terms that seem to abolish the rights of actual science. Speaking of that pre-eminent social relation that is language, he put it forward as a principle[2] that we are not able to understand the functioning of our own language, nor can we separate ourselves from the pseudo-evidence this gives rise to and enter into a true knowledge of other languages, unless we first build up a picture of the 'ideal form' of language and the modes of expression that must pertain to it in order for it to be language. Only then can we understand how German, Latin, Chinese each participate in their own fashion in this universal eidetic, and define each of these languages as a specific mixture, in its own proportions, of universal 'forms of meaning', a 'blurred' and incomplete realization of 'general and systematic grammar'. Actual language was thus to be reconstructed by an operation of synthesis, starting with the essential structures of any possible language which enfold it in their pure clarity. Philosophical thought appeared as something absolutely autonomous, capable – and the only thought capable – of yielding true knowledge by recourse to the essences that provided the key to things.

It could be generally said that the whole historical experience of social relations is put in question here in favour of the vision of essences. This experience certainly presents us with 'social processes', with 'cultural formations', forms of law, art and religion, but in so far as we remain at the level of these empirical realizations, we do not even know the meaning of these rubrics under which we classify them, still less, therefore, whether the historic becoming of a particular religion or form of law or art is really a function of its essence, and provides a judgement of its value, or whether on the contrary this law, art or religion still contains other possibilities. Husserl said at this time that history could not judge an idea, and when it did in fact do so, this 'evaluative' (*wertende*) history borrowed surreptitiously from the 'ideal sphere' the necessary connections that it claimed to derive from the facts.[3] As for those 'world views' that resigned themselves to being simply the balance of that which it was possible

2. *Logische Untersuchungen*, II, 4te Untersuchung, p. 339. (*Logical Investigations*, trans. with an Introduction by J. N. Findlay, New York: Humanities Press, 1970. *Editor's note*)

3. 'Philosophie als strenge Wissenschaft', *Logos*, I (1910), p. 325. (English translation in *Phenomenology and the Crisis of Philosophy*, ed. and trans. Quentin Lauer, New York: Harper & Row, 1965. *Editor's note*)

to think at the particular moment, taking into account the findings of science, Husserl certainly admitted that these posed a real problem, but in such terms that they prohibited themselves from seriously resolving it. The problem arises from the fact that philosophy would lose its sense if it refrained from judging the present. Just as a morality that was 'interminable and transfinite on principle' would no longer be morality, so a philosophy that abandoned on principle taking any position in the present would no longer be philosophy.[4] The fact is, however, that in their desire to confront current problems, 'to have their system, and enough, in time to live afterwards',[5] the philosophers of the *Weltanschauung* school miss the whole point: they can bring no more rigour to the solution of these problems than can other men, since they live like them in the *Weltanschauung*, and lack a *Weltwissenschaft*, and by exhausting themselves in thinking out the present, they deprive genuine philosophy of the unconditional devotion it demands. Once this has been constituted, however, it will make it possible to think the present as well as the past and the eternal. To go straight to the present is thus to let go of the solid and grasp the illusory . . .

When Husserl came back to problems of history in the second part of his career, and primarily to that of language, we no longer find the idea of a philosophical subject, in command of all possibilities, who has first to discard his own language in order to rediscover beyond all actuality the ideal forms of a universal language. The first task of philosophy in relation to language now seems to be to discover for us our adherence to a certain system of speech, which we use quite effectively for the simple reason that it is as immediately present to us as is our body. The philosophy of language no longer opposes empirical linguistics as an attempt at a total objectivization of language against a science constantly threatened by the prejudices of the mother tongue; on the contrary, it is the rediscovery of the speaking subject at work in opposition to a science of language that inevitably treats language as a thing. H. Pos[6] has shown very well

4. ibid., p. 332.   5. ibid., p. 338.

6. H. Pos, 'Phénoménologie et linguistique', *Revue internationale de philosophie*, January 1939.

how, in opposition to the scientific attitude, or the attitude of observation, which is oriented towards language already expressed, grasps it in the past, and breaks it down into a series of linguistic facts in which its unity disappears, the phenomenological attitude is now that which provides direct access to language as it is actually living and present in a linguistic community – which does not just use language to maintain itself, but also to base, envisage and define a future. Here, therefore, language is no longer broken down into elements that are seen as assembled together bit by bit; it is rather like an organ whose tissues all work together in a single functioning, however diverse might be their provenance, and however fortuitous their original insertion into the whole . . . Now, if it really is the specific task of phenomenology to approach language in this fashion, then this task is no longer that of the synthetic determination of all possibilities; reflection is no longer the return to a pre-empirical subject who holds the keys to the world; it no longer possesses the constitutive elements of the actual object, no longer encircles them. It has to become aware of the object in a contact or frequentation that at first passes beyond its ability to understand. The philosopher is in the first place he who discovers that he is situated within language, that he *speaks*. Phenomenological reflection is then no longer confined to listing with complete clarity the 'conditions *sine qua non*' without which there would be no language; it has to reveal what it is that gives rise to speech, the paradox of a subject who speaks and understands, oriented towards the future, despite everything that we know about the accidents and slips of meaning which have made language what it is. There is thus in the here and now of speech a wisdom which is not to be found in any merely 'possible' expression; there is in our linguistic 'field of presence' an operation which serves us as a model for conceiving other possible systems of expression, far though it is from being a particular case of these. Reflection is no longer the passage to another order of reality which re-absorbs that of the here and now, it is primarily a more intense awareness of our deep-rootedness in the latter. The absolute condition for any valid philosophy is henceforth its passage via this here and now.

150 Maurice Merleau-Ponty

In point of fact, Husserl's disavowal of formal reflection can be seen before his recognition of the *Lebenswelt* as the primary theme of phenomenology. Whoever has read *Ideas I* will have noted that eidetic intuition was already here an 'assertion', and phenomenology an 'experience' (Husserl said that a phenomenology of vision had to be constructed on the basis of a *Sichtigkeit* which we first had to experience in practice, and he generally rejected the possibility of a 'mathematics of phenomena', a 'geometry of lived experience'). It is just that he did not always stress the progress towards this. It is almost as if thought based itself on its factual structures in order to extricate its possible structures: a quite imaginary variation would draw a treasure of eidetic assertions from the infinity of its experience. When, as in Husserl's last writings, recognition of the world of lived experience, and thus also of language as experienced, became a characteristic of his phenomenology, this was only a more resolute way of expressing that philosophy is not fully in possession of the truth of language and of the world, that it is rather the recovery and the initial formulation of a scanty *logos* in our world and in our life, tied to the concrete structures of the latter – this '*logos* of the aesthetic world' which already appears in Husserl's *Formal and Transcendental Logic*. When he wrote in a posthumous fragment that its embodiment in language transports the transitory interior phenomenon into an ideal existence, Husserl did no more than complete the movement of his whole former thought.[7] This ideal existence, which had originally for Husserl to provide a basis for the possibility of language, is now the most particular possibility of language itself . . . But if philosophy is no longer the transition to an infinity of possibilities, nor yet the leap into absolute objectivity, if it is first and foremost contact with the here and now, we can understand how it is that certain investigations in linguistics already anticipated those of Husserl, and that certain linguisticians, without knowing it, were already treading the ground of phenomenology. Husserl does not say this in so many words, neither does Pos, but it is difficult not to think of

7. 'Ursprung der Geometrie', in *Revue internationale de philosophie*, January 1939, p. 210. (Reprinted in this volume, pp. 42–70. *Editor's note*)

Saussure in this respect when he demands a return from objecti-fied language to speech.

In reality, the entire relationship between philosophy and history is transformed with the very movement of reflection that seeks to free philosophy from history. The more he reflected on the relation between eternal truths and factual truths, Husserl was obliged to replace his original definitions with a much more simple relationship. His meditations on transcendental reflection and its possibility, carried out over a period of at least twenty years, show clearly enough that in his eyes this term did not refer to a distinct faculty that it would be possible to pin down, point to, and actually isolate, alongside other modalities of experience. Despite all his trenchant formulations constantly stressing the radical distinction between the natural and the transcendental attitudes, Husserl was well enough aware right from the start that these in fact impinged on one another and that every *act of consciousness* carries the transcendental within it. As far as the relation between fact and essence is concerned, at any rate, even such an early text as *Die Philosophie als strenge Wissenschaft*, after distinguishing the 'ideal realm' from his-torical fact, as we have already seen, expressly refers to the over-lapping of the two orders, stating that, if historical criticism really shows that a certain order of institutions is devoid of substantial reality and is in the last analysis only a name for referring to a mass of facts which have no internal relationship, this is because empirical history itself contains sketchy intuitions of essence, and because criticism is always the other side, or the emergence, of a positive assertion that is already there ... In the same article, Husserl already admits that history is precious for the philosopher, in so far as *it reveals to him the Gemeingeist*. It is not so difficult to move from these initial formulations to the later ones. To say that history teaches the philosopher what the *Gemeingeist* is, is to say that it gives him the means to think communication be-tween subjects. It confronts him with the need to understand that there are not just minds that are each bearers of a perspective on the world, and which the philosopher can inspect one by one, even though it is not permitted, let alone prescribed, for him to think them *together*; there is rather a community of minds co-existing for each other and hence each invested with an outside by which they become visible. This is in such a way that the philosopher can no longer talk of mind in general and deal with all and each under the same name, nor pride himself on constituting them; he has rather to see himself as part of the dialogue of minds, each with their own particular situation, and recognize their dignity as constitutive agencies at the same time as he claims this for himself. Here we are very close to the enigmatic formula that Husserl arrived at in his texts on the *Crisis of European Sciences*, when he wrote that 'transcendental subjectivity is intersubjectivity.' Now if the transcendental is intersubjectivity, how can we avoid a breakdown of the boundaries between the transcendental and the empirical? For in relation to other people, everything that the other sees of me, my entire facticity, becomes reintegrated into subjectivity, or at least posed as an indispensable element of its definition. In this way the transcendental descends into history, or, what is meant by this, the historic is no longer an external relationship between two or several subjects endowed with absolute autonomy; it has an inside, it forms part of their own definition, and each knows himself a subject not just for himself, but also for the others.

In the unpublished writings of his last period, the opposition of fact and essence is explicitly mediated by this idea that the purest reflection discovers a 'genesis of meaning' (*Sinngenesis*) immanent in its objects, the necessity of a development, of a 'before' and an 'after' in its expression, of a series of steps or progressions which follow on from one another, each of which can not be 'at the same time' as the other but rather presupposes it as the horizon of the past. Of course, this intentional history is not the mere sum of expressions taken in isolation: it resumes and orders them, it revives and rectifies, in the here and now of a present, a genesis which would otherwise prove abortive. But it can do this only in contact with the given, in finding its themes in this. It is no longer just an unfortunate accident that the study of meanings and the study of facts impinge on one another: a meaning would be empty if it did not condense in itself a certain becoming of the truth.

It is to be hoped that we shall soon be able to read, in Husserl's complete works,[8] the letter that he wrote to Lévy-Bruhl on 11 March 1935 after having read *La mythologie primitive*. Here he seems to admit that the philosopher cannot directly arrive at the universal by simple reflection, that he is not in a position to dispense with anthropological experience, nor to construct, by a simply imaginary variation of his own experiences, what it is that makes the meaning of other experiences and other cultures. 'It is a possible task, and one of great importance', he writes; 'it is a major task to project ourselves (*einzufühlen*) into a humanity closed in on its living and traditional sociality, and to understand in what way, in its total social life and on the basis of this, this humanity possesses the world, which is not for it a "representation of the world", but the world that is real for it.' Now, access to archaic worlds is barred to us by our own world: Lévy-Bruhl's primitive peoples are 'without history' (*geschichtslos*), their life is one 'which is simply the flowing present' (*ein Leben, das nur strömende Gegenwart ist*). As for us, we live in a historic world, one that 'has a future in part already realized (the national "past") and in part still to be realized'. An intentional analysis that would recapture and reconstitute the structures of the archaic world could not confine itself to making explicit those of our own, for what gives meaning to these structures is the milieu, the *Umwelt*, of which they are the typical style, and we can thus understand them only if we understand how time flows and how being is constituted in these cultures. Husserl goes so far as to write that 'on the path of this intentional analysis, which has already been in large measure developed, historical relativism has its incontestable justification, as an anthropological fact . . .'

What, then, does he make of philosophy? The last lines of this letter make this clear: philosophy must accept all the findings of science, which represent the beginnings of knowledge; it must

8. In course of publication by Martinus Nijhof of The Hague, under the direction of H. L. Van Breda. We have had no authorization from the editors to quote the few unpublished extracts that are printed here. We therefore ask the reader to see these simply as a foretaste of the texts which the Husserl Archives at Louvain are preparing in the only authorized edition.

thus accept a historical relativism. As philosophy, however, it cannot simply confine itself to recording the variety of anthropological facts: 'Anthropology, just like every positive science and the sciences as a whole, if it gives us the first words of knowledge, does not have the last word.' Philosophy would have its autonomy, but after positive science rather than before. The philosopher is not dispensed from gathering up everything that anthropology can give us, essentially, that is, testing our actual communication with other cultures; philosophy could not in any way undermine the competence of the scientist open to its research methods. It would simply set itself up in a dimension in which no scientific knowledge could challenge it. Let us try to define this dimension.

If the philosopher no longer claims the unconditional ability to simply think his own thought through and through (for it turns out that his 'ideas' and 'evidence' are always to some extent naïve, and that, embedded as they are in the tissue of the culture to which he belongs, they cannot be really known simply by examining them and varying them in thought; they must rather be confronted with other cultural formations and be seen on the basis of other prejudices), does he not then abdicate his rights in favour of the positive sciences and empirical investigation? Not at all. The same historical dependence that forbids the philosopher claiming immediate access to the universal and eternal, forbids the sociologist putting himself in this role and giving the scientific objectification of the social an ontological value. The concept of history, in its deepest sense, does not mean confining the thinking subject to a fixed point of time and space: he can only appear so confined in relation to a thought itself capable of escaping from every spatial and temporal determination in order to see him in his space and his time. This, however, is precisely the prejudice of an absolute thought that the meaning of history discredits. There can be no question of simply transferring to science the magisterial authority that is refused to systematic philosophy, in the way that historicism does. The sociologist says to the philosopher, you believe you are thinking for ever and for the whole world, while all you are doing is expressing the prejudices and pretensions of your own culture. That is true, but it is just as true of dogmatic sociology as it is of philosophy. And as for he who speaks in these terms, *where does he speak from*? The sociologist can only form this idea of a historic time that contains philosophers like a box contains its contents by placing himself in turn outside of history, and claiming the privilege of an absolute spectator. In fact, it is just this conception of the relations between the mind and its object that the historical awareness invites us to refashion. It is precisely the fact that my thought belongs for someone else to a particular historic situation, and beyond this, to other historical situations that interest him (since it is a product of the objective relationships that science provides us with), that makes knowledge of the social a knowledge of myself, and evokes and legitimizes *a view of intersubjectivity as my own intersubjectivity* which science forgets even while making use of it, and which is the specific property of philosophy. If history envelops us all, it is up to us to understand that whatever truth we are able to reach is not obtained in opposition to our historic belonging, but rather through it. Considered superficially, this would seem to destroy all truth; considered radically, however, it founds a new idea of the truth. In so far as I stick to the ideal of myself as an absolute spectator, of a knowledge without its own standpoint, I can only see in my specific situation the root of error. But once I recognize that it is only through my situation that I connect with any action or knowledge that can have any meaning for me, and that this situation contains ever more nearly everything that can have being for me, then my contact with the social in the finitude of my situation reveals itself to me as the point of origin of all truth, including that of science, and, since we have an idea of the truth, since we are in truth and cannot escape from it, it only remains for me to define a truth in the situation. Knowledge is thus founded on the irrefutable fact that we do not exist in the situation like an object in objective space, and that, for us, the situation is the root of curiosity, investigation, interest in other situations as variants of our own, then in our own life as illuminated by others and now considered as a variant of others; finally, it is that which binds us to the totality of human experience no less than that which separates us from it. What we call science and sociology is now the attempt to construct certain variable ideals that objectify and schematize the functioning of this actual communication. What we call philosophy is now the awareness that we have to preserve the open and successive community of living, speaking and thinking *alter egos*, in one another's presence and all in relation with nature, such as we understand it behind us, around us and in front of us, at the limits of our historical field, as the ultimate reality whose functioning is traced in our theoretical constructions and which these constructions cannot be substituted for. Philosophy is thus not defined by a particular domain of its own: all it speaks of, just like sociology, is the world, men and the mind. What distinguishes it rather is a certain *mode* of the awareness that we have of others, nature or ourselves: it is nature and man in the present, not 'flattened' (Hegel) in a secondary objectivity but as they offer themselves in our everyday business of knowledge and action with them – nature in us, other people in us, and us in them. In this respect, we not only have to say that philosophy is compatible with sociology, we have also to say that it is necessary for it, as a constant recall to its tasks, and that each time that the sociologist comes back to the living sources of his science, to what it is that operates in him as the means of understanding even the most distant cultural formations, then he is spontaneously already engaged in philosophy ... Philosophy is not a particular science, it is the vigilance that does not let us forget the source of all science.

We are not claiming that Husserl would ever have accepted a definition of this kind, for, right to the end, he always considered the return to living speech and history, the return to the *Lebenswelt*, as a preparatory voyage, still to be followed by the specific task of philosophy, that of universal constitution. It is still a fact, however, that in his last published work rationality is seen simply as one of two possibilities with which we are confronted, the other being chaos. And it is precisely in the awareness of a kind of anonymous adversity that threatens rationality that Husserl seeks something that can stimulate knowledge and action. Reason as an appeal and a task, 'latent reason' that has itself to be transformed and made to realize its potential, becomes the criterion of philosophy.

It is the only way to decide whether the *telos* which was inborn in European humanity at the birth of Greek philosophy – that of humanity which seeks to exist, and is only possible, through philosophical reason, moving endlessly from latent to manifest reason and forever seeking its own norms through this, its truth and genuine human nature – whether this *telos*, then, is merely a factual, historical delusion, the accidental acquisition of merely one among many other civilizations and histories, or whether Greek humanity was not rather the first breakthrough to what is essential to humanity as such, its *entelechy*. To be human at all is essentially to be a human being in a socially and generatively united civilization; and if man is a rational being (*animal rationale*), it is only insofar as his whole civilization is a rational civilization, that is, one with a latent orientation toward reason or one openly oriented toward the entelechy which has come of itself, become manifest to itself, and which now of necessity consciously directs human becoming. Philosophy and science would accordingly be the historical movement through which universal reason, 'inborn' in humanity as such, is revealed.[9]

Thus the human essence is not given, nor its necessity unconditional: it will come into play only if the rationality whose idea was left to us by the Greeks, instead of remaining an accident, proves itself to be essential by the knowledge and action that it makes possible, and comes to be recognized by irrational humanities. The Husserlian essence is now borne by an 'entelechy'.

The role of philosophy as the awareness of rationality within contingency is not an insignificant remainder. It is only the philosophical awareness of intersubjectivity, in the last analysis, that enables us to understand scientific knowledge. Without this, science remains indefinitely suspended, always deferred until the conclusion of discussions about causality which, bearing on man, are by nature interminable. We may ponder, for example, whether social relations are, as a psychoanalytic sociology would have it, simply the enlargement and generalization of the drama

9. *Die Krisis der europäischen Wissenschaften und die transzendentale Phänomenologie*, I, *Philosophia*, Belgrade, 1936, p. 92; *The Crisis of European Sciences and Transcendental Phenomenology*, trans. B. Carr, Evanston: Northwestern University Press, 1970, pp. 15–16.

of sexuality and aggression, or whether on the contrary this drama itself, in the form that psychoanalysis describes it, is not just a particular case of the institutional relationships of Western societies. The interest of these discussions lies in their provoking sociologists to observation, revealing facts, arousing analyses and intuitions. But they lead to no conclusion so long as they remain on the terrain of causal and 'objective' thought, since it is neither possible to reduce one of these causal chains to nothing, nor to think them both together as causal chains. The only condition on which it is possible to hold both of these views as simultaneously true, as they in fact are, is that we move on to an acausal mode of thought, which is philosophy: it is necessary to understand both that the individual drama takes place between *roles* already inscribed in the institutional constellation, and that therefore the child proceeds right from the beginning of his life, by way of simple perception of the care given him and the utensils that surround him, to a deciphering of meanings, which from the very beginning generalizes his own drama and makes it into the drama of his culture, and that, despite this, the entire symbolic awareness only elaborates, in the last instance, what the child experiences or does not experience, suffers or does not suffer, feels or does not feel, in such a way that there is not even the most individual detail of his history that does not bring something to this meaning of his that he will display when, after having first thought and lived according to what he believed it good to do, and having perceived according to the vision of his culture, he finally comes to reverse the relationship and to slip into the meanings something of his own speech and his behaviour, to convert these into culture, down to the most secret details of his experience. The standpoint of causality does not allow the centripetal movement and the centrifugal movement both to be possible together. It is only the philosophical attitude that makes these reversals conceivable or even visible, these 'metamorphoses', this proximity and this distance of the past and the present, of the archaic and the 'modern', this involution of cultural time and space, this perpetual overdetermination of human events which, whatever might be the singularity of local or temporal conditions, makes social facts always appear to us as variants of a single life, of which our own life also forms part, and makes every other person for us an other ourself.

Philosophy certainly still involves a break with objectivism, a return from *constructa* to lived experience, from the world to ourselves. It is only that this indispensable progress, and he who characterizes it, no longer transports us into the rarified atmosphere of introspection or into a realm that is numerically distinct from that of science; it no longer puts us in a state of rivalry with science, since we have recognized that the 'interior' which it brings us back to is not a 'private life', but an intersubjectivity which links us up ever more closely with the whole of history. When I come to realize that the social is not just an object, but first and foremost my own situation, and I awaken in myself the awareness of this sociality of mine, then my entire synchrony becomes present to me, and through it the whole of the past, which I become capable of thinking as the synchrony that it really was in its time, as well as the whole convergent and discordant action of the historical community which is actually given me in my living present. Renunciation of the explanatory apparatus of the system does not lead to philosophy being relegated to the position of an auxiliary or propagandist of objective knowledge, since it does have its own dimension, that of coexistence – not as an accomplished fact and object of contemplation, but as a perpetual event and the milieu of universal *praxis*. Philosophy is irreplaceable because it reveals to us the movement by way of which lives become truths, and the circularity of this singular being which, in a certain sense, *is* already everything that it *comes to think*.

8 Alphonse de Waelhens

The Human Sciences, the Ontological Horizon, and the Encounter

A. de Waelhens, 'Sciences humaines, horizon ontologique et Rencontre', *Existence et Signification*, Louvain: Nauwelaerts, 1958, pp. 233–61.

Translated by David Fernbach

To investigate the philosophy that appears on the horizon of the human sciences is a difficult task, and can give rise to several ambiguities. To start with, there can be a considerable difference between the philosophy that the *Geisteswissenschaftler* avows, and believes he is using or verifying, and the philosophy that it might actually be possible to extract from his work. The danger of this confusion becomes particularly intense when, for example, we rely on the philosophical declarations of particular scientists in order to discover the ontological conception of man that the sciences of a given epoch appear to imply. Should we then establish a separation of domains and powers, by decreeing that the scientist has no philosophical competence, and that he must carry on with his work in history, sociology, linguistics, or even physiology or psychoanalysis, without concerning himself with an object that is outside his reach: the specifically human mode of being and existing? This separation could only be a myth. It may well be that the scientist, at least sometimes, has no philosophical competence, but he does have a philosophy, whether he says so or not, and whether it is true or false. And even if he claims to have reduced this philosophy to the status of a conclusion, and believes he has a method for investigating the facts of his domain without letting himself be influenced by this philosophy, we know that this is not in fact the case. We know that this 'philosophy' is secretly at work in the selection and interpretation of facts; we know, for example, that the claim to possess a philosophically 'neutral' research method already derives from a perfectly well constituted and identifiable philosophy, just as governments that claim not to engage in politics do so regardless, and always the same kind. Let us take two examples. If the revolution that was eventually to bring about gestalt psychology nearly proved abortive at an early stage, this was because certain of the original gestalt psychologists stuck to conceiving their forms as things, and on this basis tried to refer the existence of privileged forms in human perception to the actual presence of figures of this kind in the cortical system. What is today the prevailing thesis, to the effect that the privileged character of these forms is a function of the *meaning* that they have for human behaviour and the idea that this realizes, was not acceptable to Wertheimer and Köhler because the philosophy that inspired them made it inadmissible for a meaning to be able to act on a behaviour, i.e. for them, on the operation of nervous mechanisms. To take another related example: the first attempts to constitute a science of sociology met with little success – in any case a success very small in proportion to the efforts made – and this is because the first sociologists conceived the science whose pioneers they were as a social *physics*, in other words they remained prisoners of the preconceived idea that all reality was composed of atomistic elements whose interaction and interference had to be observed according to the methods developed by the natural sciences. However, the idea that man is a natural being, and that he simply participates in nature along with all other beings in a sort of *omnitudo realitatis*, is evidently a philosophical idea, even if the idea of a bad philosophy.

We thus see that our problem cannot be simplified by leaving aside the philosophical ideas that scientists have of the object of their investigations, and confining ourselves to presenting the philosophical conceptions that the science in question makes use of, actually if implicitly, in its results. For these very results, although they can up to a point correct the philosophical prejudices of the scientists involved, do not necessarily succeed in doing so, as we have seen in the case of gestalt psychology: in fact, they are themselves a product of ideas which, in orienting investigation, draw limits both for research and for discovery which can only be broken by starting from a *different* perspective. Perhaps progress consists precisely in the possibility of the new perspective which is then acquired. This is what is verified by the example of gestalt psychology, and also by that of psychoanalysis. It is clear that Freud's original philosophical perspectives prevented psychoanalysis from attaining in the work of its founder the meaning that it has for the philosophers and psychologists of today. What remained the decisive obstacle for Freud was his spontaneous conviction, bound up with the medical 'philosophy' of his epoch, that the impulses or drives that make up the unconscious take the form of 'forces'. The very work of Freud, however, shows us that this conception is erroneous and that this 'force' must be understood as the necessity of a meaning. At the present time, as can be seen for example by reading Hesnard or Lacan, the 'view' of man which is going to orient the further progress of psychoanalytic investigation is changing. The new conception is already leading to distinct advances. Undoubtedly it will some day be apparent that, relative to the great success of these new investigations, the philosophical concept of man that prevails among the psychoanalysts today is still inhibiting or inadequate, but not sufficiently so that successful results, even if incomplete ones, have not been reached, and are now preparing a new philosophical revolution in psychology, as is already attested to by the writings of the authors just mentioned.

These considerations inevitably lead us into very great difficulties. We cannot content ourselves with mere words, and say for example, without any other explanation, that the philosophical concept of man that we find on the scientific horizon is the result of a dialectic born of the permanent tension between the explicit meaning of the prevailing conception and the implicit meaning advanced by discoveries that have been obtained in the light of this prevailing conception. This is undoubtedly true. But the real question is to understand precisely what this tension consists of, which are the factors that provoke it. In its turn, and by a movement analogous to that which we are studying here, the solution of these difficulties makes us wonder what is meant when it is claimed that the scientist employs a 'philosophical' conception in order to guide his research, and that the result of this research can lead to a philosophical conception very different from the original one? What is involved in a science that is born of a philosophy and in its turn engenders one? And what is involved in this philosophy that evolves under the influence of factors that are theoretically foreign to it?

It seems evident to me that these questions cannot be left unanswered if we want to tackle in a fruitful way the problem of the particular philosophy that is visible on the horizon of the present human sciences. On the other hand, however, we cannot hope, even in the most schematic fashion, to deal with all these problems in the framework of a single essay. I shall therefore confine myself here to pointing out a few directions in which a solution might be sought.

Rather than deal with everything at once, let us start by tackling a concrete case, that of sociology. It is not by chance that I have chosen this as an example. For both Husserl and Merleau-Ponty have considered this question, and they have done so from perspectives very close to those which we are following here.

It is easy to say, of course – and in a certain sense true – that philosophy is not science and science not philosophy. A sociology that claims to be positive science shares in this opposition. We have also seen sociology, in its early days, demand and grant itself a total autonomy in relation to philosophy. We do not want to challenge this here. The point, however, is to know what meaning should be ascribed to it. If this autonomy is supposed to consist, as has been the case, in a pure and simple mutual ignorance between philosophy and sociology, then they are simply made incomprehensible to each other, and a state of permanent crisis arises in culture.[1] The basis of this pretended ignorance that philosophy and sociology feign in relation to one another is a well-known fact. It is on the one hand a conception of philosophy which reduces this simply to the consideration of the mind by itself, and on the other hand, the claim to bring sociology back to the notation and enumeration of positive facts that are said to be free from any interpretation. It is only too clear that these two ways of understanding the work of philosophy and sociology respectively, widespread as they may be at the theoretical level (since the whole of idealism, on the one hand, and the whole of the positive sociology of a certain epoch, on the other hand,

1. M. Merleau-Ponty, 'The Philosopher and Sociology', above, p. 142.

accept them), have always been refuted in practice. Every philosophy is reflection *on* a reality that everywhere and always displays the dependence of the mind on something outside itself, and which places the becoming of this mind in reference to the other. Conversely, in the case of sociology, every attempt to grasp facts becomes meaningful only by its insertion into a perspective that transcends these facts, and is possible only on the basis of an ontology that the scientist need not necessarily explain but is fatally constrained to assume. When positivist sociology thinks it can exclude every ontological presupposition and remain philosophically neutral by describing human behaviour as one describes the properties of a chemical substance, it actually takes up a position and contests that man exists in the fashion of a thing. That this is by no means always explicitly affirmed does not show that there is no such assumption, but simply that the scientists in question consider it as absolutely natural and *selbstverständlich*; in such a way that they lose all awareness of having put it forward as a specific solution – and as it happens, most likely a bad one – of the problem of the ontological status of their object. The question, then, is to know whether the facts, disturbed as they are by the application of this perspective, will not end up, regardless of the explicit intervention of the scientist, by imposing a modification of the status that their original description initially presupposed, thus bringing sociology, as the most recent history of this science already shows, into the dialectical movement which we have already spoken of.

Since our example is that of sociology, let us examine in what direction this is being achieved. Faithful to the prejudice that we have outlined, sociology initially demanded that the sociologist treat 'social facts as if they were something foreign to him, as if his study of them owed nothing to the experience of intersubjectivity that he has as a social subject'.[2] It would say that this natural experience of intersubjectivity was of no use, since the development of sociology itself led it to show that our social relationships, such as we are aware of them, are only particular cases or variants 'of a dynamic process, whose existence we did not originally suspect',[3] and that we learn about via statistics and

2. ibid., p. 144.   3. ibid., p. 144.

the comparison with another series of facts, possibly provided by other disciplines. Undoubtedly. But this transformation, this discovery of the *true* meaning of social relations by sociology, can still be formed only 'by analogy or by contrast'[4] with the experience of social relations that we have ourselves lived; without this, we would not even know what the science we are studying was speaking about. It is thus true to maintain that geology teaches us what a mountain, a valley and a river really are. But if we have never been on a journey or to the countryside, then we do not exactly know what it is that geology is explaining. The conclusion we draw from this example is that every scientific thesis or explanation refers back, possibly by a series of intermediate steps that are susceptible to analysis, to an experience of the lived world of perception. This does not mean that the thesis in question cannot maintain something different from what this original experience puts forward, but scientific knowledge is still necessarily the explanation of an aspect of the experience of the life-world.

This leads us on to an initial and very interesting discovery. In fact, whether it wants to recognize it or not, science starts off by referring to the experience of the lived world, and, since we are dealing here with sociology, to the lived experience of social life. The mode of being that this science is therefore led to attribute to man starts off as that which man attributes to himself in this same lived experience. It seems to me that these conclusions have a general validity and that they must be extended to all the human sciences. We can sum them up as follows: in fact, all the human sciences start off by referring back to a lived experience, at least an implicit one, and they provide a certain explanation of this. The mode of being that they are thus constrained to put forward for man is the same as that which a phenomenological analysis of lived experience would discover, one that was undertaken with the specific goal of bringing to light this mode of being.

We must still guard against a possible misunderstanding. In the first place, the lived experience that we are speaking of here does not correspond to any genetic phase in the evolution of the concrete human individual. It is thus not a question of primitiveness or infancy. This is not the place to explain what phenomenology

4. ibid., p. 144.

understands by reduction to the life-world. We shall confine ourselves here to pointing out that this life-world turns out to be, in the last instance, the object of intention aimed at in any kind of human behaviour, even if it does not form the concrete content of any particular human act. This aim, which can be discovered at the ultimate source and foundation of all possible human intentionality, irrevocably supposes a certain fashion of conceiving the being of man that is implied in it. It is this conception that we have also to rediscover at the origin of all the human sciences.

There is still, however, and this is the second point, a further possible confusion, though the preceding explanations should already help to allay this. When we say that sociology as a science is necessarily based on a natural experience of intersubjectivity and on the mode of being that this implies in the human mind, i.e. on this set of experiences, the 'theses' that all social life actually puts forward, whether it is conscious of it or not, we do not mean to claim that the sociologist, if he studies the life and customs of the Papuans, will succeed only if he has participated in some way in these. What we say is that the sociologist will manage to reach an understanding of the various practices and customs of these peoples, and what they actually mean, only if he sees these practices as polymorphous and variable realizations of certain basic possibilities bound up with all social life, possibilities whose significance the sociologist can only grasp relative to an actual experience of intersubjectivity such as he himself has had. Undoubtedly, the facts discovered by anthropology are very different from those that form the tissue of his own cultural milieu. For example, the description of systems of kinship among certain Australian or South American tribes provides a tabulation that seems hardly to recall what we refer to as kinship ties. In reality, however, it is indispensable for us to refer to our own experience of kinship, in order that, in these data that are at first sight bizarre and absurd, we can discover and understand 'the style of kinship which all these facts allude to, *in what sense* certain subjects in this culture perceive other subjects of their own generation as their "parents", [and thus] . . . the basic personal and interpersonal structure, the institutional relationships with nature and with other people, that make possible the established correlations'.[5]

We can take a further example, also borrowed from Merleau-Ponty, this time referring to a domain that concerns the psychoanalyst and the anthropologist.

On the basis of the Freudian conception of pregenital sexuality, we can build up a table of the various possible modes in which the child's bodily orifices can be emphasized, and in this table, those which are actually emphasized in our own cultural system and have been described by Freudian analysts will figure as particular variants out of a large number of possible alternatives which may well be selected by cultures still unknown to us. But a table of this kind tells us *nothing* about the relations with others and with nature that define these cultural types, unless we refer back to the psychological significance of the mouth, the anus or the genital apparatus on the basis of our own lived experience, so as to see, in the different uses that different cultures make of these, different crystallizations of an original polymorphism of the body as vehicle of being-in-the-world. This table provides us only with an invitation to imagine, on the basis of our experience of our own bodies, other bodily techniques.[6]

We will certainly admit that the possibility of corporeal being that we ourselves realize is never just a mere possibility *among* others, since it is on the basis of this that all the others acquire their meaning for us and that we understand this ability of the body, the role that this structuring bodily being has in the entirety of our experience. But it is only with reference to the lived exercise of this possibility, a privileged one for us, that we are in a position to understand how the phenomena that we describe as psychoanalysts or as sociologists are really the expression of another fashion of exercising the structuring potential that the body has for the entirety of a given experience.

These considerations, if they seem to require a close collaboration between the scientist and the philosopher, do not for all that end up by amalgamating their respective tasks. The task of the scientist is to gather together facts, i.e. both to choose them and to interpret them. But he can only do this by employing, *de facto*, a certain conception of man. And this conception of man, which

5. ibid., p. 145.   6. ibid., p. 145 f.

the scientist does not have to give any philosphical exegesis of, is that which is implied and put to work by the exercise of the natural experience of subjectivity – in the case of sociology, the natural experience of intersubjectivity. It is up to the philosopher – and we would say more specifically to the phenomenologist – to extract this conception of man and the type of being that it attributes to him.

We can say that, if the findings of sociology, to keep to the same example, have not measured up to the immense efforts and means deployed in the early years of this century, this is primarily because the sociologists have done all that they could to turn their backs on the conception of man that is actually implied in the exercise of natural experience, and to conceive the human world on the model of the physical object; they have thus sought to pursue their supreme ambition of applying to humanity the methods of the positive sciences whose striking success has been the glory of the last few centuries.

As the second part of this study, we are now going to try and carry out this work of extraction. It goes without saying that we have to confine ourselves to presenting the most essential features, and do not lay claim to any originality on this fundamental subject of all phenomenology. We shall, however, set out to conduct our presentation in such a way as to take particular account of our initial example, i.e. that of sociology.

There are a thousand ways of undertaking a presentation of the conception that man has of himself in his natural experience, but the most significant, and also that which seems most appropriate for our present perspective, is to centre the presentation on the idea of incarnation. For the body – but not the body as a thing – is itself at the centre of our sociality. We can in fact conceive neither a society of pure minds, nor yet a society of beings that would lack any form of intersubjective relationship, a society of things or objects. It is thus the body – in the specifically human sense of this word – that enables the reality of our incarnation to be a social reality.

The existing human being manifests himself, first and foremost, as being-in-the-world. This expression, one generally used by phenomenologists, brings together a number of assertions. It does not simply mean that man figures among the variety of observable realities which together comprise the cosmos. It also seeks to imply that this relationship is a transcendental one, in other words that man, at the same time as he *is* a presence by himself, *is* also the practical or theoretical aim of things (initially practical), either actually so or at least virtually so. Human existence is thus not purely withdrawn into itself. It is not like the pure spirit that moves within itself without going out of itself, νοησις νοησεως. Nor is it like things which are simply that which they are. This is very well illustrated by the typically human notion of *behaviour* (for it is only by analogy that we can speak of animal behaviour). What we call behaviour is the manner of being of an existent (a being), in so far as this existent (being), while showing itself to be a consistent reality, also establishes in itself and on behalf of itself a meaning that transcends its pure consistency; in so far, also, as this meaning only arises in it by virtue of an actual relationship towards things, which also contributes to the foundation of significance. It is possible, on the basis of this provisional and still deplorably abstract formula, to gather together the series of features that comprise the typical being of human reality, in the form that this presents itself and lives itself spontaneously at the beginning of all its activities; in the form, too, that it must necessarily take at the foundation of any sociology, if this sets out to be the science of inter-human relations.

Let us try to explain these features. Firstly, in order for an existent to behave, it must enjoy a certain consistency, which it must be able to recognize as its own by the meaning that it gives to it. This first point already contains several assertions. To start with, we reject the idea that human experience, as it actually is here and now, can offer us a subjectivity that is not from the beginning a *real* subjectivity, i.e. one that, by a dimension of its being, has an immediate place in the *omnitudo realitatis*. This is the truth of realism (*chosisme*). But it is a truth that is acceptable and fertile only if it is immediately completed by something else that appears inseparably together with it. This thing that I am, I recognize as my own by the meaning that I give it, a recognition that immediately also transcends and supersedes its existence as a thing. It thus ceases to belong simply to the *omnitudo realitatis* at the very moment that it appears. For the recognition of a thing by itself is the negation of its status as a thing. But what is this recognition? This also does not confront us as simply an internal act, of the kind that a certain philosophical tradition claims to discover everywhere in man, and which in fact we never come across. Firstly, let us note that if the act by which I assume my body – since this is what we are talking about – was simply an internal act, subjective in the classic sense of the term, it would not be what it claimed to be: the recognition of myself as a dimension of externality. It would then be rather the mysterious affirmation of the association that unites a consciousness with a thing, an affirmation that would open the way not to the experience that a man actually has of himself, but to the contradictions of parallelism and dualism that pervade both rationalist and empiricist doctrines.

This is why what we have called the recognition of myself in the dimension of externality takes the form of the foundation of a meaning that I give myself, that I fix in myself. This meaning is not simply that which I claim myself to be; on the contrary, it is before all else a significance built in me, for a moment or for ever, by my actual relation to things, something which, as psycho-analysis teaches us, can be in radical contradiction with what I say of myself.

Before translating this into a more concrete language, we have to pursue the analysis of our 'definition' of behaviour. For all its component parts are intimately bound together, and any attempt to present them *in isolation* in a more concrete language runs the risk of distorting them.

We would say, then, that this recognition of myself as objective existing reality is, of itself, the establishment of my own meaning, but a meaning that is also universally accessible by the fact that this meaning is inscribed in my reality. This inscription, however, this revelation that I carry out with my body by recognizing myself in it, stands in a relationship to the things that surround me, in such a way that these things themselves come to exhibit a sense of their own. To say that the human being is a being endowed with behaviour thus directly amounts to asserting that this existent, man, is the being that is, *par excellence* and by nature, the *revealer of meaning*. This is in fact what radically distinguishes human being from all other being, and if it is said, following a long tradition, that man is essentially a being of reason, what this refers to is this capacity for revelation, of which the various historic forms of rationality are only particular modalities.

What we have to do now, however, is express ourselves more concretely. We do not believe it is an exact description of the human existent, in the experience that he has of himself, if we present him as an internality who conceives thoughts or representations in the secrecy of his consciousness, and who somehow inexplicably experiences this internality as associated with a bodily object, the object of the anatomical and physiological sciences. This manner of seeing things, far from being imposed by our experience of ourselves, seems to us on the contrary to be the fruit of a philosophical and scientific tradition which, instead of taking heed of natural experience, has undertaken to reform this, even though in fact it can itself only rest on this natural experience, if it wants to be anything at all. In reality, however, man initially appears, and appears to himself, as a creature of the world who addresses himself to the world. That he addresses himself to the world means that, in his necessary and spontaneous orientation towards the world, he everywhere brings forth a sense that things may have contained before him, but did not always do so, and which is illuminated and becomes manifest via their encounter with him. Conversely, man himself, by this work of revelation, gives a sense to his own existence and to reality. In short, with man, meaning appears everywhere. But what do we mean by this 'meaning' or 'sense'? This is the chief problem, and a very difficult one, since it requires us to speak somehow about what it is that enables speech. Let us try, anyway.

To take the problem firstly at its simplest level, let us try to determine what is understood by that minimum that psychologists analyse under the name of the sensation or content provided by the 'senses'. For classical psychology, sensation exists; it presents itself to us as an attribute of the subject, or even, if we are not afraid of this expression, as a mode of being of the latter. This is a mode of being that can quite well be isolated from others, and it is held to be a *mental thing*, an actual ingredient that is not susceptible to any further analysis, and is the basis on which all the higher-level contents of consciousness are composed. The origin of sensation is moreover explained by way of a recourse to causality, firstly to physiological antecedents, then to physical ones.

This kind of language, however, as we have already shown, is totally unintelligible. Seen in this way, sensation is considered as an objective event[7] taking place in an objective world, one whose texture at least we believe ourselves entirely familiar with, the world of physical and physiological science. But this world is itself built up by us on the basis of perceptions which we experience as being of an entirely different structure. When the physical physiologist speaks of stimuli, of nervous connections, of efferent and afferent transmission, of cortical zones, and so on, he does so on the basis of experiences which, in the last instance at least, are supplied to him by his own 'perceptions', which then appear after a completely different fashion from that described by the psychologist under the name of sensation. Now it is impossible to challenge the former in the name of the latter, since this latter, sensation, only arises together with a world built up on the basis of 'perception' and 'sense' in the other respect, which we call the natural one.

We therefore have to describe the latter directly. If we can have faith in the world of science, 'it is first of all because we have present at this moment to us a perceptual field, a surface in contact with the world, a permanent rootedness in it, and because the world ceaselessly assails and beleaguers subjectivity as waves wash round a wreck on the shore. All knowledge takes its place within the horizons opened up by perception.'[8] We see then that each of the states of consciousness that the psychologist refers to as a *quality*, redness, roughness, sound, taste, etc., arises only as an aspect of a certain behaviour, and bound up with this. Undoubtedly, this insertion is not in the normal state of things very

7. Though still with the exception of an unmentionable point which is precisely constitutive of subjectivity as such.

8. M. Merleau-Ponty, *Phenomenology of Perception*, London: Routledge, 1962, p. 207.

striking, because redness, for example, is only one dimension of the given – the woolly carpet that I couldn't slide on – and because the conduct that it involves is itself also only one aspect, and one difficult to isolate, of an overall behaviour that responds to the overall situation. But once illness or an artificial situation enables this testing of a quality to take place in a state of more or less isolation, then we see clearly that it does arise only in relation to behaviour. For example, Goldstein and Rosenthal, who made a particular study of this question, have shown that a certain movement – raising the arm – is 'differently modified in its sweep and its direction according as the visual field is red, yellow, blue or green. Red and yellow are particularly productive of smooth movements, blue and green of jerky ones; red applied to the right eye, for example, favours a corresponding stretching of the arm outwards, green the bending of the arm back towards the body. The privileged position of the arm – the one in which the arm is felt to be balanced and at rest – which is farther away from the body in the patient than in the normal subject, is modified by the presentation of colours: green brings it back nearer to the body.'[9]

These qualities are thus not only the sensation of a certain state, they also appear in a certain attitude towards the world, for example attraction or retreat. They are thus not islands, kaleidoscopic points of lived experience. On the contrary, they attain and solicit in me a certain 'fit' which makes me a being-in-the-world and directs me towards it, not in a neutral or indifferent way, but in celebrating it and making me in a certain sense a being for it. Greenness relaxes, blue yields to our gaze, as Goethe puts it, red excites, yellow is distressing. In entering these paths, the subject reveals himself as a potential for being born together (*co-naître*), as Claudel says, with a certain milieu of existence, and synchronizing himself with it.[10]

This amounts to putting in question the dichotomy of the in-itself and the for-itself. Feeling gives rise both to my connivance with things and to a certain way of designing them or of letting myself be oriented by them, so that they attain in me the fullness

9. Goldstein and Rosenthal, 'Zum Problem der Wirkung der Farben auf den Organismus', pp. 3–9. Quoted by Merleau-Ponty, op. cit., p. 209.

10. M. Merleau-Ponty, op. cit., p. 211.

of their own being. 'As I contemplate the blue of the sky I am not *set over against* it as an acosmic subject; I do not possess it in thought, or spread out towards it some idea of blue such as might reveal the secret of it, I abandon myself to it and plunge into this mystery, it "thinks itself within me", I am the sky itself as it is drawn together and unified, and as it begins to exist for itself; my consciousness is saturated with this limitless blue.'[11] These elements that are mutually external to one another, these things, these dead expanses, are now seen to be endowed with sensibility towards one another, united together and made into a whole all of whose members evoke one another. In a word, they take on a sense, and the first sense which they are capable of. The first of man's abilities is to be the revealer of the universe, even before he really gets to know these things and this universe.

This is because meaning, in the sense that we now understand it, and which is the primary one, is not yet the full bloom of knowledge but rather its origin, as well as that which permits knowledge to be not just the work of a disembodied understanding, but to be rooted in a coexistence. Conversely, the subject that shapes and exercises itself in this initial sketch of revelation is not yet an *ego*, freely relating its acts to itself, but the birth of an ego in an anonymous power of feeling. We can thus understand how it is that this power does not provide the immediate foundation of a history, that the subject who appears in it is born and dies with each experience, while still pursuing the thread of a life which is not yet explicitly present to him. And above all, we see that the various fields of revelation in which a meaning is expressed, which I shall later on refer to as the life of my eyes, my hands and my ears, have their first beginnings by imposing themselves as 'so many natural selves'.[12] All this also helps to explain how it is that the *I*, fully conscious and making its own decisions, that will arise later on in the work of reason, will already have behind it 'the density of earlier experience', which will always prevent my thought from dealing with a material and a past that are absolutely transparent to it.

On the other hand, the first meaning that presents itself to me is a *partial* one. If I am not yet quite complete in my eye, in my

11. ibid., p. 214.   12. ibid., p. 216.

finger or in my ear, this is because the visible, tangible or audible world is not the world in its entirety. If each datum appears to me to be inexhaustible in its own order – there is always more to see than I actually do see – it also proves to be inexhaustible in so far as this order evokes other orders which are not yet there. The transparency of crystal evokes a certain sound, the texture of a kind of wood or material evokes a certain flexibility or a certain way of falling and making folds. Conversely, I never pass completely into any one of these acts; they are as it were the deeds of a 'specialized me' immersed in a single faculty.

The conclusion we must draw from this is that every grasping of a sense perception is already in its way a 'situating'. The subject that presents itself in it appears there both as organizer and as organized, in a grouping that is still incomplete and in which every element discovers itself for what it is by a more or less explicit reference back to all the others, a reference that is more or less precise and in which there are different degrees of clarity. This is precisely what we mean in the French language when we use, for both the two conventional meanings that are here bound together, the single word *sens*. I am not sure whether the idea of constitution is applicable to this operation; for if it is true to say that this grouping – the visible for example – is given, it is also true to maintain that its unity only arises by the appearance of a revealer, man endowed with sense.

On the other hand, this manner of posing our problem also has the advantage of making us understand the *reality* of the pluralism and multiplicity that is evident to our senses. This pluralism and multiplicity is not simply a pallid and fictitious differentiation of the notional unity towards which, in the intellectualist conception, everything converges to the point of actually being absorbed, but rather an irreducible beginning which the understanding, whose work can never come to an end, has to take as its foundation.

This fragile sketch of an analysis of what we mean by the experience of sense – in the dual meaning of this word – still has to be completed on certain essential points. We cannot undertake to do this in the present essay. But such as it is, it already shows how ambiguous is the position of a science that, on the pretext of dismissing all ontological problems or of maintaining a total neutrality towards them, seeks to construct itself on the basis of regarding man as if he were a thing. This situation becomes far worse once it is not simply a question of a science of the individual human being, but a science of inter-human relationships, since what is now involved is not only man as a being who reveals and establishes meaning, but man as a being who carries out this operation in and for an intersubjectivity. We have to understand then, that this organization of the world, which we saw born in the solitude of a real contact which transcends itself in order to become manifest, develops and displays itself with others and for others. It is certainly true to say, though it is a rather limited truth, that the transition from subjectivity to intersubjectivity is also that from sense to reason. But in point of fact, there is really no such transition, and all subjectivity is already intersubjective, all establishment of a sense already the promise and dawn of reason. The idea of behaviour, such as we have tried to describe it, essentially shows that the significances which our behaviour is made up of, and which it arouses in things, are established and abstracted from the private secrecy of a consciousness reduced to itself. They are therefore, from a certain point of view, so many questionings addressed to others, even though from another standpoint it has also to be recognized that they are born in me from the fact of the existence of others, which the initial proposition always refers back to; there is in fact no perception which is not the seizure of an object already informed and invested by others with a certain meaning. The experience of intersubjectivity is therefore first and foremost the experience of an exchange of significances that are advanced and recaptured in bodily actions, themselves significant, undertaken towards the things in our surroundings. This exchange gives rise, without this even having to be desired, to a new layer of significances, still more distant from the basic senses that we have described, and which no longer refer to the relationship of men to things or to what each person does with himself in this relationship, but rather, superimposed on all these relationships, to a certain level reached by the relations of men among themselves, and to the meanings that they give to these relations. If I look at how someone lives in his

Alphonse de Waelhens 177

apartment or house, I do not just see him recognize or constitute the sense of the objects that surround him, I do not just see him receive this sense and propose modifications in it, I do not just see him reveal himself in all these operations and proposals (his lack of culture, his disorder, his good breeding, his manner of familiarity or of uprootedness), but I also see that all of this reveals and establishes a certain sense of interhuman relations and of the level that these have reached in the society in question. To eat all the ingredients of a meal out of the same dish, never to bolt one's door or draw the curtains over one's window, to live with bare walls, etc. are not simply acts that establish and express the sense of those particular things that are food, crockery, curtains, locks and wallpaper; they are not only acts that reveal me to be crude, refined, trusting, suspicious, insensitive, etc. . . .; they are also acts in which are inscribed, besides a certain practice of social relations, also an idea of the meaning that these relations have acquired in a given culture or milieu.

It is true that it is up to the sociologist, for example, to select and interpret these facts, and to tell us what are the forms and rites of marriage in the various societies known to us. But sociology will only manage to do this if it understands that man is not a natural species but a historic idea,[13] i.e. an existent whose being it is to give sense to the world, to himself and to others. Sociology will then see marriage rites for what they really are: a thousand different ways of giving human copulation a sense that transcends the natural fact and makes it significant not only for itself (so that it expresses the union of the two spouses, the domination of man over woman, the primacy of the family over the individual) or in relation to things (the dowry, the wedding feast, costumes), and, ultimately, to the entire universe, but above all in respect to the relations between people (relation of man to woman, relation of each of those involved to their family and to that of their partner, relations between families, relations between the husband and other men and women of the tribe, relations between the wife and other men and women). Thus wedding ceremonies express the meaning of a natural act, the meaning of objects selected to have a link with this fact, the meaning of

13. F. J. J. Buytendijk, *La Femme*, p. 22.

human existences that are involved in it (I note here, for example, that in our culture the type of marriage contract selected reveals in its own way the meaning that an individual attaches to marriage and therefore the meaning of his own existence), the meaning of human relations in general and finally the level of meaning reached by the culture in question.

The sociologist's task is to investigate what are these various ceremonies and institutions; it is also to determine, from the standpoint we have put forward, the meaning of each of the forms encountered. But these problems will only raise themselves for him and be soluble by him on the basis of a certain conception of the being of man. If he takes man to be the representative of a natural species, then these problems will seem to him to be so much verbiage; in turn, his sociology will be no more than a collection of statistics and a dictionary of bizarre facts. But from where is the sociologist going to obtain this conception of man that he can use as the guiding thread and foundation of his investigations? As I said at the beginning, various hypotheses are possible. We do not have the space here to examine them all, or to study the complications that they introduce into history and the development of the sciences. These are problems that we have already alluded to. Let us therefore end by stating that, in our view, the conception of man that the anthropological sciences must accept as the ground on which to build their own edifice is that which man himself actually puts to work, though not explicitly, in his behaviour. It is not the scientist's mission to extract this conception; he can leave this up to the person upon whom this task has devolved, that is the philosopher, and more specifically the phenomenologist.

We can see, then, that this way of seeing things, if it is generalized, implies a certain notion of relations between the sciences and philosophy. These relations are neither ones of subordination, nor of simple coexistence. The task of the philosopher is to extract the ontological status of the human existent in the form that this status expresses itself in actual existence. But this task is possible only by examination of the facts in which this existence is constituted, that is with the collaboration of the scientist. Conversely, the scientist can discover and understand facts only on the basis of a conception of the being of man that alone enables him to determine what it is that he has to look for and what dimension of intelligibility is appropriate to apply to the object of his investigation.

It is only too clear that these relations mark out a circle. What we have here is the circle of existence itself, which cannot understand itself without being, nor be without understanding itself.

9 Maurice Natanson

Phenomenology as a Rigorous Science

M. Natanson, 'Phenomenology as a Rigorous Science', in *International Philosophical Quarterly*, Vol. VII, March 1967, pp. 5–20.

The impact of Husserl's thought on continental philosophy today is indisputable; its relevance for the American scene remains uncertain. To be sure, some accommodation has been achieved. There are now fashionable if not set attitudes for responding to phenomenology: do it instead of talking about how it's done; drop the jargon and pick up the problems; set aside textual involution and attend to issue; forget programmatic manifestos and turn to concrete and manageable items of business. The gesture of response which seems to accompany such attitudinal directives is that, stripped of its esoteric language and its positional claims, the actual results of phenomenological work often turn out to be not unlike what goes under the label of 'conceptual analysis'. From this suggestion, it is only a short hop to the way station of linguistic analysis and the claim that Husserl's 'program is, in fact, not very different from that of modern British and United States analytic philosophy'.[1]

Once labelled in this way, the specimen seems harmless enough. If it is asked what there at least seemed to be in phenomenology which aroused some harsh responses, we are reassured that talk of essence and the transcendental never really mattered in any very radical way. 'Husserl's fundamental contributions', J. N. Findlay claims, 'are much simpler than they at first appear to be. Thus there is little more to his transcendental and examination of essences than a determination to examine the meaning of com-

1. J. N. Findlay, article on 'Phenomenology', *Encyclopedia Britannica*, 1964; cited in *Readings in Twentieth Century Philosophy*, ed. William P. Alston and George Nakhnikian, New York: The Free Press of Glencoe, 1963, p. 630.

mon concepts and ordinary beliefs rather than to add factual detail to our knowledge.'[2] I am going to argue that Husserl's results are inseparable from his methods, that the 'commonness' of concepts and the 'ordinariness' of beliefs are root problems which become thematic for Husserl only through phenomenological method, and that, in the end, his fundamental contributions are, if anything, more complex than they at first appear to be. The context in which these ideas will be examined will not be that of a debate between phenomenological and analytic philosophy. Instead, I propose to turn to the issues directly with the hope that an indirect polemic will succeed in unsettling some of the contentment which threatens to obscure the radicality of phenomenology. My procedure will be unfashionable, for I propose to talk about methodology. Even worse, I'll use the language of phenomenology. By way of compensation, I'll dispense with texts and manifestos.

I

Phenomenology begins with the strangeness of experience. Within the natural attitude, living in our acts, as Husserl puts it, the world and our experience in the world are taken directly; they bear the inflections of an underlying sense of familiarity. The unusual appears within the horizon of a taken-for-granted normality or ordinariness. But the unusual is not the strange in the strong sense at issue in phenomenological attitude. Something noted as odd, peculiar, not quite right, etc. is not at all primordially strange. The unusual is merely a special feature of mundane disposition.

Let me illustrate the difference between the unusual and the strange. Some years ago, walking in New York, I came across a group gathered at a street corner, huddled busily over the grating of a sewer near the curb. One man was lying face down on the gutter, extending his arm through the grating into the sewer. It was evident that he was not one of that band of street wanderers who seek to recover change and valuables with an apparatus of

2. ibid.

cord, weights, grease, and other bits of inventiveness. What this prone gentleman *was* doing – relayed to me with great animation by his audience – turned out to be an effort to recover his teeth. Apparently, he sneezed while crossing the street, and the force of that nasal blast was sufficient to rocket his false teeth out of his mouth and into an orbit which terminated with the dentures ensconced in the nearby sewer. Even in a city noted for the remarkable happening, I found that scene unusual. But to call the event strange is to use the word in a diluted sense.

I prefer to reserve the strange for stronger fare. Consider another story. There is an archetypal New Yorker in search of directions and an archetypal correlate of direction-giver. Thomas Wolfe has anatomized both in his story 'Only the Dead Know Brooklyn'. Encountering direction-seeking and direction-giving individuals in the subway is hardly unusual and certainly not strange. I once happened to be standing near a man who asked how to get to some distant address in the city. Several people tried to be of help, but their suggestions for trains, transfers, etc. did seem complex and not altogether certain. The man persisted in asking others for help. Finally, he received an authoritative and absolutely definitive response from a person who not only knew the city thoroughly but who was able to give directions in simple yet complete terms. If ever a subway questioner was answered in unmistakable and resolute form, our man was so rewarded. After receiving the perfect set of instructions, he turned immediately to someone else standing near by and repeated his original request for directions. To say that this was unusual hardly meets the point; it was rather quite strange, and the specific character or quality of that strangeness was the recognition by the group around this man that he was not really seeking directions but was interested solely in asking his question. In fact, the question was not a question at all but what seemed to be a compulsion to ask. By the time my train came along and most of the original group had departed on theirs, the man was still asking. Here, then, the strange transcends the unusual as a quality of the agent rather than a feature of the event. Primordial strangeness in the phenomenological sense goes a qualitative step further.

In suggesting that the teeth-seeking was unusual and the

question-asker strange, I assume that the event and the person at issue were parts of my world and the world of the witnesses to those scenes. *We* already on hand, in the current of daily affairs, crossing intersections and pausing on underground platforms – *we* attended to what transpired. But there was nothing unusual or strange in having a point in space and time, a place of orientation in terms of which what occurred was there for view. What was picked out of experience as worthy of notice and notation had an unstated backdrop, a reality 'rootly' presupposed and unavailable for inspection, let alone analysis. That mundanity in terms of which our attending to event and person assumed the character of a-something-possible remained utterly immanent to awareness. Displaying it for view, rendering it evident, involves the transformation of familiarity itself into a fundamental strangeness.

Such transformation has a larger and a narrower significance. In generalized terms, rendering experience strange characterizes philosophy as a whole. It involves a radical stance, a remarkable way of looking at things. That experience cannot be taken straightforwardly, that it is to-be-understood, introduces a mode of reversal into the ordinary and unreflective acceptance of the mundane course of affairs: a philosophical turn of mind signifies a shifting of perspective from simple placement in the world to wonder about it aslant it. Philosophy in this sense begins with the critique of mundanity. The narrower sense of transformation of familiarity into strangeness involves the phenomenological attitude. We are brought to the centre of Husserl's methodology.

The suspension of the general thesis of the natural attitude and the assumption of a genuinely egological standpoint make it possible for strangeness to show itself. From the slogan 'To the things themselves!' to the givenness of those 'things' is the movement from the methodological directive to the urgency of the phenomena presented by way of the directive. The primordial strangeness we have been exploring turns out to be the presence of the phenomena in their unmediated and originary manifestation to consciousness.

Why should the phenomena prove to be strange in this sense, and what is really involved in that strangeness? Before these questions can be answered it would seem that a prior caution must be attended to: in what sense is there anything philosophical to say about 'strangeness'? In providing an answer we must note the following elements: first, a philosophical description and analysis may be approached by way of a reconstruction of the phenomenon given to the ego. Such reconstruction includes a precising of the elements of meaning necessary for the possibility of the phenomenon; second, there is a recursiveness involved in the philosophical scrutiny of strangeness, i.e. the ego turns toward its awareness-of what is given, moves toward its having awareness in being able to reflect on its own procedure; third, the givenness of the phenomenon signifies the conceptual enclosure in which reflexive analysis is done: the givenness and the examination of it are features of a unitary domain defined by the intentionality of consciousness. The strangeness we are concerned with, then, is not a product of psychological response to some event or state of affairs but rather the direct presentation of what there is, bare of its encrustation of prior interpretation and already formed attitudes. The phenomenon is strange in virtue of its bleakness, its dispossession of the already anticipated and the already identified. Involved in the strangeness is a situation which frames the phenomenon and gives valence to its presentative character. But what of the strangeness itself? Can it be penetrated and can it be portrayed? Some examples are necessary. We shall pick them up in the context of certain situations.

Looking at a fellow man is ordinarily simply seeing him as there before me, potentially responsive to my talk and movements. Seeing him as *there*, incarnate in the world, as a being like myself, capable of seeing me as I see him, above all, seeing him as a creature in reality having an identity which stands before me as knowable – that seeing is encircled with strangeness and articulates the quality of being given in the world as a person for other persons. Seeing a fellow man, in this sense, is not a perceptual act but an expression of human presence. The strangeness of seeing the Other is structurally different from imagining the Other, but the experiential distance between them is especially significant. Seeing the Other in his immediacy – as though one were seeing for the first time – is being present to his 'weight' as a creature, the substantial fact of his being *this* one in and against the world. There is a difference, then, between seeing the Other in life-immediacy and imagining the Other as, say, a fictive being in a story. As James Agee puts it:

In a novel, a house or person has his meaning, his existence, entirely through the writer. Here, a house or a person has only the most limited of his meaning through me; his true meaning is much huger. It is that he *exists*, in actual being, as you do and as I do, and as no character of the imagination can possibly exist. His great weight, mystery, and dignity are in this fact. As for me, I can tell you of him only what I saw, only so accurately as in my terms I know how; and this in turn has its chief stature not in any ability of mine but in the fact that I too exist, not as a work of fiction, but as a human being. Because of his immeasurable weight in actual existence, and because of mine, every word I tell of him has inevitably a kind of immediacy, a kind of meaning, not at all necessarily 'superior' to that of imagination, but of a kind so different that a work of imagination (however intensely it may draw on 'life') can at best only faintly imitate the least of it.[3]

The actual, in-the-world seeing of the concrete Other before me crystallizes as this-seeing as distinct from an act of this type. Nor is it merely the instantiation of a type of act or event. This-givenness is a feature of primordial strangeness, a way in which strangeness shows itself, because the resources the natural attitude otherwise draws upon, its reliance on the materials of familiarity, are unavailable. Without perceptual crutches consciousness is left to struggle in walking and must, in a sense, learn how to walk. The situational context provides the clue to what can be 'said' about strangeness in the seeing of persons. The initial and the decisive point to be made is that whatever can be said presupposes some acknowledgement and concern with what was originarily given in that strangeness I've called seeing the Other.

Suppose one were to reduce the line of discussion advanced so far to the following summary: whatever the precise differences may be between them, there is some sensible distinction to be made between the unusual and the strange, but that can best be gotten at by turning to what one would say about the two.

3. James Agee and Walker Evans, *Let us Now Praise Famous Men*, Boston: Houghton Mifflin, 1941, p. 12.

Presumably talk about the unusual would have some similarities and some differences in contrast with talk about the strange. As to primordial strangeness, couldn't it be suggested that occasionally we do have an extraordinary sense of being alive, of coming into contact with other people, or something of the sort, but that such fugitive moments of life are rather bizarre feelings best left to the artist or the psychologist? To the extent that we can understand each other when we discuss that sort of experience, we might, were we interested, turn to the language of our accounts and try to explore its logic.

II

Is anything beyond this summary involved in my discussion of the unusual, the strange, and the primordially strange? It is my contention that indeed something more *is* involved: the very meaning of phenomenological reduction and, consequently, of phenomenology itself. The turn to the phenomena in Husserl's sense hinges upon the acknowledgement of an experiential order, borne by consciousness, in which and through which objects, events, and relations achieve their status as features of awareness. Not what can be said about strangeness but the experience of strangeness is the locus of the phenomenon; the experience itself is the subject and object of phenomenological concern. And the experience itself is located in a situational frame, an intentional matrix through which its features and texture are specified. If we cannot 'speak reality', we can attend to what is substantive and nuclear in its givenness. To elicit the meaning proper to the experience would then require a language infinitely sensitive to the form and character of the experience, and such language would present rather than represent what was experienced. With Agee we might speak of a 'language of reality'. He writes:

The language of 'reality' . . . may be the most beautiful and powerful but certainly it must in any case be about the heaviest of all languages. That it should have and impart the deftness, keenness, immediacy, speed and subtlety of the 'reality' it tries to reproduce, would require incredible strength and trained skill on the part of the handler, and would perhaps also require an audience, or the illusion of an audience, equally well trained in catching what is thrown . . .[4]

The phenomenological attitude, I am saying, is in search of a language adequate to the comprehension of the phenomenon and not phenomena yielded, in a secondary manner, through what is said. Relinquishing the former in favour of the latter, turning to what is said instead of the originary givenness which occasioned the saying, represents, from the phenomenological standpoint, experiential refusal.

The situation of primordial strangeness, then, must be attended to on its own, examined in its givenness, and expressed in language which is finely sensitive to the meaning it seeks to articulate. The 'language of reality' does more than report; it reconstructs, and it does so through a rhetoric which is resonant with its object. The forms such language takes vary from the poetic force Agee commands to the relentless beating of a stylistically unimpassioned but philosophically harassing jargon Husserl employs. At both extremes attending with infinite patience to the shape of the phenomena, the authors confront the phenomena by way of a methodological transcension of the natural attitude. Phenomenological reduction is an integral moment in the descriptive, analytic, and reconstructive process. Without reduction, the strangeness we have discussed would be translated into the 'concept' of strangeness or 'beliefs' about strangeness. With the reduction, 'ordinariness' associated with concepts and beliefs comes into question, and phenomenology becomes an accusatory discipline.

Now it might well be suggested at this point that I have given a partial interpretation of the reduction and that by emphasizing the strangeness at issue in the phenomenological attitude I have weighted the discussion in favour of an existential reading of Husserl. There are, in fact, many Husserls, among them the philosopher who sought to make philosophy a rigorous science. Strangeness seems a far cry from the tone of the *Logical Investigations*. Husserl's concentration on detailed, painstakingly close descriptive studies of problems in perception, etc., would seem

4. ibid., p. 236.

to be part of another philosophical world. I don't believe that the Husserl I have presented so far is alien to the thinker who deemed rigour to be a prime philosophical virtue. If there are several Husserls, it doesn't follow that they are implacable antagonists. Rather, as I hope to show, the different Husserls are necessary outcomes of the complexity of phenomenology's fundamental contributions. The agreement between them is far more interesting than the opposition.

III

The Husserl who sought to make philosophy a rigorous science was also the Husserl who sought to make phenomenology a rigorous science. In fact, the first was to be accomplished through the second. And the second was to be accomplished, in turn, by establishing a complete and thoroughgoing inventory of all eidetic structures underlying the full range of knowledge and experience, including the essential meanings at the foundation of all special disciplines embracing the social as well as the natural sciences. Moreover, the inventory of essences was to be established in such a way that their constitutive grounding in intentionality was in turn to be shown in absolute and complete detail. The bedrock for all descriptive and analytic reports concerning eidetic structure was to be the direct presentation of noetic-noematic unities in intentional consciousness. The 'in-person', utterly first-hand and direct presentation of the phenomena and the descriptions and analyses proper to them was the fundamental business of phenomenology.

The scope for such a science was obviously enormous and its pace of accomplishment necessarily tortuously slow. The effort was to be universal, encyclopedic, and absolute. In the course of its development it would pick up and carry forward what was, for Husserl, valid in all prior searches for a *mathēsis universalis*, in the positive insights of British empiricism, and in the transcendental philosophy of Kant. Husserl writes:

It is the distinctive peculiarity of phenomenology to include all sciences and all forms of knowledge in the scope of its eidetic universality, and indeed in respect of its eidetic universality, and indeed in respect of all that which is *immediately transparent* in them, or at least would be so, if they were genuine forms of knowledge. The meaning and legitimacy of all the immediate starting-points possible and of all immediate steps in possible method come within its jurisdiction. Therefore all eidetic (all unconditionally and universally valid) forms of knowledge lie enclosed in phenomenology, and through them the root-problems of 'possibility', as bearing on any science or form of knowledge one may care to consider, receive an answer. As applied, phenomenology supplies the definitive criticism of every fundamentally distinct science, and in particular there with the final determination of the sense in which their objects can be said to 'be'. It also clarifies their methodology in the light of first principles. It is therefore not surprising that phenomenology is as it were the secret longing of the whole philosophy of modern times.[5]

It is necessary to understand, then, that the detailed, close inspection of concrete problems often taken as indicative of what is best in phenomenology is, in truth, part of a gigantic enterprise which, in its ultimate formulation, attempts to trace back the constitution of all details of meaning to sources in transcendental consciousness. The results of phenomenological description are bound to the procedure Husserl is exploiting, and the radicality of his descriptive efforts comes clear when it is understood that phenomenological rigour is the consequence of accepting the meaning of reduction. Those who would argue that it is unnecessary to be overly concerned with what Husserl says about phenomenology, that instead it is more important to look to his results – those who argue that phenomenological practice is independent of phenomenological theory – end up with a residue of descriptive results which may be 'clean' in terms of their current credentials but are only a surface fragment of what Husserl intended.[6] Let me give one illustration.

Husserl's argument in the fifth *Cartesian Meditation* can be summarized or outlined without enactment of reduction, i.e. reduction can be talked about, but the results of reduction, indeed the very terms of the argument, demand a phenomeno-

5. Edmund Husserl, *Ideas: General Introduction to Pure Phenomenology,* trans. W. R. Boyce Gibson, New York: Macmillan, 1931, pp. 182–3.
6. Cf. *Readings in Twentieth Century Philosophy,* p. 630.

190 Maurice Natanson

logical performance on the part of the one who seeks to understand Husserl's claims. The sense of Other, of what might be called 'alterity', requires a special reduction within the transcendental sphere so that the fundamental intentionality relating to other subjectivities is not presupposed in a domain where it is precisely in question. In getting at the *alter ego* it is not possible, for Husserl, to take for granted relatedness of consciousness to the sense of Others. 'In the natural, the world-accepting attitude,' Husserl writes, 'I find differentiated and contrasted: myself and others.'[7] It is necessary to render this sense of 'myself and others' thematic for analysis, and this requires that within transcendental subjectivity the intentional reference to otherness be bracketed. Husserl writes:

As regards method, a prime requirement for proceeding correctly here is that first of all we carry out, *inside the universal transcendental sphere, a peculiar kind of epochē* with respect to our theme. For the present we exclude from the thematic field everything now in question; we *disregard all constitutional effects of intentionality relating immediately or mediately to other subjectivity* and delimit first of all the total nexus of that actual and potential intentionality in which the ego constitutes within himself a peculiar ownness.[8]

Stripped of phenomenological performance, this advice might appear to be little more than a recommendation that we should be concerned with getting clear about the meaning of saying 'there are other people in the world besides me'. Nor will any more sophisticated reformulation of this statement make any essential difference. The point is that Husserl is calling into radical question the constitutive sense of 'otherness' and arguing that even in pure consciousness the fundamental directedness of the ego to fellow men is presupposed. To get clear about the fundamental intentionality of the involvement of the ego with Others, it is necessary to perform the special *epochē* he describes. The results of the analysis which follow in the fifth meditation not only presuppose the theory of reduction but are unintelligible without the practice of reduction. The results are as much bound

7. Edmund Husserl, *Cartesian Meditations: An Introduction to Phenomenology*, trans. Dorion Cairns, The Hague: Nijhoff, 1960, p. 93.
8. ibid.

to one as to the other. And even in the realm of practice, what is involved is effecting reduction, not conclusions gleaned from phenomenological practice.

IV

We are brought to the following focus: the Husserl of rigorous philosophizing is not all that distant from the Husserl of philosophical strangeness. Understanding the former means recognizing the rootedness of descriptive results in the constitutive origins in transcendental subjectivity, and grasping the latter means performing the reduction. It was that performance, that methodological involvement, though, which was the entrance we took into the encounter with the primordial strange. Far from the Husserl of rigorous science avoiding in hawk-like precision the dove-like strangeness of phenomenology as an attitude, the conclusion we come to is that phenomenology as a rigorous science is built on a transcendental foundation uncovered in strangeness. Reduction remains the vital principle in Husserl's practice, because it is inescapably central to phenomenological theory. His fundamental contributions indeed then turn out to be more complex than was at first imagined, for not only is there a greater richness in the idea of rigorous science but some genuinely troubling paradoxes. I shall turn to those paradoxes shortly; for the moment I'm concerned with some of the implications of the integrity of phenomenological theory and practice for which I have been arguing. Phenomenology is shortchanged, I have suggested, if some of its 'results' are taken apart from the procedures which led to those results. In fact, without actively engaging in phenomenological analysis through reduction, there are no results, merely reports about 'results'. The stubborn streak in Husserl's philosophizing, what I've called the radicality of his thought, is his insistence on direct seeing, which means active doing of phenomenological work. Method is the instrument through which the doing is effected. It is the phenomenological razor's edge.

Two stories may help to illustrate the dangers of accepting a weakened version of phenomenology or seeking to amalgamate it in a philosophical trade union. Not long ago I presented a paper to a group of philosophers, one of whom told me afterwards that he thought my discussion was not altogether hopeless, that there was an idea or two in the paper which might be developed into something worthwhile. Overcome by a spirit of good will, he offered me this advice: 'Look,' he said, 'you're really saying something in this paper, but what you need to do is to get rid of all that phenomenological garbage.' But there is something besides translation into a different idiom: the idea that fragments or pieces of philosophical work can be taken over into another domain and fitted into a new pattern, that a truth here and a truth there can be turned into a truth everywhere. In the old country, a certain rabbi was visited by a husband and wife who had severe marital troubles and sought advice. The rabbi spoke first to the wife, who recounted a long history of wrongs and evils her husband was guilty of. She justified her own conduct with great force. Finally she said, 'Tell me, Rabbi, am I not right?' The rabbi pondered the problem, stroked his beard, and finally said, 'Yes, I think you're right.' The husband then told his side of it: the horrors he had endured from a shrewish wife, the suffering and embarrassment she had caused him, his own loving patience and good sense, his forbearance, and so on. At the end of his report he also asked the rabbi, 'Am I not right?' After careful thought, the rabbi replied, 'Yes, I think you're right.' As soon as the couple left, the rabbi's wife who had overheard everything, rushed in and cried, 'How can you tell them they're both right? They tell contradictory stories. If one is right the other is wrong. They can't both be right.' The rabbi listened patiently, stroked his beard and answered finally: 'Yes, there's a good deal of truth in what you say. You're right too!'

V

Insisting on the radicality of phenomenology and the integral relationship between method and results does not automatically cleanse Husserl's thought of internal difficulties. His fundamental contributions, I've hinted, are more complex than appears to be the case, and that complexity harbours certain paradoxes. What I have in mind is that the idea of phenomenology as a rigorous science contains two motives: the first is directed toward establishing a universal discipline whose results have apodictic force; the second, intimately bound to this goal, involves the discipline of the phenomenologist and requires that he return to his basal sources, that he be a perpetual beginner in philosophical work. If a rigorous science of phenomenology is possible, it depends on the possibility of there being a concomitant science of the phenomenologist. I suggest that in Husserl's own terms this is not possible. At least it may be said that there cannot be a science of the phenomenologist in the same sense in which a science of phenomenology is projected.

The reasons are these: the results of phenomenological work are not additive; they cannot be 'taken over' from previous efforts; they are not assured once and for all in the sense in which the results of formal deduction can be absorbed in the development of logic or mathematics. Beginning for the phenomenological philosopher means a perpetual renewal of sources, a continual return to origins, and a necessary persistence in reconstructing the edifice upon which other phenomenologists have worked. Far from being destructive to the idea of rigorous science, the paradox of the phenomenologist and phenomenology reveals a deeper meaning of rigour. The phenomenologist must attend directly to the phenomena given *to him* and must do so by way of a reduction which establishes the primordial strangeness of his experience. The intentional life which is opened up by the reversal of the ordinary reveals both the essences which structure the phenomena and the constitution and recovery of those essences by way of the meditating ego, the phenomenologist. The rigour with which the phenomenologist does his work, then, has a double pull: it points to the noetic-noematic character of intentional acts but also the activity of the ego engaged in confronting and delineating the phenomena. Husserl's own dissatisfaction with his various solutions to the question of who does the phenomenological work, his proliferation of egos, his notion of the 'phenomenological observer', are symptoms of the struggle he had in coming to terms with the achievements of rigour in what might be termed the phenomenologist's role.

VI

The paradoxes of phenomenology as rigorous science may be taken as evidence of the richness as well as the problematicity of Husserl's thought. Those who would turn away from the Husserl of phenomenological strangeness to the Husserl of rigorous science will find the former in the latter just as the latter was already sedimented in the former. One is an inescapable corollary of the other. A rag-picker's version of phenomenology, one which scouts around for useful odds and ends, results in an abandonment if not a betrayal of Husserl's mission.

These considerations lead to a larger thesis. The significance of phenomenology today is a function of its double tendency, its turn to the strangeness in terms of which direct givenness is encountered and its ideal of universal science. The impact of Husserl's thought on literature, the arts, psychology and psychiatry, as well as existential philosophy, cannot be fully understood apart from the commitment of the phenomenologist to attend with full patience and care to the implosive texture of experience. At the same time, the search for rigour arises as much from the phenomenologist's role as it does from the demands of a universal science. I find, then, a congenial relationship between phenomenological approaches to and interpretations of literature and the arts and hard-line phenomenological analysis. The language of strict and purified analysis has its image reflected in what Agee called the 'language of reality'. What the phenomenological attitude contributes to art, to literature, let us say, is a means for getting at the directness of experience through a reconstruction of language possible to the experience. The starting point and the point of control is the experience; the language then is mobilized to empower the self to comprehend its own involvement. There is a recursive function of language involved here which needs further comment.

The phenomenologist's role, I've said, turns out to be richly problematic to the meaning of phenomenology as science. The strangeness which reduction makes possible allows the phenomena to present themselves in their originary cast. In trying to describe and analyse the phenomena of direct givenness, the phenomenologist utilizes language not only to report what he has seen but also to embody his own constitutive relationship to his intentional life. In strangeness, the person before me seen directly as *this*-man, *this*-fellow being, stands forth as to be granted independence, epistemic freedom, in my acknowledgement of him. What I say about him, the reports I give, the language I employ to point back to him – such discourse is only secondarily concerned with the phenomenon-for-me; the initial problem is to comprehend and express the relationship between the language of report and the reporter utilizing language.

To speak of a recursive function of language here is to suggest that the phenomenologist is committed to attending to the circumstances and conditions of his own procedures. Phenomenology demands an internal criticism of itself. 'All transcendental-philosophical theory of knowledge', Husserl maintains, 'as *"criticism of knowledge", leads back ultimately to criticism of transcendental-phenomenological knowledge* . . . and, owing to the essential reflexive relation of phenomenology to itself, this criticism also demands a criticism.'[9] Between the phenomenologist's entertainment of the phenomenon and his report about it there exists, I am saying, a relationship of reflexive enclosure. The 'language of reality' is a rhetoric of phenomena, an attempt to rebuild the intensive relationship between the ego and what is given to it in intentional life. The thickness of much phenomenological writing may be understood as a means of tracing out the elements and patterns sedimented in perceptual life. A turning toward the shape of what is given is facilitated by a building-up, in language, of its manifold strata and strands of meaning. This is hardly intended as an excuse for bad writing; it is an hypothesis concerned with the linguistic order in which reporters and their reports rebound off each other in curious ways. It is necessary also to differentiate between phenomenological reports which are presented in the natural attitude and at least the possibility of

9. ibid., p. 152.

phenomenological reports given *through* the phenomenological attitude.[10] The limits of language here would appear to be defined by a circuit of criticism involving the phenomenologist's originary experience and the effort he makes to have his report inform as well as describe what was given to him. In exploring the recursive function of language the phenomenologist is probing the outlines of the rigour possible to his role.

VII

A summary statement of what I've tried to do here may help to clarify the line of argument advanced as well as point to its conclusions. My claims are these: first, Husserl's fundamental contributions cannot be understood apart from the revolutionary methodology which not only made them possible but guarantees their very significance. Second, phenomenological reduction is the clue to the radicality of Husserl's thought; as the gateway to intentionality it makes possible the encounter of the self and its world on the ground of a root strangeness. Third, far from romanticizing phenomenology, the concern with strangeness turns out to be essential to the meaning of phenomenology as rigorous science; for rigour, in Husserl's sense, involves a return of the phenomenologist to his own sources, a return stamped with essential strangeness. Fourth, the complexity of Husserl's thought is based on the unsuspected richness as well as paradoxical character of his conception of science: the science of phenomenology presupposes the activity of the phenomenologist at the same time that no science of the phenomenologist is possible. Fifth, the significance of Husserl's thought for the intellectual and artistic domain today lies in the dual tension coiled in phenomenology, for it is at once a universal and absolute discipline and also what we may now term an art of the phenomenologist. Finally, I have tried in an oblique way to suggest that the phenomenologist's concern with language arises from a direct commit-

10. See Juan David Garcia Bacca, 'E. Husserl and J. Joyce or Theory and Practice of the Phenomenological Attitude', *Philosophy and Phenomenological Research*, 9, 1949, 588–94.

ment to an insistent confrontation with immediately given experience, that attending to the experience is not reducible to reflection on what one may say about the experience, that it is turning to the shape and texture of the situationally ordered experience which is the prime responsibility of the phenomenologist, that what may be said about the experience cannot replace it. To give up the phenomenon because it is apparently easier to present arguments about the linguistic characterization of the phenomenon (the stronger charge against phenomenology being that 'the phenomenological method with its ultimate appeal to intuition, not to the logic of language, makes *argument* impossible')[11] – to turn away from the phenomena at the expense of a struggle to deal with them as features of a living world inhabited by men seeking to understand themselves in the world, to avoid the clash of philosophy with mundanity, is to evince a failure of nerve.

The attempt to rescue Husserl from what existentialists and literateurs have made of what are taken to be his genuine contributions to philosophy is at best a partially valid enterprise. At worst, the attempt to domesticate phenomenology leads to a scandalous ignoring of what Husserl himself insisted on as the foundation of phenomenology: transcendental subjectivity, intentionality, and the theory of the reductions. There *are* valid existential themes to be found in phenomenology, and as the discipline of subjectivity it could hardly avoid one of the richest expressions of consciousness, the domain of art. I discovered recently that Husserl and Oskar Kokoschka knew each other in Vienna and later met in Prague. According to Kokoschka, what brought the two men together was the occasion of Kokoschka's first public lecture, which he gave in Vienna as a young man in 1912. The lecture was entitled 'On the Nature of Visions'; Husserl's interest in it in turn led to his taking an interest in the artist. It would be an infinitely hazardous thread upon which to hang an argument to suggest that Husserl's cordiality to Kokoschka's lecture was evidence for the resonance between phenomenology and art. I would not think of making so dubious a claim. Rather, I close with the independent recommendation that

11. *Readings in Twentieth Century Philosophy*, p. 630.

what Husserl heard from Kokoschka over fifty years ago was a distinctively phenomenological insight phrased in terms of an almost visual poetry. Kokoschka said: 'Consciousness is the source of all things and of all conceptions. It is a sea ringed about with visions.'

Maurice Natanson 199

10 John O'Neill

Can Phenomenology be Critical?

J. O'Neill, 'Can Phenomenology be Critical?' in *Sociology as a Skin-Trade*, London: Heinemann, 1972, pp. 221-36.

What is the task that I mean to set for myself in asking whether phenomenology can be critical? I am raising the question whether we can be authentically aware of the reflexive limits of the corpus of social science knowledge due to its implicit ties with the order of history and politics. The very question is evidence of a certain uneasiness, but also of a determination to dwell within its circle at least as much as to drive for a solution. How shall I proceed then? For to begin, I cannot settle for you the nature of phenomenology. Of course, I am aware that I might attempt to set out some of the principal features of Husserlian phenomenology. But the nature of the auspices for such an exposition should not be confused with its method of historiography and reference whose very intention of making its appeal public invites criticism and reappraisal, and is ultimately the same thing as philosophical argument. The question of the authoritative procedures for introducing phenomenology is made even more problematic by the developments in phenomenology from Husserl to Heidegger, Scheler, and Jaspers; or through Sartre and Merleau-Ponty; not to mention Schutz and the ethnomethodology of Garfinkel and Cicourel. Faced with a similar problem, Merleau-Ponty has remarked that 'we shall find in ourselves, and nowhere else, the unity and true meaning of phenomenology'. In other words, we must take our own context, namely, our gathering out of mutual concern with the contemporary issues in the social sciences, as the topic for phenomenological theorizing.

What is the occasion, then, which provides the resource for my own theoretical effort? I take it that it is not simply a by-product of my academic *curriculum vitae* which yields a certain kind of documentary evidence of my concerns with the topic of our symposium. I want also to assume that this occasion is not the simple production of a symposium under the rule of dialectical or trinitarian postures of argument and torture of the truth. However, I would not deny that these may well be contingent features of performances such as a symposium. Clearly, though, there is some kind of rule which is a constitutive feature of our symposium. It is the rule which provides for the dramatization of the assumption that there are issues in the social sciences which are philosophical and which are as such in dispute from a variety of standpoints, but in a manner which does not preclude exchange and mutual exploration of common concerns. This is an enormously important assumption which is threatened nowadays by certain highly subjectivist and solipsistic postures as well as political ideologies which invade classrooms and conferences and threaten to turn the modern mind into an armed camp, a result which, as Camus has remarked, would separate us from the Greeks.

I want to develop a phenomenological conception of critique and argument under a rule of limit and cosmic order which is simultaneously the ground of political order and rebellion. Habermas has argued[1] that Husserl's critique of positivist science does not go far enough in simply denying the separation between knowledge and the life-world. In so far as science and philosophy, including the social sciences, separate the activity of theorizing from the world of human interests, both rest upon a positivist ontology. The prescriptions for this separation constitute the rule of methodological objectivity or segregation of subjective interests and values. The unfortunate practical consequences of the separation of science and values can only be corrected through an understanding of the true relation between knowledge and interest, in other words, of *praxis*. Husserl's critique of the objectivism of science and the natural attitude which is its pre-scientific ground, may be taken as an obvious sense in which phenomenology is critical. But it does not go far enough to free transcendental

1. Jürgen Habermas, 'Knowledge and Interests: *A General Perspective*', appendix to his *Knowledge and Human Interests*, trans. Jeremy J. Shapiro, London: Heinemann Educational Books, 1971.

phenomenology itself from practical interest. Habermas invokes the etymology of θεωρια in order to trace a development in the concept of theory from the original activity of the representative sent by a polis to witness the sacred festival of another city to the philosopher's μιμησις or representation in the order of his soul of the natural κοσμος.

Husserl rightly criticizes the objectivist illusion that deludes the sciences with the image of a reality-in-itself, consisting of facts structured in a lawlike manner; it conceals the constitution of these facts, and thereby prevents consciousness of the interlocking of knowledge with interests from the life-world. Because phenomenology brings this to consciousness, it is itself, in Husserl's view, free of such interests. It thus earns the title of pure theory unjustly claimed by the sciences. It is to this freeing of knowledge from interest that Husserl attaches the expectation of practical efficacy. But the error is clear. Theory in the sense of the classical tradition only had an impact on life because it was thought to have discovered in the cosmic order an ideal world structure, including the prototype for the order of the human world. Only as *cosmology* was *theoria* also capable of orienting human action. Thus Husserl cannot expect self-formative processes to originate in a phenomenology that, as transcendental philosophy, purifies the classical theory of its cosmological contents, conserving something like the theoretical attitude only in an abstract manner. Theory had educational and cultural implications not because it had freed knowledge from interest. To the contrary, it did so because it derived *pseudo-normative power* from *the concealment of its actual interest*. While criticizing the objectivist self-understanding of the sciences, Husserl succumbs to another objectivism, which was always attached to the traditional concept of theory.[2]

Whether or not Husserl neglected the original connection between θεωρια and its consequences for the philosophical way of life, as Habermas argues, it is important to stress the ambivalence in classical philosophical knowledge with respect to the idea of Beauty and Goodness. Habermas tends to overlook this tension. Miss Hannah Arendt, however, has argued that the subordination of life in the pursuit of human affairs (βιος πολιτικος) to the 'theoretical way of life' (βιος θεωρητικος) is a

2. ibid., pp. 305–6.

result of the Platonic subordination of the contemplative love of the true essence of Being, under the idea of the Beautiful, to the idea of Good, or an art of measurement which provides a rule to the philosopher's potential disorientation in everyday political life.[3] In other words, there is an essential ambivalence in western knowledge between the values of the recognition and domination of Being which has been consequential for its political tradition, particularly when the pattern of domination is based upon modern scientific knowledge which breaks once and for all the connection between κοσμος and θεωρια.

Modern social science knowledge has reduced its independence as a form of theoretical life to a rule of methodology founded upon the auspices of technical rationality. This results in a disenchanted objectivism or rationalization of the interests and values which guide technological domination as a form or 'conduct of life', to use Max Weber's phrase. However, Weber's formal rationality, so far from resting upon 'value-free' auspices, is in fact an historical constellation whose precondition is the separation of the orders of knowledge, work, and politics. In the period of the bourgeois ascendency, the value-free conception of rationality furnishes a critical concept of the development of human potential locked in the feudal world of 'traditional' values. Weber makes a fatality of technical rationality, thereby identifying its historical role with political domination as such,[4] whereas Marx's critique of classical political economy showed the critical limits of economic rationality.[5] Social science knowledge needs to be grounded in a limited but authentic reflexivity through which it recognizes its ties to individual values and community interests, notwithstanding its attempts to avoid bias and ideology. Habermas himself furnishes five theses which I shall interpret as the auspices of a limited reflexivity responsible to the project of *homo faber*.

3. Hannah Arendt, *Between Past and Future*, Six Exercises in Political Thought, Cleveland and New York: Meridian Books, 1963, pp. 112–15.

4. Herbert Marcuse, 'Industrialization and Capitalism in Max Weber', *Negations*, Essays in Critical Theory, Boston: Beacon Press, 1968.

5. See Chapter 16. ('On Theory and Criticism in Marx', in John O'Neill, *Sociology as a Skin Trade*, London: Heinemann, 1972. *Editor's note*)

(i) The achievements of the transcendental subject have their basis in the natural history of the human species.

(ii) Knowledge equally serves as an instrument and transcends mere self-preservation.

(iii) Knowledge-constitutive interests take form in the medium of work, language, and power.

(iv) In the power of self-reflection, knowledge and interest are one.

(v) The unity of knowledge and interest proves itself in a dialectic that takes the historical traces of suppressed dialogue and reconstructs what has been suppressed.

Together these five theses reveal the axiological basis of human knowledge as a pattern of communication, control, and decision, predicated upon man's self-made and thus largely symbolic project of creation and freedom. The human project is a structure of biological, social and, I would add, libidinal values, which are institutionalized through the media of language, work, and politics. The vehicle of the human project is a common tradition and identity tied to speech, creation, and citizenship which relate individual expressions to everyday social life and culture.[6] In each of these realms there is practical metaphysics of the relation of particulars to universals, within the limits of common speech, the exchange of labour and the pursuit of the common good. Moreover, there is, as Habermas argues, an essential relation between the orders of language, work, and politics. The man who is not free in his labour is not free to speak and thus freedom of speech presupposes an end of economic exploitation as well as of political repression. Dialogue and poetry are therefore the primary expressions of the bond between speech and politics; it is through them that knowledge achieves reflexive awareness of the values of the human community to which it belongs and is thus able to play its role in the constitution of the body politic.[7] I have mentioned the work of the poet in the politics of freedom because he, as well as the novelist and musician, is the guardian of tradi-

6. See Chapter 11. ('Embodiment and History in Hegel and Marx', in ibid. *Editor's note*)

7. See Chapter 6. ('Authority, Knowledge and the Body Politic', in ibid. *Editor's note*)

tion and creativity. I think it is necessary to relate the knowledge-constitutive interests to the expressive, libidinal interests of the body politic in order to extend political dialogue into the street, the songs and everyday confrontations within the body politic. For these are the life-world understandings of the traditions of need and rebellion.

Modern consciousness is tied to the standpoints of anthropology and historicism which reveal that all knowledge about man, including scientific knowledge, presupposes some metaphysical position on the relation between human facticity, knowledge, and values.[8] Thus we can only speak of the reflexive ties between subjectivity and the regional ontologies of the worlds of science, economics, politics, and everyday life, and not of a naïve realist, subject/object dichotomy.

It may help to clarify the conception of limited reflexivity which I am proposing as the auspices for a mode of political theorizing which has its community in the body politic, if I contrast it with the consequences of a total reflexivity of absolute knowledge. There is, for example, a conception of reflexivity which is very close to the limited notion I am fostering, but which is quite alien to it in its consequences for the orders of language, thought, and politics. I have in mind the sociological conception of reflexivity as the awareness of the infra-structures of knowledge in culture, class, and biography. At first sight, the consequences of the sociology of knowledge and ideology might appear to make for a moderation of political argument through an understanding of the intervening circumstances of class and history. But in practice it has brutalized political awareness and obscured the science of politics for which Mannheim had hoped. It was to these issues that both Husserl and Weber addressed themselves in their reflections on the vocations of science and politics. Both were concerned with the nihilism that was a potential conclusion from historicism and the sociology of knowledge. Husserl and Weber approached these problems in terms of an inquiry into the very foundations of western knowledge or science. Let us recall briefly

8. Ludwig Landgrebe, *Major Problems in Contemporary European Philosophy*, From Dilthey to Heidegger, trans. Kurt F. Reinhardt, New York: Frederick Ungar Publishing Co., 1966, p. 11.

Weber's reflections, which are perhaps better known to socio-logists and political scientists, and then turn to Husserl's struggles with these problems in *The Crisis of European Sciences*.[9]

At first sight, the connection between Weber's reflections on the vocations of science, politics, and capitalism are not evident. Superficially, modern economics, politics, and science present us with an exotic competition of goods and values without a rational standard of choice. We accumulate knowledge much as we do money, and the result is a vast obsolence of commonsense knowledge and values. Any attempt to introduce order into this process is as disturbing to it as the occasions for these very attempts, so that our politics is snared in a polytheism of value. 'And with this,' says Weber, 'we come to inquire into the meaning of science. For, after all, it is not self-evident that something sub-ordinate to such a law is sensible and meaningful in itself. Why does one engage in doing something that in reality never comes, and never can come to an end.'[10] Weber's question about the auspices of modern science is simultaneously a question about the grounds of modern community and personality in a world from which God is absent and order thereby an enigma to a disenchanted world of value accumulation. Weber compares his own questioning of the meaning of science with Tolstoy's ques-tion about the meaning of death in the modern world, where man is pitted against himself in a self-infinitude of want and desire. 'And because death is meaningless, civilized life as such is mean-ingless; by its very "progressiveness" it gives death the imprint of meaninglessness.'[11] In this way Weber made sociology aware of its own reflexive need to embed in a community of purpose whose institution is as much a charismatic hope as a goal of rationality.

Weber's conclusions, though they do not satisfy Marcuse's con-

9. Edmund Husserl, *The Crisis of European Sciences and Transcendental Phenomenology, An Introduction to Phenomenological Philosophy*, trans. David Carr, Evanston: Northwestern University Press, 1970.

10. Max Weber, 'Science as a Vocation', *From Max Weber*, Essays in Sociology, translated, edited, and with an Introduction by H. Gerth and C. Wright Mills, New York: Oxford University Press, 1958, p. 138.

11. ibid., p. 140.

ception of critical theory, are in striking contrast with the Parsonian interpretation of Weber which serves to make sociological knowledge an irony of functionalist practice. That is to say, the Parsonian version of sociological knowledge invents a utopia of social system and pattern variable action congruence in order to embed its own instrumentalist rationality as a precipitate of utilitarian culture. Whether it starts from Hobbes's nasty vision or from Luther's excremental vision, Parsonian sociology reduces the problem of its own reflexivity to the anodyne of instrumental knowledge, hoping thereby to substitute affluence for the glory of love's risen body. While we cannot dwell upon Parsonian sociology in any detail, it may not be amiss, in view of its adoption into political science, to comment that Parsons' latest generalization of the instrumentalist vision based upon the master metaphor of money as the most generalized means of exchange and efficacy, only serves to further mystify the grounds of political order by neglecting the ways in which the behaviour of money is nothing else than the algebra of the system of stratification and exploitation for which Parsons pretends to account. In short, and in contrast with the critics of Parsonian ideology, I would argue that it is Parsons' conception of theorizing as an activity grounded in the means-end schema which generates his intrinsic notions of social structure and personality as a functionalist utopia of congruent orders of individual and collective reality.[12] Yet the unconscious merit of Parsons' classical study of the corpus of utilitarian social science knowledge[13] is to have focused on the ambivalence of the instrumental and ritual values of human knowledge, subordinated to the *a priori* of individual interest.

I have turned my argument towards the topic of sociological reflexivity not for the purpose of engaging in criticism as it is conventionally understood, but for the purpose of coming to terms

12. See Chapter 13. ('The Hobbesian Problem in Marx and Parsons', in John O'Neill, op. cit. *Editor's note*)
13. Talcott Parsons, *The Structure of Social Action*, A Study in Social Theory with Special Reference to a Group of Recent European Writers, New York: The Free Press of Glencoe, 1964.

with the very phenomenon of sociological reflexivity, namely, *how it is that we can show the limits of sociology and still be engaged in authentic sociological theorizing*. This is the question that I began with when I set myself the task of asking whether phenomenology could be critically aware of its own limits and its implicit ties with history and politics. I shall now pursue this topic in Husserl's later writings, acknowledging that my reading of them is a continuation of an earlier reading by Merleau-Ponty. More concretely, my reading of Husserl and Merleau-Ponty is essentially a borrowing from them both, continuous with everything else we borrow in life. For, indeed, as Merleau-Ponty remarks, 'I borrow myself from others; I create others from my own thoughts. This is no failure to perceive others; it is the perception of others.'

We need a conception of the reflexive grounds of social science knowledge which will be grounded in the facts of institutional life and yet remain equally true to the claims of science and poetry, or to what is general as well as what is unique in our experience. Reflecting upon the crisis of the European sciences, Husserl remarked that '*the dream is over*' of there ever being an apodictic or rigorous science of philosophy. Some have thought that it is only those who set such goals for philosophy who are likely to turn to philosophical disbelief and despair. In such circumstances, it is the task of phenomenological philosophy to take its historical bearings, to acknowledge its debts to the life-world which it presupposes so long as there is no total threat to civilization, but which must then concern it.

The philosopher, says Husserl, 'takes something from history'. But history is not a warehouse, or a rummage heap from which we can take 'things', because facts, documents, philosophical, and literary works are not palpably before us, apart from our own indwelling and interpretations. Furthermore, we do not, strictly speaking, transmit or hand down a scientific, literary, or historical tradition. We may be Renaissance historians without having read or researched every aspect of the Renaissance, just as we may be Platonists without a concern for every word of Plato, so that we might as well speak of a 'poetic transmission' which owes as much to us as to fact. And yet none of this need imperil the teleology of knowledge, of science, history, or philosophy.

Let us be more precise. I know, of course, what I am striving for under the title of philosophy, as the goal and field of my work. And yet I do not know. What autonomous thinker has ever been satisfied with this, his 'knowledge'? For what autonomous thinker, in his philosophizing life, has 'philosophy' ever ceased to be an enigma? Everyone has the sense of philosophy's end, to whose realization his life is devoted; everyone has certain formulae, expressed in definitions; but only secondary thinkers who in truth should not be called philosophers, are consoled by their definitions, beating to death with their word-concepts the problematic *telos* of philosophizing. In that obscure 'knowledge', and in the word-concepts of the formulae, the historical is concealed; it is, according to its own proper sense, the spiritual inheritance of him who philosophizes; and in the same way, obviously, he understands the others in whose company, in critical friendship and enmity, he philosophizes. And in philosophizing he is also in company with himself as he earlier understood and did philosophy; and he knows that, in the process, historical tradition, as he understood it and used it, entered into him in a motivating way and as a spiritual sediment. His historical picture, in part made by himself and in part taken over, his 'poetic invention of the history of philosophy', has not and does not remain fixed – that he knows; and yet every 'invention' serves him, and can serve him in understanding himself and his aim, and his own aim in relation to that of others and their 'inventions', their aims, and finally what it is that is common to all, which makes philosophy 'as such' as a unitary *telos* and makes the systems attempts at its fulfilment for us all, for us (who are) at the same time in company with the philosophers of the past (in the various ways we have been able to invent them for ourselves).[14]

Merleau-Ponty remarks how well Husserl's term *Stiftung*, foundation or establishment, captures the fecundity of cultural creations by which they endure into our present and open a field of inquiry to which they are continuously relevant.

It is thus that the world as soon as he has seen it, his first attempts at painting, and the whole past of painting all deliver up a *tradition* to the painter – *that is,* Husserl remarks *the power to forget origins* and to

14. *The Crisis of European Sciences and Transcendental Phenomenology*, pp. 394–5.

give to the past not a survival, which is the hypocritical form of forgetfulness, but a new life, which is the noble form of memory.[15]

Through language, art and writing, what was only an ideal meaning in the mind of an individual achieves an objective and public status, enters a community of thinkers, which is the presupposition of truth. Thus we witness the event of that circuit of reflection in which what was first recognized as neither local nor temporal 'according to the meaning of its being', comes to rest upon the locality and temporality of speech, which belongs neither to the objective world nor the world of ideas.

Ideal existence is based upon the document, not, of course, as a physical object, or even as the vehicle of one-to-one significations assigned to it by the language in which it is written, but upon the document in so far as, again by an 'intentional transgression', it solicits and brings together all lives in pursuit of knowledge – and as such establishes and re-establishes a 'Logos' of the cultural world.[16]

We need, then, a conception of the auspices of philosophical reflexivity that is consistent with 'poetic invention' (*Dichtung*), as well as with the community in which we philosophize. Such a notion may be present to us in the concept of *reflexivity as institution* rather than as transcendental constitution. By means of the notion of institution we may furnish a conception of reflexivity which, instead of resting upon a transcendental subjectivity, is given in a field of presence and coexistence which situates reflexivity and truth as sedimentation and search. We must think of reflexivity as tied to the textual structures of temporality and situation through which subjectivity and objectivity are constituted as the intentional unity and style of the world.[17] 'Thus what we understand by the concept of institution are those events in an experience which endow it with durable dimensions, in relation to which a whole series of other experiences will acquire meaning, will form an intelligible series or a history – or again those events

15. M. Merleau-Ponty, *Signs*, trans. Richard C. McCleary, Evanston: Northwestern University Press, 1964, p. 59.

16. ibid., pp. 96–7.

17. See Chapter 7. ('Situation, Action and Language', in John O'Neill, op. cit. *Editor's note*)

which sediment in me a meaning, not just as survivals or residues, but as the invitation to a sequel, the necessity of a future.'[18] The institution of reflexivity is founded upon a series of exchanges between subjectivity and situation in which the polarities of means and ends or question and answer are continuously established and renewed, no less than the institution of ideas, truth, and culture. Reflexivity, therefore, is not an *a priori*, but a task which we take up in order to achieve self-improvization, as well as the acquisition of a tradition or style of thought which is the recovery of an original auspices opened in the past. To this we bring a living expression, or the inauguration of a world and the outline of a future, which is nothing else than ourselves, 'borne only by the caryatid of our efforts, which converge by the sole fact that they are efforts to express'.[19]

The notion of *critique* which we may derive from the concept of reflexivity as institution is one which is grounded in a contextual environment which lies open horizontally to the corpus of social science knowledges rather than through any transcendental reflection. This notion of critique is the result of abandoning Husserl's attempt to construct an eidetic of any possible corpus of knowledge as the correlative of a universal and timeless constituting reflexivity and the problems it raises for intersubjectivity, rationality, and philosophy itself. The corpus of the historical and social sciences is not, properly speaking, constituted through any object or any act of reflection. It arises from a continual production or verification (*reprise*) which each individual undertakes according to his situation and times. Thus each one's work must be continually reviewed to unearth its own auspices sedimented in the archaeology of human science. This is not a simplistic argument for eternal starts, any more than a crude rejection of the accumulation of human knowledge. It is rather an attempt to interpret the *rhetorical* nature of the appeal of knowledge and criticism through which tradition and rebellion are made.

'Reading' a text is inevitably an essay in rhetoric, that is to say

18. M. Merleau-Ponty, *Themes from the Lectures at the Collège de France 1952–1960*, trans. John O'Neill, Evanston: Northwestern University Press, 1970, pp. 40–41.
19. *Signs*, p. 69.

if we follow Aristotle, leaving aside Plato's insistence on the mastery of truth, it requires a profound knowledge or care for the souls one seeks to persuade. This concern to suit one's speech or argument to the other person's soul is the anthropological ground of all talk, argument, and criticism. It is at the heart of what is serious in our concern to discuss with one another, to correct and persuade. It is for this reason that we elaborate upon one another's speech and thought. And we never argue so fiercely as between ourselves, because what is at stake is the utopian connection between truth, justice, and beauty. We sense implicitly the style of the world from a manner of speaking and thinking, so that we are drawn by its resonance, or else confused and repulsed. The error in modern communication and information theory is that it overlooks the rhetorical vehicle of speech, reading and writing. It does this because in turn it lacks any conception of the intention to institute solidarity and a just social order in the relations between the partners to human speech.

What emerges from these examples is that the universality and truth aimed at by theoretical consciousness is not an intrinsic property of the idea. It is an acquisition continuously established and re-established in a community and tradition of knowledge called for and responded to by individuals in specific historical situations. Understood in this way, history is the call of one thought to another, because each individual's work or action is created across the path of self and others towards a *public* which it elicits rather than serves.[20] That is to say, history is the field which individual effort requires in order to become one with the community it seeks to build so that, where it is successful, its invention appears always to have been necessary. Individual action, then, is the invention of history, because it is shaped in a present which previously was not just a void waiting to be determined by the word or deed, but a tissue of calling and response which is the life of no one and everyone. Every one of life's actions, in so far as it invokes its truth, lives in the expectation of an historical inscription, a judgement not of its intention or consequences but of its fecundity, which is the relevance of its 'story' to the present.

20. 'Materials for a Theory of History', in *Themes from the Lectures at the Collège de France*, pp. 27–38.

True history thus gets its life entirely from us. It is in our present that it gets the force to refer everything else to the present. The other whom I respect gets his life from me as I get mine from him. A philosophy of history does not take away any of my rights or initiatives. It simply adds to my obligations as a solitary person the obligation to understand situations other than my own and to create a path between my life and that of others, that is, express myself.[21]

The object of human knowledge is not, strictly speaking, an object; it is the institution within human space and historical time of artefacts, tools, services, institutions which are depositaries of what men before us have thought, needed, and valued. Cultural objects, in this sense, are the vestiges of embodied beings who live in society and communicate with one another as embodied minds.[22] It is such human beings who have opened up for us the hearth of culture and institutions, which it is our first duty to tender. And this we do, not as mere drudgery, but as the cultivation of our own growth, the basis for our departures and the source to which we return for fresh inspiration. Human institutions are the ground of our common and individual achievements, enriching us and impoverishing us with a legacy which was never quite intended for us and yet never totally rejected by us, even when we refuse it. This human legacy is never fully ours until we learn to alter it through our own inventions, our personal style.

Human experience and vision accumulates only in the circle of social relations and institutions, which enlarge and deepen the sense of our sentiments, deeds and works through the symbiosis of solidarity and personality. Human action is essentially the unfolding of a cultural space and its historical dimensions, so that in a strict sense we never accomplish anything except as a collective and historical project. For the individual action involves, therefore, a constant dialogue with others, a recovery of the past and the projection of breaks which are never entirely successful. But this is not a source of irremediable alienation; it is the feature of our experience which calls for its completion through a collec-

21. *Signs*, p. 75.
22. John O'Neill, *Perception, Expression and History*; The Social Phenomenology of Maurice Merleau-Ponty, Evanston: Northwestern University Press, 1970.

tivity, with a history that knows a tradition as well as a future. Such a collectivity or institution is never wholly reified; it is made and unmade, with a particular grain in each of us who lives and alters what he draws upon for his life. And this is a feature not only of human institutions, but of our thoughts, our sentiments and, above all, of human talk. Understood in this way, human institutions are the sole means that we have of keeping faith with one another, while being true to ourselves.

The ultimate feature of the phenomenological institution of reflexivity is that it grounds critique in membership and tradition. Thus the critic's auspices are the same as those of anyone working in a community of language, work and politics. In the critical act there is a simultaneity of authorship and authenticity which is the declaration of membership in a continuing philosophical, literary, or scientific community. The critic does not alienate himself from his community, which would be the consequence of an absolute knowledge and ultimate nihilism. This is not to say that the critic is not rebellious; it is to remark upon the consequences of solitude and solidarity as the starting points of criticism.

Criticism in our sense is very close to Camus' conception of rebellion and order under the sun. Criticism reflects an aspiration to order under the auspices of the things that are present and of our fellow men, under a limit which is reflexively the recognition of solidarity and a rule of memory as an antidote to revolutionary absurdity.

At this meridian of thought, the rebel thus rejects divinity in order to share in the struggles and destiny of all men. We shall choose Ithaca, the faithful land, frugal and audacious thought, lucid action, and the generosity of the man who understands. In the light, the earth remains our first and our last love. Our brothers are breathing under the same sky as we; justice is a living thing. Now is born that strange joy which helps one live and die, and which we shall never again postpone to a later time. On the sorrowing earth it is the unresting thorn, the bitter brew, the harsh wind off the sea, the old and the new dawn. With this joy, through long struggle, we shall remake the soul of our time, and a Europe which will exclude nothing. Not even that phantom Nietzsche, who for twelve years after his downfall was continually invoked by the

West as the blasted image of its loftiest knowledge and its nihilism; nor the prophet of justice without mercy who lies, by mistake, in the unbelievers' pit at Highgate Cemetery; nor the deified mummy of the man of action in his glass coffin; nor any part of what the intelligence and energy of Europe have ceaselessly furnished to the pride of a contemptible period. All may indeed live again, side by side with the martyrs of 1905, but on condition that it is understood that they correct one another, and that a limit, under the sun, shall curb them all. Each tells the other that he is not God; this is the end of romanticism. At this moment, when each of us must fit an arrow to his bow and enter the lists anew, to reconquer, within history and in spite of it, that which he owns already, the thin yield of his fields, the brief love of this earth, at this moment when at last a man is born, it is time to forsake our age and its adolescent furies. The bow bends; the wood complains. At the moment of supreme tension, there will leap into flight an unswerving arrow, a shaft that is inflexible and free.[23]

I have tried, then, to outline a notion of criticism as a mode of theoretical life which is reflexively tied to the institutions of philosophy, art and the sciences. The heart of this conception is its adherence to the presence of the things around us and of our fellow men in recognition of the institutional life which they share through the work of language, labour and politics. It is a notion of critical theorizing whose auspices lie nowhere else than in the community of knowledge and value which are its claim to any contribution. The voice of such criticism is neither fanatical nor cynical, although it is in no way a simple affirmation of the claims of the community and tradition in which it belongs. What I have in mind is a conception of criticism which does not exploit the differences between the way things are and how they might be but rather leaves itself open to the experience of their reversal, to the care for what is sublime as well as of what is desperate in the human condition and the times through which it passes.

For the reasons outlined above we cannot accept the paradigmatic value of the psychoanalytic conversation, at least in so far as the passive objectivity of the analyst is false to the dialogic search in which no member of the language community is abso-

23. Albert Camus, *The Rebel*, An Essay on Man in Revolt, trans. Anthony Bower, New York: Vintage Books, 1956, p. 306.

John O'Neill 215

lutely privileged, and is therefore necessarily historical rather than clinical.[24] Moreover, we need to remember that human speech has no absolute goal of rational clarification, of disbelief, and rejection of prejudice. Human speech, dialogue, and conversation seeks just as well acceptance, or the understanding of what was already our belief, our native prejudice. This is the circle of language in which we dwell – the hermeneutic circle – which is not broken even when all come to understand our motives, our past experience. For there is nothing beyond death which alters what we have lived, although our understanding may return it to the silence of our being. There is, in other words, a naïve dogmatism underlying the liberal social science conception of understanding which still draws upon the rationalist tradition of Enlightenment unmasking. But there is nothing behind the face of the man who speaks, beyond what else he has to say or how he keeps his silence. We find meaning between words and sentences and between men; there is nothing either in the back of this or beyond it.

24. Habermas has himself provided for this conclusion in his essay 'Toward a Theory of Communicative Competence', in *Recent Sociology No. 2*, Patterns of Communicative Behaviour, ed. Hans Peter Dreitzel, New York: Macmillan, 1970.

11 Thomas Luckmann

Philosophy, Social Sciences and Everyday Life*

T. Luckmann, 'Philosophy, Sciences and Everyday Life' in *Phenomenology and the Social Sciences*, ed. M. Natanson, Evanston: Northwestern University Press, 1973, pp. 143–85.

At the end of an analysis of the extrascientific presuppositions that went into the making of modern physical science, Edwin A. Burtt wrote almost half a century ago: 'An adequate cosmology will only begin to be written when an adequate philosophy of the mind has appeared. . .'[1] This was the conclusion to which Burtt was led after a survey of historical evidence on the formation of scientific thought during the period from Copernicus to Newton. For a foundation of scientific knowledge more is required than a science that analyses 'nature' and its structure. We have such a science and its achievements are well known. What is required is also more than a science that analyses man as part of nature. We have such a science as this, too, and its results, considerable even today, promise to become more impressive in the future. But what is required in addition is a science that analyses man as that peculiar part of nature that is not only capable of understanding 'nature' but also of understanding itself as part of it. We do have sciences that are beginning to grapple with this peculiarity of man's position in nature, but it must be conceded that our knowledge here is uncertain and there is much confusion about the methods appropriate to such sciences. And, finally, what is required is a philosophy that provides clear and reliable methods of reflection on the nature of the evidence on which these various sciences are founded, *and* on the nature of the evidence on which such a process of reflection itself can be firmly based. Burtt postulates

* Abbreviated by the author.

1. Edwin Arthur Burtt, *The Metaphysical Foundations of Modern Physical Science*, 1924; revised ed., Garden City, N.Y.: Doubleday, n.d. [1932], p. 324.

the need for a critical theory of knowledge, 'critical' to be understood as an extension of the Kantian sense of that word. Obviously, this need has not been fully met to this day, but it is my conviction that under certain conditions phenomenology, and especially the programme and the achievements of Husserl's last work, can satisfy it.[2]

Husserl saw that modern science, having separated itself from philosophy, no longer provided answers to certain elementary questions that men have asked at all times. He also saw that the empiricist tradition in modern philosophy and modern science was beginning to formulate as a problem something that to him too was a problematic consequence of the separation of science and philosophy, i.e. the naïve self-sufficiency of science and its inability to examine its own presuppositions. But Husserl was convinced that this tradition was not radical enough in its attempt to clarify the foundations of science, and that it would not be able to resolve the 'crisis' of modern science, its divorce from basic questions of human life.[3]

There is an urgent need, then, for philosophical clarification of the human activities in which cosmologies originate – including that apparently indubitable cosmology that is associated in the popular mind with modern physical science. Like its mythological and theological predecessors, this scientific variant of cosmology

2. Edmund Husserl, *Die Krisis der europäischen Wissenschaften und die transzendentale Phänomenologie*, The Hague: Nijhoff, 1962; English trans. David Carr, *The Crisis of European Sciences and Transcendental Phenomenology*, Evanston: Northwestern University Press, 1970; hereafter cited as *Crisis*.

3. 'In this perspective empiricism seems to contain a tendency to the scientific discovery of the life-world which is familiar to everyday experience and yet unknown to science ... Here it must suffice to note that the achievements of the mathematical sciences, and more generally, of all sciences committed to a physicalist approach necessarily became problematic to empiricism as it directed its attention to the concretely experienced, historically relevant world which is the topic (human society, culture) of scientific investigation in certain scholarly traditions in the humanities. The demand for a clarification of the theoretical activities which produce the constructs of science, a clarification in the context of and in relation to the life-world, was evidently present in this situation. Such a clarification was to establish the meaning and the "scope" of science' (*Crisis* (German ed.), p. 449; my translation).

is self-sufficient, i.e. it claims to provide a satisfactory account of its own foundations. It thus evidently believes that it has already answered the need stated by Burtt, if indeed it is at all inclined to admit the legitimacy of that need. But it is precisely this naïve, metaphysically motivated self-sufficiency that cannot stand up to critical philosophical examination, any more than could its mythological and theological predecessors. No critical theory of science can accept the assumption that the scientific cosmology has found the Archimedean point from which both an understanding of the universe *and* an understanding of this understanding can be reached in one single move. And, in contrast to mythological and theological cosmologies, the modern, self-sufficient scientific cosmology has not even succeeded in providing plausible answers to the human quest for a subjectively meaningful location of the self in the universe.[4]

We are, of course, certain of the productivity of scientific methods, and we cannot doubt that useful knowledge has accumulated in various sciences. And yet we remain uncertain of the basis of such knowledge, and doubts linger on as to the extent to which scientific methods are capable of reaching the realities of human life. To put it simply, each science taken singly is impressive; all sciences put together make for a sorry cosmology. It is no solution at all to the problem to declare cosmological questions meaningless and to reduce science to the status of a cognitive technology. This merely leaves the field to the irrational ideologies of scientism and antiscientism. The philosophy of science has wider obligations than those to which, in recent times, it thought it could limit itself as a result of the technical specialization of the sciences and the academic compartmentalization of philosophy.

4. In an appraisal of Husserl's view of science, Herman Lübbe puts it succinctly: 'In its modern form European science for the first time no longer fulfils its old function to provide man with a reasonable grasp and reasoned consciousness of his existence in the whole of being. To the contrary, it successively dissolved this consciousness. It thereby released man to metaphysical disorientation. In a manner of speaking it threw the individual subject back upon himself and his isolated certainty of himself' ('Husserl und die europäische Krise', *Kant-Studien*, XLIX, 1957–58, 228; my translation).

This is not to denigrate the usefulness of the contributions that have issued from recent philosophy of science within its self-imposed 'professional' limits. The reconstructed logic of science, as Abraham Kaplan aptly calls it,[5] tends to an idealization of the complex structure of scientific knowledge. But reconstructions may effectively influence constructions: it is the quality of the reconstruction, not the fact that it is reconstructed, that is important. If the reconstructed logic stands in a sensible relation to what Kaplan calls the logic-in-use, and to what Norwood R. Hanson describes as the logic of theory-finding as opposed to the logic of theory-using,[6] it can help to reveal the syntax by which statements in the sciences are constructed and aid in the clarification of the canons by which the validity of conclusions is evaluated. Having overcome its early inclination to ignore the processes of concrete scientific inquiry, the philosophy of science may contribute to the formulation of rigorous methodologies for science. It may help in the description of the theoretical activities that constitute science as currently carried on. But these contributions form only one part of its legitimate task.

The philosophy of science must not stop short of an investigation of those activities that are the basis for theory of any kind, including scientific theory. These are the activities that it is nowadays fashionable to call *praxis*, referring to the full range of human conscious activities in the intersubjective and historical world of everyday life. Only a clarification of this universal basis of theory can hope to show the significance of scientific knowledge for human life and establish its legitimate place among other forms of knowledge. Karl Popper describes clearly the common theoretical interest of science and philosophy:

There is at least one problem in which all thinking men are interested. It is the problem of cosmology: *the problem of understanding the world – including ourselves, and our knowledge, as part of the world.* All science

5. Abraham Kaplan, *The Conduct of Inquiry*, San Francisco: Chandler, 1964.
6. Norwood Russell Hanson, *Patterns of Discovery*, Cambridge University Press, 1958.

is cosmology, I believe, and for me the interest of philosophy as well as of science lies solely in the contribution which they have made to it.[7]

The task of the philosophy of science goes far beyond the immediate concerns of the methodologies of the physical sciences. It consists in giving a convincing account of the relation of science to theoretical activities in general, and of the relation of these activities to common sense and everyday life. It will not do to refer this task to an empirical discipline – such as the psychology of cognition, or even the sociology of knowledge – for *final* adjudication. Such a procedure leads to an obviously vicious circle.

An attempt to avoid that circle involves the search for a controlled, independent perspective on both science and common sense. The question about the foundations of science, its place among other forms of knowledge, and their common origin in everyday life is, first of all, a question about an appropriate method of answering questions of that kind. Clearly, the method must be at least as reasonable and subject to control as the methods of scientific reasoning – but it must also be reflexive and give an account of its own presuppositions. Much depends on the initial view of the problem. One can easily relapse into the circularity of scientific rationalism instead of retaining the controlled reflexivity of a critical theory of knowledge. This danger, I think, is what Burtt had in mind in juxtaposing a philosophy of the mind to a cosmology.

Husserl made what appears in retrospect as a strategic decision: not to accept the claim of modern science to be the ultimate form of human knowledge. In three of his major works, one early and two belonging to a later phase of his thought, Husserl investigated the foundations of formal logic.[8] By the method, first, of pheno-

7. Karl R. Popper, *The Logic of Scientific Discovery*, New York: Basic Books, 1959, p. 15 (italics mine).

8. *Logische Untersuchungen*, 1900; Tübingen: Niemeyer, 1968; English translation by J. N. Findlay, *Logical Investigations*, New York: Humanities, 1970; *Formale und transzendentale Logik*, Halle: Niemeyer, 1929; English translation by Dorion Cairns, *Formal and Transcendental Logic*, The Hague: Nijhoff, 1969; *Erfahrung und Urteil*, 1938; 2nd ed., Hamburg:

menological psychology and later of transcendental phenomenology, he traced the origins of logical and mathematical thinking
to the activities of consciousness in what he came to call the
Lebenswelt, that is, the pretheoretical and theoretical levels of the
world of everyday life. But it is his last work, the *Crisis*, which
initiated a new phase of philosophical reflection on science. In it
he effectively demolished the 'ultimacy' pretensions of the modern scientific cosmology. For superficial if not silly reasons, and
often from sheer ignorance, this has been taken as an 'attack' on
science.[9] It should not be necessary to stress that Husserl does
not question the validity of science – as far as it goes. The question remains, how far *does* it go?[10]

It is significant that in answering this question Husserl immediately confronts the problem of method. In this respect, at
least, his importance equals that of Descartes and Kant. If Husserl initiated a new phase in philosophy and in the philosophy of
science, it is as much by having developed a method for determining the validity of science as by having destroyed the 'ultimacy' pretensions of the scientific cosmology. The elementary
phenomenological epoché, the various reductions, eidetic varia-

Claassen and Goverts, 1948; English translation by Spencer Churchill and
Karl Ameriks, *Experience and Judgment*, Evanston: Northwestern University Press, 1973.

9. Some years ago Maurice Natanson warned against the misappropria-
tions and misrepresentations of phenomenology: 'In particular, the legend
of the *Lebenswelt* lends itself or has been made to lend itself to a critique of
rationalism and natural science which is, I think, not only mistaken but
inimical to phenomenology' ('The *Lebenswelt*', *Review of Existential
Psychology and Psychiatry*, IV, spring, 1964, 134). Things have taken a turn
for the worse in the meantime.

10. Aron Gurwitsch puts it concisely: '*It is the historical significance of
Husserl's Galileo analysis to challenge and even to abandon the acceptance of
science as an ultimate fact and rather to see in it a problem.* Husserl is far
from questioning the technical, or, more precisely, the intrinsic validity of
science, and nothing could have been further from his mind than dismissing
it in any sense. What is in question is not science itself, nor any particular
scientific theory, but the interpretation of science' ('Comments' on Herbert
Marcuse, 'On Science and Phenomenology', *Boston Studies in the Philosophy
of Science*, Vol. II: *In Honor of Philipp Frank*, ed. Robert S. Cohen and
Marx M. Wartofsky, New York: Humanities Press, 1965, p. 294; italics
original).

tion, and so on, combine in accounting or being able in principle to account for the presuppositions of phenomenological psychology and transcendental phenomenology – which, in turn, have clarified or are capable of clarifying the constitutive structures of conscious activities upon which everyday life as well as science is founded.[11] In short, Husserl developed a method of philosophical analysis that is rationally controlled *and* reflexive. The method permits an approach to the question 'How far *does* science go?' that does not end in a vicious circle.

It is perhaps more obvious to this generation than it was to its predecessors that this question goes far beyond the boundaries of a single academic discipline. It is a fundamental philosophical question for modern man. In an age when science – which, after all, *is* a human activity – is either deified or satanized, it is also an eminently political question. Far from being destructive of science, Husserl's demolition of the 'ultimacy' claim of the scientific cosmology and his attempt to establish firm foundations for science provide a sound basis for determining its human significance.

The Cosmological Paradigm in Social Science

Both the general problem, i.e. the cosmological validity of science, and the question about the proper way to approach this problem are particularly urgent when 'cosmology' is taken to refer not only to a systematic explication of the physical universe, but also to a theoretical account of the social world. The reasons why

11. I know of no résumé of the methods of phenomenological analysis that could adequately substitute for the study of Husserl's work. Dorion Cairns's systematic presentation of Husserl, which served as a source of instruction to a generation of students, has not yet found its way into print. Discussions of Husserl in the work of Alfred Schutz, Aron Gurwitsch, and other first-generation phenomenologists were rarely expository. Among the numerous brief introductions, one that is particularly clear and useful is Maurice Natanson's 'Phenomenology: A Viewing', in his *Literature, Philosophy, and the Social Sciences*, The Hague: Nijhoff, 1962; see also Herbert Spiegelberg, 'The Essentials of Phenomenological Method', in *The Phenomenological Movement: A Historical Introduction*, 2nd ed., The Hague: Nijhoff, 1965, II, 655–701.

this should be so are obvious, at least in a general way. They have been taken up under different headings in what is by now a voluminous literature.[12] Nevertheless they will bear some discussion from the point of view I am taking here.

To begin with, one should register profound wonder that anyone should ever have wanted to exclude the social world from the theoretical concern of cosmology. The world of man *was* included in mythological and theological cosmologies, as a matter of course *and* as a matter of overwhelming interest, during most of the history of human thought. This changed in Western thinking after Galileo. Since his time, some philosophers and scientists have excluded the reality of human activities from cosmology. It is my contention that they do so for reasons that are not subjected to critical reflection. The distinction between a 'physical universe' and other domains of reality, e.g. a 'social world', is derived from the metaphysical presuppositions that went into the making of the modern scientific cosmology. It must therefore not be exempt from critical examination. The division of reality into a physical world and a world of human affairs occurred as part of a global process of 'rationalization'. It was a milestone in the depersonalization of mythological views of the world, a process described by Max Weber as *Entzauberung*.

This division of reality stands at the end of concatenated theological, philosophical and scientific traditions, and at the beginning of a historical movement of thought that led to the situation characterized by Husserl as the 'crisis' of modern science. The motives for this division had their source in the theological cosmology of the Middle Ages. To say that man attains a divine level of knowledge by virtue of mathematics was not merely a *façon de parler* for Galileo. Nor did his opponents underestimate the possibilities inherent in his view. In a universe whose reality is guaranteed by its mathematical structure, man as well as God becomes problematic in a way that was entirely alien to the older

12. Two examples of the literature I have in mind here are the hundreds of books and, probably, thousands of articles on historicism and on the so-called value freedom of social science. For a good overview of the latter, see Hans Albert and Ernst Topitsch, eds., *Werturteilsfreiheit*, Darmstadt: Wissenschaftliche Buchgesellschaft, 1971.

cosmologies, however much they may have differed among themselves in other respects. In the new vision of reality man requires *ad hoc* explanations just as much as God.

The ontological and epistemological sources (to the extent that it is possible to isolate these more technically philosophical components from the general cultural background) that fed into the stream of the new cosmology can be traced to shifting patterns of influence of opposing philosophical traditions; in Galileo, Platonism won over Aristotelianism.[13] However, reference to the complex origins of these perspectives tells only part of the story; the other part consists of the unique blending of these perspectives into a new vision of the universe. This new vision became clear with Copernicus, who postulated the mathematical structure of the universe. Against the opposition of traditional empiricist philosophy, this postulate was transformed into an article of belief which is taken for granted in the modern cosmology. It did not become entirely immune from critical examination, but philosophical questioning generally proceeded along the innocuous line that the postulate should, perhaps, not be given an ontological but 'merely' an epistemological interpretation.

The cosmological plausibility of this view was decisively strengthened when it was combined with Galileo's doctrine of primary and secondary qualities, and still later, with Newtonian mechanics. Galileo's idea of primary and secondary qualities is expressed in his famous statement that 'Whoever wants to read a book, must know the language in which that book is written. Nature is a book and the characters in which it is written are triangles, circles and squares.'[14] It can be paraphrased less elegantly as follows: Only the primary qualities can be expressed exactly, i.e. mathematically; the real, objective, absolute reality consists of primary qualities; only what can be expressed mathematically is truly, objectively, absolutely real. This is not much of a syllogism and it probably was never formulated in quite that

13. Alexandre Koyré, 'Galileo and Plato', in *Roots of Scientific Thought*, ed. Philip Wiener and Aaron Noland, New York: Basic Books, 1957, pp. 147–75.

14. Quoted in Gurwitsch, 'Comments', p. 300 (see Galileo Galilei, *Il Saggiatore*, Florence: Edizione Nazionale, 1965, VI, 232).

manner. It is an example of what C.S. Peirce analysed as abductive reasoning.[15] According to Peirce, abduction is a form of reasoning which guides many common-sense procedures and is also an important strategy of theory-finding in science. In this particular instance abductive reasoning on a grand scale seems to have been involved in the historical construction of a cosmology.

The Copernican postulate of the mathematical structure of reality, the Galilean doctrine of primary and secondary qualities, and the notions of causality generally associated with Newtonian mechanics (Newton's own strong strain of prudent empiricism notwithstanding) combined to produce a new view of reality whose persuasiveness was probably based as much on its extraordinary aesthetic appeal as on its continuous popular verification in the successes of applied science and technology. As is the nature of systematically articulated views of the world, the cosmology was expansionistic within science and imperialistic outside of it. New areas that were to be investigated scientifically were subordinated to the new cosmology.[16]

In contradistinction to older cosmologies, the expansionism of the new scientific cosmology was checked, at first, by the problem of fitting man into its scheme. The conception of man was more resistant to change than was the conception of the universe. As long as man was cut from the pattern of the old cosmology, he could not be fitted into the tight clothes of the new. Descartes did not hesitate to deliver the human body (and the poor beasties) to the icy winds blowing in the new universe. But not, alas, the human soul.[17]

15. C. S. Peirce used the terms 'hypothesis', 'abduction', and 'retroduction' to describe the process of abductive reasoning. See his *Collected Papers*, 8 Vols., Vols. I–VI, ed. Charles Hartshorne and Paul Weiss, Cambridge, Mass.: Harvard University Press, 1931–5, especially II, 372–88; V, 112–31; and VI, 311–32. For abduction as an interactional phenomenon, see Richard Grathoff, *The Structure of Social Inconsistencies*, The Hague: Nijhoff, 1970, especially pp. 40–75.

16. 'The conviction that sooner or later all science is mechanics dies hard: for three centuries science has been dominated by notions of inertia, impact and resultant velocities. This has affected our understanding of causation' (Hanson, *Patterns of Discovery*, p. 65).

17. A very special act is required to account for the human soul: 'I had described after this the rational soul and shown that it could not be in any

For some time the cosmological situation was thus character-ized by uncertainty, inconsistency and incipient implausibility. What was traditionally connected as part of one comprehensive reality was split asunder. Radically different styles of thought which were completely incompatible with one another were pres-cribed for the knowledge of man (and God) and for the knowledge of the rest of the universe. This split had been prepared for a long time. Judaism, a major step in the *Entzauberung* of the mytho-logical universe, had already singled out man, the member of the elect tribe, as standing in a special compact with God.[18] But the Thomistic reconciliation of Christianity with Greek philosophy successfully refitted man into the over-all scheme of creation. Meanwhile, beneath the official doctrines the world view of the folk tradition had always retained the essential structure of the old mythologies. The separation of man from the universe in the newly emerging cosmology, on the other hand, gave rise to a metaphysical disorientation that within a century or two had repercussions in the culture of all social classes.

In order to cope with this cosmological inconsistency, attempts were begun to justify the expulsion of Adam from the new cos-mology or to recast the conception of man so that he would fit into it smoothly. The attempts carry the trade-mark of abductive reasoning; they are neither inferences nor deductions but leaps from familiar premises to an unknown order of things that is made comprehensible by assimilation to the premises. Such move-ments are not entirely unlike leaps of faith. It is therefore not surprising that two contradictory ways of resolving this cosmo-logical inconsistency emerged in the course of time.

One solution runs as follows: Man is part of nature; nature consists of primary qualities; man is reducible to primary quali-ties; there is no world of human affairs for which scientific under-standing is not possible, in principle, through a reduction to the

way derived from the power of matter, like the other things of which I had spoken, but that it must be expressly created' (René Descartes, *Discourse on Method*, trans. Elizabeth S. Haldane and G. R. T. Ross, Cambridge University Press, 1931, I, 117–18).

18. See Max Weber, *Ancient Judaism*, trans. and ed. H. Gerth and D. Martindale, Glencoe: Free Press, 1952.

mathematical manifold of space and time. The leap to the other solution takes off from the other foot: Man is not reducible to primary qualities; the special origin of his soul – or the uniqueness of his experience – cannot be mathematized; man is not part of reality in the sense in which nature is real (this is one of the sources of the Cartesian difficulty); therefore there can be no science of man (except of course under the wholly subordinate aspect of man as a 'machine').

These 'conclusions' are at the heart of the methodological controversies of social science. It hardly needs to be added that these controversies are the social science variant of the general crisis of modern science. I shall not here ask to what extent phenomenology, by clarifying the origins of theoretical activities in the world of everyday life, provides a philosophical foundation for all science. I shall instead look closely at one important part of the wider question, the elementary problem of social science methodology. I hope I have already shown the historical context of the ideas that prevented the emergence of a social science which did not try to follow the precepts of the new cosmology. Copernicus, Galileo and Newton are *malgré eux* the main figures, not of social science, but of the methodology of modern social science. Their new cosmology severed social science from its ancestry.

The rapid growth of social science in the past quarter-century, the specialization of disciplines and the increasing technical sophistication of their methods, the attempts at extending paradigms across disciplinary boundaries and at constructing a unified theory, as well as the urgency of the social problems that can only be resolved – or so it is commonly thought – if social science reaches the 'maturity' of, and collaborates with, physical science and technology: all this may explain, and, perhaps, partly justify, the loss of memory that is widespread among contemporary social scientists. The long tradition of systematic reflection on human conduct in society is no longer alive. The historian will no doubt trace some contemporary theoretical paradigm by way of Marx and Hegel to a Gnostic source. In a playful mood, he may point to a similarity between some idea of Veblen's and a half-forgotten observation of Saint-Simon. A political scientist may appeal to hallowed ancestors in Aristotle, Pomponazzi, or Machiavelli. A linguist may make his reverence before Panini, a sociologist may bow to Montesquieu. But these ritual invocations are usually mere frills and ornaments in scholarship, whose viable intellectual sources are much more recent. To the average social scientist the idea of a specialized history of social science appears stranger than did the need for a professional history of physical science to the ordinary physicist of pre-Sartonian days; he sees himself as the practitioner of a science that is in its infancy. Social science as we know it today is a child of Modernity writ large. It traces its descent into the nineteenth, perhaps as far back as the late eighteenth century. Beyond that begins the prehistory of social lore and isolated philosophical speculation.

I do not intend to examine here all the reasons for this peculiar partial amnesia. My reminder here has a different purpose. I want to stress an important consequence of the modernity-image that prevails in social science today. In sharp contrast to physical scientists, social scientists find that they cannot look backward to an autonomous tradition of philosophical reflection on their enterprise. The most promising candidates to membership in such a tradition, Vico, for example, are sweepingly disqualified as mere speculative 'metaphysicians'. The methodology of *social* science is a child of Galilean *physical* science.[19]

The 'Crisis' of Social Science

Most social scientists and almost all those philosophers who like to instruct social scientists on their business persist to this day in allowing the Copernican-Galilean-Newtonian view of the world to impose upon them the basic perspective in which they look on themselves and on the goals of their theoretical activities. They

19. I am using the term 'Galilean science' in the sense employed by Husserl in *Crisis*. Gurwitsch puts it as follows: 'Husserl, when he speaks of Galileo, does not mean the historical figure of that name who lived at a certain time, any more than by Galilean science he means the scientific work actually done by that historical figure. Rather Galilean science denotes the science inaugurated by Galileo. The name is used as a symbol for the historical development of modern science from, roughly speaking, 1600 to 1700, that is, the constitution of classical physics and even beyond' ('Comments', p. 292).

continue to take for granted the assumptions that the universe is deceptive yet fully knowable; that the appearances given to pre-scientific man, an inferior 'subjective' species easily befuddled by secondary qualities, hide a structure of 'objective' primary qualities; and that discovery of this ultimate reality depends on the supreme and autonomous form of knowledge, (numerical) mathematics. Despite Hume and others, they cling to an apparently ineradicable push-and-pull notion of causality to explain how it all hangs together. Revolutionary elements of seventeenth-century philosophy and science, abductively transformed into an eighteenth-century cosmology, almost routinely transmitted to the nineteenth century as a paradigm of physical science, thus form the unexamined background of methodological reflection in social science well into the second half of the twentieth century.

The same paradigm, however, gave rise to elementary methodological positions in social science which seem to their adherents to be irreconcilably opposed. It should be recalled that the early phases of the new cosmology were characterized by an elementary inconsistency which stimulated abductive reasoning along two main lines, depending on whether the inconsistency was to be eliminated or legitimated. The fundamental methodological controversy in social science is at best a continuation and at worst a petrification of these efforts.

On one side of the controversy man is subordinated to the newly found principles. He *cannot* be merely a bundle of secondary qualities, he *has* to be part of nature. And because 'nature' is the mathematical manifold representing the primary qualities of true reality, the hunt for the primary qualities of human existence is on. The Cartesian reservation on the human soul is given up and an intrinsically consistent man-machine solution replaces it. Through analogy with astronomy and mechanics, a plausible interpretation of anatomical and even physiological findings appears possible. But while the solution appears logical, the application of the logic to the study of human affairs leads to results whose absurdity is not diminished by the fact that they form part of the routine background of our thinking as social scientists. No matter how sophisticated the technical discussion of the logic and the logistics of science, the guiding vision of social science on this side of the methodological controversy is of a closed mechanical universe whose objective qualities are numerical.

Failure of the vision has resulted in two varieties of frustration. The inability to determine the primary qualities of man as a social, political and historical being by transforming him into a walking inventory of instincts or drives, into a *homo oeconomicus, homo sociologicus*, game-strategist, personality subsystem of an action system, and the like, inspires recurrent movements of cosmological reductionism. The man-machine becomes a symbol of hope to those proponents of reductionism who must try to secure unlimited extensions of credit for their programme. The other variety of frustration is that of the sensitive souls who, after an early training in some self-consciously 'scientific' discipline, develop ideological guilt feelings or aesthetic phobias about the language of cybernetics, systems analysis, simulation, or even old-fashioned structural-functionalism. They are easily converted to the soft-belly faction of the other side of the methodological controversy.

On the other side of the controversy, the absurdity of the consequences is seen and the applicability of the premises of the new cosmology to man denied. The premises are at the same time uncritically accepted for the rest of creation. Man therefore has to be removed as far as possible from nature, 'nature' being nothing but a measurable space-time manifold. Furthermore, the pushes and pulls of vulgar matter cannot apply to the 'historicity' and the 'uniqueness' of the human mind. Therefore there can be no social *science*, there can be only intuitive reconstructions of the unfolding of the mind. The idiographic narratives have to have a logic, a style different from the man-machine analysis of human affairs. The inapplicability of the new cosmology to human affairs provokes not merely a legitimate rejection of a numerical-mechanistic conception of social science, but an enduring inability to reexamine the problem of formalization and mathematization.

Neither party possesses a common programme. Neurath's claim that 'empiricists' and 'rationalists' have joined in a movement of 'unified science' whose platform could be called 'logical empiricism' or 'empirical rationalism' was exaggerated when it was originally made in 1938, and the movement has not become any more unified since then.[20] Since the seventeenth century, philosophers have presented a wide variety of positions on logic, scientific method, causality, inference and so on, which followed most of the imaginable combinations of Baconian empiricism and Cartesian rationalism. Nevertheless, logical empiricism serves to designate the modern philosophical centre of this party. In science, it combines with various philosophically more or less purified versions of 'positivism'. It is not *necessarily* reductionist, but it often is; it is not *necessarily* behaviourist, but again it often is.

Meanwhile, the other party can be characterized, in a general way, as Neo-Platonistic and idealistic. Among its more extreme adherents the Hegelian heritage is obvious. Roughly speaking, one may consider the historicists, Dilthey, most Neo-Kantian philosophers, e.g. Rickert, idealistic phenomenologists, and the 'picture-book' variety of phenomenologists as belonging here. Winch's interpretation of Wittgenstein,[21] as well as so-called 'critical sociology' in Germany and some Neo-Marxists in other countries have their *methodological* origins on this side of the divide. Seen through Neo-Kantian and idealistic interpretations Max Weber can also be placed here. But despite the inconsistencies in his methodological rhetoric, Weber seems to have passed more successfully than any other major social scientist the Scylla and Charybdis of the cosmological paradigm in social science.[22]

In sum: the search for a *mathēsis universalis* of human affairs was abandoned by both sides. One side stopped looking because it thought it had found it already, and was content to let the concrete problems and the recalcitrant 'facts' of the social sciences look out for themselves. The other side never started looking

20. Otto Neurath, 'Unified Science as Encyclopedic Integration', in *International Encyclopedia of Unified Science*, ed. Otto Neurath, Rudolf Carnap, and Charles Morris, Vol. I, no. 1, 1938; 2nd ed., Chicago: University of Chicago Press, 1955.

21. *The Idea of a Social Science*, New York: Humanities Press, 1965.

22. For a recent critical appreciation of Weber see W. G. Runciman, *A Critique of Max Weber's Philosophy of Social Science*, Cambridge University Press, 1972.

because it was convinced there was nothing to find. Both sides thus contributed to the social science variant of the crisis of modern science.

The crisis is not to be confused with the 'reactionary' and 'revolutionary' attacks on the limited but, within this limitation, necessary and legitimate autonomy of science. Nor is it simply a matter of romantic impatience with the also limited but legitimate rationality of science. Attacks of this kind are not new, and despite their present vociferousness they are probably less dangerous today than earlier in the century when they were associated with powerful totalitarian political forces. The crisis of social science is not caused by its technological implications, despite the recurrent fear, recently reacting to Skinnerian chimeras, that social science is about to find the key to the total manipulation of the human mind. Nor is it a crisis of substantive theory or of research procedures, if these terms are understood narrowly. The logical and logistic problems of the organization of ideas arising in social science, as in any similarly complex social institution concerned with the acquisition and transmission of knowledge, are so normal that they hardly deserve to be called 'crises', though it is true that the ideological, technological, theoretical and procedural problems connected with social science appear more serious at the present time than ever before.[23] In part this impression may be attributed to the well-known generation effect: every generation views the state of the world with more profound concern than did the previous one. In part, however, these contemporary alarms are genuine symptoms of the 'crisis' of social science in the sense in which I am using it, i.e. in strict analogy to Husserl's application of the term to Galilean physical science.

The fundamental function of theory is to suggest meaningful solutions to basic problems of everyday life, to help men in their orientation to the universe. One would hope that science would do this more successfully than its cosmological predecessors. In order to perform this function, however, theory must first give

23. A thoughtful discussion, by a physical scientist, of some of the recent Doomsday prognostications about science can be found in Harvey Brooks, 'Can Science Survive in the Modern Age?', *Science*, CLXXIV, 1 October 1971, 21–30.

a meaningful account of the concerns of everyday life. Description and explanation are inextricably interwoven. Furthermore, scientific theory is distinguished from the mythological and theological accounts from which historically it emerged (and which vestigially survive in it)[24] by its degree of *explicit* systematization and formalization of knowledge and by its commitment to a teachable and public method for the acquisition of knowledge. The empirical acquisition of knowledge, its rational interpretations, and its public transmission are to be controlled by a community of investigators, to borrow an apt Peircean reformulation of the old concept of the republic of scholars. Communication within this community, however, and just as importantly, with the larger community of noninvestigators, is founded in some presumably determinable manner on the intersubjectivity of ordinary experience. In short: scientific theory is description as well as explanation; communication in science rests on communication in everyday life.

This has an important consequence for social science. The subject matter of social science, the sociohistorical reality of everyday life, is not only a problem in the sense in which 'physical nature' as a universe of 'objects' is a problem to science, but a problem of epistemological reflexivity as well. According to Husserl, the crisis of science resulted from the alienation of the idealized and formalized products of theoretical activity, of 'logic' and 'mathematics' reified as structural principles of nature, from their sources in the *Lebenswelt*. I submit that, because of the peculiar reflexivity of social science, its estrangement from its sources is a bigger threat to its elementary theoretical function than reifications in physical science are to *its* cosmological purpose. In social science it is not only the products of theoretical activities that are uncritically reified; under the prevailing cosmological paradigm the producers themselves are in constant danger of reification.

It is of course not enough merely to speak of 'alienation' and 'crisis' in a general way. I hope I have succeeded in a more specific

24. See Ernst Topitsch, 'Mythische Modelle in der Erkenntnislehre', *Studium Generale*, XVIII, no. 6, 1965, 400–18.

diagnosis by tracing the present symptoms in the methodology of social science to an underlying cause. The cosmological paradigm of Galilean science was imposed, for a number of reasons, on social science and on the philosophy of social science, and kept them in a state of double naïveté.[25] In the first place, the sources of science in the theoretical activities of idealization and mathematization, and the foundation of these activities in the praxis of everyday life, were suppressed. This is a form of blindness which social science shares with physical science. Social science not only very properly took over the logical form of reasoning (the historic achievement of the combination of empiricism with rationalism) from physical science; it also very improperly pretends to the same (illegitimate) *epistemological* autonomy of scientific knowledge (which is its historical *hubris*). The second aspect of naïveté is the exclusive property of social science. It is a blindness concerning the nature of the subject matter of social science.

I am reasonably confident that the diagnosis is correct. I must confess that I am much less confident of the cure than of the diagnosis. Nevertheless, having come this far in the identification of the problem, I should like to try to suggest the direction in which I think the solution is to be found. In pointing to it I shall use as signposts certain important suggestions in Husserl's *Crisis*[26]

25. In *Crisis* Husserl distinguishes the naïveté of Galilean science and logie from the naïveté of the natural attitude of everyday life. See also *Cartesian Meditations*, trans. Dorion Cairns, The Hague: Nijhoff, 1960, especially pp. 152–3.

26. The reader beware! I think that the extrapolation of the suggestions which I am taking mainly from *Crisis* can be justified. But Husserl probably would not accept these extrapolations as being within the frame of transcendental phenomenology. In *Crisis* there are passages which suggest a train of thought with which my proposal is incompatible. See, e.g.: 'For the realm of souls there is in principle no such ontology, no science corresponding to the physicalistic-mathematical ideal, although psychic being is investigable in transcendental universality, in a fully systematic way, and in principle in essential generality in the form of an *a priori* science' (*Crisis*, p. 265); 'for an objectivity after the fashion of natural science is downright absurd when applied to the soul, to subjectivity, whether as individual subjectivity, individual person, and individual life or as communally historical subjectivity, as social subjectivity in the broadest sense' (p. 337). Much depends on what one means by 'after the fashion of natural science'.

and in the opus of Schutz.[27] Again I shall leave aside the general problem of the crisis of science, to whose solution Husserl devoted his last work, and concentrate instead on the methodological consequences of the second aspect of the naïveté of social science mentioned above.

A solution to the crisis of social science might be found if the search for a formalization of social reality in science were taken up again. I maintain that a *mathēsis universalis* of the *social* world has not even been programmatically established in what, roughly speaking, is the positivist tradition. I also maintain, however, that the cosmological goal of a *mathēsis universalis* must include human conduct on all its levels; the Human Exclusion Act is unconstitutional. The goal of a *mathēsis universalis* for human affairs cannot be reached by simple analogy to the ideal of mathematization in Galilean cosmology. This ideal is too closely tied to a numerical conception of what is 'objective' and 'empirical'. A *mathēsis universalis* appropriate to the social world will have to be truly independent of Galilean cosmology. It will have to be based on the premise of the epistemological reflexivity of a science of human conduct. A science that describes and explains the constructions of social reality must be able to develop a programme of formalization (and a theory of measurement) that is appropriate to the constitutive structures of everyday life.[28]

The diagnosis of an illness is not its cure, nor is the naming of a medicine that is not yet on the market. Yet I think that these

---

If it refers to Galilean science, *d'accord*. But a 'science' *a priori*, a transcendental eidetic phenomenology is not the only alternative. For an interesting discussion of ambiguities in Husserl's notion of *Lebenswelt* and correlative ambiguities in his view of an (*a priori*) science of the *Lebenswelt*, see Natanson, 'The *Lebenswelt*', especially pp. 130–32.

27. See especially 'Common-Sense and Scientific Interpretation of Human Action', *Collected Papers*, I, 3–47; 'Concept and Theory Formation in the Social Sciences', ibid., pp. 48–66; and 'Phenomenology and the Social Sciences', ibid., pp. 118–39.

28. This, I take it, is the wider aim of Aaron Cicourel's *Method and Measurement in Sociology*, New York: Free Press, 1964. At this stage of methodological discussion his book admittedly and understandably has a programmatic flavour. Cicourel's detailed critique of the unreflected use of (numerical) mathematics in various research procedures is particularly valuable.

two steps are important, at least for redirecting attention from symptoms to causes.

The existence of a crisis in social science is not generally perceived. This does not strengthen my case, but it does not necessarily weaken it. If the diagnosis is correct, both sides have good reason to ignore the existence of a crisis. It is more flattering to assume that it is not social science but the opposing side that is in critical condition.

The controversies among various schools of thought *do* concern genuine issues of substantive theory and occasionally also of methodology. But because every indication of the critical condition of the patient is attributed to a serious but localized infection (structural-functionalism, *structuralisme*, neopositivism, 'critical theory', transformational grammar, symbolic interactionism, statistical historiography, ethnomethodology, etc.), the scattered symptoms are not recognized as forming part of a syndrome which has a single cause.

I have already indicated that in my view the solution to the crisis of social science lies in the formulation of a *mathēsis universalis* appropriate to human affairs. Because of the illustrious history of the concept of *mathēsis universalis* the statement of the programme in the abstract makes it appear even bolder than it is. I shall come back to what I see as its main promise and its most serious difficulties. But first it should be recognized that the need for such a programme is not widely felt, which is not surprising. Empirical theory and research are only possible on a foundation of things taken for granted. It is impossible to make everything problematic at the same time. In addition, the reluctance of the practitioners to make their methodological naïveté a topic for reflection is not only understandable, it is a secondary indication of the crisis we have been discussing. But the intrascientific difficulties of methodological communication have a parallel in the intraphilosophical difficulties of communication *about* social science (and social reality) – not to speak of the traditional difficulty of communication between philosophers and social scientists.

I would not be surprised if logical empiricists and positivists of various persuasions should forget their differences and agree on

Thomas Luckmann 237

the absurdity of the goal I have advanced. Is not the mathematization of nature including, of course, social reality already achieved in principle? Why should there be an intrinsic relation between the algorithms of theoretical operations, i.e. the generalized syntax of science, and the interpretations of the algorithms with respect to particular domains, i.e. the semantics of specialized sciences? The Galilean paradigm suggests obvious answers to these questions. The need for taking into account the epistemological reflexivity of social science will be denied. As for the implied question about the 'conditions of the possibility' (to apply the Kantian expression) of social science, that is an impermissibly idealist and transcendentalist query. The history, psychology, and sociology of science including, of course, social science, and of philosophy including, of course, the philosophy of science, will provide an empirical account of the conditions under which science and philosophy originate and operate.[29] That must suffice. And as for the sense and import of social science, that is a matter of value judgements, political decisions about social uses of knowledge, and so on, which science can treat as empirical facts and analyse for their consequences. That, again, must suffice. Need I say that the chief weakness of this line of reasoning lies in its faith in the Münchhausen trick of pulling oneself out of a swamp by one's own pigtail? Respect for rationalism and empiricism as essential elements in the historical 'rationalization' of cosmologies is one thing. It is another thing to accept as an article of faith the 'ultimacy' claim of science and resign oneself to the viciously circular theory of knowledge that claim entails.

Transcendental phenomenologists, on the other hand, will find the programme superfluous. They will maintain that Husserl's conception of the universal structures of the *Lebenswelt* is only meaningful in connection with his idea of transcendental phenomenology as a rigorous *a priori* science. What can social science add to this? Physical science can be presumably left to its naïve theoretical *technē*. But any programme for social science other than one that makes it part of a transcendental eidetic enterprise is a relapse into a naïve naturalism.

29. See Richard Bevan Braithwaite, *Scientific Explanation*, 1953; 3rd ed., Cambridge University Press, 1956, pp. 20 f. •

I have already stated some of the reasons for my reluctance to adopt a position which postulates a supreme 'discipline of all disciplines' and anticipates an ultimate 'fulfilment' of science and philosophy. It is one thing to consider the crucial question of the transcendental conditions of knowledge and to adopt a rigorous method of philosophical reflection grounded in immediate experience. It is another thing entirely to abandon the unity of science in its cosmological sense and its basic logical structure for the sake of an illusory quest for absolute and total certainty of knowledge. To do this, it seems to me, is to abandon the idea of a descriptive-phenomenological foundation of cumulative empirical sciences, confusing it with that of a perennial 'first philosophy'.[30]

Universal and Historical Structures of Everyday Life

The programme of a *mathēsis universalis* for social reality is stated provocatively. It should be made clear at the beginning, however, that the aims of the programme are weaker as well as stronger than the two terms *mathēsis universalis* may suggest separately and jointly. The aims of the proposal, stated one way, are to institute a search for possibilities of formalization that are genuinely independent of the Galilean cosmological paradigm. Stated in another way, the aims are to generate some principles for the construction of a metalanguage into which the observational languages of the various social sciences could be translated with a controlled decrease of historical specificity and without loss of the intrinsic significance of observational statements. 'Formalization' and 'metalanguage' describe the goals of the programme but they do not specify them exactly; I am using the terms in a sense that is not identical with their common employment in technical discourse. Before clarifying my use of these terms, however, I want to anticipate an even likelier misunderstanding by stating explicitly that the proposal does not imply a revival of notions concerning a separate 'logic' of social science.

Kant's critique of the 'transcendent' use of concepts provided a transcendental foundation of knowledge in the activities of

30. See Natanson, 'The *Lebenswelt*', pp. 133 f.

human consciousness. In its historical context, however, Kant's critical theory of knowledge can be seen as an attempt to purify the epistemology of physical science of the powerful traces of Galilean cosmology. After Kant – and Hume, who woke Kant from his 'dogmatic slumber' – the merger of rationalism and empiricism from which was fashioned the hard core of modern science was obliged to meet higher standards of epistemological sophistication.

The attempts to provide a philosophically adequate foundation for social science, however, generally still took a Galilean view of physical science, and that well into the first half of the twentieth century. It was this view that was either adopted uncritically or rejected completely. Up to the generation of Rickert, Dilthey, and Weber – and in some quarters for a generation beyond them – the conviction prevailed on both slopes of the methodological Big Divide that in social science one had to opt for the Galilean model or against it. Those who rightly decided that the model offered neither theoretical nor procedural solutions to the problems they were facing therefore searched for a special form of logic which would permit generalized interpretations of unique, value-oriented human actions and the equally unique products of human action as, for example, art. This search led into one of the major dead-end streets in the philosophy of social science. As far as I can judge, no plausible argument was advanced that justified a radical distinction between a *general* logic of explanation in social science on the one hand and in physical science on the other.[31]

31. The question of a special logical form of social science was recently revived by Karl-Otto Apel (see especially 'Szientistik, Hermeneutik, Ideologiekritik', *Man and World*, I, 1968, 37–63; and 'Wittgenstein und das Problem des hermeneutischen Verstehens', in *Zeitschrift für Theologie und Kirche*, LXIII, no. 1, 1966, 49–87) and Jürgen Habermas (see his 'Zur Logik der Sozialwissenschaften', in *Philosophische Rundschau*, special publication 6, Tübingen, 1967, and *Knowledge and Human Interests*, trans. Jeremy J. Shapiro, Boston: Beacon Press, 1972). Apel and Habermas subject the foundations of the Galilean cosmology to legitimate criticism but present their discussion, at least by implication, as a general analysis of physical science and its philosophical foundations. No doubt they are right in pointing out the serious shortcomings of 'positivist' methodology in social science. To their view of a reductionist physical science, based on a

But with Dilthey and even more so with Weber the first signs announcing a shift in orientation appear. The question of a special logical form of the social and historical sciences receded into the background. Weber himself clearly recognized it as a pseudo-problem and in his rebuttal of Stammler's 'refutation of material-istic history' insisted on the generality of the 'logic' of explanation in science.[32] Slowly there emerged another question, in various formulations, in which words as heterogeneous as 'meaning', 'in-tention', 'purpose', 'motivational nexus', 'rationality of goals and ends', 'semiotic context', 'sign-oriented behaviour', 'norms', and 'roles' appeared as key terms. With Dilthey's programme of a general descriptive historical psychology and Weber's systema-tic combination of the 'interpretation' of human action with 'causal' explanation, the new question began to replace the search for special logical forms as a central issue in philosophical

---

manipulative and operationalist theory of measurement, they oppose a discipline of hermeneutic interpretation of cultural configurations of meaning. Their perspective is not entirely dissimilar to that of Wittgenstein as described by Winch. Habermas sometimes comes close to the notion of a protosociology (analogous to the protophysics of Lorenzen) but shies away from it, mainly, I think, because he finds it difficult to conceive of a theory of measurement appropriate to sociohistorical reality. Both Apel and Habermas take the methodological leap into language as the transcendental 'condition of possibility' of intersubjectivity, of knowledge, and of science. This leap is motivated in part by their serious concern with the epistemo-logical reflexivity of social science. I agree that the 'professional' philosophy of science cannot serve as a substitute for a critical theory of knowledge. But I do not find their solutions plausible. I cannot agree that the epistemo-logical reflexivity of social science entails a radical dichotomy between social and physical science – let alone a dichotomy based on differences in 'logical form'. The insistence of Apel and Habermas on the radical difference between the two kinds of science has other than purely methodological motives. It derives from a number of premises on the nature of 'nature' as against 'history'. It is also connected with the curious assumption that physical science is founded on a technological, essentially capitalist praxis, whereas 'critical' social science is to become a historical praxis of emanci-pation.

32. Max Weber, *Gesammelte Aufsätze zur Wissenschaftslehre*, Tübingen: Mohr (Siebeck), 1922, pp. 291–359. Incidentally, this essay should be reread by all those social scientists who have been hypnotized by the recent up-surge of discussion in English and American philosophy on the meaning of 'following a rule'.

reflection on social science. The question is how the 'field' of social science is to be identified and how the constituent elements in the 'field' are to be recognized and defined. Kaplan puts it quite simply: 'Behavioural science is occupied with what people do, but the "what" is subject to two very different kinds of specification.'[33] It is a mistake to bypass answering the question by pointing to some higher rationality presumably at work in forming the tradition- and context-bound but apparently decisionist definitions of problems by scientists in a given discipline, or even worse to refer it, by default of a critical philosophy of science, to the academic division of labour. It is also a mistake to trivialize the question about the identification of constituent elements or 'units' by referring it exclusively to the level of specific investigative techniques, such as participant observation, coding, and the like.[34]

The answer to this question should bring out whatever it is that distinguishes social science from physical science and whatever is common to the various social sciences. It is not a matter of logical form. The logic of social science is the logic of science – if various rather general modes of explanation can indeed be given this designation because of their common origin in human logic as an idealized form of theoretical activity and because of their common cosmological purpose. There are, however, more specific styles of explanation which are determined by specific explanatory aims. These are associated with various disciplines. The specific styles of explanation, while themselves instances of more general modes, are tied to the substantive theoretical prob-

33. Kaplan, *Conduct of Inquiry*, p. 358. Kaplan introduces here the useful terminological distinction between act and action. To say that social science is interested in the explanation of *actions* does not imply that in their explanatory frames data from ecology, ethology, neurophysiology, and so on are not to be used in a full causal analysis of a given problem. It does, however, state a level of interest, and withdraws credit from metaphysical reductionism. For an interesting attempt to work back to that level of explanation from reductionist positions, see George A. Miller, Eugene Galanter, and Karl H. Pribram, *Plans and the Structure of Behavior*, New York: Holt, Rinehart, and Winston, 1960.

34. This seems to be the tendency of Hans Albert in his interesting and polemical 'Hermeneutik und Realwissenschaft', *Mannheimer sozialwissenschaftliche Studien*, III, 1971, 42–7.

lems which the various disciplines confront, and the problems derive in their turn from the subject matter with which a discipline is concerned. I suggest that the family likeness in the explanatory problems faced by the disciplines of social science, from history to linguistics is due to the peculiarities of the areas over which they claim academic jurisdiction, and that these peculiarities originate in the structure of the domain over which social science implicitly, at least, also claims cosmological jurisdiction. The domain is the domain of human action and of its objectivated results. It is the constitution of the domain and the explanatory aims that are bound to it, rather than the logical form by means of which the domain is explained, that account for the difference between social and physical science.

It should not be, but it probably is, necessary to add that this does not mean that the domain (and its science) is to be considered autonomous within the over-all paradigm of cosmological 'causal explanation'.[35] It certainly does not imply that human action is the only thing of interest with respect to man or, for that matter, that an account of human action need not take in data from other explanatory frames. What it does mean is that there is an autonomous theoretical interest in a level of explanation that is irreducibly that of human action. The identification of the domain of social science is determined by the human interest in the understanding of human action. The interest is theoretical but prescientific; the theoretical interest, in turn, originates in the praxis of everyday life. This interest is cosmological, legitimate and ineradicable. The theoretical interests of social science must represent this interest in the logical form of science.

The identification of the domain and of its constituent elements is not merely a matter of several levels of analysis in a 'unitary' science, in the sense that different aspects of phenomena may be deducted and placed in a 'deductive system'. It is that, but in a way which is trivial in the present context: the domain *does* happen to be the domain which is the foundation for the production of cosmologies of science and of operational-instrumentalist de-

35. See Weber, *Zur Wissenschaftslehre*, especially pp. 322–34 and 509 f.; cf. also Geoffrey Madell, 'Action and Causal Explanation', *Mind*, LXXVI, 1967, 34–48.

cisions on levels of analysis. No doubt the domain, and the production of cosmologies, and the decisions on levels of analysis, can be and should be made objects of empirical analysis. But even the most sophisticated sociology of knowledge is an insufficient answer to the problem of epistemological reflexivity in social science.

An alternative and methodologically controlled, reflexive account of the constitution of the domain and its elementary structures is provided by the phenomenology of the *Lebenswelt*. The radical return to the immediate evidence of conscious experience provides an evidential starting point unavailable in common sense and scientific theory. The method of reduction permits controlled reflexiveness on the presuppositions of the method, of the evidence, and of their communication to others. The circle, as Husserl fully recognized, remains. But it is not viciously naïve.

The programme for a *mathēsis universalis* of social reality is a proposal for a phenomenology of the universal structures of everyday life; it is to serve a methodological purpose in social science by supplying a matrix for the empirical analyses provided by the disciplines that deal with and 'explain' the concrete historical structures of everyday life. The matrix is not 'theory', i.e. it has no direct connection to the logic of explanation. Nor is it merely a regional taxonomy based on classificatory decisions. It is founded on a rigorous method that uncovers and clarifies invariant structures of the conscious activities in which human action is constituted.

It is now easy to see why it is somewhat inexact to describe the programme of a *mathēsis universalis* for social reality as a proposal for formalization appropriate to human affairs. Formalization generally refers to the establishment of systems of symbols and of rules governing the combination of symbols. When I speak of formalization in the present context I am not thinking of the general logic of the rules that govern the combinations of symbols. I am not thinking of a general logistics of operations on statements about social reality as distinct from a logistics of operations on statements about some other kind of reality. Just as I see no reason to accept the claims in favour of a special logical form in social science, I cannot easily conceive of a need for (or indeed the possibility of) a special algorithm for the universe of human action. It may well be that there are serious difficulties in the 'recasting of verbal theories as causal models',[36] and that the specific mathematical operations performed on statements about social reality within some explanatory paradigm leave a large residue of dissatisfaction. This is surely due in some measure to the inappropriateness of the specific operations. But in large measure such dissatisfaction can be traced eventually to unsatisfactory solutions to the problems of identifying the 'field' and defining the 'units' in the field. I suspect, in other words, that the dissatisfaction stems from a frustration of the theoretical interest in the level of human action and its objectivations, not from a failure of the mathematics involved.[37] And that leaves us again with the problem of the constitution of social reality in human action. The formalization of 'the rules of the game' presents no intrinsic difficulty – for any particular game in 'nature' or 'social reality'. The difficulty arises from the fact that in society everybody is playing many games at the same time, and that the rules define the players, and the players define the rules.[38]

36. Hubert M. Blalock, Jr., *Theory Construction*, Englewood Cliffs: Prentice-Hall, 1969, p. 27.

37. 'Mathematical techniques can often be applied to good effect even when the known facts have to be somewhat distorted to feed them into the mathematical machinery. But in the case of current algebraic grammar the amount of distortion, while not great, conceals just the most important fact about natural human languages: the fact that they are (technically speaking) "ill-defined" systems, like table-manners or football or governments, rather than "well-defined" systems like logic or mathematics.' Thus Charles F. Hockett, disowning gracefully substantial parts of his own essay 'Language, Mathematics and Linguistics' (*Current Trends in Linguistics*, Vol. III: *Theoretical Foundations*, ed. Thomas A. Sebeok, The Hague: Mouton 1966) in an author's précis of the essay published in *Current Anthropology*, IX, April-June, 1968, 128. Presumably all 'natural systems' are ill defined, more or less. It is of course the 'more or less' which offers room for further debate on what it is that is being defined.

38. The point is made by Ernest Gellner: '*The constraints, the "rules" within which social life is played out, are themselves a consequence of the game* ... A "structural" account of a society is an account of how this comes to be: how the game itself generates and sustains the limits within which it is played. This is the really crucial fact about sociological method. This manner of formulating it shows why the task is so much harder than

Furthermore, the proposal for a *mathēsis universalis* appropriate to social reality has no *direct* bearing on the question of quantification in social science. In principle, counting noses and performing operations on numerical items are methodologically rather harmless; taken in isolation, the practice is no more dangerous in social science than anywhere else. But it does become methodologically explosive because it is tied to the identification of the units in the field. It has to be decided *what* is to be counted. Indirectly, then, the problem of quantification, like the problem of formalization, is connected with the problem of the constitution of the domain and the level of explanation that is pertinent to a given explanatory interest.

I am led to suggest that what appears as a triad of the simplest theoretical activities: identification (observation)-counting-classification, is anything but that. A burning methodological issue centres around the implicit theory of measurement. This issue is most acute in disciplines with a general explanatory aim, such as sociology and social anthropology, which try to account for *all* the games, less acute in disciplines with a relatively restricted region of investigation, such as linguistics, and least acute in disciplines with a sharply defined explanatory interest, such as economics. But in all social science disciplines the theory of measurement carries the imprint of the Galilean cosmology.[39] A methodologically legitimated decision on what is to be counted is generally avoided. The researcher unwittingly adopts individual or official, bureaucratic, common-sense taxonomies. Such deci-

---

that of a chess analyst, who has no need to explain just why the players will not knock over the board, why the rook will not move diagonally, and so forth' ('Our Current Sense of History', *European Journal of Sociology*, XII, no. 2, 1971, 170; italics original).

39. 'The terms of classical Newtonian theory are, like those of social science, all concepts referring to what can be observed. The relatively simple structure of such a powerful theory has, to put it moderately, not yet been deployed to its fullest advantage by social scientists' (May Brodbeck, 'Models, Meaning, and Theories', in Gross, *Symposium*, p. 401); 'Talking about the meaning of people's movements does not suggest that the way of ascertaining its presence is not the same as the way of ascertaining the meaning of anything else' (Quentin Gibson, *The Logic of Social Enquiry*, New York: Humanities Press, 1960, p. 52).

sions do not produce data whose comparability is warranted. All too readily the problem is glossed over by post hoc technical 'validation' and submerged in displays of numerical mathematics whose items originated in 'coding decisions'.[40]

No Galilean primary qualities having been discovered in human conduct, assortments of secondary qualities are measured as if they directly represented primary ones. The consequence of social science naïveté concerning its epistemological reflexivity is, on the hidden level of 'operationalized' research procedure, measurement by fiat.[41]

Hochberg defines formalization as the replacement of descriptive signs in an axiomatic system by mere marks.[42] The proposal of a *mathēsis universalis* for social reality is thus not a proposal for full formalization but merely for partial formalization. The 'descriptive signs' are statements on human conduct in ordinary language or, if one wishes to become technical about it, in an observational language in which the statements of actors are reformulated in one translation step and linked to statements of (actor-)observers.[43] These are to be 'represented', not by mere marks, e.g. geometrical figures, but by statements on elementary structures of human conduct. It must be added immediately that the specific form of attentiveness to the ordinary language of the actors that characterizes some traditions in social science such as, for example, some symbolic interactionists and ethnomethodologists in sociology, ethnoscientists, 'cognitive' anthropologists, etc. in social anthropology, and ethnographers of communication and componential analysts in anthropological linguistics, does

40. For an excellent discussion of this and of related problems, see Cicourel, *Method and Measurement*, especially Chapter 1.

41. The term was used by Warren Torgerson (*Theory and Method of Scaling*, New York: Wiley, 1958, p. 21) and taken up critically by Cicourel (*Method and Measurement*, pp. 12 f.).

42. 'Axiomatic Systems', p. 427.

43. Even Felix Kaufmann's well-known phrase 'every interpretation of social facts presupposes a fundamental interpretation, namely, that of the underlying physical fact as a social fact' does not specify adequately the complex constitution of 'social facts' and of the recognition of social facts (*Methodology of the Social Sciences*, 1944; 2nd ed., New York: Humanities Press, 1958, p. 166).

not presuppose an established matrix of universal, invariant structures of everyday life which rigorous phenomenological analysis should yield. Nor does such attentiveness suffice in and by itself to generate such a matrix – but such traditions find direct methodological justification in this matrix. This does not mean that other traditions are to be excommunicated by some new methodology, but their research procedures can be shown to be more naïve than absolutely necessary in the matter of operational definitions of the field and its units. Moreover, to the extent that unit-identification procedures, partial formalization of units, theoretical explanation, and methodological reflection on the entire theoretical enterprise are empirically connected, this naïveté does have repercussions.

The proposal of a *mathēsis universalis* for social reality is thus a proposal for formalization only in a loose sense of that term. In fact, it is a proposal for a *mathēsis universalis* in a restricted metaphorical sense. Its basic aim can be stated as the formalization of a matrix of elementary and universal structures of human conduct. The proposal takes up Husserl's notion of a science of the *Lebenswelt* and reformulates it as a proposal for a phenomenological foundation for the methodology of social science, inasmuch as that methodology cannot avoid being concerned with the peculiar problem of the structure of the domain that is undeniably constituted in human action.

The motive for and the foundation of the programme are one:

as soon as we consider that the life-world does have, in all its relative features, a *general structure*. This general structure, to which everything that exists relatively is bound, is not itself relative. We can attend to it in its generality and, with sufficient care, fix it once and for all in a way equally accessible to all. As life-world the world has, even prior to science, the 'same' structures that the objective sciences presuppose in their substruction of a world which exists 'in itself' and is determined through 'truths in themselves' (this substruction being taken for granted due to the tradition of centuries); these are the same structures that they presuppose as a priori structures . . .[44]

The descriptive phenomenology of the *Lebenswelt* is ultimately based on the phenomenological method of radical reduction and

44. Husserl, *Crisis*, p. 139 (italics original).

attention to the experience of intentional acts in originary evidence. It is thus philosophically legitimated by a reflexive account of the knowledge of experience. In other words, the descriptive phenomenology of the natural attitude in everyday life has its methodological foundation in phenomenology as a transcendental critique of knowledge. For this reason it satisfies the need for a 'philosophy of the mind' described by Burtt. It can offer the guarantee of continuous epistemological reflexivity, which is an essential condition of the philosophical foundation of social science.

It is legitimate to suggest a more specific function for the descriptive phenomenology of the invariant structures of the world of everyday life: to provide the general matrix, appropriate to the level of human action, for statements on human conduct articulated in historical vernaculars. Such a matrix offers a satisfactory solution to a fundamental problem of social science, the problem of the comparability of historical data. And, obviously, all the data of social science are historical.

To put it more precisely:

(1) The data of social science are preinterpreted.[45] Interpretation of experience (and action) is a constitutive element of the data; we do not have 'raw' data to which are added commonsense interpretations which are to be discarded by means of some 'purifying instrument', if only we could find one.

(2) Interpretations are made in, and bound to, ordinary historical languages. The data of social science are therefore from the outset irrevocably part of historical worlds of everyday life: they are constituted in human action and experience as historically specific contexts of significance and motivation.

The universal structures of everyday life could serve as a matrix for such data, as a metalanguage for the historical languages in which data on human action must necessarily be presented.

Such a matrix must meet two requirements. It has to meet the criterion of subjective adequacy in the sense in which Weber introduced the term. The 'translations' of the statements (but not

45. In several methodological writings Schutz clarified the interdependence of the interpretations and preinterpretations that constitute the data of social science.

necessarily of their theoretical explanations) from the historical languages into the metalanguage or, more appropriately, the protolanguage would have to be plausible in principle if not in immediate fact to the speakers-actors who produced the statements. The matrix also must consist of genuinely universal structures of the world of everyday life. It is not sufficient to generalize some apparently elementary features of a given common-sense view of man and society. This procedure cannot substitute for the phenomenological *epochē*, as witness the ethnocentric 'picture-book phenomenology' of the twenties and, I might add, of the sixties as well.

The protolanguage consisting of the phenomenological account of the universal structures of the world of everyday life would thus represent a formalization (in the sense that it would not be another ordinary historical language) of statements on human conduct articulated in ordinary languages. The proposal is neutral with respect to the problem of logical form of explanation and of theory construction, except that it is motivated by and subordinated to the cosmological interest in the explanation of human action. At the same time, the proposal is intimately tied to a demand for a theory of measurement in social science. Measurement of human actions and their objectivations must be based on a two-level account: of the invariant structures underlying typifications of social reality (and thus co-constituting social reality), and of the invariant structures underlying linguistic articulation of historically variant concrete typifications of human action in human experience.

This programme for the solution of a central problem of the methodology of social science is still just that: a programme. Nevertheless, some important prerequisites for accomplishing the aims of the programme have been met. Husserl himself, Gurwitsch, Schutz and some other phenomenologists have been filling in the over-all contours of the *Lebenswelt* originally sketched out by Husserl. Still, much work remains to be done there. As for the specific use of descriptive phenomenology in methodological reflection, this essay is a tentative step in that direction. And finally, as for the replacement of the implicitly Galilean theory of measurement in social science by an epistemologically reflexive one, work on this task has begun in various movements in social science that are close to or even claim descent from phenomenology (symbolic interactionism, ethnomethodology, ethnoscience and others), as well as in other quarters that have no particular inclination to look for philosophical foundations in phenomenology, as in the increasingly rewarding work on universals in language by linguists of various theoretical persuasions, anthropological linguists working on ethnographies of speaking, and others who would perhaps dislike to be labelled.

A synthesis of these varied efforts will require more than an addition of individual results. It will require continual reflection on the sources and consequences of epistemological reflexivity in social reality and social science.[46] Without such reflection the relevance of science in general and social science in particular can be assumed but not explicated.

Postscript on the Circle

Alas, there are no absolute certainties and there are no definitive resolutions of fundamental 'crises'. My argument which contained as an important step in its chain of reasoning a critique of a historical process of cosmological abduction relies in its proposal for a solution to the crisis in social science on abductive premises. Nonetheless I suggest that it offers clarification for the scientific-cosmological enterprise. It does not resign itself to the inner circle of viciousness that characterizes the thinking of the

46. I refer here only to the contribution to the theory of measurement. It is not my purpose to evaluate in detail the merits of the various approaches in producing accurate and relevant descriptions, although I may say that in my opinion some of the best work in this regard is being done in the approaches that pay attention to the 'indexical' (to borrow Garfinkel's expression) features of communication. Nor am I proposing to assess the respective contributions of these approaches to theory, and thereby to the cosmological purpose of science. I would merely like to offer my opinion that some of these approaches are lapsing into a new empiricism. This empiricism differs significantly from the old 'positivistic' empiricism in its descriptive sophistication, but its anti-theoretical self-sufficiency makes its more extreme versions almost as much of a threat to the cosmological purpose of science as its 'positivistic' opposite.

modern descendants of the scientistic theory of knowledge. It is only fair, however, to let the reader judge whether the outer circle is not as tightly closed as the inner.

The physical and social sciences are engaged in a common cosmological enterprise. The enterprise follows certain general rules whose structure is analysed in the logic of science and whose origin can be reconstructed historically. On that level it can be decided whether the sciences have the structure of hypothetico-deductive systems, whether notions of verification should be replaced by the concept of corroboration, whether or not over-all paradigms change in a revolutionary fashion, and so on.

These theoretical activities presuppose still more general activities of the mind. The idealized rules for these activities can be 'operationalized' in a logistic system and traced back to their origins in everyday activities. In radical philosophical reflection following a precise rule of evidence (transcendental reduction, i.e. attending to phenomena as they 'present' themselves), the structures of theoretical and pretheoretical activities are clarified and traced back to their foundation in active and passive syntheses of consciousness. This is a process of explication that starts with and returns to the most direct evidence available: inspection of immediate experience. The analysis points at all levels of the foundational structure of experience to its embeddedness in the *Lebenswelt*, the world of everyday life.

The descriptive phenomenology of everyday life which is ultimately founded on this radical method describes the universal structures of subjective orientation and action: lived space, lived time, the elementary structure of face-to-face situations, the levels of anonymity, the biographical-historical subscript to all experience, the lived intersubjectivity of communication in everyday life, and so on. To the most general discoveries of the 'geology' of the *Lebenswelt* these 'geographic' analyses of a descriptive phenomenology thus add some basic surface contours.

But now one discovers 'correlates' of these descriptions in the descriptive results of 'naïve' empirical sciences and, indeed, of aesthetically filtered common-sense observation. That discovery is an invitation to embrace the pretheoretical immediacy of the

Lebenswelt or to join the traditional cosmological enterprise of 'naïve' science. There is no reason to decline the invitation, individually, as long as the differences in cognitive style, method, universe of discourse, and purpose are not extinguished.

And here another round starts. Theory in all sciences involved in the cosmological enterprise takes a number of things for granted which become problematic upon reflection:

(1) The unity of experience among men in different societies throughout the course of history. Philosophically speaking, this refers to the problem of whether 'mankind', a 'transcendental ego', an 'empirical species', or whatever, is the transcendental subject of knowledge.

(2) The givenness and the possibility of communication. Philosophically speaking, this refers to the problem of the *mathēsis universalis*.

Social science rests upon an additional presupposition: that the ordinary, culturally and historically highly variable commonsense definitions of reality are 'objective' data (sales, suicides, fathers, presidents and so on). Philosophically speaking, this is the problem of the epistemological reflexivity of social science and of the human constitution of the domain under investigation.

With this problem we are back with the *Lebenswelt* as the foundation of science, *and* as the foundation of the field of social science. And we start with reflection on the presuppositions of a particular historical enterprise, science, in which our elementary cosmological interest is historically invested. The method of reflection must be 'rational' and must be based on immediate evidence. That is where we came in!

The solution to the epistemological reflexivity of social reality and social science which I proposed is not definitive. It starts a process of reflection, however, in which the quest for certainty about 'starting points' – to be found in a radical philosophical method – is abductively joined to the cosmological interest in understanding the universe of which we are part – to be satisfied, more or less plausibly, more or less effectively, and perhaps *less* naïvely, by science.

Part Two
**Contributions to the Theory of Social Action,
Communication and Symbolic Realities**

12 Alfred Schutz

Some Structures of the Life-World*

A. Schutz, 'Some Structures of the Life-World', in *Collected Papers*, Vol. 3, The Hague: Nijhoff, 1966, pp. 118–39.

The following considerations concern the structure of what Husserl calls the 'life-world' in which, in the natural attitude, we, as human beings among fellow-beings, experience culture and society, take a stand with regard to their objects, are influenced by them and act upon them. In this attitude the existence of the life-world and the typicality of its contents are accepted as un-questionably given until further notice. As Husserl has shown, our thinking stands under the idealities of the 'and so forth' and 'I can do it again'. The first leads to the assumption that what has proved valid thus far in our experience will remain valid in the future; the latter to the expectancy that what thus far I have been able to accomplish in the world by acting upon it I shall be able to accomplish again and again in the future. Therefore we can speak of fundamental assumptions characteristic of the natural attitude in the life-world, which themselves are accepted as unquestionably given; namely the assumptions of the con-stancy of the structure of the world, of the constancy of the validity of our experience of the world, and of the constancy of our ability to act upon the world and within the world.

What is given as unquestionable is in first approximation to be designated as that which we take for granted as familiar; as such it is the form of the understanding which we have in the natural attitude of both the world and ourselves. But it belongs to the nature of what we accept as unquestionably given that at any moment it can be put in question, just as that which all along we have taken for granted might at any moment prove unintelligible. Even the assumptions of constancy are valid only until further

* Translated from the German by Aron Gurwitsch.

notice: Expectancies based on the constancy of the structure of the world may be disconfirmed, what has been valid may become doubtful, what has appeared as feasible may prove unrealizable. What had been accepted as unquestionably given then becomes a problem, a theoretical, practical or emotional problem, which must be formulated, analysed and solved. All problems arise on the background of what had been given as unquestionable (it is the latter which in the proper sense of the word becomes questionable) and all solutions of problems consist in transforming, by the very process of questioning, that which has become questionable into something new which now in turn appears as unquestionable. Already that which without being questioned is accepted as a matter of course has its open horizons, both inner and outer horizons, which in the natural attitude are given to us as susceptible of possible exploration. To solve the problem, whether of a practical or theoretical nature, which results from the fact that that which thus far had been taken for granted has become questionable, we have to enter into its horizons in order to explicate them. As soon as we have attained knowledge we deem sufficient of that which has become questionable, we discontinue that endless task and by an arbitrary decree consider the problem as solved in a way sufficient for our purposes. How does it happen that a problem arises at all, that is to say, how does it happen that that which has become questionable for us appears as worth being questioned? What is relevant for the solution of a problem? When does it appear to us as 'sufficiently solved' as far as our purposes are concerned so that we discontinue further investigations?

All these questions point to different meanings of the concept of relevancy, some of which will be analysed in the following. First of all, we have to consider succinctly some fundamental structures of the life-world accepted as unquestionably given. This unquestionedness and familiarity are by no means homogeneous. Our knowledge about it and our ability to act in it and upon it exhibit manifold stratifications.

Let us consider the stratification of the life-world in a spatio-temporal respect. There is, to begin with, a stratum of the life-world experienced or experienceable which is now within my actual reach (reach of hearing, seeing, manipulation, etc.), a world of which I have or can have direct perception with or without the aid of instruments of all sorts, of which I know that it acts upon me immediately, and upon which I can act immediately – with or without the aid of instruments. I also know of the world which formerly was, but no longer is, within my reach. Here we still have to distinguish as to whether my experience of that world includes the expectancy that, at least in principle, I can bring it back within my actual reach, or whether this is not the case. If it is within my ability to restore my previous reach, e.g. by returning to the point from which I had taken my departure, then with reference to the idealizing assumptions of the 'and so forth' and 'I can do it again', I accepted as unquestionable that within the restored reach I shall on principle find again the same world which I had experienced previously, when it had been within my actual reach, perhaps with the modification 'the same but altered'. The third zone is the segment of the world which neither is nor was within my actual reach, which, however, I might bring within my actual reach. This zone too has its peculiar degree of familiarity. In the first place, I take it as unquestionable that its typical structures will be the same as the regions which I actually experience or have experienced. In the second place, the problem of the structure of the social world intervenes here in so far as I take it for granted that the world within your actual or restorable reach is, in principle, the world within my potential reach although, on account of my biographical situation, my experiences of it will differ from yours, which correspond to your biographical situation.

The stratification of the world into zones of actual, restorable and obtainable reach already refers to the structure of the life-world according to dimensions of objective temporality and their subjective correlates, the phenomena of retention and protention, recall and expectancy, and to the peculiar differentiations of the experience of time which correspond to the manifold dimensions of reality. Here we can not deal with these highly intricate problems.

One word must be added as far as the structuring of the social world is concerned. The social life-world within our reach will be called the domain of direct social experience and the subjects encountered in it, our fellow-men. In this domain we share with our fellow-men a common span of time; moreoever, a sector of the spatial world is within our common reach. Hence the body of my fellow-man is within my reach and vice versa. This central domain is surrounded, as it were, by the world of my contemporaries whose subjects coexist with me in time without, however, being with me in reciprocal spatial reach. Contemporaries know about one another in multifariously articulated typified ways which admit of all degrees of fulfilment and emptiness, intimacy and anonymity, and whose description is the task of a philosophical sociology. Notwithstanding all social distance, contemporaries are in principle able to act on one another. The world of contemporaries contains, of course, regions which consist of former fellow-men – whether these may or may not again become fellow-men for me – and potential fellow-men. Furthermore, there is the world of our predecessors which acts upon us while itself being beyond the reach of our action, and the world of our successors upon which we can act but which cannot act upon us. The former is given to us as a problem, to be interpreted by means of more or less specific and concrete typifications, the latter is in principle a region of complete anonymity.

All these stratifications belong as unquestionably given to our naïve experience of the socialized world. Even the typifications and symbolizations on terms of which we distinguish the several strata of our social world, construe and interpret their contents, determine our action in it and upon it and its action upon us according to all degrees of ability, are predefined as unquestionably given by virtue of the socially conditioned schemata of expression and interpretation prevailing in the group to which we belong and which we used to call the 'culture' of our group. It too, above all, is part of our life-world which we take for granted. It co-determines what within our culture is accepted as unquestionable, what can become questionable and what appears as worthy of questioning; it also co-determines the delimination of the horizon to be explicated, that is, the conditions under which for purposes of social life an emerging problem can be considered as solved.

This is so because only to a very small extent does the knowledge of each individual originate from his personal experience. The overwhelming bulk of this knowledge is socially derived and transmitted to the individual in the long process of education by parents, teachers, teachers of teachers, by relations of all kinds, involving fellow-men, contemporaries and predecessors. It is transmitted in the form of insight, beliefs, more or less well founded or blind, maxims, instructions for use, recipes for the solution of typical problems, i.e. for the attainment of typical results by the typical application of typical means. All the socially derived knowledge is, to begin with, accepted by the individual member of the cultural group as unquestionably given, because it is transmitted to him as unquestionably accepted by the group and as valid and tested. Thus it becomes an element of the form of social life, and as such forms both a common schema of interpretation of the common world and a means of mutual agreement and understanding. This leads us to the next step, namely the question of the structuring of all knowledge about our life-world in its multiple articulations.

As William James has already seen, in the naïve attitude of our daily living there corresponds to the afore-mentioned structuring of the spatial-temporal and social-cultural world, partly overlapping it, a differentiation of our knowledge about it.

He made the fundamental distinction between 'knowledge of acquaintance' and 'knowledge about'. 'Knowledge about' refers to that comparatively very small sector of which everyone of us has thorough, clear, distinct, and consistent knowledge, not only as to the what and how, but also as to the understanding of the why, regarding a sector of which he is a 'competent expert'. 'Knowledge of acquaintance' merely concerns the what and leaves the how unquestioned. What happens when we operate the dial of the telephone is unknown to the non-expert, it is incomprehensible to him and even immaterial; it suffices that the partner to whom he wants to speak answers the telephone. We assume that the apparatus, the procedure, the recipe, the maxim of our practical conduct will, in the normal course of things, stand its test in the future as this has thus far been the case, without our knowing why this is so and upon what this confidence of ours is based. The zones of our 'knowledge about' and 'knowledge of acquaintance' are surrounded by dimensions of mere belief which in turn are graded in multiple ways as to well-foundedness, plausibility, likelihood, reliance upon authority, blind acceptance, down to complete ignorance. Among all these spheres of knowledge it is only the 'knowledge about' that stands under the postulate of clarity, determinateness and consistency. All other spheres, notwithstanding their inner contradictions and incompatibilities by which they are affected, belong to the realm of what is not questioned and, therefore, unquestionably accepted, briefly to the realm of what 'is taken for granted', as long, at least, as such knowledge suffices to find through its aid one's way in the life-world. It must be noted that these forms of our knowledge concerning the life-world, whose 'ideal types' we have sketched rather roughly, are differentiated in manifold ways and that they perpetually change for the individual, from individual to individual, from individual to the social group, for the group itself, and finally from one group to the other. The content of what is known, familiar, believed and unknown, is therefore relative: for the individual relative to his biographical situation, for the group to its historical situation. A further fundamental category of social life is the inequality of the distribution of knowledge in its various forms among the individuals belonging to the group and also among the groups themselves. This fundamental category deserves to be made the central theme of a sociology of knowledge which is aware of its true task.

Now, what determines this differentiation of knowledge in its several forms? The answer to this question immediately leads us to the theme of relevancy.

Let us call the knowledge which at a certain moment of time the individual has at his disposal in the way described above his stock of knowledge, and its several gradations, its degrees of familiarity. If we briefly examine how the individual experiences its structure, we discover as subjective correlates of the several forms of knowledge corresponding zones of interests by which the individual is motivated. The individual finds himself perceiving, thinking, acting in the world which he, as a spontaneous being, apperceives. Leibniz has rightly defined spontaneity as the capacity to proceed from apperception to ever new apperceptions. If, however, the individual lives naïvely, it is not that the world of nature, culture and society is given to him in its entirety, for him to find his way in it, to master it by action or thought. The articulation of the world, as sketched in the beginning, into strata of different reaches implies that the individual living in the world always experiences himself as being within a certain situation which he has to define. Closer analysis shows that the concept of a situation to be defined contains two principal components. The one originates from the ontological structure of the pre-given world. To make a glass of sugared water, Bergson says, I must wait until the sugar has dissolved. The other component which makes it possible to define certain elements by singling them out of the ontologically pre-given structure of the world originates from the actual biographical state of the individual, a state which includes his stock of knowledge in its actual articulation. What belongs to the former, the ontological component of the situation, is experienced by the individual as imposed upon, and occurring to him, as a condition imposed from without upon all possible free manifestations of spontaneity. The biographical state determines the spontaneous definition of the situation within the imposed ontological framework.

To the experiencing subject's mind, the elements singled out of the pre-given structure of the world always stand in sense-connections, connections of orientation as well as of mastery of thought or action. The causal relations of the objective world are subjectively experienced as means and ends, as hindrances or aids, of the spontaneous activity of thought or action. They manifest themselves as complexes of interest, complexes of problems, as systems of projects, and feasibilities inherent in the systems of projects. The system of these complexes, which are interwoven in manifold ways, is subjectively experienced by the individual as a system of his plans for the hour or the day, for work and leisure; all these particular plans being integrated into one supreme system which, without being free from contradictions, encompasses all the other plans. We shall call the supreme system the 'life-plan'.

Be it noted that we use the word 'plan' in an enlarged sense which does not necessarily involve the element of deliberateness. There also exist plans which are imposed.

The life-plan thus determines the particular plans which, in turn determine the current interests. The interest prevailing at the moment determines the elements which the individual singles out of the surrounding objective world (whose articulation has previously been described) so as to define his situation. It is by virtue of the same interest that out of the pre-given stock of knowledge those elements are selected as are required for the definition of the situation. In other words, the interest determines which elements of both the ontological structure of the pre-given world and the actual stock of knowledge are *relevant* for the individual to define his situation thinkingly, actingly, emotionally, to find his way in it, and to come to terms with it. This form of relevancy will be called '*motivational relevancy*' because it is subjectively experienced as a motive for the definition of the situation.

Motivational relevancy may be experienced as imposed from without or else as a manifestation of inner spontaneity of any form (from a dark urge up to a rational project). It can be experienced in all degrees of evidentness or else, it can be unconscious in the sense of Leibniz's '*petites perceptions*' and even in that of modern depth psychology. The degree of clarity of the insight in which motivational relevancy is experienced depends upon the structure of the actual stock of knowledge from which the elements required for the definition of the situation are selected.

The actual stock of knowledge is nothing but the sedimentation of all our experiences of former definitions of previous situations, experiences which might refer to our own world in previously actual, restorable, or obtainable reach or else to fellow-men, contemporaries, or predecessors. In the light of our foreknowledge the situation to be defined may appear as typically alike, typically similar to a situation previously defined, as a modification or variation of the latter or else as entirely novel, and all this in what Husserl has called synthesis of recognition in all its species. The reference of the situation to be defined to the stock of knowledge may concern elements of the 'knowledge about', 'knowledge of acquaintance', mere belief or ignorance. If the elements of our stock of knowledge, which are at our disposal in the mentioned gradations, suffice for the definition of the situation, as far as motivational relevancy is concerned, then the definition takes place as a matter of course in the form of the unquestionably given. Such will be the case in all affairs of routine. However, it may happen that not all motivationally relevant elements fore-known in sufficient degrees of familiarity are adequate, or that the situation proves to be one which cannot be referred by syn-thesis of recognition to a previous situation typically alike, simi-lar, etc. because it is radically new. In such a case it becomes necessary to 'know more about' these elements, be it that new knowledge must be acquired, be it that the knowledge at hand must be transformed into higher degrees of familiarity. Such an element will become relevant for further acquiring of knowledge and hence, relevant also for the definition of the situation. This relevancy, so founded upon motivational relevancy, still differs totally from it. Now the relevant element is no longer given as unquestionable and has to be taken for granted: on the contrary, it is questionable but also worth questioning, and for that very reason it has acquired relevancy. That relevancy will be called *'thematic relevancy'* because the relevant element now becomes a theme for our knowing consciousness, a process which in tradi-tional psychology has usually been treated under the heading of 'attention'.

What makes the theme to be a theme is determined by motiva-tionally relevant interest-situations and spheres of problems. The theme which thus has become relevant has now, however, be-come a problem to which a solution, practical, theoretical or emotional, must be given. We now turn to the thematically rele-vant problem which, though it may genetically have been mo-tivated by more encompassing problems, interests and plans, after it has been constituted as thematically relevant, is detached from its context of motivation and becomes interesting and therefore worth questioning in its own right, so to speak. Yet this way of expression is not sufficiently precise. The motivationally relevant contexts continue remaining as outer horizons of what has be-come thematically relevant: we can turn to them again, we can question and explicate them, and we do so in fact to find the point at which we have to abandon any further investigation of the thematically relevant, because our knowledge of it has become sufficiently clear and familiar for the thematic problem at hand to be considered as solved with regard to the encompassing context. The total motivationally relevant interest-situation determines when our 'curiosity' to scrutinize the thematically relevant has to be considered as satisfied. In a different respect, however, the total situation merely forms the background or the margin of the actually relevant theme. The theme alone, as we say, is in the focus of our interest: the problem involved in it must be solved before we can turn to other things. We say 'first things first' – 'the most important first' – giving thus in colloquial language an excellent definition of the thematically relevant.

The thematically relevant is the problem and, as we said, as such it is worth questioning and is also (for reasons of motivational relevancy) questionable. It solicits us to penetrate into its inner and outer horizons, to bring it, in a synthesis of recognition, to coincidence with elements contained in our stock of knowledge and, first of all, to discover its typical pertinence to preconstituted and therefore typically familiar world phenomena. There arises here a series of important connections with other domains of phenomenological research which we can not study more closely within the present context. We merely want to point out briefly three spheres of research: (1) Husserl has shown that, from the outset, the pre-predicative experience of the life-world is fundamentally articulated according to types. We do not experience the world as a sum of sense data, nor as an aggregate of individual things isolated from and standing in no relations to one another. We do not see coloured spots and contours, but rather mountains, trees, animals, in particular birds, fish, dogs, etc. What Husserl has not explained in his published writings, however, is that this typification takes place according to particular structures of relevancy. In pre-predicative typification I can perceive my dog Fido in his typical behaviour as healthy or sick, as an individual, a German shepherd dog, a typical dog in general, a mammal, a living creature, a thing of the external world, a 'something at large'. Which typical structure I choose depends upon the thematic relevancy which this object has for me. Contexts of a similar kind appear in the sphere of predicative judgement, at least in everyday thinking. Every judgement of the form 'S is p' is by necessity elliptical, since 'S' is never exclusively 'p', but besides many other things like 'q' and 'r', 's', 't' ... it is also 'p'. In the biographical moment under consideration in which I pronounce the judgement 'S is p', 'S-being-p' is thematically relevant for me, because it is thus constituted by the motivational relevancies which in their totality are referred to in abbreviated form by the expression 'in the biographical moment under consideration'.

(2) How in the field of transcendental subjective consciousness – after the performance of the phenomenological reduction – the relations between theme, horizon and margin are arranged, how they condition one another and how they shift, has been excellently analysed by Aron Gurwitsch.[1] Though Gurwitsch believes that his use of his term 'Relevancy' differs from mine, I fully endorse his analysis. It seems to me that his concept of 'relevancy' is a special case of my concept of 'thematic relevancy', mine being more encompassing in so far as I am concerned with a phenomenology of the life-world, with which man in the natural attitude has to come to terms not only in thought but also emotionally and in action, whereas Gurwitsch's analyses only deal with transcendental consciousness after the reduction has been performed and hence the 'world has been bracketed'.

(3) Furthermore, Husserl has established the important distinction between open and problematic possibilities. After the thematically relevant has become a problem it can be considered both within the general framework of the ontologically pretraced spheres of incompatibility and with respect to alternatives between which a choice has to be made, that is – in Husserl's language – as a problematic possibility. In the latter case a choice can be made between but a finite and comparatively small number of possible solutions, each one of which carries its own weight. The thematically relevant problem is solved as soon as it can be decided under which of the available alternatives it has to be

1. *The Field of Consciousness*, Pittsburgh: Duquesne University Press, 1964.

subsumed, a process which, in turn, is determined by the more encompassing system of motivational relevancies.

Under all circumstances the solution of the thematically relevant problem involves the reference to the actually present stock of knowledge, as ordered beforehand according to degrees of acquaintance, of familiarity, of belief in the manner already described. However, not all the elements of the stock of knowledge are equally 'relevant' for the solution of the problem involved in the theme. The bulk of our foreknowledge is without bearing upon the theme and, therefore, immaterial for its being grasped and elaborated. Obviously, in the present context the term 'relevant' is used in a new sense – a third one – which shall be called '*interpretational relevancy*'.

In associationist psychology the complex mechanism of the interpretational relevancies and their relationship to motivational and thematic relevancies is simply posited as unquestionably given and, on this unclarified basis, the well-known principles of spatial and temporal contiguity, of similarity and difference are established. But how the associative combination of the acquired knowledge with what is thematically relevant comes about remains unclarified. The insight into the previously sketched structure of our stock of knowledge according to degrees of familiarity may be of help. If we ask, first of all, how the structuring came about, we find that our foreknowledge consists in material that was previously of thematic relevancy, material which, now given in the form of the unquestioned, is no longer given as a theme but merely as a horizon and, more particularly, in the form of a habitual acquisition. The transformation of the thematic-problematic into what henceforth will be possessed as unquestioned has genetically taken place by virtue of motivational relevancies conditioned by factors of biography and situation, motivational relevancies which determine the condition under which the problem involved in the theme could be considered as solved: that is, the point at which further investigation has become thematically irrelevant, because the knowledge obtained was sufficient for the definition of the previous thematic situation. As we have briefly shown before, our knowledge of the life-world, whether prepredicatively given or formulable in predicative judgements, is knowledge of the *typicality* of the objects and events in the life-world. The typicality, in turn, is determined by the exigencies of the previous thematic situation which had to be defined so as to come 'to terms with it'. The same exigencies also determine the degree of familiarity of the elements of knowledge which by the accomplished solution of the thematic problems have been transformed into habitual acquisitions. This acquired knowledge of the typicality of the life-world has its proper style in every degree of familiarity. All typification is relative to some problem: there is no type at large but only types which carry an 'index' pointing to a problem. If, by syntheses of recognition, an actually relevant theme is brought to coincidence as typically known, typically familiar, typically alike, with a type which pertains as habitual to the horizonally given stock of experience and displays the same degree of familiarity, then this foreknown type becomes interpretationally relevant with respect to the actual theme. We then say with reference to that theme that we have already experienced 'something of that sort' or heard about it, or that we know in a casual way what is in question. We say, furthermore, that we have reason to assume, that we believe, suppose, deem it probable or possible, hope, fear that the situation now to be defined has typical familiarity with the one experienced before: the present situation, to be sure, is '*atypical*' in some respect or other, yet by and large it has the same typical style. The term 'atypical' is ambiguous: it may mean that the 'atypical' condition as experienced in the present situation is incompatible with the previously experienced typifications of situations with which the present one is compared, or that it could be, or could be made, compatible with them if one of the two types were brought to a higher level of familiarity, or finally, that what is now thematically relevant displays completely novel features which cannot be brought into coincidence with any elements of the previously acquired stock of knowledge.

The elements of the horizonally given stock of experience which are interpretationally relevant are brought to bear upon the solution of the thematic problem, prove to be knowledge organized beforehand in several degrees of familiarity and according to different styles of typification, knowledge which derives from the fact that material which had previously been thematically relevant has been transformed into acquired knowledge now accepted as unquestioned. Because of this previous ordering, moreover, the elements that are interpretationally relevant at a particular time stand in a specific sense-connection with one another which is conditioned both biographically and ontologically and has its origin in motivational relevancies which are the same as the ones in which the now thematically relevant originates. Just this common origin in motivational relevancy seems to us to explain the enigmatic possibility of 'effective coincidence by synthesis of recognition'. We may assume that further analysis of the context will throw some light upon the secret of association. Perhaps Kant had something similar in view when, in the first edition of the *Critique of Pure Reason*, he distinguished the threefold synthesis of apprehension in intuition, of reproduction in imagination and of recognition in the concept, a tripartition, which in the second edition is unified in the synthesis of apperception.

The 'effecting of coincidence' between the actually thematic and the horizonally given elements of the stock of experience, which hereby become interpretationally relevant, is by no means always, nor even preponderantly, a passive process. To a large extent, the selection of the material which at a given moment of time becomes interpretationally relevant is a result of learning. As early as in childhood we have to learn what we have to pay attention to and what we have to bring in connection, so as to define the world and our situation within it. The selection and application of interpretationally relevant material, even after it is once learned, and has become a habitual possession and a matter of routine, still remains biographically, culturally and socially conditioned. The same life-world lends itself to a magic interpretation by primitive people, a theological one by the missionary, and a scientific one by the technologist. It could also be shown to what extent the system of interpretational relevancies depends upon the structuring of the world into zones of reach and into the different dimensions of social experience. The systematic investigation of this wide domain is still lacking. We still do not possess the high art

Leibniz has demanded, which would teach us to avail ourselves of what we know (*l'art de s'aviser de ce qu'on sait*).

What has been said thus far needs some important supplementation in order to prevent possible misunderstandings. First of all, the relationship between typification and interpretational relevancy must still be clarified. What we find in our stock of knowledge as typified experience is nothing but material which had previously been sufficient to transform, with the help of tested and interpretationally verified foreknowledge, thematically relevant problems into unquestionedness. This process of acquisition of experience had led to the sedimentation of the stock of knowledge prearranged according to types and degrees of familiarity. One might also say that, after the thematic problem has been solved, the typifications related to it and already inserted into the stock of knowledge form the line of demarcation between those horizons of the previously thematic problem as are explicated and those that remain unexplicated. But this way of putting it is still inaccurate, since no allowance is made for the fact that no particular problem is ever isolated: all problems are connected with one another, all thematic relevancies form systems, because all motivational relevancies are subjectively experienced as systems of plans subordinate to the life-plan of the individual in question. Because these systems of motivational relevancies determine not only the systems of thematic relevancies but also the corresponding interpretational relevancies, the latter also stand in a systematic context, and the same holds for the typifications originating here from and for the corresponding degrees of familiarity of our stock of knowledge.

These questions are obviously related to the genesis of the stock of knowledge and its specific individual structure. And every moment of our life, the stock of knowledge in all its stratifications as to systems of relevancy, typifications, degrees of familiarity exists and is available within certain limits. As such it is an element of the biographical situation at the moment in question. It forms the unquestionably given background and basis for the definition and mastery of the surrounding worlds – articulated as to zones of reach – of nature, culture and society. This world as a whole is, in principle, opaque, as a whole it is neither understood nor understandable. By virtue of the systems of relevancy and their structures, sense-connections, which to a certain extent can be made transparent, are established between partial contents of the world. For the business of life it means a great deal to see problems even if they cannot be transformed into unquestionableness. Here originate the aporetic categories of that which is unknown but knowable, of that which is known to be unknowable. The former leads to the possibilities – predetermined as to type – of filling empty places in our stock of knowledge; the second leads to several domains of reality, superposed upon that of the life-world, which by means of symbols are referred to the life-world and interpreted within it.

A further necessary supplement to what has previously been said concerns motivational, thematic and interpretational relevancies. As long as in the natural attitude man experiences his life-world and unreflectingly directs himself to it in his actions, thoughts or feelings, the differentiation into several systems of relevancy does not come within his view at all. As Husserl expresses it: he lives in his acts, directed to things and events, and in so doing he, so to speak, has the relevancies 'in his grasp'. He lives not only in his acts, directed to their objects, but also lives 'in' the corresponding relevancies in terms of which the questionable is distinguished from the unquestionably given. A reflective turn is required to see the relevancies themselves and their differentiation into several systematic connections. This turn, however, does not call for the disinterested attitude of the onlooking observer, not to speak of the scientist or the philosopher. Every consequential decision in the life-world brings man face to face with a series of thematic relevancies of hypothetical nature, which have to be interpreted and questioned as to their motivational insertion into the life-plan. A theory of projected action and decision in the life-world requires an analysis of the underlying systems of relevancy. Without such a theory no foundation of a science of human action is possible. The theory of relevancies is therefore of fundamental importance for the theory of the social sciences.

It is also essential from other and still more important points of view. In the first place, it is a task of the social sciences to investigate to what extent the different forms of systems of relevancy in the life-world – motivational, thematical and, most of all, interpretational systems – are socially and culturally conditioned. Already the typification of acquired knowledge, that is of the conditions under which problems can be considered as sufficiently solved and the horizons as sufficiently explicated, is to some extent socio-culturally co-determined. Not only the vocabulary but also the syntactical structure of common colloquial language, the 'inner form of speech', as Wilhelm von Humboldt has called it, contains the system of typifications and hence interpretational relevancies which by the linguistic community are considered as tested and verified, consequently as given beyond question, as approved and valid until further notice, and which, in the process of education and learning, are therefore transmitted to new members of the group. The same holds for the several means which every culture makes available for the typical orientation in, and the mastery of, the life-world, such as tools, procedures, social institutions, customs, usages, symbolic systems. All knowledge concerning those means determines motivational, thematic, and interpretational relevancies which the individual member of the given social group inserts into his stock of knowledge as an unquestionably given background – imposed upon him or lying within his ability – for his individual definition of his situation in the life-world.

In the second place, every communication with other men in the life-world presupposes a similar structure of at least the thematic and interpretational relevancies. This similar structure will occupy a privileged position within the social domain involving fellow-men in face-to-face situations because the sector of the spatial life-world, common to the partners, by necessity makes some elements to be of equal thematic relevancy for both partners, and furthermore because the body of the partner with his field of physiognomic expression, his gestures, his actions and reactions discloses an interpretationally relevant field which otherwise would not be accessible to the same extent. It is the task of a philosophical sociology to study the modifications which these common or similar systems of relevancy pertaining to fellow-men in face-to-face situations undergo in the interpretations of the world of predecessors and anticipations of the world of successors. For such a philosphical sociology the phenomenological analysis of the structures of the life-world has to secure the necessary preconditions.

13 Benita Luckmann

The Small Life-Worlds of Modern Man

B. Luckmann, 'The Small Life-Worlds of Modern Man', *Social Research*, Vol. 37, No. 4, 1970, pp. 580–96.

Husserl speaks of 'our everyday life-world' (*unsere alltägliche Lebenswelt*) as the world which man experiences at every point of his existence as immediately and simply given.[1] Comprising objects, trees, animals, men, values and goods, it is an intersubjective, i.e. a social, world in which man experiences the whole round of his life. It is a world of practical interest to man, a familiar world, a world taken for granted.

The everyday life-world extends indefinitely in space and time. Man's interests, however, focus on 'that sector of the world of his everyday life which is within his scope and which is centred in space and time around himself'.[2] Embedded in the *Lebenswelt* which in various degrees of closeness and distance surrounds them as a 'darkly perceived horizon of undetermined reality',[3] these sectors of everyday life are only sub-universes of human existence. They are not separate and independent social 'wholes'. In different ways – directly and indirectly – they are connected and bound to larger and still larger 'outside worlds'. Living in his 'small life-worlds', man may perceive the receding horizons of the *Lebenswelt* acutely or dimly. They may represent 'outside worlds' of which his small community appears to be an integral part, as in the case of traditional societies. They may also be con-

1. Edmund Husserl, *Ideen zu einer reinen Phänomenologie und Phänomenologischen Philosophie*, Vol. I, The Hague: Nijhoff, 1950 (first edition 1913), especially §§ 27, 28, 29, 30; and *Krisis der Europäischen Wissenschaften und die transzendentale Phänomenologie*, The Hague: Nijhoff, 1954, especially §§ 9 and 33 ff.

2. Alfred Schutz, 'On Multiple Realities', in *Collected Papers*, The Hague: Nijhoff, 1962, p. 222.

3. Edmund Husserl, *Ideen*, op. cit., § 27, p. 58 (my translation).

ceived of as non-human worlds of animals, ghosts, demons, which surround and threaten or protect the existence of the tribal isolate. In late industrial society the segment of the life-world actually 'inhabited' by man consists of many small worlds. These are located within the 'private' as well as the institutional spheres of existence. Though of different degrees of importance and necessity to man's existence, none of them represents a 'whole' life-world in which all of man's life unfolds. One can rather speak of man's part-time existence in part-time societies. To describe tentatively the multi-dimensional nature of everyday life in contemporary society I shall speak of the small life-worlds of man.

The historically predominant life experience of man has taken place within the more or less well defined limits of small communities. The tribe, the clan, the village, the small town represented kinds of small worlds within which all of man's living was done. Of these small life-worlds with distinct territories, a high degree of self-sufficiency and shared beliefs in what constitutes the good life, man possessed detailed and intimate knowledge. He knew all or most of the other inhabitants as fellow-hunters, chiefs, guardians of the sacred lore, relatives, neighbours, witches, dog catchers, beggars, grocers, etc. whom he encountered in his daily rounds in face-to-face relationships. He knew his own 'pre-ordained' place in the community and could predict the actions and reactions of his fellow-men with considerable certainty. He knew about the 'right order of things' in his community and it 'made sense' to him. He knew that this *right order of existence* to which he was 'attuned'[4] through his life within the community was approved by the gods and should not be disturbed, lest it be destroyed, or he himself cast out, which 'would be like death'.[5] The fears and anxieties originating mainly in the surrounding world of nature, and the conflict situations of his social life notwithstanding, traditional man moved within his small life-world

4. Cf. Eric Voegelin, *Order and History*, Vol. I: *Israel and Revelation*, Baton Rouge: Lousiana State University Press, 1956, pp. 4, 9.

5. Essence of the answer of a peasant respondent ('tradition-minded') to the question where he would like to live if he could not live in his native village. Reported by Daniel Lerner in *The Passing of Traditional Society*, New York: The Free Press of Glencoe, 1964, p. 25.

with a certain ease and safety. Acting in accordance with the generally recognized norms and expectations which emanated from the common world view, he participated in a continuity of being which transcended not only his own life but that of his family – in most instances that of his community as well.

While representing separate existential and political units the traditional communities were at the same time parts of larger societies. To these they were connected by stronger or weaker – but always intermediary – links: the feudal landlord who dispensed the justice of the king; the starosta of the mir who collected taxes for the tsar; the distantly related bureaucrat who as a minor official in the capital could intervene in behalf of a deserving cousin; the travelling salesman who told his tall stories of the Babylonian wonders of the city; the visiting opera company which performed the legendary events of the cosmological myths, etc. The filtered knowledge about the larger society was incomplete and fragmentary. In the slow process of passing from one institutional level to the next – on a vertical as well as on a horizontal plane – social knowledge, while being absorbed and transformed, was fitted into the already established conceptual framework of the small society. In a reverse but synchronized process the little community was fitted into the plan of the larger society and beyond it into the order of the cosmos or the universal God.

To be sure, life in the communities of traditional society is seen 'looking backwards' as to a 'finished product' – when the actual communities have already disappeared, are disappearing or undergoing fast and dramatic changes. Aristotle, at the imperial court of Alexander the Great, wrote about the 'good life' of the polis after its fall; Redfield wrote about the 'wholeness' and 'homogeneity' of 'folk culture' in Chan Kom when the village had already 'chosen progress'. The classical sociologists (Tönnies, Durkheim, Maine and others), trying to provide systematic presentations of industrial society, did so against the backdrop of an ideal-typical construct of traditional society. Other social scientists of different schools of thought and methodological persuasions in trying to make visible and understandable life in communities of pre-literate and classic societies have in most instances presented it in self-sufficient isolation or cosmic harmony: The 'small, closely integrated social units'[6] are seen as 'cosmions', 'illuminated with meaning from within',[7] existing 'for all the business and pleasure of living'.[8] Very much as a jeweller would lovingly display a precious stone on a velvet tray and in the best of lights, anthropologists and sociologists present traditional small life-worlds against the stated or implied 'urbanism', 'disorganization', 'heterogeneity', or 'segmentation' of modern 'mass' society.

The bi-polar systems of explanation (*Gemeinschaft-Gesellschaft*; mechanical-organic solidarity, status-contract, sacred-secular, folk-urban, collectivistic-individualistic societies, etc.) explicitly or implicitly point to the loss of unity, meaning, harmony, satisfaction in the transition from traditional to modern life. But theoretical constructs meant to generalize and to compare are not found existing in their 'pure form'. They are not to be confused with the social reality as actually experienced by man living in traditional small communities. There is no doubt that, as for all men, life in traditional societies, too, has had its share of burdens, anxieties and frustrations. The fear of hunger, disease, wild animals, thunder, eclipse, drought, floods; the worries and terrors about mistakes in ritual performances which might not have sufficiently pleased the gods or assuaged the demons; the temptations of the Devil and the wrath of God must have been very real and disruptive experiences of traditional or 'primitive' man. This is not to underestimate the actual structural and cultural differences between traditional and modern societies, nor to minimize the changes in the perception of social reality as more or less meaningful to individual existence.

The intricate and complex process of industrialization which

6. Ralph Linton, *The Study of Man*, New York: D. Appleton-Century Co., 1936, pp. 283–4.

7. Eric Voégelin, *The New Science of Politics*, Chicago: University of Chicago Press, 1952, p. 27.

8. Robert Redfield, 'How Human Society Operates', in *Man, Culture and Society*, ed. Harry L. Shapiro, New York: Oxford University Press, 1960, p. 345.

led to a segmentation, specialization and 'rationalization' of institutions also eroded the beliefs in a cosmological order[9] of traditional societies. Separate institutional spheres acquired a degree of autonomy which permitted them to develop their own 'rationally' founded legitimations and to withdraw, as it were, from a hierarchically interlocked system of representations of society as a whole.[10] The accompanying increased division of labour, the increase in specialized role performances, the diversification of loyalty claims, to mention but a few manifestations of modernization, have accordingly affected the coherence of individual biography as well as the microcosmic character of the small communities. Both have lost their 'wholeness'.[11]

Contemporary man no longer 'naturally'[12] sees himself as a useful and necessary member of a social whole geared into a meaningful plan of existence within the totality of a cosmic or divine order. The transcendence-continuum which in traditional society reached out from the centre of individual life within the community, through the various spatial units of outer society into the encompassing order of the cosmos has been broken. We may speak of a *transcendentia interrupta* which perhaps more than any other single phenomenon of modern life accounts for the 'great feeling of meaninglessness, a search for something to grab hold of, some unifying thing',[13] experienced by modern man.

The separate institutional spheres which appear to function according to their own laws and pursue their own separate goals alternately or in combination dominate various parts and particles of man's daily life. Like a Kafka-esque creation man may try to

9. Cf. Voegelin, *Order and History*, op. cit., Vol. I, pp. 1–52.

10. Cf. among others Ralf Dahrendorf, *Class and Class Conflict in Industrial Society*, London: Routledge & Kegan Paul, 1968, in which he develops the term 'institutional isolation'.

11. Cf. Arnold Gehlen, *Sozialpsychologische Probleme in der industriellen Gesellschaft*, Tübingen: Mohr (Siebeck), 1949.

12. Cf. Max Scheler's concept of the 'relative-natural world view' (*relativ-natürliche Weltanschauung*), as developed in *Die Wissensformen und die Gesellschaft*, Berne: Francke, 1960 (first published 1925).

13. Quoted from an interview reported by Steven V. Roberts in 'The Better Earth', *New York Times Magazine*, 29 March 1970.

come to terms with them to get them in his grasp and fight imaginary and losing battles against them in the process. They continue to make compelling demands on him. Yet none of them provides him with knowledge and guidelines for fitting his whole life experience and eventual death into the order of larger society and beyond it. After satisfying the institutional claims, he is left free – a freedom, it would seem, for which in the course of history man has fought persistently and passionately – to pick up the loose strands of his existence and fit them together as best he can.

The domains of freedom interpenetrating the institutionally controlled life of modern man have come to be called his 'private sphere'.[14] A relatively recent dimension of the social structure and of human existence, it is located between and within the institutionally defined 'spheres of interests' and represents a 'no man's land', unclaimed by the powers that be. Within its confines man is free to choose and decide on his own what to do with his time, his home, his body and his gods.

Lacking institutional means[15] to define new cultural goals and thereby to give the uncertainties of his life and the certainty of his death a unity and meaning which could enable him to transcend them, man can turn to the 'idea market' in which industries, ideologies, prophets, cranks and 'beautiful people' compete in their offerings of 'meaning', 'fulfilment', 'happiness', 'oblivion', 'truth' and 'togetherness'. In his socially undirected and uninhibited (though certainly not unlimited) freedom he can choose to 'freak out on Jesus' to satisfy his 'spiritual hunger',[16] to join 'man's most advanced school of the mind' and through Dianetics 'rid himself of unwanted feelings and sensations, and achieve a new enthusiasm toward life', or to wind up with an 'oom' feeling at Esalen. He can take an 'acid trip' to overcome his loneli-

14. Cf. Thomas Luckmann, *The Invisible Religion*, New York: The Macmillan Co., 1967; also, John Kenneth Galbraith, *The Affluent Society*, Cambridge: Houghton Mifflin Co., 1958, esp. Chapter XVIII.

15. Cf. Robert Merton, *Social Theory and Social Structure*, Glencoe: The Free Press, 1959, esp. Chapter IV.

16. From an interview reported by Edward B. Fiske in 'New Youth Groups "Freaked Out" on Jesus', *New York Times*, 22 February 1970.

ness, alienation, mistrust, his 'horrible state of misery',[17] and he can chant with the Soka Gakkai and achieve 'a natural high, an essential high, a universal high' (he can also chant for a bass fiddle or a new refrigerator).[18] He can take to the streets 'in a show of strength and determination and hope' and 'stay in the streets' where he can be together with others who share his food, his music and his thoughts.[19] He can 'tune in' rather than 'out' to participate in the mysteries of 'The Poetry of the Rock'. He can order the *Whole Earth Catalog* to provide him with 'tools . . . to conduct his own education, find his own inspiration, shape his own environment and share his adventures with whoever is interested'.[20]

With man's innate, biologically founded sociality, his corresponding 'gift' in constructing meaningful social realities,[21] his long historical experience of life in small communities, he proceeds to create within his private sphere and around the various roles he performs a variety of small universes of existence. Choosing and rejecting among the prefabricated parts of the vast array of 'existence kits' offered and available to him, man proceeds to build them into the small existence units which constitute his actual life-worlds. Very tentatively one might say that the construction of small life-worlds takes place on two levels:

(1) On the institutional level, where they are built around the specific institutional roles the individual performs. On this level they are limited by the institutionally imposed restrictions.

(2) On the level of the 'private sphere' in which:

17. Description of socio-psychological state of youth addicts by Dr Donald H. Louria, President, New York State Council on Drug Addiction, as reported by Lacey Fosburgh in 'Experts Predict a Flood of Heroin in U.S. Schools', *New York Times*, 5 February 1970.

18. '2,000,000 Americans Attracted to Buddhist Sect', *New York Times*, 8 March 1970.

19. Invitation leaflet to join the 'Bobby Seale Contingent' in the 15 April 1970 Moratorium against the War in Vietnam in Cambridge, Mass.

20. From an interview reported by Steven V. Roberts in 'Mail Order Catalogue of the Hip becomes National Bestseller', *New York Times*, 12 April 1970.

21. Cf. Peter L. Berger and Thomas Luckmann, *The Social Construction of Reality*, New York: Doubleday, 1966.

a. life-worlds are being constructed from modern as well as traditional elements of small-world existence patterns, or,

b. in which attempts are being made to create *new* designs for 'whole and lasting communities', using hedonistic, theoretical, 'scientific', but also romanticized historical 'models' of communal life.

The life-round of modern man is not of one piece. It does not unfold within one but within a variety of small 'worlds' which often are unconnected with one another. Within a lifetime – within the round of one day – the individual is alternately, consecutively or simultaneously a participant of variegated groups of communities which, in many instances, he is able to leave at will. He can – at least theoretically – change his job, he can in effect become a member of another social club, political party or church; he can sell or redecorate his house, move into another slum or suburb, divorce his wife and establish a new family. He can adopt a new sub-cultural style of clothes, appearance, gestures, language, love-making; he can create a new 'image' of himself or buy a new personality from his psychoanalyst. Instead of being a full-time member of one 'total and whole' society, modern man is a part-time citizen in a variety of part-time societies. Instead of living within one meaningful world system to which he owes complete loyalty he now lives in many differently structured 'worlds' to each of which he owes only partial allegiance.

Most of modern man's existential universes are *single-purpose communities*.[22] They are built around one specific role of the individual. The definition of this role – which all members of the community perform – is clearly understood and fully accepted. There is no doubt that X is a co-expert on fifteenth-century Mongolian history even though one might disagree with him on the original meaning of the name and the actual location of the place at which the Chinese General Chu, having been lured deep into Upper Mongolia by Bunyaširis warriors, was defeated in 1410. One's disagreement might be violent. Yet, within the

22. Cf. also the concept of 'segmentally rather than totally relevant' reference groups as developed by Ralph H. Turner, 'Reference Groups of Future-Oriented Men', in *Social Forces*, 1955, 34, 130–6.

small world of Mongolian studies one does after all speak the same language, one shares the same students, reads the same texts, goes to the same meetings, quarrels over the same footnotes whose paramount importance is not appreciated by anybody else. Other historians and scholars may be concerned with Mongolian history, but in ever-decreasing degrees of intensity. Their professional worlds might touch and from time to time overlap in part with one's own. But *they* will always be clearly distinguished from the experts on Mongolia. The highly formalized and routinized kind of interaction which provided 'security' and 'peace of mind' to man in traditional communities may also be found, though of a more limited variety, in the small lifeworlds of modern individuals, at least for the duration of their stay in any particular world.

The new existential universes of the private sphere may be *freely chosen* or *deliberately* (though not necessarily reflectively) *constructed*. They are not *given* in the sense in which traditional man is born into a community of 'the living and the dead'. While traditional man takes for granted that he will live and die in the community of his birth, the modern individual can exchange one of his several life-worlds for another without having to fear punishment or repercussions. He may, for example, exchange his 'food world' for an 'anti-food world', and move from the gourmet club set of his 'graciously living' friends into the 'slim-gym' togetherness of fat ladies who are trying to reduce their 'whole and total' weight of 3875 pounds to that of 3475 in six months of 'mutual friendship, support and encouragement'.[23] He cannot, even though supported and driven by the implications of the mobility ethos, move as easily from one job to another. The new small life-worlds, of the private sphere at least, are interchangeable but not when the 'exchange' creates a conflict with the 'rational' laws of the individual's 'institutional existence'.

Not unlike the traditional communities, the modern life-worlds are *small, comprehensible* and *knowable*. Inside a particular typing pool of this large corporation whose policies do not interest me and whose goals I only vaguely understand, I know the girls with whom I work. I know about their families, their hobbies, their

23. Communication of a friend.

biographies. I know the pool supervisor and the five or ten men whose letters I type. I recognize their voices as they come out of the dictating machine. I connect these voices with the individual people who sit in their cubicles down the hall. I know that X and Y are bachelors worth dressing up for. I know that Z and W always have second thoughts about their formulations and make you retype letters. I know that V's wife always calls at 5 o'clock to check up on her husband, etc. I know where the coffee machine is kept and whom I can meet there when. I know when the man who sells doughnuts and candies comes around. I have that little routine in the ladies' room where I go with the girl from the pool with whom I am friendly; we exchange notes on dates, clothes, plans and the current office gossip. I am equally familiar with the members, the rules, the inadequacies, the intrigues of my tennis club, my local church, the PTA of my children's school. All of them represent some of the small worlds within which my life unfolds and in which I participate for some limited ends. Inside these small worlds I feel quite safe. I feel 'at home'. There are not many uncertainties. Things make sense to me. I understand them.

The 'residence' within these small worlds is not always durable: I get married and quit my job in the typing pool; my husband does not play tennis and I take up golf so we can play together; the children grow older, go to college, I am no longer a member of the PTA, and I have become converted to Catholicism. 'Residence' is frequently of a *temporary* and always of a *migratory* character. The existence of the small worlds themselves is restricted and limited. So is individual participation. The individual is a temporary and part-time member, precisely because he is also a temporary and part-time member of other small life-worlds.

The *multi-world existence* of modern man requires frequent 'gear-shifting'. As he moves from one small world into the next, he is faced with at least marginally different expectations, requiring different role performances in concert with different sets of people. The small life-worlds of modern man belong to different 'jurisdictions' and different realms of meaning.[24] They pursue

24. Alfred Schutz, op. cit.

different goals, aim at the attainment of a different 'good', are differently organized, require different forms of behaviour, satisfy different 'needs' of man, make different kinds of demands upon him. Unlike the small communities of traditional society and similar to the autonomous institutional spheres, the small life-worlds never claim the total individual. Modern man lives in a set of small worlds. The connection and cohesiveness among his various life-worlds are provided solely by the biographical coincidence of his memberships.

Man, who creates and improves his small life-worlds, also attempts to arrange and fit them into at least a biographically reasonably meaningful whole. For this purpose he usually singles out one or two which seem of greatest permanence and importance to him. This one, or these few micro-universes will become the nucleus around which his other life-worlds can be arranged. The existence units predestined to constitute the *navel* of the small world clusters of existence are those which traditionally have carried out major functions in fitting the individual for life in society and providing individual existence with a sense of permanence. They are the family and the ecological community. Though of more recent origins, man's work world must also be included.

These three *omphalic* small worlds have undergone and are undergoing significant changes in the process of modernization. Though the family still socializes the young it no longer teaches them clearly defined patterns of behaviour, supported by firm beliefs which would prepare them for life in a correspondingly stable society. In a way one can say that the family socializes its young for the multi-dimensional existence in potential sets of part-time worlds by socializing them into the family itself as an instance of small-world existence – but also by the 'world-openness' of anticipatory socialization. The socialization process is further carried on in some of the other partial universes.

Biologically and economically of vital importance for man's early survival, emotionally the most stable and satisfying life-world, and at the same time the most durable one, the family continues to occupy a central position among the small life-worlds of modern man. This being so, the family is presumed to gratify expectations that in traditional society were the concern of other associations and institutions, but mainly of a multi-generational and extended family. One such expectation is to provide 'fulfilment' of an almost religious nature to the lives of the marriage partners[25] and by implication a meaningful integration of their multi-world existences. Another is the sustenance of a 'transcendence-promise', inherent in the family's procreation and socialization functions, for which, in traditional societies, whole symbolic universes had been created, frequently administered by specialized personnel. These 'societal' burdens placed upon a significantly changed and reduced family may strain its resources and overtax its functional limitations, thereby endangering its very continuity.

The ecological community, like the family, has preserved a number of its traditional functions, though they too have been modified and recast. Even more so than in the case of the family, a vigorous community ideology based on old symbolic associations has survived, at least on the rhetorical level, correspondingly supported by politicians on all levels of government. Though day-to-day decisions of local political institutions are made on 'rational' grounds (the scope and nature of 'rationality' usually being determined by supra-local institutional spheres in which the 'local branch' of government represents but a small constitutive unit)[26] these decisions may be reached and carried out in the traditional political style of the small town – while preserving the latter's old 'small world' character.

A contemporary citizen of a village, small town, faubourg, suburb, quarter or ghetto, decidedly 'modern' in his style of life, 'rational' on the job and in business, 'progressive' in his economic beliefs – and sometimes even in his private morals – may fight with conviction against the removal of an old (and ugly) historical monument which is a traffic hazard to boot. He may vigorously oppose the felling of an old tree which keeps the sunshine out of the nursing home, and the moving in of a new 'dirty'

25. Cf. Thomas Luckmann, op. cit., pp. 112–13.
26. Cf. Arthur J. Vidich and Joseph Bensman, *Small Town in Mass Society*, Princeton University Press, 1958.

industry which holds the promise of an economic boost for the city's dwindling resources.[27]

The survival of historical landscapes, the 'character of a village', city profiles, old communal rituals[28] may provide a 'sense of community' and continuity which is not warranted by the range of functions performed nor the amount of political control exercised by the ecological communities. The very fact of 'settling down', of buying a house, planting a rose bush, competing with one's neighbours over the least amount of crabgrass in one's lawn, or upbraiding the owners of 'uncurbed' dogs on the streets of one's neighbourhood, creates bonds which may make the prospect of moving away something more than just a problem of packing and frantic wives. Even the ghetto of one's childhood which one has left with joy and shame may be rediscovered as the 'stake' of one's 'black future', because 'Watts is my home'.[29]

The fact that working serves other than strictly economic functions is an amply substantiated truism.[30] This holds true for professionals and white-collar workers as well as for managers, craftsmen and tradesmen, the service occupations and the skilled and semi-skilled industrial workers. An overwhelming majority of employed men in a national sample stated, for example, that they would continue working even if by some chance they inherited enough money to live comfortably without work.[31] They explained that they enjoyed working, and also that work kept them occupied, justified their existence and enhanced their self-respect, and that without it they would 'feel lost' and 'go crazy'.[32]

27. Cf. Benita Luckmann, *Politik in einer deutschen Kleinstadt*, Stuttgart: Ferdinand Enke, 1970.

28. Cf. W. Lloyd Warner, *The Living and the Dead*, New Haven: Yale University Press, 1959.

29. Stanley Saunders, 'I'll Never Leave the Ghetto', *Ebony*, Vol. 20, No. 10, August 1967.

30. Cf. among others in this field Elton Mayo's classical study, *The Social Problems of Industrial Civilization*, Cambridge: Harvard University Press, 1945. Mayo describes the stabilizing influence on members of a clique in the workshop as against the anomic effects of their neighbourhoods.

31. Only among the unskilled workers one half wanted to quit work.

32. The actual withdrawal from the work-world at retirement may, like widowhood, produce reactions of anomie. See Nancy C. Morse and R. S. Weiss, 'The Function and Meaning of Work', in *Man, Work, and Society*,

The work ethos internalized along with other values of the Protestant ethic in America,[33] but equally strongly stressed in all other industrializing countries, has been carried over into life patterns of late industrial society. There it fills that part of leisure time – by 'do-it-yourself' occupations and the immersion in 'hobby worlds' – which is not passed 'educationally', 'informatively', 'enjoyably' or 'boringly' in viewing television.[34] Work being a dominant value-theme of industrial society, the rejection of work is analogously experienced as a rejection of society, followed, in turn, by the negative evaluation on the part of the 'working class' of 'bearded do-nothings', 'hairy parasites', etc.

As occupation has become the dominant status indicator for modern man, the work-world has become central for 'establishing' him in many of his other life-worlds in and outside the institutional spheres. A number of professions and occupations also may foster hopes and aspirations for extending the limits of one's physical existence by books written, students taught, pictures painted, services rendered, 'empires' built, etc.

The omphalic small life-worlds meet basic biological needs and perform equally important social functions. Enhanced by the residual 'traditional prestige' and supported by modern institutional ideologies as well as diffused 'general values' of society, the omphalic life-worlds are viewed as potential carriers of the incoherently articulated values of 'unity', 'meaning' and 'sense of permanence'. At the same time on the level of experimentation the search is on for 'total' and 'lasting' life-worlds, small and

---

ed. Sigmund Nosow and William H. Form, New York: Basic Books, 1962, pp. 29–35; also E. A. Friedmann and R. J. Havighurst, 'Work and Retirement', ibid., pp. 41–55. Cf. also Pierre Bourdieu, 'Le Désenchantement du monde: Travail et travailleurs en Algérie', mimeographed monograph of the Centre de Sociologie Européenne, Paris, 1966.

33. The qualities and aspirations of the 'Protestant ethic' imputed to the Puritan settlers seem to be analogous to those guiding the economic activities of Catholic refugees (from former German territories or settlements) forcibly settled in a predominantly Protestant town in Southern Germany at the end of the Second World War. Cf. Benita Luckmann, op. cit. Part I, 6.

34. Television programmes can and do provide bases for fantasy-life worlds which may, in turn, give 'meaning' to one's everyday life.

universal. This is true particularly among the young who in their 'confrontations' with existing society have in stages become disappointed, frustrated, disgusted, enraged and estranged from what they designate as a 'meaningless', 'anonymous', 'abstract', 'sick', 'bureaucratic' and 'repressive' society. In a dialectical interplay between 'activism' and 'turning-off' (possibly, but not necessarily involving different sets of people), in alternating phases of 'creative destructionism'[35] and 'dropout', the period of new world construction is ushered in.

While the 'rejection' of the old world is usually marked by non-conventional appearance and manners, offensive speech, the spurning of established morals, etc., its symbolic 'break-down' is played out in acts of violence aimed at the destruction of objects symbolizing modern society: the wrecking of a computer, the burning of banks, the decimation of files, the bombing of corporation office buildings, etc. The 'old world' is also exorcized and 'overcome' through witchcraft, magic, mystical cults – usually of Oriental origin – drug cultures, etc. What follows is the search for 'one's identity', 'one's thing', new and ever newer life-worlds. Everybody is 'running for the woods' and 'taking to the hills'. Communes are sought out or built up: American style, i.e. basically 'religious' and 'tribal' despite the anarchical intentions of their founders; Scandinavian style: promiscuous at first and boring later; 'functional' ones – those mostly conceived by women in cities in order to save money, divide labour, share babies and gain more free time. 'Scientific' communities are being produced 'with available behavioural technology' which should, in the words of the man who has provided the blueprint,[36] make it 'possible for any group of men of goodwill to construct a good life'. Western towns are being resurrected to 'discover things for oneself'; Blacks 'build a community of love . . . among blacks', in which 'the white man no longer exists'.[37] Ecology is becoming

35. Term coined by Michael Bakunin. Cf. his *Gosudarstvennost' i anarkhiya* (Statism and Anarchism), Zürich and Geneva, 1873.

36. From interview of B. F. Skinner by Richard Todd, '"Walden Two": Three? Many More?', *New York Times Magazine*, 15 March 1970. Cf. also Skinner's book, *Walden Two*, New York: Macmillan Paperbacks, 1962.

37. Stokely Carmichael, 'Towards Black Liberation', *Massachusetts Review*, autumn 1966.

'a whole way of life' which 'gives unity to experience' and some day 'might be as important as rock'n'roll'.[38] 'The future is a blank screen you can play your phantasies out on'[39] in 'looking for life's reality'.[40]

All this seems to indicate at least two things. 'Life's reality' is something that the traditional systems of meaning transmitted and that the 'big' social institutions of modern society fail to transmit for large numbers of individuals. Modern society does not provide the 'links' for fitting the totality of individual existence into the order of the industrial universe. On the other hand, modern man possesses enclaves of 'freedom' in which he can arrange his private life in almost any way he likes. This does not mean that his private life is solitary; on the contrary. In his quest for 'order and meaning' modern man seems to be creating for himself a small-world existence again in which the complex, bewildering and often frightening outside world is placed more or less effectively in parentheses.

The life of man in modern industrial societies does indeed differ in many important and less important, in obvious and hidden respects from the life of man not only in prehistoric and 'primitive' societies but also in traditional and even early industrial societies. Yet there are some intrinsic continuities in the manner in which he arranges his life or at least in the manner in which he seeks and finds meaning in such arrangements. Modern man continues to live in small worlds which are comprehensible and manageable to him. These small worlds are not 'whole' but partial; they are not life-long but part-time; they are less 'naturally-given' than 'intentionally chosen'; there is no single small world but many of them.

38. From interviews as reported by Steven V. Roberts in 'The Better Earth', op. cit.

39. From an interview of Stewart Brand, creator of Whole Earth Catalog and owner of Whole Earth Truck Store, as reported by Steven V. Roberts, op. cit.

40. From an interview of Scott Ross, thirty-year-old former disc jockey turned Pentecostal: 'I went the political route, and then through the drug trip. Others get into meditation or Hare Krishna. We're all looking for life's reality.' *New York Times*, March 1970, 'Many Youths turn to Pentecostals'.

14 Burkart Holzner

The Construction of Social Actors: An Essay on Social Identities

B. Holzner, *The Construction of Social Actors: An Essay on Social Identities*, MSS.

Introduction

Several recent intellectual developments have brought the concept of identity under closer scrutiny by the social sciences (DeVos, 1969; Isaacs, 1967; Parsons, 1968; Erikson, 1967).[1] These developments arise from the puzzles of modern history which have exposed certain previously taken for granted aspects of social existence as problematic. For example, conceptions of the 'society' as the encompassing framework within which social processes occur have become questionable as national societies and intersocietal, even intercivilizational, processes themselves become objects of study (Nelson, 1968). That nations are constructed and that national societies are shaped through historic actions and their consequences is for us an obvious fact. Indeed, the practical concerns of social scientists and politicians with nation and institution building have demonstrated the simple fact that such collectivities are not simply givens but are in part devised through deliberate actions and strategies.[2]

The various attempts to understand modernization as a process converging in all parts of the world upon the highly technological and liberal society have encountered with puzzlement the fact that divergencies are as frequently observed as convergencies. Indeed, we must recognize a world-wide trend towards the reaffirmation of primordial ethnic and racial identities, a reaffirmation which, in part, results from deliberate acts and strategies. The belief in a shared cultural tradition, a community of fate, often linked to the belief in common biological descent which is

1. For full references, see pp. 309 f.
2. One may think, for example, of the recent notion of 'nation-building'.

characteristic of ethnic groups, has proved a significant focus in the forming of individual and collective identities. We are today compelled to accept the fact that there appear to be strong reasons which make individual or collective actors affirm various communal as against national identities, instilling in them the deliberate purpose to use modern political and technical instrumentalities for widely divergent ends. The realignment of the international system of status and prestige, which is the necessary consequence of the world-wide movement towards modernization, also has given rise to movements aiming to change the feeling of self-worth, of authority, and the conditions of power of disadvantaged groups. In the context of such social movements we can observe the processes of identity construction with particular clarity. For an example we may refer to the black power movement in the United States and its profound consequences for the public conception of the collective and personal identities of American blacks (Himes, 1973).

The turbulence of modern history, brought about by drastic realignments of power and the opening up of previously undreamed of possibilities, have also produced a multiplicity of hard constraints which compel persons and groups to seek shelter and support in collective identifications. Communal, ethnic, and racial clashes around the world have taken a fearsome toll in human life (Richardson, 1960; Gurr, 1970). Again and again the analysis of such constraints which reinforce, or sometimes weaken, collective identities points up the complexity of the process which cannot be resolved by simplistic conceptions of economic determination, or theories of social deviance, or even straightforward theories of political strategies for power. Something else is at stake here, and it appears that the conceptual apparatus of social science – which after all developed in the context of rising European nationalism and hence tended to reify conceptions of the society as an encompassing framework, and thereby drifted into simplistically unidirectional models of development – is as yet insufficiently equipped to deal with it. We do have a great deal of relevant and important knowledge about the formation of groups, the establishment of their boundaries, the forming of coalitions and more, but we have not as yet assembled it in a way appropriate to the understanding of the phenomenon at hand: the construction of social actors and the forming of social identities.

Another set of considerations must be mentioned as well. In the highly modern, that is technology- and knowledge-based, societies of today we find that many of the practical constraints, imposed by scarcity, which in the past buttressed social conceptions of individual identity have become less compelling. This is the result of a multiplicity of means and a shift of scarcities from traditional patterns to entirely new ones. In this context many individuals face the burden of choice and deliberation in the construction and maintenance of their identity in a most practical sense. Whereas it was the general pattern of traditional and industrial societies to present their members with a strictly limited array of possible models for one's social existence, the knowledge-based society offers a large surfeit of them. Paradoxically this increased concern with conscious choice of life style in the explicit awareness of the problem of social identity goes hand in hand with increased knowledge of the social and psychological determinants involved in the shaping of personalities, groups, institutions and societies. Indeed, Talcott Parsons argues that such awareness of new determinants of social existence poses a perceived problem of freedom and increases the feeling of alienation (Parsons, 1968). Clearly, social models of personal identity have become problematic in contemporary society, a condition which has inspired a considerable volume of intellectual production on this subject.

In the social sciences themselves, scrutiny has been extended to encompass increasing domains of otherwise taken for granted aspects of social life. Important currents in social psychology, sociology and phenomenology have converged in the study of processes of the social construction of reality (Berger and Luckmann, 1966; Holzner, 1968). We now know that the intersubjective confirmations which buttress our sense of reality experience and our specific interpretations of situations are themselves social in character and can be subjected to systematic study and explication. In this spirit it may be worth our while to extend this point of view from the concern with an understanding of the social processes which lead to the construction of a meaningfully interpreted world of objects to the concern with the construction of social actors themselves (Coleman, 1973).

When we do this, we may expect to shed some light on such diverse matters as the relationship between individual and society, which the prevalent conception of institutionalization sees largely determined by primary socialization, the patterns of certain types of identity building social movements, and even the impact which the construction and maintenance of identifiable collective or individual actors may have on directions of historic development. In this view social change is always seen as a consequence of action, produced by actors compelled to face constraints and opportunities and developing rationales for doing so. However, actors are not necessarily individuals, nor is one individual necessarily only one actor; we must now explore the nature of actors as social constructs.

Actors as Social Constructs

The concept 'actor' is used here to refer to some entity which is the source of a pattern of action. Clearly, this concept differs from the concept 'organism' which refers to a concrete physical-biological entity, whereas the concept 'actor' does not. There are no actors known who are not in some way based on human organisms, and thereby constrained and limited by biologically defined capabilities. However, states, armies, industrial firms and other collectivities must in certain respects be treated as actors and are so treated in everyday discourse and by the law; it would be absurd to call them organisms.

Neither is the term 'actors' synonymous with the concept 'personality'. We mean by personality a system of relatively enduring behavioural dispositions which are in part genetically, in part socially determined. A given personality structure may well be compatible with sustaining a variety of actors in our sociological sense. In fact, while there are extreme situations in which the enactment of an actor-model absorbs the total resources of a personality, as may be the case in the artistic genius or the religious virtuoso, social actor constructs are rarely that demanding. Each individual personality is capable of playing a variety of roles, and indeed is compelled to do so. Where clusters of such roles are bundled into divergent or possibly even incompatible patterns which are enacted by the same individual at different periods of time or in alternation, we must recognize that an individual is capable of sustaining several individual actors, let alone his ability to participate in a variety of collective actors.

We are thus dealing with the concept 'actor' in the strictly sociological sense as the focal source of social action. That is, the social environment affords an actor simultaneously status as an object – he must be a social entity of some kind, and as a subject, i.e. actors are believed to be conscious and deliberate (Parsons, 1951).[3] This fact poses not too great a problem when we deal with individuals as conscious subjects who engage at least at times in deliberate actions. However, we attribute subjectivity also to collective actors. Common parlance has it that a nation, or an organization, takes a particular 'point of view', 'feels' that their objectives are being thwarted, 'hopes' for a victory and the like. In taking such notions seriously it should be treated as obvious that we do not wish to reify metaphysical constructions such as 'collective consciousness' or 'collective unconscious'. But there are specific and explicable processes through which the reality construct of a deliberately proceeding collective actor with attributes of objectness is being created and sustained, and the understanding of these phenomena may prove to be of considerable significance.

Actors, then, taken as the focal points of action must be treated from the point of view both of their being an object and of their being a subject. Every actor, individual, or collective must reckon with a number of specific constraints, most of which we do not need to explore here. We will briefly deal only with some of them, namely the demands of responsibility, authority, trust, and identity, in order to pinpoint certain compelling demands for articulating symbolically the nature of the actor as an object and the frame of reference and point of view of his subjectness.

The term responsibility implies that others have the power to hold an actor accountable for the consequences of his action over

3. See especially 'Categorization of actor-units in object roles' and 'Classification of orientation-role types', pp. 142–5 in Parsons, 1951.

a considerable period of time. To what extent an actor is taken as accountable, in the sense that his resources may be called upon to undo damages caused by his previous action is a matter of wide variation. However, to the extent that an actor wishes to be able to call upon the dependency and cooperation of others, he is compelled to demonstrate the scope and the limitations of his responsibility. In doing this, he creates important symbolic determinations of himself as a social object. It may be taken for granted that efforts to maintain responsibility will be abandoned when compelling reasons to do this disappear. One very important source of such reasons rests in claims to authority, the right to direct others and marshal their resources for some collectively legitimated goal.

Authority enables the concentration of diffuse resources on particular objectives and thus not only concentrates but also creates genuine increments of power. The possibility to construct an authority structure and to maintain it rests both on the control of the means of coercion and the nature of legitimacy; in both senses it is always finite and compels depending upon the strategic situation, the drawing of social boundaries. Again, we see occasions which compel the symbolic articulation of a social entity; when challenged, authority must be able to specify from where its rights come and how far they reach.

By trust we mean the predisposition of others to count, implicitly, on the responsibility, rightfulness, regularity and therefore reliability of the actor's actions. The absence of trust imposes such degrees of uncertainty that others may well be motivated to take coercive measures against the untrustworthy actor (Luhmann, 1968; Holzner, 1973). Taken together, the imperatives of responsibility, authority, and trust inherent in action constrain an actor to present symbolic indications of his identity. Viewing these constraints not only as general concepts but in their concrete historical shape will go several steps towards clarifying the specific nature of the identity constructs an actor must develop.

The emphasis on constraints and necessities in the previous sentences should caution both ourselves and readers against the possible misunderstanding that the construction of actors is a somehow ephemeral phenomenon subject to whimsical change through alterations of one's consciousness or ideological state. This is most emphatically not the case. We are discussing processes of massive force whose direction and patterning are not easily deflected from their course and which are governed by scientifically discoverable natural laws. In fact, the rearrangement of presently available knowledge resulting from the point of view suggested here may allow us to connect facts and principles in such a way that we may be able to take steps towards further understanding of the necessities governing social activity.

The construction of a social actor, whether individual or collective, thus requires the definition of a social object of specifiable attributes which has a place in physical and social space, and in physical and social time, and thus can be said to enter into determinate relations with other social objects. Similarly, it requires the development of a frame of reference and point of view compatible with this location or a trajectory of locations. It appears inherent in what has been said that the conception of using the socialization process as a model for the construction of actors would be mistaken. Indeed, from this perspective primary socialization would be a process of organismic modification, learning, personality development, which is in part determined by an already existing image of a responsible, competent, and trustworthy actor. Similarly the process of role learning in secondary socialization is not the appropriate model for the understanding of the process. Rather, we are referring to the construction of personal identity which occurs partly determined through socialization, partly through strategic interactions relating to one's social position. More dramatically, we should include the processes of role innovation and the construction of novel models of identity. Most clearly the process of actor construction can be seen in the context of certain social movements and the construction of collectivities. We are thus focusing less on the learning of established models and culture patterns, more on the strategic occasions in which an identity construct must be either revealed or created in order to satisfy a challenging or dangerous situation (Nelson, 1965 and 1969).[4]

4. For some most suggestive leads toward the understanding of these processes see certain formulations of Benjamin Nelson.

All the processes that impinge on the construction of actors in some sense can be considered developments. There is a useful sense in which we can speak of the development of responsible citizens, or the development of a state. However, whereas the use of socialization as the model for these processes would lead us into the conception of a predetermined outcome, the model advocated here sensitizes us to possibly divergent outcomes which result from strategic choices in the determination of actors as social entities, performed under conditions of varying constraints.

Object Construction and Subject Construction: The Place of Identity in Relations of Action

We have been speaking of the reflexivity of actors, the fact that they must be treated as objects and subjects at the same time but in different respects. To discuss processes of object and subject construction implies that there are degrees to which something or somebody can be an object or subject. Probably this comes as a surprising notion since we are accustomed to dealing with objects as things and subjects as consciousness, neither of which seem to be matters of more or less. If one considers this, however, it does become quite readily apparent that there are indeed degrees of objectness. A social entity may vary from a fuzzy aggregate with nebulous boundaries and barely articulated characteristics, to a sharply delineated organized group (Campbell, 1958). The degree to which a social entity becomes an organized object clearly depends on the sharpness with which its boundary is drawn, its internal coherence, its tendency to remain identical with or similar to what it once was under varied external conditions, and its capacity to offer resistance against intrusion.

Similarly we are able to speak of degrees of subjectness. Not only in the sense that our consciousness may not be sharp and wide awake, so that we live in the realm of the unconscious or semiconscious, but in the analytically more appropriate sense of varying degrees of articulation of the subject aspect in an actor. This subject aspect of an actor appears to require a relatively organized frame of reference which locates the acting subject in a context and enables it to perceive given occasions from its point of view. It further implies reflexivity and self-hood – all of which very clearly are matters of degree. Actions, we might say, become more clearly understandable the farther the crystallization of the actor as a subject has progressed so that actions may appear to another either as inchoate and incomprehensible, so that they can be described and explained but not understood, or else they appear as transparent in their motivation and relation to the actor's point of view (Schutz, 1972).[5]

In speaking of the subject and object aspects of an actor, we are venturing into an area in which misunderstandings are easily possible. It should be quite clear that we do not have any reference to the by now outdated controversy in the social sciences concerning the superiority of 'objective' over 'subjective' methods (or the reverse). Nor do we wish to perpetuate any notion of a sharp dichotomy between objectivity and subjectivity. In fact, in general we prefer to avoid the terms objective and subjective but find them in this context altogether unavoidable. The conscious actor both treats himself in certain respects and is treated by others as an object, an entity of some kind, while at the same time he experiences himself in the first person as the locus and source of action and is in that sense perceived by others as a 'free' and conscious person or quasi-person.

Thus the object and subject aspects are interdependent and even interpenetrate in a peculiar way. Georg Simmel discussed this matter in the following passage in his *Philosophy of Money*:

Subject and object are born in the same act: (a) logically, in that the purely conceptual, ideal constituents are, on the one hand, given as the content of representation, and, on the other, as the content of subjective reality; and (b) psychologically, in that the as yet self-unrelated representation, containing both subject and object in a neutral state, undergoes internal differentiation and thereby gives rise to a contrast between the self and its object, through which each of these is first endowed with the character that sets it apart from the other. This process, which eventually brings about our cognitive model of the world, also goes on within our volitional experience . . . insofar

5. The point of view taken in this paragraph clearly is much influenced by the work of Alfred Schutz, giving it an empirically oriented interpretation.

as the human being receives gratification from anything, there occurs an entirely unitary act (that is, subject and object are not distinguished) . . . the possibility of desire (however) is the possibility of the object of desire. Such an object – characterized by contrast with the subject, and constituted as object by that contrast – the desire for which the subject simultaneously endeavours to gratify and to set at rest, is for us a value. (*Wolff*, 1959)

The interpenetration of subject and object in an action and the emphasis on the social process of their differentiation as aspects of the actor is the main point we accept from Simmel's statement. However, we must maintain that any actor, not just the individual, develops the subject aspect. In collectivities, this process has been dealt with under the heading of consensus, with often misleading results. The specific social arrangements whereby individual personalities are motivated to commit part of their cognitive modes to a collective actor's frame of reference or system of relevance and to assess situations from that actor's point of view is far more complex and often substantially different from what the search for consensus would lead us to believe.

We can now say several general things about the construction of identities by which indeed we mean the delimitation of actors. We may speak here of actors in *statu nascendi*, social entities endowed with some minimum objective base and a minimal sense of subjectivity. Such nascent actors will encounter compelling occasions in which an identity must be declared, as if in a password, or limitations must be acknowledged and dealt with even if they are painful. The place of the actor in relation to others, and in relation to time and space, must inevitably be assessed and conceptions of past, present, and future develop. Thus, as there emerges an entity that others can treat as an actor object there develops with compelling necessity a definition and codification of the actor's subject aspect. We assume, as stated above, that such articulations of what and who an actor is are only undertaken when circumstances demand such effort. There will be tendencies on the part both of others and of the actor to develop a relatively coherent typification (Schutz, 1972) that satisfies as best possible external and internal demands. On the external side the typification will include such things as boundary, time duration of the actor, status and the like; on the subject side they will include a frame of reference and point of view. The construction of such typifications is an exceedingly onerous process especially in those stress situations in which it is most demanded. Therefore there will be a high proclivity to accept culturally available models of identity and their various components, including especially models of conscience which include solutions to questions of responsibility as well as authority (Moore and Anderson, 1966; Nelson, 1968; Marx and Holzner, 1973).[6]

The way in which an actor becomes differentiated from others and a separate and identifiable entity will depend not only on the general state of social differentiation, but very largely on the existence of scales and devices of social assessment or measurement. Indeed, such scales and devices to assess, for example, an actor's power or his wealth or prestige will differ vastly depending on the nature of the symbolism available, and depending on the prevalent nature of organization.[7] Any rejection of a scale as inappropriate and the attempt to replace it authoritatively by a different scale is a typical strategy of rebellion and revolution.[8] In either case, however, the existence of such scales of social assessment will define positively or negatively possibilities open for identity construction. That these processes involve large motivational energies has been under-emphasized this far, but should go without saying. Identity determinations may not only involve matters of relative security and insecurity but the very continued existence of the actor. The mechanisms through which motivation is channelled towards symbolized identity constructs,

6. The concept 'model of identity' and the more specific (component) 'model of conscience' were formulated on the basis of the work of Moore and Anderson on 'folk models' and 'cultural objects'. Nelson's work on models of conscience in relation to cultural revolutions is most important here. Other aspects of the concept 'model of identity' are explored in a 1973 paper by Marx and Holzner.

7. Again, this point was most forcefully made in Simmel's *Philosophy of Money*. There is some awareness of these issues also in the literature on 'social indicators', for example in Raymond Bauer, 1966.

8. This process is at work, for example, in the religious movements of salvation among 'parish people' (Weber), and especially in the drastic restructuring of values involved in the 'rejection of the world' (Weber, 1920).

mechanisms of identification and mobilization cannot be discussed here.

The Construction of Collective Actors as Objects

In the following we will speak of the construction of collective actors with primary reference to those collectivities like states, churches, value-oriented movements that present the claim to be grounded on urgent and vital needs of their actual or potential constituents and that therefore make a comprehensive claim for allegiance. Such collectivities are transformed from mere categories of persons into collective actors through some form of organization and articulation of their identity that tends to arise in response to specific and compelling occasions. We assume that the central process in this respect is the assembling and maintenance of authority which necessarily on one side involves the mobilization of loyalties and on the other side strategies for conflict and potentially the formation of coalitions.

The most fundamental determination of such a collective actor involves legitimation of its boundary, basically in terms of territoriality or else in terms of social domains of allegiance. The testing of where the boundaries are will determine fundamental attributes such as sect-like withdrawal as against imperial quests for domination. Secondly, there need to be determinations of placement of the collective actor in relation to significant others, with respect to the most salient domains of values. The inequality and the distribution of values among actors makes coming to terms with stratified systems an inescapable aspect of identity formation. What the collectivity is as defined by its boundaries, and where it is located in the scheme of other actors having differential access to desired values are probably the basic foundations of identity construction. Which values are salient will determine the response to such placement – but more about this later.

Another basic determination of the actor's nature as object involves its position in time. The duration of a collective actor's existence may be a matter of dispute but it is of large significance for the way in which others will respond to the collectivity. The outcomes of occasions for tests will decisively influence the assessment of the actor's power, a particularly salient dimension of placement. All of these are relatively obvious and straight-forward assessments of a social object. However, historic circumstances may lead to rather diverse profiles of different collectivities along these dimensions. Where physical and social boundaries are clear and unambiguous, we face one situation which presents opportunities for strategies of identity construction drastically different from those in which this is not the case. Disparities among the different dimensions of placement and assessment are likely to reduce the collective actor's qualitative interpretation in terms of significance and degree of uniqueness. Such interpretations are often based on the construction of a coherent or collective fate, symbolized by visible landmarks. Out of such interpretations arises the quality profile of the collective actor's authority and power, scope and limitation of responsibility, trustworthiness, and predictability, and the assessment of its value significance. It should be noted that such qualitative interpretations are likely to be strongly influenced by the models of the social object implemented in the construction of the collective actor.[9]

The Construction of Collective Actors as Subjects

The determination of the collective entity as an object, sketched before, clearly has strong implications for the development of its subject aspect. The central problem is the emergence of a coherent frame of reference and point of view, and its anchoring in the solidarity and commitment of constituent actors, be they in turn collectivities or ultimately individuals. The drawing of collective boundaries, and the placement of a collectivity in a stratified order, its temporal duration, claims to power and significance and uniqueness must be of such a nature in order to ensure that they can effect large transfers of motivation and alterations of frames

9. Such processes and their consequences are particularly visible if one studies the history of European nation states, and the construction of models for nations in the politico-legal conception of the sovereign nation state, with concomitant models of citizenship.

of reference on the part of the constituent actors. Thus, the subject aspect of the actor in turn imposes stringent constraints on the kinds of responses which enter into object determinations of what the actor is.

Solidarity in the sense of an unproblematic sharing of everyday definitions of reality and actions rarely encompasses the entire domain of a large collectivity. Symbolic transfers of loyalty to landmark symbols of the collectivity are essential. These are likely to be successful only under the condition that they offer a significant store of value to constituent actors in terms of security, welfare, feelings of self-worth or other value dimensions. It is in the context again of meeting specific occasions of challenge that landmarks of collective experience are constructed which become the enabling ground for coordinating expectations and the transfer of loyalty.

The quality of the actor subject does involve the establishment of a frame of reference acknowledging but not necessarily accepting the objectness of the collective entity, presenting models of rationality and problem solving and linked with the legitimacy base of the authority structure. Ultimately it is in this context that the symbolic articulation of collective identity becomes most significant. Such symbolic articulations with their constructions of past, present, and future and their relations to models of decision making that are considered appropriate can be seen as the central structure determining interpretations of the collective fate and of desirable actions. In this sense the symbolization of collective identity becomes a code for the collectivity (Parsons, 1968).[10]

More specifically the dual exigencies of maintaining the actor in relation to others and maintaining the collectivity through constant mobilization of resources from its constituents will give rise to the construction of a collective ideology and myth (Geertz, 1964).[11] Most significantly such a collective ideology must include not only responses to the challenges from the external environment but must also offer models of subjectivity, and models of

10. The conception of a 'code' in this sense is specified in Parsons' paper 'The Position of Identity in the General Theory of Action' (Parsons, 1968).
11. The term 'ideology' is here used in the sense used by Clifford Geertz.

conscience for its constituents. Which form such models will take will vary depending on the base of strength from which strategies are formulated for the solution of specific problems. Such a base of strength may be a highly developed state apparatus, or a highly developed sense of communality among constituents, or some other relatively secure domain from which problematic situations can be tackled. The range of permissible models of individual identity and especially conscience will vary considerably when the collectivity has, for example, the ability to pay for services in money, or must rely on dedication to military values, or has command of a moral system. We consider it, however, unlikely that the dynamics of collective identity formation and maintenance do not have a direct impact on the range of individual identity formations and think it possible to discover the specific ways in which this connection comes about.

Models of Personal Identity

From what we have said before it is now clear that personal identity construction is a process which cannot even be considered merely within the framework of individual developmental psychology, nor even within the framework of the social psychology of socialization. It must take into account, among other things, the dynamics of collective identity construction prevalent in a person's social field and the demands thereby imposed upon him, as well as the actual social structuring of situations which demand determinations of responsibility, personal authority and competence, trustworthiness, and thus impose certain external demands for formulating various responses to the question who one is.

In addition to collective identification demands, we thus are compelled to deal with the distribution of authority and demands of responsibility in the society, and their relation to networks of unreflected social relations, as in the family. Where relations of family-like security determine many of the responses to demands to identify one's self, they are likely to give rise to very specific strategies of social interaction and rather specifically limited modes of identity construction. Such basic identity constructs are of a different nature from the identity constructs of a purely relational and competence based variety such as those that enter into the modern occupational world (Isaacs, 1967).[12] It is probably the interface between that realm of not primary socialization but primary relations and the realm of fluid social relationality that most significantly influences the salience of primary familistic, ethnic, and racial identifications. Again the assumption must be that such identifications are constructed and maintained through necessities and a sociological task becomes to discover what these are.

These reflections lead us to search for the conditions that give rise to the construction and subsequent dispersion of specific models of personal identity of which social history shows considerable, but not random, variety. We are likely to discover such conditions when we focus our attention on those situations in which an individual or collective actor is confronted with the compelling demand to identify himself. There are, for example, certain economic situations in which responsibility must be demonstrated in order to become eligible for credit. We would expect to find rather wide variation in socially anchored notions as to what constitutes a satisfactory test of such responsibility. Obviously, a property- or even more so a land-oriented society will be more likely to emphasize family or clan memberships in determinations of economic responsibility than a performance- and income-oriented system in which demonstrated and preferably even certified capabilities of the actor matter more.

However, the reference to the granting of credit should be taken as an illustration of a type of situation in which identification demands become inescapable; more fundamental may be determinations of contract-worthiness and reliability. Where the conception of responsibility and work reliability refers to learnable and therefore in principle detachable skills, certification procedures arise which support the identification process as in the modern professions. Indeed, under these circumstances highly stylized models of identity and corresponding procedures for presenting such identities and their associated claims to responsi-

12. The relationship between the 'primordial' domain and other modes of identity construction is especially explored in the work of Harold Isaacs.

bility develop as in the varied conceptions of the professional. The structure of an economic system therefore gives us leads as to the distribution of such identification demands and their preferred solutions in a society. Similarly, the structure of a political system will expose individual and collective actors systematically and repeatedly to demands to declare and defend their claims to authority. Indeed, the modern conception of citizenship in its varied specific legal forms is one of the most obvious results of such demands. Corresponding notions of the official or leader are constructed in interaction with such identifications. Finally, the establishment of trustworthiness requires a demonstration of basic competencies as well as solidarities which must be credibly expressed and for which appropriate symbols exist.

It appears quite clear that the highly differentiated and interdependent modern society with rapid rates of social change produces with greater frequency demands to establish who and what one is than a stable segmented society with lower interaction rates. The problem of actor construction and models of identity then is directly related to the Durkheimian problem of the transformation in forms of solidarity in the context of modernization. Indeed, it seems reasonably clear that each identification demand can be fulfilled only by pointing symbolically to some solidarity which can be said to be willing to back up the claims an actor makes about himself. The nature of such certifying solidarities, however, has obviously undergone rather drastic change. Patterns of solidarities, then, may be seen as drawn upon in order to solve actors' identification problems (with the term 'identification' here always meant in the straightforward sense of revealing oneself as in a password and thus establishing one's responsibility, authority, trust, and thus one's identity).

This circumstance of the interdependence between an individual actor's identifying performance and his solidarities again reminds us of the interdependence between individual actor constructs and collective actor construction. The mobilization of collectivities which will typically take the form of the construction of a collective actor not only will back up individual actor's identification performances, but it will also introduce new demands. Specific definitions of the scope of authority and types of responsibilities must be enforced by the leadership of the collectivity in order to marshal the commitments and social energies required by the collective actor. Hence, identity models will be produced in the process of an intersection between structurally distributed demands faced by individual actors to establish the scope and limits of their responsibilities with the force field of collective actors (Allardt, 1970/71). Models of conscience then come to be matters of primary importance and provide rationales for the resolution of competing claims.

It should be noted that, hand in hand with the study of the distribution of situations in which responsibilities must be demonstrated and therefore identities must be credibly presented, we find situations and indeed actors that are exempt from such demands. Indeed, it is precisely the type of society in which responsibility is vested in an individual actor that is likely to create a multiplicity of conceptions of non-responsible actors. The systematic introduction of the conception of childhood, for example, in social history would be an indication of this process. Further, the delimitation of situations which have decidedly no bearing on the determination of responsibilities becomes a more deliberate and clearly stated matter (see, for example, Freidson, 1972).

Conclusion

We have in this paper explored a point of view to consider social actors as constructions which are shaped through culture-production in order to satisfy certain systematically arising situational demands for identification and the delimitation of the actors as both object and subject. We feel this point of view may be fruitful for the study of certain otherwise puzzling processes in contemporary social history. It directs our attention to a systematic investigation of those situations in which compelling determinations of the nature and identity of an actor must be made, whether the actor be collective or individual. It is sociologically obvious but not trivial that such situations do not occur randomly but are systematically produced by the prevailing social structure and hence give rise to specific types of actor identity constructs. The processes through which these constructions are accomplished are inadequately understood but a fruitful research strategy for the exploration can be easily imagined. Detailed descriptive case studies of the way in which actors in *statu nascendi* develop strategies for dealing with identification demands and the way in which their subjectness in frame of reference and point of view are structured appear to be in order. Beyond this a social historical investigation of prevalence and incidence of certain describable models of identification would be useful. Finally, one can imagine an approach to the study of social movements in which the interplay between collective and individual actor constructs is the focus of the investigation, instead of the up to now not very fruitful concern with personality and institutions.

References

ALLARDT, Erik, 1970/71, 'Culture, Structure and Revolutionary Ideologies', *Journal of Comparative Sociology*, Vol. 11–12, 24–40. Esp. the section 'The psychological background to the culture-building element in ideologies'.

BAUER, Raymond A. (ed.), 1966, *Social Indicators*, Cambridge, Mass.: The MIT Press.

BERGER, Peter L., and LUCKMANN, Thomas, 1966, *The Social Construction of Reality*, Garden City: Doubleday.

CAMPBELL, Donald P., 1958, 'Common Fate, Similarity and Other Indices of the Status of Aggregates of Persons and Other Social Entities', *Behavioral Science*, 3, 17.

COLEMAN, James S., 1973, 'Loss of Power', *American Sociological Review*, 38 (February), 1–17.

DEVOS, George, 1969, 'Minority Group Identity', in Joseph C. Finney (ed.), *Culture Change, Mental Health, and Poverty*, Lexington: University of Kentucky Press.

ERIKSON, Erik H., 1967, 'Identity', in *New International Encyclopedia of the Social Sciences*, New York: Macmillan.

FREIDSON, Eliot, 1972, *The Profession of Medicine*, New York: Dodd, Mead.

GEERTZ, Clifford, 1964, 'Ideology as a Cultural System', in David E. Apter (ed.), *Ideology and Discontent*, New York: The Free Press.

GURR, Ted Robert, 1970, *Why Men Rebel*, Princeton University Press.

HIMES, Joseph S., 1973, 'The Black Mystique', Chapter 4 in Himes, *Racial Conflict in American Society*, Columbus: Charles E. Merrill Publishers.

HOLZNER, Burkart, 1968/72, *Reality Construction in Society*, Cambridge, Mass.: Schenkman Publishing Co.

1973, 'Sociological Reflections on Trust', *Humanitas* (November).

ISAACS, Harold R., 1967, 'Group Identity and Political Change: the role of color and physical characteristics', *Daedalus*, 96, 2, 353–75.

LUHMANN, Niklas, 1968, *Vertrauen*, Stuttgart: Ferdinand Enke.

MARX, John, and HOLZNER, Burkart, 1973, 'The Social Construction of Strain and Ideological Models of Grievance in Contemporary Movements', unpublished manuscript.

MOORE, O. K., and ANDERSON, A. R., 1966, 'Models and explanations in the Behavioral Sciences', in Gordon J. DiRenzo (ed.), *Concepts, Theory and Explanation in the Behavioral Sciences*, New York: Random House.

NELSON, Benjamin, 1965, 'Self Images and Systems of Spiritual Direction in the History of European Civilization', pp. 49–103 in S. Z. Klausner (ed.), *The Quest for Self Control: Classical Philosophies and Scientific Research*, New York: The Free Press.

1968, 'Scholastic Rationales of "Conscience", Early Modern Crises of Credibility, and the Scientific-technocultural Revolutions of the 17th and 20th centuries', *Journal for the Scientific Study of Religion*, VII, 2 (Fall), 157–77.

1969, 'Conscience and the Making of Early Modern Cultures: the Protestant Ethic beyond Max Weber', *Social Research*, 36, 1 (February), 4–21.

PARSONS, Talcott, 1951, *The Social System*, Glencoe: The Free Press.

1968, 'The Position of Identity in the General Theory of Action', pp. 11–23 in C. Gordon and K. Gergen (eds.), *The Self in Social Interaction*, New York: John Wiley & Sons.

RICHARDSON, Lewis, F., 1960, *Statistics of Deadly Quarrels*, Pittsburgh: The Boxwood Press.

SCHUTZ, Alfred, 1972, *Reflections on the Problem of Relevance*, ed. Richard Zaner, New Haven and London: Yale University Press.

SIMMEL, Georg, 1900, *Philosophie des Geldes*, Leipzig: Duncker und Humblot.

WEBER, Max, 1920, 'Zwischenbetrachtung' in *Gesammelte Aufsätze zur Religionssoziologie*, Tübingen: Mohr, Vol. I, 536 ff.

WOLFF, Kurt, 1959, *Georg Simmel, 1858–1918*, A Collection of Essays, with Translations and a Bibliography. Contributors Howard Becker *et al.*, Columbus: Ohio State University Press, 226–7.

15 H. Taylor Buckner

Transformations of Reality in the Legal Process*

H. T. Buckner, 'Transformations of Reality in the Legal Process', in
Social Research, Vol. XXXVII, No. 1, spring 1970, pp. 88–101.

'Reality' is not always constructed according to the same rules
and processes. People construct their sense of everyday reality in
differing ways, and there are many specific enclaves of reality
wherein certain formalized rules prevail over common-sense rules.
'There is a right way, a wrong way, and the Army way.' In most
of our experiences acts are routinely interpreted within the reality
in which they arise, and no threat of differing interpretations dis-
turbs the participants. In other cases, such as cross-culture con-
tacts, acts are interpreted in completely divergent realities, and
no alignment takes place, or alignment takes place only after
a great deal of effort. In yet other cases, an act will occur within
one reality and then will be reinterpreted within the framework
of another reality. When such reinterpretation is done it may be
carried out pell-mell or by a system of formalized rules, which is
the case in the operation of the legal process. All reality on a
group level is formed by independent actors coming to agree to
a common set of concepts, within a common frame of reference.
The legal system provides a very formal example of the process
of group reality formation: its procedures and precedents for
coming to agreements are recorded and stand as guides for the
formation of further agreements within the frame of reference of
legal reality. This paper examines the rules for transforming
everyday reality into 'legal reality'.

Acts are without inherent meaning. All meaning is socially

* Revision of a paper read before the Sociology of Law Section of the
Annual Meeting of the American Sociological Association, Boston, August
1968. I would like to thank Leo Van Hoey, John Lennon, and Peter Berger,
who read and commented on earlier drafts of this paper. (*Author's note*)

assigned to acts by the individuals who come to know of them, on the basis of their own understanding of the acts' relationship to their sense of 'reality'.[1] An act may be taken to serve as an indicator of the subjective intent of the actor, an indicator of greater or lesser clarity, whether or not the act was *intended* to stand as a sign of his subjective intent by the actor.[2]

In law, for an act to constitute a crime, there must be unity of act and intent (except in the case of criminal negligence).[3] The act is basic and must only be linked to the perpetrator, while proof of intent, which is an aspect of the subjective reality of the perpetrator, must depend either on his own linguistic objectification of his intent, or upon an inference from the conditions surrounding the act, as they were perceived, which tends to support the assertion of intentionality. For most acts the ordinary consequences of a voluntary action are presumed to be intended, and if the act itself was unlawful, unlawful intent can be presumed.[4] For other acts such as libel, specific intent must be proven.

The problem in an assertion of criminality is twofold. First, it must be proven that the actor committed the act and that he intended to do so. Second, it must be proven that the act itself constituted a specific crime. The procedures for proving these two contentions consist of a set of rules for transforming perceived acts into linguistic objectifications and comparing these with linguistic descriptions of prohibited acts so as to determine whether the two are the same. As a control over this process there are provisions in law for reviewing the application of the transformational rules to determine whether they were 'correctly' applied to the specific case.

1. In other words acts are apperceived by consciousness through typifications derived from subjective realities. See Peter Berger and Thomas Luckmann, *The Social Construction of Reality*, New York: Doubleday, 1966, *passim*.

2. ibid., p. 34.

3. *California Penal Code*, Section 20 (hereafter cited as *Calif. P.C.*). Most states' basic laws are somewhat similar, as they are all codifications of common law.

4. *Calif. P.C.*, 21.

Divergent Realities Produce Divergent Typifications of Acts[5]

An act may be typified differently in many distinct realities. In each case, elements of the act relevant to its typification in a specific reality are attended to and selected out in the typification process. The typifications of an act are therefore not isomorphic between realities. Consequently, assessments of the act based on these several typifications will differ markedly.

Take, for example, a narcotics addict seeking something to steal which he can sell so that he may buy heroin. Late at night he sees a portable television set through the window of a house. He finds a spade and uses it to force open the locked window, climbs in and picks up the television set. As he is leaving the house via the window, with the television under his arm, a patrol car flashes its spotlight down the side of the house and the officer sees him. The addict is apprehended and taken to jail to be charged with burglary in the first degree.

The addict, up to the time of his apprehension, had considered his burglary to be an instrumental act. He needed money and no legitimate source could supply enough. Though he had committed many burglaries he thought of himself as an addict, rather than as a burglar. He knew that most of the houses he burglarized were insured, and he assumed that the owners added fictitious losses to those he caused when they reported the burglaries, so he felt that the owners were no less criminal than he. As he entered the house he felt a sense of excitement and fear. He was thankful that no one awoke when he pried up the window. As he was leaving he saw the spotlight and knew that flight was hopeless. He felt the cool ground as he dropped to it, and the

5. The word 'typification' comes from the work of Alfred Schutz. When Schutz uses the term, he means that we experience a world which has mountains, trees, animals, and fellow-men, not a world which is a 'mere aggregate of colored spots, incoherent noises, centers of warmth and cold' (*Collected Papers*, Vol. 1, The Hague: Nijhoff, 1962, pp. 7–8, 208). Berger and Luckmann define typification as 'schemes in terms of which others are apprehended and "dealt with" in face to face encounters' (op. cit., p. 29). In the course of this paper I am interested in the attribution of criminality on the basis of actions, which involves complex typification procedures that vary radically with the typifier's subjective reality.

handcuffs when the officer put them on. Then he began to think of what would become of him. This is his reality.

The officer was patrolling his beat. He was flashing his light up alleys and between houses because a rash of burglaries had occurred on his beat, and from the *modus operandi* they seemed to be the work of an opportunistic 'hype-burglar'.[6] When he saw a man leaving a window with a television set under his arm, he immediately assumed the man was, and typified him as, a burglar, probably the man he was looking for. Stopping his car, he drew his revolver, and jumped out. He ran along the side of the house and shouted to the burglar to fall to his knees, which he did. The officer then searched his prisoner, and locked him in the back seat of the patrol car. He picked up the television set and put it in the trunk as evidence, explaining to the occupants of the house, who had appeared, that it would be returned later. He then began to examine the scene of the burglary. Starting with the idea that he had captured a burglar, he searched for the means of entrance. Finding the pry marks and the spade, he radioed for a police photographer to take photographs, and he began to make out his report. When the patrol wagon came in response to his call, he sent the burglar to jail. These are some elements of the officer's reality, and explain his typification of the person he caught as a burglar.

In this example the possible interpretations of the act do not vary as widely as they might in the case of riots or demonstrations, where each side has a complex system of justifications for its actions, and a hostile typification of the other side.[7]

6. A 'hype-burglar' is a heroin addict who steals to support his habit. Typically, he is involved in thefts from automobiles and the theft of anything which can be eventually converted into narcotics.

7. On rare occasions there will be a reciprocal typification wherein both the officer and the offender will define the situation in remarkably similar ways, given their divergent realities. The frequently arrested alcoholic and the arresting officer may both come to view his usual state as being 'drunk and incapable'. This reciprocal typification speeds the offender's acceptance of the officer's view. Another situation which frequently occurs is the exact opposite of reciprocal typification. Unilateral typification often takes place when the legal framework had never even occurred to the 'offender', that is, in his reality the possibility of a legal construction of the meaning of his

It is rare in situations such as burglary that ideas of the act committed will differ greatly, but the meaning of the act is quite different for the offender and for the officer. Since the officer is society's agent, his view is provisionally upheld by the legal system. It gives him the right to arrest and detain persons, using all force necessary, when he has 'reasonable cause to believe that the person to be arrested has committed an offense in his presence'.[8]

After arrest and charging, the offender, who is now a defendant, consults with his attorney, or with the public defender, to ascertain the possibility of having the officer's typification of the situation set aside, the re-enforcing of his own no longer being relevant. His attorney examines the evidence and the crime that his client is charged with to see if it has the elements which are usually associated with such crimes. The attorney may then, if the crime is not unusual, propose to his client the possibility of a 'deal' whereby the burglary charge may be reduced to 'petty theft', a lesser offence, but still an offence, in return for a guilty plea.[9] If the client accepts this offer he will go to jail or be put on probation, albeit for an incomplete characterization of his act, and the officer's typification of him as a burglar is upheld by default.[10]

Should the defendant be atypical or should the crime be atypical, or should he refuse to make a deal, to 'cop out', his case will go to trial and the typification procedure of the officer will be called into question. If the officer were to have made a gross

act had never entered his mind. Law, however, establishes its precedence among realities in such situations through the dictum: 'ignorance of the law is no excuse.'

8. *Calif. P.C.*, 836.

9. David Sudnow, 'Normal Crimes: Sociological Features of the Penal Code in a Public Defender Office', *Social Problems*, 12, 3, winter 1965, pp. 255–76, discusses this process in detail. See especially p. 260.

10. Another typification process, based on the officer's report and on the routine defendant's characteristics, is employed to see if the present burglar is a burglar 'like others', which involves: 'regular violators, no weapons, low-priced items, little property damage, lower class establishments, largely Negro defendants, independent operators, and a non-professional orientation to the crime'. Sudnow, ibid., p. 260. These are the attendant elements of reality in the work life of the Public Defender and District Attorney.

error in his original apprehension, the district attorney would probably drop the charges. Thus those cases which do go to trial tend to be procedurally correct, so far as is known.

The Officer's Typification Process is Compared with a 'Common Sense' Typification Process

The officer must state the means by which he came to judge that the defendant was a burglar. He is required by law to have had 'reasonable cause' to believe that the defendant was a burglar before he arrests him. Reasonable cause is defined for police officers as 'that state of affairs which would lead a reasonable man to a strong suspicion that the offender had committed a crime'.[11] By introducing the 'reasonable man' and *his* typification procedures, a *societal* control is placed on the extensive socialization of the police officer to police perceptions. The 'reasonable man' supposedly uses 'common-sense' knowledge when making inferences about possible criminality, not the specialized perceptions and knowledge of the police officer. In the burglary case mentioned, the officer might state that he saw a man leaving a building with a television set, via a window, late at night, and from these observations he inferred that the man was a burglar, as would any reasonable man. Had he simply stopped a man on the street for no reason at all, and searched him, finding evidence of criminality, the evidence so discovered would not have been admissible (in California). If police officers were allowed to arrest citizens without any justification, and a 'common-sense' justification of 'reasonable cause' appeals to most people as a fair one, the officers would be independent actors rather than social agents in their apprehensions.

The importance with which this conformity to the typification processes of the 'reasonable man' is viewed may be seen from the fact that higher courts routinely reverse convictions of people who have been proven guilty, if the essential evidence was gathered by

11. Field notes from police training lectures. The police were studied by participant observation in the course of research for my doctoral dissertation, 'The Police: the Culture of a Social Control Agency', unpublished Ph.D. dissertation, University of California, Berkeley, 1967.

any procedure which cannot be justified in terms of 'common sense'. While society gives the police officer the warrant to typify behaviour as criminal, it restricts him, in theory, to typification methods which an ordinary member of society would use in a similar situation.

In the courtroom the act which is under discussion is quite remote. All the people concerned are in the courtroom, not on the street, it is daytime, and the accused burglar is wearing a business suit and tie.

In order to test the officer's typification procedure against common sense, the court must know what it was. The only way in which it can be made present is by being linguistically objectified (that is, made into a linguistic object) and introduced. The entire series of acts is linguistically objectified by the various participants from their different perspectives, in order to bring to the reality of the court the 'legally relevant' aspects of the reality of the street. Reality at the court level consists almost entirely of linguistic objectifications of past experiences, which are taken in law as constituting the 'facts' of the case.[12]

There are three uses for the linguistic objectifications which are brought into the reality of the court.

First, the officer must objectify his thoughts and actions in the situation. This may be exceedingly difficult because many elements of the situation, elements to which the officer attended without being aware of it, are hard to put into words. It may be that elements of the act which excited his attention were subliminally perceived – smells, manner of walking, the way the suspect looked at him, strange sounds – and never brought to his conscious awareness.

Second, the officer must demonstrate the isomorphism of his objectifications and typifications with the presumed 'commonsense' typifications which a 'reasonable man' would have made in a similar situation.[13]

12. *Calif. P.C.*, 1126. Berger and Luckmann, op. cit., p. 38, point out the role of linguistic objectifications in making 'present' people from the past and in bridging realities.

13. In fact, the specialized perceptions of the officer tend to be taken for granted. Learning what elements of a situation to notice automatically takes

Third, the prosecution must demonstrate that all the elements of the crime as specified in abstract language in the Penal Code have been proven by the linguistic objectifications, that is, it must prove that the two sets of words, one describing the act and one quoted from the Code, correspond in all particulars.[14] Suppose that our burglar were caught while it was still dark outside and first degree burglary were charged because the crime was committed at night.[15] Suppose further, however, that the defence could prove that the act actually took place five minutes after 'official' sunrise, even though it was still dark. Situationally, the offence is the same, a man was burglarizing a house in the dark, but legally it is no longer a first degree burglary, because the two sets of words no longer agree.[16]

Linguistic Objectifications Must be Accurate or the Transformation is Defective

Since the crucial link between the act and its assessment in court is the *quality* of the linguistic objectifications of the participants, and since, in adversary proceedings a person might be motivated, in consideration of his own interests, to falsify or distort his testimony, regardless of which side he is on, it has been found necessary to establish both general and specific rules and punishments to control the quality and veracity of these objectifications.

In general, the quality of testimony is ensured by the prohibition against the introduction of hearsay evidence. Hearsay evidence is evidence of a statement that is offered to prove the truth of a matter which was made other than by a witness, while he is

years of experience. If an ordinary person were in the situation with a police officer who pointed out the clues to which he was attending, he might come to the officer's conclusions, but he almost certainly would not do so alone. Witness the number of people who have seen crimes in progress without noticing that anything unusual was happening.

14. Harold Garfinkel, 'Conditions of Successful Degradation Ceremonies', *American Journal of Sociology*, LXI, March 1956, item 4, p. 423.

15. *Calif. P.C.*, 460.

16. *Calif. P.C.*, 463. In practice this 'legal' distinction might be overlooked.

testifying at the hearing. Were the rule enforced without exception, it would allow only the people who actually witnessed an act, and who were also in the court and sworn to testify, to speak of it. There are numerous exceptions which take into account the special nature of utterances, or the special conditions which might not allow the speaker to appear. Thus dying declarations, spontaneous declarations, evidence of inconsistent statements by a witness, and so forth are often admissible.[17] These necessary compromises allow the work of the court to continue when it would be impossible for it to do so under a strict interpretation of the hearsay rule. With these exceptions all evidence offered by witnesses is a direct recounting of their own experience. Thus, at the trial, the act is recreated in legal reality by the participants from their own subjective realities. (A defendant, of course, may choose not to testify, not to bring his own reality into the court, if he feels that it might tend to incriminate him.)[18] This direct testimony becomes the 'facts' of the case in legal reality. Note, however, the incredible number of 'facts' from everyday reality which are prohibited entrance into legal reality for one reason or another.

Specific laws to keep witnesses from lying about their experiences, perjury laws, have been enacted to provide penalties for falsifying objectifications.[19] In the reality of the court where all evidence is objectified, perjury is decided by the weight-of-numbers of objectifications. Thus the testimony of two witnesses,

17. *California Evidence Code*, 'Hearsay'.

18. Fifth Amendment, *Constitution of the United States*, *Calif. P.C.*, 1323, Uniform Code of Military Justice, Art 31.

19. One of the oldest rules against perjury is 'Thou shalt not bear false witness against thy neighbour', *Exodus*, 21:16. *Calif. P.C.*, 118, reads: 'Every person who, having taken an oath, that he will testify, declare, depose, or certify truly before any competent tribunal, officer, or person in any of the cases in which such an oath may by law be administered, willfully and contrary to such oath, states as true any material matter which he knows to be false and every person who testifies, declares, deposes, or certifies "under penalty of perjury" in any of the cases in which such testimony, declarations, depositions, or certifications is permitted by law under "penalty of perjury" and willfully states as true any material matter which he knows to be false, is guilty of perjury.' The punishment for perjury, a felony, is one to fourteen years in the state prison. *Calif. P.C.*, 126.

or of one witness combined with corroborating circumstances, in other words two agreeing linguistic objectifications, are required to prove the perjury of a witness.[20]

In combination, the hearsay rule and the perjury laws are attempts to ensure that the transformation from experience to objectification is made correctly so that the jury (or the court in some instances) is presented with the 'facts' in such a way that it can assess the defendant's guilt, that is, determine whether the officer's typification of criminality is correct.

Because a jury of ordinary men, not lawyers, judges or policemen, is the trier of fact, another societal 'common-sense' control is imposed on the nature of the typifications and their construction, which can be offered into evidence. The specialized perceptions of the police officer must be explained before a rotating jury, in terms which will make the officer's 'reasonable cause' appear 'reasonable' to these ordinary men. This provides a direct control, in each case, over society's agents, the police.

Preparations for Reality Transformation by Defendants and Officers

The defendant in a criminal action is not usually highly experienced in restructuring his subjective reality into the precise forms required by legal reality. His attorney will guide him and, to a certain extent, substitute for the expertise he lacks in making this transition. For example his attorney will prevent him from being examined if he thinks that the result will be perjury or an admission of guilt. The attorney will concentrate on attacking the existential grounds of the officer's typification process, pointing out flaws and non-common-sense assumptions made by the officer. He operates within legal reality to help his client as best he can to overcome his lack of preparation for making the switch between realities.[21]

20. *Calif. P.C.*, 1103a.
21. Defendants may introduce aspects of their own subjective reality in explaining their actions. If this subjective reality is congruent with the experiences of the members of the jury, that is, if the jury finds the defendant's actions 'reasonable' in the circumstances, a possibility of acquittal exists. Cf. Garfinkel, op. cit., item 3, p. 423.

Given the fact that defendants in examples such as I have given are usually guilty, if the defence cannot find flaws in the testimony of the officer and other witnesses, or find a mistake of procedure, the only possibility left open is to commit some form of perjury.

For the officer, on the other hand, appearance in court is routine. He is prepared by his training and experience for the possibility of testifying in court, and he has the second-hand experience of his fellow officers to draw on. John Minderman, a ten-year veteran of the San Francisco Police Department, commented in a personal communication:

> The defense is entitled to a copy of the incident report prior to trial. Many officers are experienced and adept enough to only fill in the barest legal skeleton of the offense while keeping crucial and damning details unwritten in their minds, thus keeping information from the defense.

The officer has objectified his subjective reality before, and he has practised applying court rules to acts he sees. For example, while working as a police officer, I was instructed in the proper method for filling out an arrest form for drunks. First, I was to write down my 'reasonable cause' for being interested in the person, e.g. I saw him staggering in the park. Second, I was to give the evidence of my senses, e.g. bloodshot eyes, smell of alcoholic beverage on his breath, vomited on clothes, urinated in trousers. Third, I was to give the interpretation which I made from those observations, i.e. that he is incapable of caring for himself, which constitutes the legal cause for arresting him.[22] The drunk has no such training, and can hardly offer a defence against such a methodical charge.

The officer generally knows what evidence is admissible and what is not. He knows what he must do to *develop* 'reasonable cause' that will *appear* to be reasonable to the common sense of the jury. He orients his investigation around the production of admissible evidence, and the production of 'common-sense' reasonable cause.

In some cases the press of the immediate situation makes it imperative for the officer to act at once, in the absence of 'reasonable

22. *Calif. P.C.*, 647 f.

cause' that would pass a common-sense test. If his actions result in evidence of criminality he can then 'back up' and figure out the way to proceed which will make his evidence admissible. If no such way exists, he may retroject into the situation the necessary elements to support the common-sense basis of his typification of criminality.[23] Since the officer is linguistically objectifying his own subjective reality, there are many ways in which he can stretch it in the light of his present knowledge. He can find what *would* have constituted reasonable cause had he thought of it at the time, and simply say he *did* think of it at the time. He can testify to things he did not see which were there. He can anticipate the court's review and put in his initial report items which would have given him reasonable cause had they happened.[24] Finally, and without much danger, he can simply perjure himself. Very few of his fellow officers will testify against him, and no one else is likely to be able to.

Appeal Controls the Application of Transformational Rules

Matters of fact (linguistic objectifications) are assumed in law to be adequately brought out and decided during a trial. Questions of law, i.e. procedure, which arise are dealt with by the court in the progress of the trial.[25] An appeal by the defence must be based on a matter of law.[26] One of the most common bases of appeal is the question of whether or not the officer truly had common-sense reasonable cause to typify the behaviour as criminal, regardless of its true criminality. It is toward the standards

23. Berger and Luckmann, op. cit., p. 147, suggest this process goes on among converts who have switched realities, and reinterpret their old reality in terms of the new.

24. For example, Drunk Arrest forms tend to be 'over-written'. Far fewer drunks actually urinate in their pants than the forms indicate, but when it comes to court who is to say? The drunk can't remember, and the officer has it down in writing. 'Over-writing' is common, in my experience, when the officer knows in his subjective reality that the offender is guilty but also knows that he cannot prove it in legal reality with evidence legally gathered.

25. *Calif. P.C.*, 1124, 1126.

26. *Calif. P.C.*, 1259.

of appellate review that officers often orient their 'production' of reasonable cause.

At the appellate level, transcribed linguistic objectifications are the only signs of the original act. Even the defendant need not appear.[27] On the basis of the transcript of the trial and the behaviour described therein, the appellate court decides whether the officer, acting in the now quite remote street situation, had reasonable cause for his typifications.[28] The effect of appellate review is to examine the application of the transformational rules to the concrete case. If all was done correctly the officer's subjective reality is validated, it becomes socially objective reality, and the defendant is 'legitimately' typified a criminal by 'society'.

Conclusion

I have examined a burglary and the operation of the legal process whereby the interpretation of an act is *routinely* transformed between realities. In this case, and possibly in others, a routinization of the transformational process has led to the formalization of its rules and the emergence of controls to assure their correct implementation. In other transformational processes, as, for example, that which occurs between dreams and everyday reality, rules are only partially and imperfectly institutionalized in our society. In still other transformational processes, as for example, between inter-cultural subjective experiences, rules hardly exist, making each transformation an *ad hoc* process. The underlying rules for these less agreed upon, but potentially important, transformations, constitute an important area for further research.[29]

27. *Calif. P.C.*, 1255.

28. A certain amount of misunderstanding arises between the police and the courts as a result of this process. As a case moves through the courts it is 'purified' and the factual picture of law enforcement contexts is lost. (Wayne R. LaFave, *Arrest: The Decision to Take a Suspect into Custody*, Boston: Little, Brown, 1965, pp. 490–91.) The 'reasonable cause' becomes less and less reasonable to the officer as it discounts his highly accurate probabilistic knowledge of criminal behaviour.

29. It is not unreasonable to assume that mankind will sooner or later encounter an intelligent extra-terrestrial life form. What will be the rules governing the communication of experiences under these conditions?

16 Hansfried Kellner

On the Cognitive Significance of the System of Language in Communication

H. Kellner, 'On the Cognitive Significance of the System of Language and Communication', paper prepared for the 7th World Congress of Sociology, Toronto, Canada, August 1974.

The investigation of social forms and structures of everyday communication commonly falls within the field of social psychology and – insofar as linguistic questions are of concern – into the realm of socio-linguistics. In the light of the conventional partition of the social scientific interests such an allocation of this object of study is self-evident and needs no further comment. Taking up everyday communication as a topic of enquiry in the perspective of the sociology of knowledge may, however, cause initially some surprise.

What aspects of communication are revealed in such a perspective depends above all upon the conceptions one connects with the sociology of knowledge as a discipline and the cognitive relevancies one is ready to concede to the processes of social communication and language. It is indisputable that there exists an intrinsic relationship between certain topics of a sociology of knowledge and the problems of an analysis of communication and language. The sociology of knowledge traditionally always aimed to clarify the structure of social knowledge and thought and to relate it to social conditions and situations, whereas the sciences of language and communication repeatedly tried to discern the influence of social communication and language upon the very structure of knowledge and cognition. In this general sense both areas of investigation share an area of study. Accordingly, the exploration of linguistic-communicative processes should be as much an integral part of the concerns of a sociology of knowledge as is the study of knowledge relevant for the sciences of communication and language.

As obvious as the above may appear to be, the sociology of knowledge nevertheless showed astoundingly little interest in any detailed study of the structure and mechanisms of social communication. Only recently P. Berger and T. Luckmann developed a position in the sociology of knowledge[1] which – inspired by the phenomenological work of A. Schutz – not only paid serious attention to communication and language processes for the first time, but also used the systematic properties of the latter as a foundation for important steps in their theoretical arguments. To grasp the astounding fact of the relative absence of language and communication analysis in the older sociology of knowledge and the shift signalled by the work of Berger and Luckmann, it is worthwhile to look shortly at some main currents of the history of that discipline. This will help to clarify the status of explorations into linguistic-communicative problems and at the same time to prepare the ground for our central task, i.e. the analysis of the system of language in social communication.

As it is well known, the main body of interests and conceptions of the traditional sociology of knowledge have evolved out of the epistemological and methodological problems of the historical sciences and the *Geisteswissenschaften* in the nineteenth and twentieth centuries.[2] It was this tradition which is responsible for the often noted tendency of the sociology of knowledge to limit itself to a sociological rendering of old epistemological and methodological preoccupations. The new version of old philosophical analyses of knowledge and thinking was a response to the doubts which arose about the older version with the social transformations associated with industrialization and enlightenment.

Ever since the scepticistic philosophy of that area, reality could no longer be viewed as independent of consciousness and human action. Consciousness and action came to be seen as constitutively

1. P. Berger and T. Luckmann, *The Social Construction of Reality*, New York: Doubleday, 1966; Penguin Books 1966.
2. For a fuller description of the sociology of knowledge, cf. R. Aron, *La Sociologie allemande contemporaine*, Paris, 1950; K. Lenk, *Ideologie*, Neuwied, 1961; and particularly H. J. Lieber, *Wissen und Gesellschaft*, Tübingen, 1952.

involved in the shaping of that reality; reality *and* cognisance of reality were no longer considered as objectively 'given' but were conceived as 'products' of subjective human activities.

As long as the social side of human activities was disregarded in this perspective, objects of experience – and thus reality – were seen largely as results of the achievements of mental operations. But these achievements were thought to rest upon the 'laws' or the 'immanent categories' of the reasoning of the human mind. This perspective found its clearest expression in the Kantian epistemology. The very moment, however, when the structure of the social world was taken into account by the *Geisteswissenschaften*, the matter appeared in a different light. The grasp of reality as a constitutive part of the human world no longer could be seen exclusively or even predominantly as dependent on the operations of the solitary mind and its categories of understanding. It also had to be viewed as an expression of social situations and relations in which the cognising subject lives and moves about. The experience of reality was bound to socially prevailing values and perspectives. These were 'selections' from a wide range of possibilities and could be understood as being determined by the social structure or motivated by social life. The world of objects presenting itself to the individual was therefore at least partially 'preselected'. A socially and historically variable, socially 'determined' conceptual sphere demanded analysis as an antecedent of individual consciousness. Whereas extensive historical and cultural research in the nineteenth century clearly demonstrated the 'relativity' in the area of social experience, many solutions were offered to the epistemological problems about the precise nature of the constitution of that experience. A discussion was thus set in motion from which emerged the sociology of knowledge as a discipline.

The prominent classical sociologists of knowledge (Marx, by implication, and later Scheler and Mannheim, in particular) inherited this epistemological problem and set out to clarify the relationship between experience and the social reality which is the domain of this experience and, at the same time, its object. Whatever the difference in their answers, the main issue remained for them the same: in which way and to which degree the shaping of social experience must be seen as a result either of 'ideal-factors' (i.e. of subjective, perhaps transcendental operations of the human faculty of understanding) or of 'real-factors' (i.e. of objective social-structural processes and relations), to use the terms coined by Scheler. The interest of the founders of the sociology of knowledge naturally focused on the 'real-factors' to which, on the whole, the governing role was attributed. In this respect they differed only in degree not in substance. This position had an important corollary. Subjective social experience and with it the formation of interests and knowledge was related – functionally or causally – to 'real-factors'. The extreme consequence of this position was that reality (i.e. the 'real' reality) did not appear in experience, but preceded it. Experience was absolutely bound to a perspective which the specific *Realverhältnisse* (Mannheim) dictated.

The obvious methodological problem, how an 'objective' social reality could be ascertained by experience, where experience was purportedly shaped by it, remained for the classical sociology of knowledge an insoluble hermeneutic problem. For Dilthey[3] – who next to Marx had a marked influence on Mannheim – the problem of understanding in the *Geisteswissenschaften* is how to disclose 'life through life' and how to cope with the inseparable unity of the living and cognising subject. After Dilthey Mannheim's sociology of knowledge took the boundedness of cognition to a 'life-world' as evidence for its basic axiom. But another implication of the fact that all cognition is cognition bound to a specific 'life-world' was ignored or pushed aside. In order to resolve the 'problem of understanding' (the hermeneutic problem of the social sciences), it must be acknowledged that a conception of reality is not only the subject matter of the sociology of knowledge, but also its own epistemic starting point. The assumption of a 'preceding' objective reality, a 'hidden' reality operating behind experience, is not justified. It is necessary and legitimate to search for the objective conditioning factors of any subjectively presented reality, but they must not be sought beyond

3. W. Dilthey, 'Ideen über eine beschreibende und zergliedernde Psychologie', *Sitzungsbericht der Kgl. Preuss. Akad. d. Wiss.*, XXIX, 1894, Vol. 2.

our human horizons. These factors must be located in the very same stratum, the stratum which contains the meaning-related forms and elements of experience in the 'social life-world' in the sense of the phenomenology of the late Husserl and Schutz.[4] A sociology of knowledge which rests its methodology on the phenomenology of the social life-world will place the meaning textures of the social world in the centre of its theory. Such a sociology of knowledge – initiated by Berger and Luckmann – does not pretend to look for the conditions of the possibility of a life-world as such but proceeds from the givenness of the life-world. It explores the objectively predefined reality of the individual as it is subjectively understood and socially expressed and constituted. It investigates, more particularly, the world of everyday life that Schutz has shown to be at the core of most sociological analysis, i.e. a world in which the individuals experience reality on the basis of meaning structures that they helped to fashion themselves, a world within which they intersubjectively plan and accomplish their actions.

The structures of everyday life are, however, not only investigated as prevailing textures of meaning that are socially and intersubjectively constituted but also as realities which are maintained by various mechanisms and are transformed, re-stabilized or dissolved in the course of everyday actions.[5] The sociology of knowledge must therefore necessarily turn to an exploration of the structures of social interaction and communication. The larger part of these constructions, transformations, and validations of the meaning of the life-world occurs in processes of social interaction and communication. Everyday face-to-face conversation is the most important form of these processes. Thus the problem of language and language use in social life becomes central. It will occupy us in the following analyses.

Before we go on to delineate some structures of the system of

4. Cf., in particular, E. Husserl, *The Crisis of European Sciences and Transcendental Phenomenology*, Evanston: Northwestern University Press, 1970; and A. Schutz, *Collected Papers*, The Hague: Nijhoff, 1962–6.

5. For a fuller description of this problem, cf. P. Berger and H. Kellner, 'Marriage and the Construction of Reality', *Diogenes*, 1964, Vol. 46, pp. 1–24; and P. Berger and T. Luckmann, op. cit., pp. 135 ff.

language in everyday communication we return briefly to a consideration of the fact that the traditional sociology of knowledge payed little attention to language in social life. This may have been due to the unwillingness of that discipline – preoccupied as it was with epistemological problems – to take everyday life and the realm of subjective experiences *au sérieux*. It is noteworthy, however, that the role of language in the structuring of experience had been pointed out by prominent scholars in the days in which the sociology of knowledge found its first systematic formulations. In the study of language within the Humboldtian tradition, for example, the cognitive significance of language had been emphasized repeatedly, and this could have hardly escaped the notice of the early sociologist of knowledge. What is particularly interesting is that the problem of language and speech in social life could have been easily formulated – for better or for worse – in the classical terms of the sociology of knowledge, as a problem of the relation between 'ideal factors' and 'real factors'. A short look at the philosophy of language of E. Cassirer will demonstrate this point.

In his *Philosophie der symbolischen Formen*[6] Cassirer set out to formulate the 'basic forms of understanding' of the world and proposed a 'theory of forms' of the mind which could be derived from an analysis of language. Language and the systems of symbols resting on it were regarded as the medium of the transcendental achievements of the operations of the mind. Cassirer thus reformulated Kant's theory of forms in terms of language as an 'autonomous ideational form'. What was performed in transcendental apperceptions according to Kant was rea ized in language – according to Cassirer. A 'representation' of the objects of experience is achieved through the 'signitive functions' of language. Thereby, according to Cassirer, reality could appear and take on a mode of objectivity. In the final consequence, the representation of objects and reality derives from the logical (grammatical) relations of a system of symbolic forms, and it was the assumption of Cassirer that an analysis of this systematic order would reveal the transcendental achievements of consciousness.

6. E. Cassirer, *Philosophie der symbolischen Formen*, 3 vols., 1923–31; see in particular Vol. 1.

As a system of symbols, however, empirical languages are relativistic. Their structures afford perspectivistic object-definitions and, therefore, posit perspectivistic truths. This perspectivity of empirical systems of symbols is the source of a relativity of propositions in various domains of life. According to Cassirer, science itself is not excluded. Science (i.e. nomological science) is thus placed next to other symbolic universes like art, myth and religion. In these domains propositions about reality are developed by means of a specific system of signs. Any reality so conceived is necessarily a 'selective' reality. Cassirer accorded a somewhat different status to the cultural sciences (*Geisteswissenschaften*). It was his view that the cultural sciences don't make propositions about reality as such but investigate formal relations between symbolic forms. They don't say anything about reality, their statements explicate logically the symbolic forms by means of which reality presents itself to an experiencing subject. Symbolic systems are therefore the transcendental condition under which an empirical, meaningful world can appear to the individual.

This position entails an acknowledgement of the relativistic moment in the experience of reality, or more precisely realities. In view of its transcendental status – as Cassirer would have it – language could be seen as an 'ideal-factor' shaping reality, yet the empirical relativism of language points in the direction of 'real-factors'. An empirical language has its own specific social history and objectivates particular forms of representation. It is a system of definitions of reality which are prior to the acts of experiencing reality – but it is a specific system of particular definitions. Epistemologically, language is in the centre on both accounts. It is the condition for the possibility of experience of a reality and at the same time it determines *which* reality becomes the object of experience.

Clearly, such a conception of language as the one formulated by Cassirer – that is by the Cassirer of the *Philosophie der symbolischen Formen*[7] – will not convince everybody. It did not

7. After his emigration Cassirer reformulated his earlier perspective and came close to a phenomenological approach to sign relations in conscious life; cf. E. Cassirer, *Logik der Kulturwissenschaften*, Darmstadt, 1961.

inspire the contemporary sociology of knowledge and could not have done so unless the inflated value it placed on language had been reduced to a more reasonable level. In that case, however, it could have provided valuable indications about the significance of language to a sociology of knowledge that tended to ignore language completely.

Cassirer used and interpreted certain kinds of data which were gathered by linguists within and without the Humboldtian tradition and which pointed to an intimate relationship between language, knowledge, and world-view. The sociology of knowledge eventually had to come to terms with these data and the theories they occasioned – either by accepting and integrating or by refusing them. Following the general paradigm of the classical sociology of knowledge one should have expected that the linguistic structures on the semantic-syntactic level should have received a prominent place among the so-called 'real-factors'. The general hypothesis of 'linguistic determinism' or 'linguistic relativity' by a number of scholars before the days of Sapir and Whorf[8] maintains neither more nor less than that the individual experience of reality is functionally, if not causally, dependent upon the language of a given society. Although the verification of this hypothesis inevitably runs into considerable methodological difficulties, a profound influence or even constraint of language upon experience generally has come to be acknowledged.

The extensive recent research on this problem refutes any flat conception of a linguistic determinism,[9] yet it remains evident that a particular language and particular contexts of speech (of a culture or a distinct social group) map out the world for the individual in differing modes of typicality and different degrees of intensity. But this must not be understood as if a linguistic sign system *per se* exerts this influence or constraint. It does so only as a result of its *use* in social situations, which is co-determined both by the social biography of the actor and by the social structures

8. In particular, E. Sapir, *Language*, New York, 1921; and B. L. Whorf, *Language, Thought and Reality*, Cambridge, Mass., 1956.

9. The literature on this subject is immense. For a concise review and critique, see H. Gipper, *Gibt es ein sprachliches Realitätsprinzip?*, Frankfurt/M., 1972.

within which linguistic action takes place. More generally, linguistic structures become cognitively significant only within socially specific relevance structures and contexts of communication. Turning to an explication of this insight it must be noted again that neither the philosophy of language which was now discussed nor the classical sociology of knowledge provides adequate paradigms. In the contemporary study of language it is widely accepted that the problem of language in social life should be approached from the side of the structures of social action and communication. This approach, it is hoped, will not only disclose the rules and patterns of linguistic behaviour and communicative strategies, but also provide answers to the question of the cognitive significance of language. It is the latter which is our primary concern now. But before we turn to a description of the structure of cognitive linguistic behaviour we must explain why we find the phenomenological perspective relevant, if not mandatory, for this description.

The conscious activities that constitute experience are the point of reference of all phenomenological investigations. It will be also our point of reference in the present task. In the study of language phenomena and social communication in linguistics, philosophy, sociology and psychology, conscious life was usually taken for granted and the analysis was carried out more or less on a functional or structural level. Inferences *were* drawn about conscious life from such analyses, but the structures of consciousness themselves were not analysed on their own account and in their own terms. An approach of considerable interest in this connection is that of Wittgenstein and his followers.[10] It can serve as a starting point from which and against which to begin our own analysis.

The Wittgensteinian conception of language is not unlike Cassirer's, in fact it looks somewhat like a sociologically more

10. This goes for the later Wittgenstein. His earlier work is not considered here. Cf. L. Wittgenstein, *Philosophical Investigations*, Oxford, 1953. Considerable changes from Wittgenstein's own positions characterize the thought of various scholars influenced by him. But much of what is said here of these positions also applies to Wittgensteinians such as J. L. Austin (*How to do Things with Words*, Oxford, 1962).

pertinent version of it. The previous language-based transcendental critique of consciousness is supplanted by a transcendental critique of language itself. The rules of the synthesis of experience are replaced by the rules of the grammar of a language, and the activities in mental life are now derivative of linguistic operations in the realm of social actions. Whereas phenomenological sociology follows A. Schutz in concentrating on an analysis of the constitution of meaning and meaning textures within the horizons of consciousness in the social life-world, Wittgensteinian philosophy focuses on a 'logical' analysis of meaning and meaning relations as they are supposedly bound up in the grammar of language. Both approaches, however, lead to an 'interpretive sociology'.[11] Sociologically they are both directed to the intersubjective realm of social action. Yet there is a difference. For a sociology in a Wittgensteinian version, the intersubjectivity of social action does not result from the 'reciprocity of perspectives' (Schutz) on the basis of intentional mental achievements, but can be directly derived from the rules of linguistic structure and behaviour. A necessary and unquestioned assumption underlying this position is that language is not essentially a system of signs but an embodiment – even in its internal structure – of social actions. The grammar of a language therefore incorporates not only references of meaning for experience, but defines also a system of rules which circumscribe affairs of social interaction as a linguistically bounded universe of communication. Wittgenstein's famous maxims that 'the meaning of a word is its use in language'[12] and that 'language-games'[13] represent 'forms of life' concisely represent this position.

Phenomenological analysis of language and communication in the context of the sociology of knowledge need not reject the Wittgensteinian paradigm entirely, but it must correct and amplify it by a description of 'intentional' conscious processes which are involved in the use of language in the world of action and experience. This is also important for an account of the changes and transformations in the conceptions of reality in everyday life. A conception of language which overestimates the rigidity of the

11. Cf. P. Winch, *The Idea of a Social Science*, London, 1965.
12. L. Wittgenstein, op. cit., § 43.   13. L. Wittgenstein, op. cit., § 23.

relations between linguistic structures and modes of reality apprehensions cannot adequately cope with such changes. This is a severe and obvious shortcoming of the language determinists but is also an implicit weakness of Wittgenstein's philosophy of language. The world of social actions is also the source of transformation of the language and its meaning structures and not solely the recipient of meaning from it. Language is constitutively important for experience and action. At the same time, it is not a cognitive cage, in which the meaning textures of human actions and cognitions are inescapably entrapped. As social beings we cannot escape using a language, but the language we use remains at our disposal. But no doubt it is also true that in using language we not only make use of it but are used by it. By means of language we produce a reality and make it available to ourselves, name it and intersubjectively communicate about it. At the same time *changing* definitions of reality emerge from social communications, flow back into the matrix of language and transform it. The forms and patterns of communication define the conditions and relevancies under which we 'thematize' various elements of language and at the same time also set up the 'relevance structures' (Schutz) by virtue of which various definitions of reality enter our language.

In order to grasp these processes in their full implication we must look closely at the processes of communication on the level of language. This description and analysis of uses of language must include the intentional processes that are involved in the conscious activities which constitute the use of language. Such a venture presupposes the analysis of the constitution and organization of the social world of everyday life as it presupposes the description of the organizational structures of the field of consciousness, a task for which we may refer to the work done in the phenomenological tradition.[14]

Our present analysis will be restricted to the question how the main features of language operate cognitively in acts of experience

14. The background for these analyses is to be found in the work of Husserl, Schutz, A. Gurwitsch (cf. esp. *The Field of Consciousness*, Pittsburgh, 1964), and more generally in the phenomenological tradition and in the sociology of knowledge of Berger and Luckmann.

and communication. We hope to contribute thereby to the problem of the cognitive relevance of language whose solution is of obvious importance for the sociology of knowledge.

*

The cognitive significance of language for experience and the apprehension of reality usually was approached from opposite directions. One approach was based on a view of language as a self-contained system of signs, the other emphasized the actualization of language in speech acts. These two approaches were not necessarily considered as independent from one another but they did pay attention to different levels of the problem and stressed different aspects. De Saussure's[15] disjunction of the total sphere of language into the correlates *langue* (i.e. language as a system of certain elements, in particular of signs) and *parole* (i.e. realizations of the *langue* in speech acts) not only provided a formal distinction for linguists, but pointed to categories of potential sociological and psychological relevance. *Langue* for him was a 'system' that existed in the 'heads' of the members of a language-community and functioned as the substratum and the condition of the possibility of speech. Although psychologically relevant, *langue* transcended the individual in that it was also a 'social institution' in the sense of Durkheim, embodying 'collective representations' from which derive the individual sign realizations. It not only makes social communication possible, but is also cognitively coercive because the individual can only have 'representations' inasmuch as they are provided by the system of the language of his society.

This kind of perspective upon language was paralleled in other linguistic schools of thought, in a more developed form especially in the Neo-Humboldtian movement of linguistics.[16] The notion of the 'system' itself and the conception of the linguistic sign

15. F. de Saussure, *Course in General Linguistics*, New York, 1959.

16. The most prominent linguists to be mentioned here are L. Weisgerber, J. Trier and W. Porzig, for a general discussion, cf. R. Hoberg, *Die Lehre vom sprachlichen Feld*, Düsseldorf, 1970. The English reader is referred to H. Basilius, 'Neo-Humboldtian Ethno-Linguistics', in J. Fishman, *Readings in the Sociology of Language*, The Hague/Paris, 1968, pp. 447–59.

that goes along with it is decisive for the way in which the cognitive influence of the system of language upon experience was conceived by the Neo-Humboldtians. Formally, the systematicity of the sign system is given in the fact that elements of a language cannot exist in isolation next to each other, but rather (with certain exceptions, as for example proper names) can only appear within structural connections with regard to each other. A linguistic sign, therefore, becomes a sign only insofar as it 'coexists' with other signs in a common system or field. Consequently a language cannot be conceived of as a store or lexicon of a large number of words and singular syntactic relations, where each element depicts referentially a singular piece of reality. The words of a language must be seen as related to the objects and events of reality only in a *mediated* form. In the 'natural attitude of everyday life' (Scheler) we use linguistic signs most of the time for non-linguistic purposes and reference, i.e. we are intentionally directed to the correlates of what we speak and communicate about. In this attitude we therefore do not fully grasp the linguistic-cognitive relations involved in our use of language. In the natural attitude it seems to us that the 'named' things and affairs of reality are totally independent of our way of referring to them. The inadequacy of this 'instrumentalistic' conviction becomes apparent if we look at the structure of the linguistic sign.

What is the relationship between the *sign* and the cognitively *signified* (Saussure's *signifié*)? In the use of a sign the signified does not coincide with the object *meant*, we refer to the object *that* is meant in a *conceptual* dimension, i.e. by a *meaning*. It is this meaning which renders the object in a particular perspective, i.e. it presents the object *as* it is meant. We are thus referred to objects and processes of reality mediately: through structures of meaning. These meanings are objectivated structures of 'appresentational pairings' and belong to the sphere of the language we are using. It is important to emphasize the 'appresentational' form by virtue of which meanings are linked to linguistic signs. 'Appresentation' is a form of intentional 'apperception' through which we 'pair' a particular sign (or more precisely a sign-vehicle) with a particular meaning. But in the same kind of intentional process this link can also be modified or abandoned. In spite of the fact that a large number of sign-meaning relations remain rather stable for an individual throughout his biography, there are other relations which are shifting almost constantly.

The remarks about the importance of the appresentational form of the sign-meaning relations were also meant to correct a conception prevalent in Saussurian and Neo-Humboldtian linguistics which tends to consider the sphere of meanings as an exclusively intralinguistic affair. According to this conception, the signs of a language are units of a particular kind in which the relations between signs and meanings are determined by the system in which they are located. The system of language, more precisely the systematicity of semantic/syntactic 'fields' in language, bestows 'meaning' upon its conceptual correlates. When he uses a sign the individual is referred from the stratum of the sign-vehicle (sounds) to a meaning content which is defined by language, and from that only he is referred to the objects meant in reality. The object *as* conceived is mediated or filtered by meaning relations that are secured in the system of language. Language, seen in this way, is an 'intermediary world' (*Zwischen-welt*),[17] to use a Humboldtian term, that is located between our cognitions and the objects known in reality. Its structure exerts cognitive constraints upon us. Clearly, such a conception verges on an 'idealistic' epistemology. It needs to be amended by taking account of the structures constituting sign relations in conscious life of apperception and appresentation.

Yet, despite the phenomenological deficiencies in the Neo-Humboldtian theory of signs, the conception of language as a system or field of signs has a certain value. Linguistic signs and meanings are not stored in language in the form of an inventory, a lexicon, existing independently each for itself. They coexist in a mutual relationship of dependence and opposition. The meaning of a word is therefore co-defined by meanings of neighbouring words arranged in common 'semantic and syntactic fields' of various kinds. In the use of a sign, the meaning referred to receives 'motivations' (Saussure) from these fields and gives it its peculiar contour. Language functions thereby as a 'system of

17. W. v. Humboldt, *Gesammelte Schriften*, Berlin, 1903–18, Vol. 7, p. 60.

indications' (or 'references'), that channel our intentional orientations to a certain extent. In the field of consciousness and its intentional horizons meaning relationships are thus linked to semantic/syntactic fields. The sense connections that obtain in our horizons of experience are partially fashioned from them.

For the sociology of knowledge such linguistic fields are especially important inasmuch as they usually also contain 'pragmatic' relations, i.e. schemes of knowledge about social affairs. The 'meaning in use' notion of Wittgenstein could be helpfully applied here, since the 'fields of use' of signs, or 'language-games' according to this perspective, are clearly related to contexts of social actions and strategies of behaviour. If the Wittgensteinian conception is taken in its original form, however, it leads to a 'contextualism' that does not give enough room to the manifold ways with which we are *intentionally* operating in linguistically articulated dimensions of meaning. It is legitimate to investigate meaning relations with regard to semantic fields and contexts of the use of signs, but speaking in social contexts does not fully coincide with contextually defined relations of meaning. In order to communicate in social contexts successfully, we must be also able to 'construct' contexts verbally by a systematic use of signs, and that presupposes that signs have to be variable over against habituated forms of their use; i.e. language must be truly 'generative'.[18]

The verbal construction of contexts of meaning in a generative sense must be accounted for by a more detailed analysis of the acts of sign realizations, i.e. acts of speech (*parole*). The distinction between language and speech is not as arbitrary as it might appear on first sight if we regard linguistic life as a whole. The meanings of signs as they are presented in their linguistic systems do not always coincide with the meanings that a speaker or listener connects with them in concrete cases of their application in social situations. To infer from this that linguistic meanings derive either solely from the use of signs or exclusively from established relations in the sign system fails to appreciate an

18. We accept the Humboldtian conception implied in Chomsky's notion of generation, but we don't think that Chomskyan linguistics is relevant to our purpose.

important structural condition of both language and speech. When we speak we do not simply select meaning relations from the given linguistic system in order to construct intended sense connections in the social situations of speech. This selection is also guided by different dimensions of meaning that emerge from the context of the social situation itself. These contextual delimitations nonetheless do not fully determine the meaning relations that are articulated in speech. In order to be able to produce verbally the intended meaning texture the individual must still turn back to the conditions of the linguistic sign system.

The interdependence of the system of signs, speech, and context becomes fully apparent if we regard it in the situation of a social communication. The speaker who intends to convey a meaning to a listener must take into consideration a variety of sense strata and relate them to each other. To mention the most important one: he must take into account the situation and the 'problem at hand' prevailing in it; he must pay attention to the (putative) intentions of the listener which he achieves by a 'role-taking process' (Mead) on the basis of a 'reciprocity of perspectives' (Schutz); and he must 'rehearse' the applied (or to be applied) sign relations and their meanings in their suitability for the purpose at hand. For the listener the same holds true inversely.

These considerations point to a structure wherein different moments and layers of language, speech, context and intentionalities meet and constitute a continuous but structured 'referential' process of signitive relations. The sociology of knowledge must of course go beyond the conception of language of structural linguistics. It must investigate the dynamics of social life and work out the referential relation of meaning structures that obtain there. What is required here is a theory of the appresentation and apperceptual processes.[19] An investigation of this order of magnitude goes beyond the scope of this paper. A few general remarks must suffice.

In most cases of the use of linguistic signs we are steadily referred to affairs which are not contained within the immediate

19. Cf. E. Husserl, *Cartesian Meditations*, The Hague, 1970, especially *Meditation V*; and A. Schutz, *Collected Papers*, op. cit., Vol. 1, pp. 294 ff.

linguistic meanings of the used signs themselves. As speakers and as listeners we are experiencing something that is not presented by the sign but appresented by it, and we apperceive the appresented affair by grasping a meaning that is *not* the meaning of the affair to which we are oriented. Through manifold kinds of appresentations a large spectrum of meaning interconnections is given that make it possible to experience reality in an orderly fashion. This universe of sense relations evidently originates in the experiences of the various dimensions of the social world and is geared to the subjective relevance structures of individuals who try to come to terms with their reality. In this universe of sense relations language occupies a privileged place as a distinct structure. It must be held against the linguistic-structural conception of language, however, that the sign relations that pertain to the area of social interaction and communication are not restricted to the semantic and syntactic 'fields' of language. They also contain social references, by way of appresentations and apperceptions, which gear into the sphere of social 'typifications' and 'interpretative schemata'. This implies that in the (active and passive) use of signs we do not only elicit meanings that are attached to the signs in a conceptual form, but also evoke horizons of understanding and interpretation about the social world relevant to us.

Inasmuch as language is a shared system of signs, it *may* also embody (appresent) shared signitive references which allow for a maximum of intersubjective understanding in communication. Signs are surrounded by horizons of meaning. When individuals communicate with each other, these horizons, too, are apprehended in a similar manner. The similarity of horizons, as apprehended in communication, depends on a variety of social factors. The basic factor is the presence or absence of 'shared experiences', whether these be due to overlapping biographies among the communicating individuals or to their participation in social relations of some closeness or affinity. It also depends on the presence or absence of shared 'social definitions' arising out of similar evaluations of social affairs, as they may exist in a closely-knit social group. Furthermore, the similarity of the horizons of meaning is based on the individuals' partially sharing a 'system of relevance' in the structure of their personalities. Finally, it is based on a common system of relevance that is regulative for them in the communicative situation. Inasmuch as intersubjective relations of these kinds were present for the individuals communicating with each other, the common language could serve as a basis for affinitive thematizations of reality. Conversely, the weaker such factors, the more difficult, although not completely impossible, are such affinitive thematizations. Even with different preconditions in the bodies of knowledge and referential relations attached to linguistic signs of the communicators, actual processes of communication can lead to an assimilation between their outlooks upon reality. Although concrete communicative processes can have such an effect, it is language which serves as a central precondition and medium for it. Provided there is a basic stock of intersubjectively shared meaning relations in the semantic and syntactic fields of the language of the communicators, usually available in a common 'mother tongue', and provided there is a certain number of common general social typifications in the subjective stocks of knowledge with which the members of a common society are normally equipped, the communicating individuals may venture into sense explications and sense apprehensions (interpretations). These processes may lead to the establishment of a high degree of mutual understanding and to common definitions of reality. What is more, such processes are the more likely the more significance the individuals invest in ongoing communications.

In the course of such communications the communicators attentively turn to each other, enter into reciprocal role-taking processes, rehearse their linguistic expressions, explore the putative horizons of understanding and relevancies of their partners, check and countercheck their thematizations and confirm and disconfirm their meaning explications. The horizons of meaning and experience are thus reciprocally unfolded for the partners and this may lead to a higher degree of mutual understanding. The underlying *topic* of these communicative processes are the social meanings pertaining to conceptions of reality. The elementary *means* of this communication is language. In so far as mutual understanding does occur, the conceptions of reality must be linked to the signs of whatever language is used. The communicating individuals establish a common 'referential system' of social typifications and definitions. If their communicative relations are to be routinized they must also learn to 'associate' ('pair') elements of this referential system with linguistic forms of conceptual meanings and expressions. This association will be proportionately more stable (and thus 'taken for granted') as this association takes on socially objectivated forms of appresentations. In order to remain stable, however, this association of linguistic form and social reality reference needs a communicative texture that is socially upheld by correspondingly stable forms of social interaction. In this way, language and communication depend on each other.

A language which is so linked to a social referential system necessarily exerts a cognitive influence on the experience of reality. This cognitive influence, however, is not of the same kind as that of the 'intermediary world' of linguistic signs in the Humboldtian sense. Its influence is not exerted through the systematicities prevailing in the semantic and syntactic fields of a language, but rather through the processes of apperceptions in the life of consciousness. Moreover, its influence is at the same time less rigidly established and deterministic than that of the so-called intermediary world. It is open to revisions that emerge from the relevance structures which guide human beings in the solution of the problems encountered in the world of everyday life.

17 Peter Berger

The Problem of Multiple Realities: Alfred Schutz and Robert Musil

P. Berger, 'The Problem of Multiple Realities: Alfred Schutz and Robert Musil', in M. Natanson (ed.), *Phenomenology and Social Reality, Essays in Memory of Alfred Schutz*, Evanston: Northwestern University Press, 1970, pp. 213–33.

Robert Musil's great novel, *The Man Without Qualities*, constitutes an entire world.[1] This world has a vast multiplicity of facets, enough to keep a couple of generations of *Germanisten* fully occupied, and certainly far too many to attempt even an overview here. There are facets of this world that clearly refer to the external, historical situation of the novel – Austria on the eve of World War I. But, from the beginning, there are dimensions of the novel's world that have nothing to do with this location in space and time. Indeed, as the novel develops, it is these dimensions that move into the foreground of attention and give the socio-historical events the quality of a largely ironic preamble. What Musil attempted in his gigantic work was nothing less than a solution of the problem of reality from the perspective of modern consciousness – a consciousness that, unlike most others who have talked about it, he not only posits but painstakingly describes. A central theme in this context is what Musil calls the 'other condition' (*der andere Zustand*) – another reality that

1. We have throughout used the edition of *Der Mann ohne Eigenschaften* by Adolf Frisé (Hamburg: Rowholt, 1952). All subsequent numbers, unless otherwise stated, refer to the pagination of this edition, which includes not only the part of the novel published in the early 1930s, but a vast bulk of material from the *Nachlass*. The edition has been severely criticized for its handling of the *Nachlass*, but has become standard nonetheless. Most of this literary controversy, of course, is irrelevant to our present purpose. To date, only the part of the novel published during Musil's lifetime is available in English – *The Man Without Qualities* (New York: Coward-McCann, 1953). The English translators have been among Frisé's sharpest critics. Cf. Ernst Kaiser and Eithne Wilkins, *Robert Musil – Eine Einführung in das Werk* (Stuttgart: Kohlhammer, 1962).

haunts the reality of everyday life and the quest of which becomes the principal concern of Ulrich's, the novel's main protagonist. It is this theme that will interest us here.

The centrality of the 'other condition' to *The Man Without Qualities* has been remarked upon by several critics and has recently been the subject of a careful monograph.[2] But it is not our aim here to engage in literary criticism. Rather, we want to show how this central theme of Musil's novel can be illuminated with the aid of certain Schutzian categories and, conversely, how Alfred Schutz's analysis of the problem of multiple realities can be effectively illustrated by means of Musil's novel.[3] Such a confrontation between Schutz and Musil has intrinsic plausibility to anyone familiar with their respective works. To what extent this could also be ascribed to the fact that they were both contemporaries and compatriots may be left open. One may recall, if one wishes, the opinion of yet another important Austrian figure of this period, Karl Kraus, to the effect that Austria served as a dress rehearsal for the apocalypse – an opinion echoed by Musil when he writes, in a note for *The Man Without Qualities*, that Austria is a particularly clear case of the modern world.[4]

The Man Without Qualities contains a veritable labyrinth of plots and sub-plots, but its major events can be easily summarized. Ulrich, a moderately well-to-do and highly promising mathematician in his early thirties (*nel mezzo del camin . . .*), decides to take a year's 'vacation from life', with the purpose of dealing with a vague but general malaise concerning his manner of living. The entire action of the novel falls within this year, between the summers of 1913 and 1914, mostly in Vienna. During

2. Ingrid Drevermann, 'Wirklichkeit und Mystik', in Sibylle Bauer and Ingrid Drevermann, *Studien zu Robert Musil*, Cologne: Boehlau, 1966. Drevermann's monograph has been useful for the present paper, but our approach to the problem, of course, is from a very different vantage point.

3. The problem, of course, is taken up in several places in Schutz's opus. We would especially refer to the following articles: 'On Multiple Realities', in *Collected Papers*, Vol. I, The Hague: Nijhoff, 1962, pp. 207 ff.; 'Symbol, Reality and Society', in ibid., pp. 287 ff.; 'The Stranger – An Essay in Social Psychology', in *Collected Papers*, Vol. II, The Hague: Nijhoff, 1964, pp. 91 ff.; 'Don Quixote and the Problem of Reality', in ibid., pp. 135 ff.

4. 1577.

this period Ulrich becomes involved in two public affairs. The one is a large-scale undertaking, sponsored by the government but centred in the *salon* of Diotima, wife of a high government official and an 'influential lady of indescribable spiritual grace'. The aim of this undertaking, begun in competition with a similar enterprise in Germany, is to celebrate the seventieth anniversary of the coronation of the Emperor Francis-Joseph in 1918 by proclaiming the true meaning of the Austro-Hungarian monarchy. The other affair is the trial of Moosbrugger, the demented murderer of a prostitute, in whose fate Ulrich and some of his friends have a mysterious interest. Both these affairs move into the background in the later stages of the novel. The turning point in Ulrich's year comes with the death of his father. Ulrich returns to the provincial city, where he grew up and at whose university his father had been a professor of law, for the funeral and the settlement of the estate. There he meets Agathe, his 'forgotten sister', whom he has not seen since childhood. Ulrich and Agathe, who has decided to leave her husband, return to Vienna and set up a common household, with the express purpose of together discovering the 'other condition' that has become Ulrich's passionate goal. What remains of the unfinished novel, including the fragmentary material from Musil's posthumous papers, deals with the unfolding relationship between Ulrich and Agathe.

Ulrich is a man standing in the very midst of everyday reality – young, successful, open to the world. It is this everyday reality that we encounter with full force in the early chapters of the novel, beginning with the first paragraph, which gives us the exact weather report for central Europe for a lovely day in August 1913. It is this reality that, throughout the novel, serves as the departure point as well as the foil for Ulrich's ventures into other regions of being – the 'paramount reality', in Schutz's sense, in which 'normal life' takes place and which persists in its massive facticity even after various breakdowns in the fabric of 'normality'.

This reality is presented by Musil in its overwhelming richness, in itself a vast assemblage of different social worlds. In a rapidly revolving kaleidoscope we meet such different milieux as that of the higher officialdom, the military, the polite intelligentsia, the international business world, as well as the dank, subterranean sphere in which Moosbrugger has his social habitat. Various figures representing these milieux are drawn by Musil with almost ethnographic exactitude – for example, Count Leinsdorf (the tolerant, rather tired dignitary who first thought up the great patriotic *Parallelaktion*, so called because of its competition with the German undertaking), General Stumm von Bordwehr (a figure drawn with loving care, who tries honestly and hard to grasp the vagaries of the civilian mind within the orderly categories of military logic), Diotima (who escapes from the pedantic bed of her husband into the intoxicating realm of ideas and of the 'soul') or Arnheim (the Prussian business tycoon, who is at the same time a man of 'soul' and intellect, and of whom Musil gives us a portrait composed with the precision of acute antipathy). It is safe to say, however, that Musil does not present us with this array of sociologically specific figures with the intention of giving us an overall picture of Austrian society at that time (in this respect, one might profitably contrast Musil with his younger compatriot novelist Heimito von Doderer). The rich reality of the sociological assembly remains a foil for what is to come, a means rather than an end. *The Man Without Qualities*, Musil notes himself, is not a 'great Austrian novel', nor a 'historical report', nor a 'description of society'.[5] Rather, this particular society is presented to us with the intention of bringing out certain key features of *any* society, that is, with the intention of delineating the essential structure of everyday reality.

While everyday reality is experienced as a totality, it is within itself variegated and stratified. Thus, for instance, Diotima and her maid Rachel (the little Jewish girl from Galicia who passionately reveres the glittering people she feels privileged to serve) share the same everyday reality, even live in the same house, yet are separated by an enormous gulf in terms of their respective social worlds. Because of this differentiation within everyday reality, the transition from one of its sectors to another can be experienced as a shock. This is felt, for instance, by Ulrich as he arrives in the cold splendour of the Hofburg for an audience with a high imperial official, or by the good General Stumm in his mounting perplexity at the intellectual debates in Diotima's *salon*.

5. 1600.

These shock experiences foreshadow the shock that accompanies any transitions *beyond* the domain of everyday reality, but they are both quantitatively and qualitatively more moderate, for the simple reason that the transition they signal takes place between sectors of *the same* comprehensive reality of the social world, that is, still takes place within the same ontological coordinates.

The world of everyday reality presents itself as self-evident facticity. In order to live a 'normal' life in society, it must be taken for granted as such. Only then can one travel through time as on 'a train that rolls down its own rails ahead of itself', thus 'move within firm walls and on a firm ground'.[6] This feat, however, requires a specific suspension of doubt – to wit, the *'epoché* of the natural attitude'. As Ulrich puts it to himself on the nocturnal walk during which he decides to devote himself fully to the investigation of the 'other condition', being at home in the world of everyday reality presupposes a 'perspectival abridgment' of consciousness.[7] Only then does that reality take on the appearance of an 'orderly, smooth roundness', within which the life of the individual becomes plausible to himself as an orderly and seemingly necessary sequence of facts.[8] Most people are satisfied with this accomplishment, because it gives them the impression that their lives have a definite course, an impression that protects them against the terrors of chaos. A life thus lived is suffused with the warm feeling of being at home that a horse has in its stable.[9]

This security in everyday reality, precisely because it rests on the continuous effort of the *'epoché* of the natural attitude', is inherently precarious. From within its own perspective, everyday reality assigns to other ontological possibilities the status of 'utopias'. Upon closer scrutiny, however, everyday reality loses its taken-for-granted character and itself takes on the appearance of a 'utopia' – that is, as the enactment of a highly artificial drama, and a poorly composed one at that. History, expounds Ulrich in a conversation with his friends Walter and Clarisse (two musical spirits who detest what they take to be his cynicism), consists of the dull repetition of the limited number of roles

6. 445.   7. 648 ff.   8. 650.
9. 1239 – '*Stallgefühl*'.

provided for in this 'world theater'.[10] History is thus based on routine and triviality, and even most murders are only performed because certain roles call for killing. As soon as this viewpoint is taken, everyday reality becomes problematic *as a whole*, over and beyond any specific problems *within* it (such as the political problem of ordering its stratified sectors – which is why Ulrich is unpolitical). Now, everyday reality is revealed as a tenuous balancing act between a multiplicity of forces bent on destroying it, 'a middle condition made up of all possible crimes',[11] a compromise in which all passions check each other and take on a comforting grey coloration.[12]

In terms of the historical situation of *The Man Without Qualities*, the world of its everyday reality moves towards dissolution. Musil's original plan had been to bring the novel to an end with the outbreak of the war. The year 1918, as the reader is ironically aware throughout the whole presentation of the *Parallelaktion*, will see not the definitive proclamation of the true meaning of the Austro-Hungarian monarchy but its cataclysmic destruction. Ulrich's central concern, however, is in another dimension. It is not with this or that problem within the reality of what he calls the 'existing system', but with the questioning of the latter's very universe of discourse – or, as he puts it repeatedly, with the 'abolition of reality'. The utopian vision of the 'other condition' lies on the other side of this abolished reality. It is glimpsed, as it were, through the openings of this reality's crumbling structures.

What are these openings? They are the points at which the '*epoché* of the natural attitude' breaks down. These points then become possible transfer stations to the 'other condition', not yet identical with the latter, but potential occasions for its attainment. While differing greatly in their experiential content, all these transition points have in common a violent breakdown of the taken-for-granted routines of everyday life and, *ipso facto*, an intimation of novel and strange modes of being.

The first allusion to this in the present text of the novel is

10. 364.
11. 474 – '*ein Mittelzustand aus allen uns möglichen Verbrechen*'.
12. 573.

instructive.[13] Ulrich, on one of his frequent nocturnal walks through the city, is attacked by a gang of hoodlums and knocked unconscious. Upon returning to consciousness, still lying in the street, he finds himself being attended to by a solicitous lady and her coachman (the lady is the ineffably silly and slightly nympho-manic Bonadea, who subsequently becomes Ulrich's mistress for a time). When the lady commiserates with him over the brutality of his experience, he launches into a somewhat feverish discourse in which he defends such brutal, totally physical experiences as most valuable in disrupting the ordinary habits of everyday living. Ulrich's discourse, which startles poor Bonadea, in its inappro-priateness to the situation, ends by comparing sports with mys-ticism and love in its capacity to transport the individual into a 'truly bottomless, suspended state', suggesting that before long a theology of sports will have to be developed.[14] While this incident is the first one in which the breach of everyday reality is alluded to within the course of the novel, it is not the first such experience in Ulrich's memory. A number of times he recalls an experience he had at the age of twenty, as a young lieutenant in the army, when he fell violently in love with the wife of a major and was so terrified by his own turbulent emotions that he fled to a distant and solitary island.[15] It was during this 'island experience', indeed, that he had his first intimation of a possible 'other con-dition', a strange and infinitely comforting peace that followed the preceding violence. Both in Ulrich's biography and in the action of the novel, then, the possibility of the 'other condition' is first encountered in a sudden interruption of everyday routine, that routine which had been 'taken for granted until further notice'.

At times such an interruption can occur in the midst of other-wise ordinary events, which, in a flash, are seen as absurd. This absurdity then undermines the taken-for-granted reality of every-day life as a whole. On one such occasion Ulrich, who, against his will, has been made secretary of the *Parallelaktion*, returns home and starts to work through a collection of memoranda sent to him by Count Leinsdorf. This includes such items as a declara-tion of the archdiocesan ordinariate against confessional mixing

13. 25 ff.   14. 29.   15. 124 ff.

in a proposed foundation for orphans and a rejection by the ministry of education of an appropriation requested on behalf of the stenographers' association. Ulrich reacts to all this by 'pushing back the package of real world' and going out for a walk, which ends in a visit to Walter and Clarisse, during which Ulrich expounds the afore-mentioned thesis of history, as a very dull and very repetitious *theatrum mundi*.[16] On another occasion Ulrich is interrogated in a police station in the wake of a street incident in which he has been unwittingly implicated. As customary in such situations, Ulrich is asked his name, age, occupation and domicile, and in a not too friendly fashion, since the street incident, created by a drunken and aggressively class-conscious worker, entailed the offence of *lèse-majesté*. All at once, Ulrich has the impression of being caught up in a machine that is grinding his customary identity to pieces, dissolving such seemingly durable elements of that identity as his scientific reputation or the sensitive complexity of his emotional life. He experiences a 'statistical disenchantment' of his person and is more shaken by this than by the immediate inconvenience of his collision with the forces of law and order. It is still under the impact of this experience, weakened in the robustness of his accustomed way of life, that he accepts Count Leinsdorf's invitation to become secretary of the *Parallelaktion* on the following day.[17]

An important place is given in the novel to sexuality and sexual experiences, in terms of their efficacy in creating breaches in the structures of everyday reality. This, indeed, is a theme that runs through much of Musil's work outside *The Man Without Qualities*, with sexuality frequently appearing as a Dionysian, chaotic and ominous force.[18] Sexuality violently interrupts the ordinary routines of life, tearing the masks of their social roles from the faces of men and women in its grip and revealing a howling animality beneath the civilized decorum. As Ulrich observes after one of his wild bouts with Bonadea, it suddenly transforms individuals into 'raving madmen', and it is in this capacity that sexual experience is 'inserted' into everyday reality

16. 363 ff.   17. 159 ff.

18. Cf., for example, Musil's first novel, *Die Verwirrungen des Zöglings Törless*, Hamburg: Rowohlt, 1959.

as an 'island of a second condition of consciousness'.[19] Interestingly enough, in the same passage, Ulrich compares sexuality with other interruptions of everyday reality, specifically the theatre, music and religion. The violent eruption of sexual frenzy into everyday life marks a threshold of a disparate sphere of reality, a 'finite province of meaning' existing as an enclave within the 'paramount reality' of everyday life, as does the raising of the curtain on the theatrical stage, the raised baton of the conductor at the opening of a concert and the introit of the liturgy. It is not surprising, then, that Ulrich is not so much sad as contemplative *post coitum*. It is after the afore-mentioned sexual bout with Bonadea, while the latter interminably prolongs the process of getting dressed and getting out, that Ulrich has a vision of Moosbrugger.[20] And it is after Bonadea has finally made her departure that Ulrich, walking through the streets, engages in a long meditation on the fictitiousness and arbitrariness of ordinary social life.[21]

Violent aesthetic experience is another mode of interruption. Musil was particularly fascinated by music in these terms. In the novel it is especially represented by Walter and Clarisse, Ulrich's friends, who exist in the midst of violent emotional upheavals, mainly directed against each other, to the accompaniment of an ongoing musical turbulence. The piano in their apartment is always open, ready to start the tumult all over again, reminding Ulrich of the bared teeth of an all-devouring idol.[22] Clarisse moves ever more deeply into this 'spirit of music' as the novel develops. It is in this spirit that she becomes fascinated with Moosbrugger (a murderer, she exclaims at one point, who is musical and must therefore be helped) and the possibility of liberating him from prison, that she is drawn irresistibly to the company of madmen, until she finally succumbs to madness herself. One should not lightly surrender to the dark power of music, Musil suggests – nor nor to that of mathematics. The quality of mathematics as an interruption of everyday reality is not developed in detail in *The Man Without Qualities* (despite the fact that Ulrich, like Musil himself, was trained as a mathematician), but the idea is already fully expressed in Musil's first novel, *Die*

19. 115.　　　20. 117 ff.　　　21. 128 ff.　　　22. 48.

Verwirrungen des Zöglings Törless. The world of mathematics, like that of sexual and aesthetic experience, establishes a separate universe of discourse existing within everyday reality as an alien intrusion, superficially contained, made into an 'island', by the habits of social routine, but always threatening to break out of this containment and to shatter the fabric of taken-for-granted 'normality'.

Everyday reality contains alien enclaves and, to protect its own integrity and the peace of mind of its inhabitants, it must control these enclaves. It is this necessity of control that is illustrated most sharply in the figure of Moosbrugger, who represents the criminal possibility found in every society and *ipso facto* threatens the 'middle condition' that is social reality. To be sure, Moosbrugger, who goes about 'senselessly' murdering people, poses a problem of social control in the trivial criminological sense. Much more fundamentally, however, he poses a problem of reality control. For the most dangerous thing about Moosbrugger is not that he murders people, but that he has no socially understandable motives for doing so and, worse still, actually feels innocent of any crime. He inhabits that 'second homeland, in which everything one does is done innocently'.[23] The law, therefore, is not just an instrument to control and punish Moosbrugger's criminal acts. More importantly, the law is the agency of society that solemnly negates Moosbrugger's *criminal reality* – a reality that, unless negated, threatens the suspension of doubt on which all social order rests. This negation is undertaken by means of the juridically precise assignment of culpability, that is, by *translating* Moosbrugger's acts from his reality to that of society. It is just this that is done by the judges in Ulrich's vision. The counter-image to the judges, society's most impressive definers of reality, is the 'dancing Moosbrugger', a mythological figure of threatening chaos.[24] Yet, ironically, Moosbrugger foreshadows the interruption of everyday reality by the collective crime of the coming war, which, in its own way, also posits another 'condition'.[25] Crime and war, then, replicate on the level of public life the reality-

23. 119 – '*eine zweite Heimat, in der alles, was man tut, unschuldig ist*'.
24. 393 ff.
25. 1496.

shattering effect of sexual and aesthetic experience in the life of individuals.

The first part of *The Man Without Qualities* ends with Ulrich's decision to take up seriously the quest of the 'other condition', in two chapters entitled 'The Way Home' and 'Turning Point'.[26] The background of the decision lies in the breach experiences just discussed, in the fully reflected-upon relativization of everyday reality brought on by these experiences, as well as in the instinctive rejection by Ulrich of inferior approximations of the 'other condition' (notably, those represented by Clarisse and Moosbrugger). Ulrich is walking in the direction of his home. It is a beautiful but dark night, the streets are empty, there is a feeling of impending events as in a theatre. Ulrich is walking along the Ringstrasse, the broad circular boulevard that encloses the inner city of Vienna. Instead of crossing it, which would take him towards his house by the most direct route, he goes off on a tangent, following a stretch of sky visible above the trees of the boulevard. He feels a sense of great peace, but immediately reflects that this very peace, this sensation of at-home-ness, is only the result of that 'perspectival abridgment' that makes 'normal' life possible – a feat that he can no longer accomplish satisfactorily. He recalls the 'island experience' of his early youth, its feeling of liberating simplicity, and recognizes that his life will never again follow a straight line, but must henceforth move on an infinitely expanding plane. It is in the midst of these reflections that he is accosted by a streetwalker. For a moment he is tempted to accept her invitation for a few moments of uncomplicated pleasure, but then he recalls that it was under just such circumstances that Moosbrugger must have met his victim. He gives the customary fee to the girl, says a friendly word to her, and walks on. It is in this instant that he understands Moosbrugger's meaning for him – 'an escaped parable of order' – and a parable to be rejected for ever.[27] And, an instant later, he says to himself: 'All this will have to be decided!' He understands that he must choose, decisively, whether to live like other men for attainable goals or to take seriously the 'impossibilities' haunting him.

26. '*Heimweg*', 647 ff., and '*Umkehrung*', 654 ff.
27. 653 – '*ein entsprungenes Gleichnis der Ordnung*'.

Ulrich hurries towards his house now, strongly sensing that an important event is about to take place. Upon coming home, he sees that the lights are on. His first thought is that a burglar has entered the house (the German word *Einbrecher* indicates the, let us say, ontological association intended by Musil), but upon entering he finds that the 'burglar' was Clarisse (who, in one of her increasingly frequent frenzies, has decided to seduce Ulrich). The real nature of the 'forceful entry' (*Einbruch*), however, is revealed a moment later, when Clarisse hands him a telegram announcing the death of his father. It is this death that inaugurates the decisive rupture in Ulrich's year of 'vacation'. It is an intriguing question whether Musil here intends an allusion to the 'death of the father' in Nietzsche's sense – the 'unintended solemnity' of Ulrich's announcement to Clarisse, 'my father has died', and Clarisse's previously expressed interest in Nietzsche give a certain plausibility to the thought.[28] In any case, the news of his father's death leads to Ulrich's fateful journey to the provincial city of his childhood, where his father is to be buried, and to the encounter with his sister Agathe. And that encounter, indeed, takes place under the shadow of this death, in a 'house of grief'.[29] It is thus in the presence of the ultimate 'interruption' of everyday reality that Ulrich's deliberate quest for the 'other condition' begins in earnest. On the night of his decision Ulrich gets rid of the inopportune Clarisse, almost absent-mindedly, and prepares himself to meet 'this business' with the same mixture of irrational peace and observant rationality that he had felt earlier on his walk home.

The presupposition of the 'other condition', at least in Ulrich's case, is the relativization of everyday reality. The theoretical content of this relativization is nicely summed up in what could be called Ulrich's negative credo, a set of propositions propounded in answer to a question by Agathe as to what he believes in.[30] It opens, systematically enough, with the statement that all existing morality is a concession to a society of savages, that none of it is correct, and that behind it glimmers 'another meaning', which

28. 655 – '*mit einiger unwillkürlicher Feierlichkeit*'.
29. 686.   30. 769 ff.

has the potentiality of consuming fire. The 'other condition', however, is not experiencing the world. As such, it is located 'tangentially' with reference attainable by means of theoretical propositions. It is a different mode of the reality of everyday life, which it 'touches' at unexpected places. It can only be entered from the domain of everyday reality by going off at a 'tangent', as Ulrich did in his nocturnal walk home. Putting the same thing in Schutzian terms, the 'other condition' constitutes a 'finite province of meaning', disparate with reference to the common-sense reality of everyday life, and possessing a distinctive 'cognitive style'. What, then, is this cognitive structure?

An indication is already given in Ulrich's first recollection of his 'island experience'.[31] There is a dissolution of differentiations, particularly of the differentiation between subjective consciousness and the objective, external world. There is a feeling of oneness with the 'heart of the world', of being carried by being as such, a cessation of movement, an overwhelming lucidity. Already here there is an explicit reference to mysticism, though Ulrich (or Musil) hesitates to fully identify his experience with that of the mystics. In Ulrich's first communication about this to Agathe there is added the element of isolation from other men, of alienation from the world and even one's own body, which, however, is not only not terrifying but acutely happy.[32] What the novel tells us about the character of the 'other condition' is then developed mainly in the ongoing communication about it between Ulrich and Agathe, particularly in the so-called 'holy conversations'.[33] It is clear that it entails a different mode of experiencing not only the world but also the self and others. The world is seen as full of hitherto unsuspected interconnections, making up an all-embracing totality that is experienced in a state of profound calm.[34] There is a feeling that nothing more can happen – and yet that everything is happening. There is further a loss of self, a surrender to the stillness of being, an abandon-

31. 125 f.   32. 723 f.
33. Beginning with 746 ff. and taken up *passim* through what remains of the text.
34. 762 f.

ment of all desire, even the desire to ask questions.[35] Very importantly, the experience is one of intense love, for all others and for the whole world, which is now understood to be founded on love.[36] The experience also includes a different mode of time (or *durée*). One now no longer lives 'for' things, but 'in' them – that is, one no longer exists in projects into the future ('moving, striving, weaving, ploughing, sowing . . .'), but in the *hic et nunc* of an eternal present.[37]

Although the passages in which the 'other condition' is described extend to impressive lengths, they are disappointing to a degree. Despite Ulrich's (or Musil's) valiant efforts to articulate what is, almost by definition, inarticulable, the reader fails to obtain a coherent idea of just what the nature of the experience is. This is hardly surprising. Language originates in and is primarily geared to the reality of everyday life. The attempt to use language to refer to experiences that are totally outside this reality is predestined to fail, almost *a priori*. It is made very clear that the 'other condition', is, if not completely the same, yet closely analogous to the experience of mystical union – an experience that, whatever its ultimate ontological status, has proven to be intensely resistant to linguistic communication. Yet it is also made very clear that Ulrich's mysticism, if such it is to be called, is a mysticism 'with all exactness' – that is, a mysticism that does not abandon itself to orgiastic ecstasies but always retains its linkage to rational lucidity.[38] It is also a mysticism without any theological presuppositions, indeed without any positive religious faith.[39]

The entrance into any reality alternative to that of everyday life requires a breach of the '*epochē* of the natural attitude' upon which the latter is founded. The new, alternative reality (that is, the reality of any 'finite province of meaning'), however, requires

35. 1143 ff. This is the chapter entitled '*Atemzüge eines Sommertags*', possibly the last one written by Musil before his death and containing the most intense description of the experience.

36. 1240 f., but also *passim* throughout the 'holy conversations'.

37. 1331 f.   38. 665 – '*mit aller Exaktheit*'.

39. 1604 – as Musil notes about the novel as a whole, '"*religiös*" unter den Voraussetzungen der Ungläubigen'.

its own 'epochē' – once more, one can only exist within *this* reality by suspending doubts about *it*. Such a secondary *'epochē'*, as we might call it, is part and parcel of the 'cognitive style' of every 'finite province of meaning'. Without it, the new reality is threatened with the same kind of collapse that it originally 'inflicted' upon the reality of everyday life. What is more, to the extent that the new reality is removed from the massive reality-confirmations of everyday life, it is *more* susceptible to disintegration than the latter, therefore *more* in need of a determined suspension of doubt. And, indeed, we find that the 'other condition' is a very fragile business. Every little interruption of the experience by the trivialities of ordinary life threatens to upset the precarious reality of the 'other condition' – and then it is 'as if a goddess were running after a bus'.[40] As the attempt is made to retain the experience over a period of time, moments of apodictic certainty alternate with the suspicion of madness.[41] Ulrich and Agathe, in their 'magic forest', experience something that they take to be eternal – and yet fear that it may dissolve into nothingness in the very next instant.[42] This contradiction increasingly preoccupies them.

The basic empirical problem of the 'other condition' is succinctly stated by Ulrich himself when he says: 'Faith must not be one hour old!'[43] But those who hold the faith are getting older every hour – older not in the timeless reality of the 'other condition' but in the concrete 'standard time' of that everyday reality in which, despite everything, they continue to live. Their problem is thus one of 'synchronization'. Put differently, they face the problem of legitimating the coexistence of the 'other condition', in which time stands still, with the world of everyday reality, in which all things continue to move through time. In this, of course, they are not alone. To the extent that, at any rate, approximations to the 'other condition' permeate everyday reality, the problem exists wherever everyday reality is 'invaded' by other realities. From the perspective of *either* reality, the old *or* the new, there is the problem of 'translating' the alternative reality into terms appropriate to the reality in which one has chosen to stand. This, as Schutz has shown, is a central problem

40. 1209.   41. 1213.   42. 1246.   43. 755.

of *Don Quixote* – the problem that Quixote himself tried to solve by his theory of the 'enchanters', those powerful magicians who can change things back and forth between the two contending realities.[44]

Seen in the perspective of everyday reality, the problem is to explain and thus to neutralize the alien presence of the 'other condition'. There are a number of ways by which this can be accomplished. One common and theoretically unsophisticated way is to look upon the eruptions of 'otherness' into everyday life as a stimulating interlude, from which one may then return, refreshed, to one's ordinary routines as one returns from a vacation.[45] The 'other condition', or whatever approximations to it are experienced under such circumstances, is trivialized as sentimentality. Its reality is accepted, without undue disturbance, 'for the duration of the vacation' (and, as Ulrich remarks, mysticism, by contrast, is the intention to go 'on vacation' permanently). This way of coping with the 'other condition' is even employed by businessmen, who, on vacation in the Alps, enter into a quasi-mystical contemplation of bucolic scenery.

On a more sophisticated and institutionalized level, organized religion has always coped with the 'other condition' by encapsulating it in ecclesiastical routines of one kind or another.[46] Ulrich, who keeps on reading classical mystical texts during the whole period of the 'holy conversations', hypothesizes that the 'other condition' represents a human capacity *older* than the historical religions. These, in their ecclesiastical organizations, have always tried to keep the 'other condition' under control. Their representatives have always viewed the 'other condition' with the suspicion of bureaucrats in the face of private enterprise and have consistently (and, says Ulrich, with apparent justification) sought to replace it by a generally understandable morality. What Ulrich refers to here is, of course, the same phenomenon as that which Max Weber called the 'routinization of charisma' – indeed, the parallel is striking. The Catholic procedure of containing mystical explosions within the 'safe' institutional enclaves of monasticism may serve by way of illustration. But, as Ulrich

44. Cf. *Collected Papers*, vol. II, p. 142 ff.   45. 767.   46. 766.

quickly points out in the same discussion, secularization has not eliminated the problem. The alien intrusions still occur and, in the absence of the old ecclesiastical 'therapies', new ways must be found to cope with this. One of these ways is provided by modern science, which can explain and thus legitimate the 'other condition' in psychiatric categories.[47] Later in the novel, in connection with Clarisse's descent into madness, we encounter this function of psychiatry in the figure of Dr Friedenthal, whose mental hospital serves as a bulwark in the defence of the 'island of sanity' that is everyday reality.[48] The psychiatric 'treatment' of reality-shattering experiences illustrates very clearly the double character of such defensive operations – the 'other condition' is physically, institutionally contained and, simultaneously, theoretically liquidated. In a much more general way, there is the peculiarly European or western methodology of 'treating' the 'other condition' by regarding it, along with the emotional life as a whole, as a preamble or accompaniment of purposeful activity in the empirical world.[49] This general orientation makes it possible to view the 'inner world' of the mind as a beautiful and profound thing (that which Diotima and Arnheim call 'the soul'), but nevertheless deal with all this beauty and profundity as mere appendages to the 'real life' of activity in the world as socially defined. Thus the 'vacation' status of all alien states of consciousness is guaranteed both practically and theoretically. By contrast, oriental cultures have much more readily made concessions to the 'other condition' as an autonomous ontological state – with arresting effects on this-wordly activity. Again, the parallel with some of Weber's analyses (specifically, in his comparative sociology of religion) is striking here.

Seen in the perspective of the 'other condition' itself, the problem of legitimation is, of course, the reverse – how to protect the fragile reality of the 'other condition' from the massive threat of the surrounding reality of everyday life. This 'maintenance' problem can be put in sociological terms by saying that the 'other condition' requires a specific 'plausibility structure' – that is, specific *social* relations that serve to confirm and sustain its

47. 767 f.   48. 1391 ff. and 1517 ff.   49. 1315 f.

reality.[50] This sociological principle (which can be elaborated theoretically not only in Schutzian terms but in terms derived from the social psychology of George Herbert Mead) is stated explicitly by Ulrich himself. Ideas require social resonance to attain and to retain their plausibility. A young man, says Ulrich at one point, sends out ideas in all directions – but only those that obtain a response from those around him come back to him and attain a certain 'density'.[51] Man is, above all, the talking animal – he even requires conversation in order to procreate.[52] It is in conversation with others that an ordered reality is built up and kept going. This social construction of reality extends to identity itself. Thus, among lovers, 'one constructs the other, as a puppet with which one has already played in one's dreams'.[53] And when Agathe asks Ulrich 'but how am I really?' he can only laugh and point to this reciprocal construction – 'I see you as I need you' – and no one can say what either of them is 'ultimately'.[54]

In the novel it is the relationship between Ulrich and Agathe, and *only* this relationship, which serves as the 'plausibility structure' of the 'other condition'. Seen sociologically, this alone will predict the extreme fragility of the latter. As Georg Simmel has shown, the 'dyad' is the most tenuous of social relationships – consequently, the reality constructed and maintained by a dyadic 'plausibility structure' will be very tenuous. Yet the presence and response of the other, specifically one who is as much a 'significant other' (to use Mead's term) as Agathe, bestows a reality-accent upon the 'other condition' that it never had for Ulrich alone.[55] During the earlier 'island experience' he could only give 'density' to the experience by writing long letters to his 'distant

50. The term 'plausibility structure', unlike the previous analytic concepts in quotation marks, is not directly Schutzian, though it can readily be integrated with Schutz's analysis of the problem of multiple realities. Cf. Peter Berger and Thomas Luckmann, *The Social Construction of Reality*, New York: Doubleday, 1966, especially, pp. 144 ff.

51. 116.   52. 1130.   53. 1131.   54. 1177.

55. In the sense of reality construction, Ulrich is truly 'married' to Agathe – quite apart from the question of incest between them. Cf. Peter Berger and Hansfried Kellner, 'Marriage and the Construction of Reality', *Diogenes*, summer 1964.

lover' – and, understandably, this effort failed very quickly. But now Agathe 'is really here'.[56] She listens, confirms and, above all, shares the experience. And precisely in moments of doubt about the whole thing, Ulrich can reassure himself by exclaiming 'how beautiful is Agathe's voice!'[57]

The relationship of Ulrich and Agathe is entered with the explicit purpose of experiencing the 'other condition' in common. It is in this sense that it is a 'journey to the border of the possible' and a 'marginal case'.[58] It is in the 'real presence' of each other's company that the 'other condition' is to be experienced and articulated. The analogy with a religious community is thus perfectly logical. Indeed, there are sections in the 'holy conversations' that have the quality of liturgical diaphony. The essential 'maintenance' problem of Ulrich and Agathe is thus similar to that of any religious community whose members must continue to live 'in the world' – but aggravated by the fact that their community, after all, has only two members.

When Ulrich and Agathe decide to live together in Vienna, after their father's funeral, they conceive of this as an 'entrance into the millennium'.[59] They will live, they say, like hermits – and already at this point Agathe is a little worried that such a millennial existence might be rather boring. Upon their return to Vienna they first plan to remodel Ulrich's house, but soon abandon this plan and decide to leave it as it is – after all, physical surroundings are irrelevant by definition to one living in the 'other condition'. It turns out that they do not quite live like hermits, partly because old friends and acquaintances (led by the indomitable General Stumm) manage to penetrate their isolation, partly perhaps because of the very boredom that Agathe foresaw. But they look upon their 'worldly' involvements as an 'interlude'.[60] Like the early Christians and sectarians everywhere, they live 'in the world, but not of it' – or so they hope. They walk through the streets together, relishing the thought that they seem like ordinary people and that nobody can suspect their secret existence.[61] They are drawn to the world of ordinary people, yet shrink from it, because any real immersion in it threatens the

56. 892 – '*Agathe ist wirklich da*'.   57. 1209.   58. 761.
59. 801.   60. 936.   61. 943.

precarious fabric of their 'holy' life together.[62] They feel that they 'ought to do something', but do not know what, and their life together is burdened by this absence of activity – that is, by the absence of the reality-giving force of *praxis*.[63] Because of this separation from *praxis* (which is the genetic matrix of language), their conversations ever again take on an accent of 'irreality' to themselves. Thus the fence around the garden of their house both separates them from and binds them to the world of ordinary life – an ambiguous and disturbing boundary.[64]

What goes on behind this barrier can well be described as 'total conversation'. For Ulrich and Agathe not only converse about the 'other condition', but literally about everything. In the course of this conversation they even re-define (or, if one wishes, re-construct) each other's respective pasts.[65] The relentless mutual openness and the loss of previously held identity that this entails frightens both of them. Both make some attempts to withdraw from this intensity, but the attempts are half-hearted and partial – they feel guilty about these withdrawals, which appear to them as betrayals, and return from them into the ongoing 'totalization' (to use a term of Sartre's) of their privileged conversation. One may say that, *mutatis mutandis*, they experience what in Catholic monasticism has been called the sin of 'particularity' – the withdrawal, sinful by definition, from the totalizing community. A lot of time is spent in reading, much of it of mystical texts. They do read books separately, but the 'particularity' of this is neutralized by their subsequent joint discussion of these books. Ulrich, in a deliberate effort to control the power of 'reciprocal suggestion' of his conversation with Agathe, starts keeping a diary, which contains highly rational and even sceptical psychological observations about what is going on between them.[66] His diary, though, perhaps by subconscious design, is left lying about in such a way that Agathe finds it. Only after they have included *it* in their end-

62. 1095 ff.

63. Schutz, of course, emphasized the centrality of practical activity and projects in the constitution of everyday reality. This can, we think, be linked with the Marxian category of *praxis*.

64. 1162 ff.   65. 953 ff.

66. 1205 ff. The diary contains, among other things, a very interesting theory of the emotions, which, however, is not of direct interest to us here.

less conversation do they feel that 'everything is in order again'.[67]
Agathe reacts to her discovery of the diary by taking revenge and cultivating a relationship from which Ulrich is excluded. This is with Lindner, a widowed pedagogue she meets on a walk in the woods during a fit of intense depression and who has the erotically tinged ambition to 'educate' her. She does not openly tell Ulrich about her meetings with Lindner – but he knows about them, and she knows that he knows. In one way or another, then, the integrity of the separate reality of the 'other condition' is maintained. At least in the material (most of it from Musil's posthumous papers) directly pertaining to the Viennese 'hermitage' of Ulrich and Agathe, the attempt to maintain the 'other condition' as a plausible reality is successful to a considerable degree.

Perhaps enough has been said to indicate that *The Man Without Qualities* contains perspectives of some interest for a phenomenology of the *Lebenswelt* and for the general problem of multiple realities. Musil's great novel, however, has a more timely significance. Ulrich, 'the man without qualities', is deliberately presented by Musil as a prototype of modern man. As has been remarked upon by several critics, Ulrich is one of the most 'faceless' characters in modern literature – and this in a novel that abounds in sharply profiled characters. This is not due to some artistic failure on the part of the author. Ulrich's 'facelessness', his deprivation of 'qualities', is deliberate and essential. The 'man without qualities' is, at the same time, the 'man of possibility'.[68] He is marked by two distinctively modern traits – an openness to all possible modes of experience and interpretation, and a persistent, highly rational reflectiveness about the world and himself. Thus Musil, in his painstaking literary delineation of this, creates a paradigm of modernity that bears striking resemblance to a number of non-literary conceptualizations of modern man – such as David Riesman's conceptualization of the 'other-directed character', Arnold Gehlen's of 'subjectivization', and Helmut Schelsky's of 'permanent reflectiveness' (*Dauerreflektion*). Only if this is seen can one grasp the true scope of what Musil attempted to do in his nearly life-long struggle with this book – and, one may say, with Ulrich.

67. 1322.   68. 1579 – '*Möglichkeitsmensch*'.

Modern man, as the 'man without qualities', is open to an indeterminate number of reality- and self-transformations. Put differently, modern man is prone to 'alternation' between discrepant worlds of reality.[69] The reasons for this (which are far from mysterious, but empirically available to historical and sociological analysis) need not concern us here. But in this sense one can view the novel as a whole (not just Ulrich's 'experiment' with the 'other condition') as a vast treatise in 'alternation'. Thus most of the important characters in the novel serve as 'embodiments' of alternate possibilities for Ulrich and/or Agathe. There is a whole 'chorus' of characters representing the constant possibility of returning to ordinary life through an abandonment of both excessive openness and excessive reflectiveness. There is Arnheim, a sort of 'master of realities', who appears *as if* he fully controlled his own life and any possible transformations in it, who manages to combine his commercial interests in Austrian oil wells with a magnificent sensitivity of the 'soul', who, indeed, seems to combine in his person all the 'qualities' that others have separately – and who, probably for this very reason, is detested by Musil.[70] There are several figures, notably Count Leinsdorf and General Stumm, who represent a conservative pessimism that sees in political order the only viable bulwark against reality-disintegrating chaos. Lindner, Agathe's semi-secret mentor, embodies the security of conventional morality and religion – a security to which, we are told, he fled in his early youth after a terrifying encounter with religious ecstasy.[71] Walter and Clarisse, and the poet Feuermaul who plays an important role in their lives, present Ulrich with the tempting possibility of Dionysian intoxication – at the end of which stands the sinister figure of Moosbrugger, the mad murderer. There are even fairly detailed representations of most timely political possibilities in the novel – a proto-Nazi romantic nationalism, represented (ironically) by the Jewish girl Gerda Fischel and her 'Aryan' boyfriend Hans

69. Cf. Peter Berger, *The Precarious Vision*, New York: Doubleday, 1961, pp. 8 ff.; and Berger and Luckmann, op. cit., pp. 144 ff. and 155 ff.

70. Cf. the poisonous portrayals of Arnheim on 26 ff., 47 ff. and 95 ff.

71. 1299 ff.

Sepp[72] – and revolutionary socialism, represented by Schmeisser, the son of the gardener of Ulrich's father.[73]

All these figures, along with Ulrich and Agathe, have one common problem that appears to be endemic to their historical situation – that of maintaining or establishing anew principles of order in the face of threatening chaos. This is also the essential problem of the *Parallelaktion*. As we know from the beginning, of course, the attempt to root order in the public reality of the monarchy fails, and Musil makes it very clear that he has no great hopes for political projects for a 'new order'. But what about Ulrich's and Agathe's attempts at order-construction in their private reality?

It is on this issue that the literary controversy over the posthumous material for *The Man Without Qualities* is interesting for us. There are two principal positions on Musil's intentions with regard to the end of the unfinished novel. In terms of literary criticism, they hinge on the status of a passage in the posthumous material, entitled 'The Journey into Paradise', that describes a journey by Ulrich and Agathe to Italy, where they commit incest and eventually become disillusioned with each other as well as with their 'experiment'.[74] Adolf Frisé, the editor of the standard edition of the novel, places the passage towards the end of the last part, *after* the 'holy conversations'. This editorial decision has important consequences in interpretation. The incestuous journey here represents the climax of the 'experiment', the decisive attempt to attain the 'other condition' through a violent break with 'normality'. The 'experiment' fails, the 'other condition' collapses, and Ulrich and Agathe return to the 'utopia of the inductive attitude', a phrase of Musil's understood by Frisé as an acceptance of the primacy of ordinary, social life. Frisé's post-incestuous Ulrich even turns his attention to political matters, such as the coming role of China on the world scene.[75] Frisé's critical position, as well as the interpretation it entails, have been sharply attacked, particularly by the English trans-

72. 307 ff. and later, *passim.*
73. 1322 ff. and 1328 ff.
74. 1407 ff.   75. 1609.

lators of the novel.[76] The latter take the position that the disputed passage was a draft discarded by Musil long before his final years, that in his later plans for the novel there was to be no incest and no physical 'journey into paradise', and therefore no collapse of the 'experiment' in the wake of such a journey. According to this position, the final plan of the novel did not envisage any developments beyond the stage of the 'holy conversations'.

Obviously, no layman who has not delved into what must be the labyrinthine depths of Musil's posthumous papers can make a defensible judgement on the issue. Equally obviously, on such a judgement hinges the decision as to whether Musil finally intended Ulrich's attempt to 'abolish' reality to succeed or fail. It is quite possible that Musil himself did not know until the end – and, indeed, that this may be at least one of the reasons why the novel remained unfinished at his death. In any case, as things are, Musil leaves us with an unanswered question. But to bring home to ourselves the import of the question it may be useful to think once more of the analogous problem of Cervantes. Ulrich and Agathe are 'Quixotic' figures in a very profound sense. It is not without interest to recall here that, at their very first meeting in the novel, they appear dressed in 'Pierrot costumes'.[77] There is a 'ludic', a 'clownish' dimension to their entire 'experiment'. The two putative outcomes of the latter can be readily put in 'Quixotic' terms. If the one outcome is posited, Ulrich's final fate is essentially the same as that of Cervantes' tragi-comic hero – in Schutz's words, 'a homecomer to a world to which he does not belong, enclosed in everyday reality as in a prison, and tortured by the most cruel jailer: the common-sense reason which is conscious of its own limits'.[78] The other outcome implies a different conclusion. It has been put eloquently by Enid Welsford in the last paragraph of her great history of the clown as a social and literary figure: 'To those who do not repudiate the religious insight of the race, the human spirit is uneasy in this world because it is at home elsewhere, and escape from the prison house

76. Cf. Kaiser and Wilkins, op. cit. Frisé has defended himself against this attack in several articles and in a postscript to the 5th printing of his edition, 1618 ff.

77. 675.   78. Schutz, op. cit., p. 157.

is possible not only in fancy but in fact. The theist believes in possible beatitude, because he disbelieves in the dignified isolation of humanity. To him, therefore, romantic comedy is serious literature because it is a foretaste of the truth: the Fool is wiser than the Humanist; and clownage is less frivolous than the deification of humanity'.[79] In that case, *The Man Without Qualities* would not be a replication of Quixote's tragedy, but a vindication of his comic triumph.

79. Enid Welsford, *The Fool*, New York: Doubleday-Anchor, 1961, pp. 326 f.

Further Reading

BERGER, Peter, and KELLNER, Hansfried, 'Marriage and the Construction of Reality', *Diogenes*, 46, pp. 1ff., 1964.

BERGER, Peter, and LUCKMANN, Thomas, *The Social Construction of Reality*, Penguin Books, 1966.

BERGER, Peter, and PULLBERG, Stanley, 'Reification and the Sociological Critique of Consciousness', in *History and Theory*, IV, 2, 1965.

BRAND, Gerd, *Die Lebenswelt: Eine Philosophie des konkreten Apriori*, Berlin: de Gruyter, 1971.

CICOUREL, Aaron, *Method and Measurement in Sociology*, New York: Free Press, 1964.
'The Acquisition of Social Structure: Toward a Developmental Sociology of Language and Meaning', in *Understanding Everyday Life*, ed. J. Douglas, Chicago: Aldine Publishing Company, 1970.

DREITZEL, Hans Peter (ed.), *Recent Sociology*, Nr. 2, *Patterns of Communicative Behavior*, London: Macmillan, 1970.

EMBREE, Lester E. (ed.), *Life-World and Consciousness: Essays for Aron Gurwitsch*, Evanston: Northwestern Press, 1972.

EMERSON, Joan P., 'Behavior in Private Places: Sustaining Definitions of Reality in Gynæcological Examinations', in *Recent Sociology*, ed. H. P. Dreitzel, Nr. 2, London: Macmillan, 1970.

FARBER, Marvin, *Philosophical Essays in Memory of Edmund Husserl*, Cambridge, Mass.: Harvard University Press, 1940; reprinted New York: Greenwood Press, 1968.
The Foundation of Phenomenology: Edmund Husserl and the Quest for a Rigorous Science of Philosophy, Albany: State University of New York Press, 3rd ed., 1967.

FINK, Eugen, *Studien zur Phänomenologie: 1930–1939*, The Hague: Nijhoff, 1966.

FUNKE, Gerhard, 'Phenomenology and History', in *Pheno-*

menology and the Social Sciences, ed. Maurice Natanson, Vol. 2, 1973, pp. 3–101.

GARFINKEL, Harold, *Studies in Ethnomethodology*, New Jersey: Prentice Hall, 1967.

GEHLEN, Arnold, *Urmensch und Spätkultur*, Bonn: Athenäum, 1956.

GOLDSCHMIDT, Walter, 'An Ethnography of Encounters: A Methodology for the Enquiry into the Relation between the Individual and Society', in *Current Anthropology*, Vol. 13, Nr. 1, 1972, pp. 57–78.

GRATHOFF, Richard, *The Structure of Social Inconsistencies*, The Hague: Nijhoff, 1970.

'Grenze und Übergang: Bestimmungen einer cartesianischen Sozialwissenschaft', in *Soziale Welt*, Heft 4, Jahrgang 23, 1972, pp. 383–400.

GUMPERZ, J. John, and HYMES, Dell (eds.), *The Ethnography of Communication*, New York: Holt, Rinehart and Winston, 1972.

GURWITSCH, Aron, *The Field of Consciousness*, Pittsburgh: Duquesne University Press, 1964.

'Comments on H. Marcuse, On Science and Phenomenology', *Boston Studies in the Philosophy of Science*, Vol. II, In Honor of Philipp Frank, ed. Robert S. Cohen and Marx M. Wartofsky, New York: Humanities Press, 1965.

Studies in Phenomenology and Psychology, Evanston: Northwestern University Press, 1966.

HABERMAS, Jürgen, 'Zur Logik der Sozialwissenschaften', in *Philosophische Rundschau*, special issue, Nr. 5, Tübingen, 1967.

HEAP, L. James, and ROTH, O. Philipp, 'On Phenomenological Sociology', in *ASR*, Vol. 38, June 1973, pp. 354–67.

HEEREN, John, 'Alfred Schutz and the Sociology of Commonsense Knowledge', in *Understanding Everyday Life*, ed. J. Douglas, Chicago: Aldine Publishing Company, 1970, pp. 45–56.

HOLZNER, Burkart, *Reality Construction in Society*, Cambridge: Schenkmann Publishing Company, 1968.

HUSSERL, Edmund, *Ideas: General Introduction to Pure Phenomenology* (*Ideas I*), New York: Collier Books, 1962.

The Phenomenology of Internal Time-Consciousness, trans. James S. Churchill, ed. Martin Heidegger, with an introduction by Calvin O. Schrag, Bloomington: Indiana University Press, 1964.

The Idea of Phenomenology, trans. William P. Alston and George Nakhnikian with an introduction by George Nakhnikian, The Hague: Nijhoff, 1964.

'Philosophy as a Rigorous Science', in *Phenomenology and the Crisis of Philosophy*, ed. and trans. Quentin Lauer. New York: Harper & Row, 1965.

Formal and Transcendental Logic, trans. Dorion Cairns, The Hague: Nijhoff, 1969.

Cartesian Meditations: An Introduction to Phenomenology, trans. Dorion Cairns, The Hague: Nijhoff, 1969.

The Crisis of European Sciences and Transcendental Phenomenology,: An Introduction to Phenomenological Philosophy, trans. with an Introduction by David Carr, Evanston: Northwestern University Press, 1970.

Logical Investigations, trans. with an Introduction by J. N. Findlay, 2 vols., New York: Humanities Press, 1970.

Experience and Judgment, trans. James Spencer Churchill and Karl Ameriks, with a Foreword by Ludwig Landgrebe and an Afterword by Lothar Eley, Evanston: Northwestern University Press, 1973.

Introduction to the Logical Investigations, trans. with an Introduction by Philip J. Bossert and Curtis H. Peters, The Hague: Nijhoff, 1975.

The Paris Lectures, trans. P. Koestenbaum, with an introductory essay, The Hague: Nijhoff, 1975.

KAUFMANN, Felix, *Methodology of the Social Sciences*, 1944; 2nd ed., New York: Humanities Press, 1958.

KOCKELMANS, Joseph, *A First Introduction to Husserl's Phenomenology*, Pittsburgh: Duquesne University Press, 1967.

Edmund Husserl's Phenomenological Psychology: A Historico-Critical Study, trans. Berndt Jager, revised by the Author, Pittsburgh: Duquesne University Press, 1967.

'Theoretical Problems in Phenomenological Psychology', in

Phenomenology and the Social Sciences, ed. Maurice Natanson, Vol. 1, 1973, pp. 225–80.

LANDGREBE, Ludwig, 'The World as a Phenomenological Problem', trans. Dorion Cairns, in *Philosophy and Phenomenological Research*, I, Nr. 1, September 1940, pp. 38–58.

Phänomenologie und Geschichte, Gütersloh: Mohn, 1968.

LÜBBE, Hermann, 'Das Ende des phänomenologischen Platonismus', in *Tijdschrift voor Philosophie*, 16, 1954, pp. 639–66.

'Husserl und die europäische Krise', in *Kantstudien*, XLIX, 1957/58, pp. 225–37.

Bewusstsein in Geschichten: Studien zur Phänomenologie der Subjektivität, Mach-Husserl-Schapp-Wittgenstein, Freiburg: Rombach, 1972.

LUCKMANN, Thomas, 'On the Boundaries of the Social World', in *Phenomenology and Social Reality; Essays in Memory of Alfred Schütz*, ed. Maurice Natanson, The Hague: Nijhoff, 1970.

'The Constitution of Language in the World of Everyday Life', in *Life-World and Consciousness: Essays for Aron Gurwitsch*, ed. Lester E. Embree, 1972, pp. 469–88.

'Aspekte einer Theorie der Sozialkommunikation', in *Lexikon der germanistischen Linguistik*, Tübingen: Niemeyer, 1973, pp. 1–13.

MARX, Werner, 'The Life-World and the Particular Sub-Worlds', in *Phenomenology and Social Reality; Essays in Memory of Alfred Schutz*, ed. Maurice Natanson, The Hague: Nijhoff, 1970.

McHUGH, Peter, *Defining the Situation: The Organization of Meaning in Social Interaction*, New York: Bobbs-Merrill, 1968.

MERLEAU-PONTY, Maurice, *Phenomenology of Perception*, trans. Colin Smith, London: Routledge and Kegan Paul, 1962.

The Structure of Behavior, trans. Alden J. Fisher with a Foreword by John Wild, Boston: Beacon, 1963.

Signs, trans. Richard C. McCleary, Evanston, Northwestern Univeristy Press, 1964.

The Primacy of Perception and Other Essays, ed. James M. Edie, Evanston: Northwestern University Press, 1969.

The Visible and the Invisible, trans. Alden L. Fisher, Evanston: Northwestern University Press, 1969.

Phenomenology, Language and Sociology, Selected Essays, ed. John O'Neill, London: Heinemann, 1974.

NATANSON, Maurice, *Literature, Philosophy and the Social Sciences*, The Hague: Nijhoff, 1962.

'Phenomenology: A Viewing', in *Literature, Philosophy and the Social Sciences*, M. Natanson, The Hague: Nijhoff, 1962.

Essays in Phenomenology, The Hague: Nijhoff, 1966.

'Alfred Schutz on Social Reality and Social Science', in *Phenomenology and Social Reality; Essays in Memory of Alfred Schutz*, ed. M. Natanson, The Hague: Nijhoff, 1970.

'Phenomenology and Typification: a Study in the Philosophy of Alfred Schutz', in *Social Research*, 37, spring 1970, pp. 1–22.

The Journeying Self: A Study in Philosophy and Social Role, Reading, Mass.: Addison-Wesley, 1970.

(ed.), *Phenomenology and Social Reality; Essays in Memory of Alfred Schutz*, The Hague: Nijhoff, 1970.

(ed.), *Phenomenology and the Social Sciences*, Vols. I and II, Evanston: Northwestern University Press, 1973.

O'NEILL, John, *Perception, Expression and History: The Social Phenomenology of Maurice Merleau-Ponty*, Evanston: Northwestern University Press, 1970.

Sociology as a Skin Trade: Essays Towards a Reflexive Sociology, London: Heinemann, 1972.

ORTH, Ernst Wolfgang, 'Philosophy of Language as Phenomenology of Language and Logic', in *Phenomenology and the Social Sciences*, ed. M. Natanson, Vol. 1, 1973, pp. 323–39.

PLESSNER, Helmuth, *Die Einheit der Sinne, Grundlinien einer Ästhesiologie des Geistes*, Bonn: H. Bouviez, 1923.

Zwischen Philosophie und Gesellschaft; Ausgewählte Abhandlungen und Vorträge, Bern: Francke Verlag, 1953.

PSATHAS, George (ed.), *Phenomenological Sociology: Issues and Applications*, New York: John Wiley-Interscience, 1973.

RICOEUR, Paul, *Husserl: An Analysis of His Phenomenology*, Evanston: Northwestern University Press, 1967.

SCHELER, Max, *The Nature of Sympathy*, New Haven: Yale University Press, 1954.

Die Wissensformen und die Gesellschaft, ed. Maria Scheler, 2nd ed., Bern: Francke, 1960.

SCHUTZ, Alfred, *Collected Papers I, The Problem of Social Reality,* The Hague: Nijhoff, 1962.

Collected Papers II, Studies in Social Theory, The Hague: Nijhoff, 1964.

Collected Papers III, Studies in Phenomenological Philosophy, The Hague: Nijhoff, 1968.

The Phenomenology of the Social World, Evanston: Northwestern University Press, 1967.

Reflections on the Problem of Relevance, ed. R. Zaner, New Haven: Yale University Press, 1970.

SCHUTZ, Alfred, and LUCKMANN, Thomas, *The Structures of the Life-World,* Vol. I, Evanston: Northwestern University Press, 1973.

SPEIER, Matthew, 'The Everyday World of the Child', in *Understanding Everyday Life,* ed. J. Douglas, Chicago: Aldine Publishing Company, 1970.

SPIEGELBERG, Herbert, *The Phenomenological Movement,* Vols. I and II, The Hague: Nijhoff, 1965.

SPRADLEY, James, *Culture and Cognition,* San Francisco: Chandler Publication, 1972.

STONIER, Alfred, and BODE, Karl, 'A New Approach to the Methodology of the Social Sciences', *Economica,* Vol. IV, 1937, pp. 406–24.

STRAUS, Erwin W., *Phenomenological Psychology: Selected Papers,* trans. in part by Erling Eng, New York: Basic Books, 1966.

SUDNOW, David (ed.), *Studies in Social Interaction,* New York: The Free Press, 1972.

TURNER, Roy, 'Words, Utterances, and Activities', in *Understanding Everyday Life,* ed. J. Douglas, Chicago: Aldine Publishing Company, 1970.

TYLER, Stephen (ed.), *Cognitive Anthropology,* New York, Chicago: Holt, Rinehart and Winston, 1969.

TYMIENIECKA, Anna-Teresa, *Phenomenology and Science in Contemporary European Thought,* with a Foreword by I. M. Bochenski, New York: Farrar, Straus, Noonday Press, 1962.

VAN BREDA, H. L. (ed.), *Problèmes actuels de la phénoménologie*, Paris: Desclée de Brouwer, 1952.

VAN PEURSEN, Cornelius A., *Phenomenology and Analytical Philosophy*, trans. Rex Ambler and amended Henry J. Koren, Pittsburgh: Duquesne University Press, 1972.

WAELHENS, Alphonse de, *Existence et Signification*, Louvain: Nauwelaerts, 1958.

WAGNER, Helmut (ed.), *Alfred Schutz on Phenomenology and Social Relations: Selected Writings*, Chicago: University of Chicago Press, 1970.
'The Scope of Phenomenological Sociology: Considerations and Suggestions', in *Phenomenological Sociology*, ed. G. Psathas, New York: Wiley, 1973.

WALDENFELS, Bernhard, *Das Zwischenreich des Dialogs: Sozialphilosophische Untersuchungen in Anschluss an Edmund Husserl*, The Hague: Nijhoff, 1971.

WEBER, Max, *The Methodology of the Social Sciences*, New York: The Free Press, 1949.

ZANER, Richard, *The Way of Phenomenology*, New York: Pegasus, 1970.

ZIMMERMAN, Don, 'The Practicalities of Rule Use', in *Understanding Everyday Life*, ed. J. Douglas, Chicago: Aldine Publishing Company, 1970.

Acknowledgements

Thanks are due to the following for use of material contained in this book:

Reading 1   *The Journal of Philosophy*
Reading 2   Helmuth Plessner and Francke Verlag
Reading 3   Northwestern University Press and Nijhoff
Reading 4   Basic Books Inc.
Reading 5   Rombach Verlag
Reading 6   Harvard University Press and Nijhoff
Reading 7   Heinemann Educational Books Ltd and
            Northwestern University Press
Reading 8   Nauwelaerts
Reading 9   International Philosophical Quarterly
Reading 10 Heinemann Educational Books Ltd and Harper
            & Row
Reading 11 Northwestern University Press
Reading 12 Nijoff
Reading 13 Social Research
Reading 14 Burkart Holzner
Reading 15 Social Research
Reading 16 Hansfried Kellner
Reading 17 Nijhoff

Author Index

Subject Index

Language – *contd*
  seduction of, 52
  in social life, 328
  and speech acts, 335
  transcendental critique of, 333
  written, 50–51
Langue, 335
Lebenswelt. See Life-world
Life-world(s), 77, 121, 263
  ambiguities in Husserl's, 236
  choice of, 283–5, 290, 293
  construction of, 281–2
  determinancy of, 79, 81
  existence of real, 123
  features of, 79–81
  fields of, 136
  modern, 278–81
  motivation to question, 138
  phenomenology of, 244
  primitive, 276–8
  regularities of, 80
  rejection of old, 289
  relativity of, 80–81, 123
  role in sociology, 166
  search for meaningful, 288–9
  separation between knowledge
    and, 201
  small, 275–90
  stratification of, 259, 263
  structures of, 257–74
  as universal aim, 167
Linguistic analysis, 181
Linguistic determinism, 331
Linguistic objectification, legal,
    317–18
Living world, ontology of, 101
Logic
  domain of, 55
  pure, Husserl's aim, 101
  of social science, 239
  of theory-finding/using, 220
  -in-use, 220

Logical deduction, 55
Logical empiricism, 231–2

Mach society, Ernst, 116
Machine
  calculating, 94
  symbolic, 75
Man, conception of, 179
Man and nature, 217, 227, 231
The Man Without Qualities,
    343–67
Marriage rites, 178–9
Materialism of Enlightenment, 102
Mathematics
  practical, devoid of
    meaning, 59
  and reality, 351–2
Mathematization of nature, 78,
    84, 87–9, 130, 224–8
  Descartes's, 72
  origin of, 76
  of social phenomena, 146
Mathesis universalis, 189, 232–7
  passim, 253
  independent of Galilean
    cosmology, 236
  as partial formalization, 247–8
  for social reality, 244
Meaning
  as consciousness of attitude, 23,
    24
  factors affecting, 339
  genesis of, 153
  man as revealer of, 172
  structures of, 336
  in use, 338
Measurement, accuracy of, 85
Measurement, theory of, 246,
    250–51
Metaphysics, 93
  and Mach, 99
Methodenmonismus, 25

Psychologism, Husserl and, 97
Psychology, phenomenological, 97

Qualitative phenomena and physics, 86–7
Questionable, transformation to unquestionable, 258
Quixote, 358

Rationality, economic, 203
Rationality, technical, 203
Reactivatability as an aim, 52–3
Reality(ies)
   abolition of, 348
   criminal, 352–3
   formalized interpretation of, 311
   interruption of, 350, 351–2, 358
   language of, 187–8
   multiple, 343–67. *See also* Other condition:
      alternation between, 364
   relativity of, 311, 330, 354
   and religion, 358–9
   selective, 330
   and social background, 326–7
   social construction of, 293, 360
   subjective, 325, 327
   transformation, legal, 311–23:
      and linguistic objectification, 318–20; preparing for, 320–22; status of rules for, 323; translation between, 357
Realverhältnisse, 327
Reasoning, immanent categories of, 326
Rebellion, 301
   and criticism, 214–15
Reduction, phenomenological, 124, 187–8, 347
   breakdown of, 348

non-additive nature of, 194
   secondary, 356–7
Reflexivity, epistemological, 244
   institution of, 211
   of social sciences, 203
Relevancy, 262–9
   interpretational, 268
   modifications of systems of, 273–4
   motivational, 264–5
   need for theory of, 272
   social conditioning of, 272–3
   thematic, 265–8
Religious monopolies, 9
Renaissance, 9
Resolution, canonical, 230
Responsibility, 295–6
Rigour and phenomenology, 181–99

Salvation, religious, 301
Science
   atomistic view of, 115–16, 117
   common interest with philosophy, 220–21
   divorce from human life, 218
   explicit/implicit philosophy of, 162
   and the life-world, 129–33
   natural, problem of success of, 122–3
   need for epistemological grounding, 58
   nomological, 330
   phases in philosophy of, 72–5
   as problem, 74
   reconstructed logic of, 220
   theoretical and practical, 75
   validity of, 222–3
Scientism, 219
Self
   in exact social science, 20

A selection of books published by Penguin is listed on the following pages.

For a complete list of books available from Penguin in the United States, write to Dept. DG, Penguin Books, 299 Murray Hill Parkway, East Rutherford, New Jersey 07073.

For a complete list of books available from Penguin in Canada, write to Penguin Books Canada Limited, 2801 John Street, Markham, Ontario L3R 1B4.

If you live in the British Isles, write to Dept. EP, Penguin Books Ltd, Harmondsworth, Middlesex.

Some books on sociology published by Penguin Books

Some reference books published by Penguin Books

A DICTIONARY OF ARCHAEOLOGY
Warwick Bray and David Trump

A DICTIONARY OF BIOLOGY
M. Abercrombie, C. J. Hickman, and M. L. Johnson

A DICTIONARY OF COMPUTERS
*Anthony Chandor with John Graham
and Robin Williamson*

A DICTIONARY OF ECONOMICS
Graham Bannock, R. E. Baxter, and Ray Rees

A DICTIONARY OF ELECTRONICS
S. Handel

A DICTIONARY OF GEOGRAPHY
W. G. Moore

A DICTIONARY OF GEOLOGY
D. G. A. Whitten with J. R. V. Brooks

A DICTIONARY OF PSYCHOLOGY
James Drever

A DICTIONARY OF SCIENCE
E. B. Uvarov, D. R. Chapman, and Alan Isaacs

Some books on anthropology and archaeology published
by Penguin Books

ANCIENT IRAQ
Georges Roux

THE AZTECS OF MEXICO
G. C. Vaillant

THE HUNTING PEOPLES
Carleton S. Coon

KINSHIP AND MARRIAGE
Robin Fox

MAGICAL MEDICINE: A NIGERIAN CASE-STUDY
Una Maclean

THE PEOPLE'S LAND:
ESKIMOS AND WHITES IN THE EASTERN ARCTIC
Hugh Brody

THE PYRAMIDS OF EGYPT
I. E. S. Edwards

RULES AND MEANINGS
Edited by Mary Douglas

WITCHCRAFT AND SORCERY
Edited by Max Marwick